Policing Citizens

Policing Citizens: Authority and Rights

P.A.J. Waddington

LONDON AND NEW YORK

First published in 1999 by Routledge

Routledge
2 Park Square, Milton Park,
Abington, Oxon, OX14 4RN

and

270 Madison Ave,
New York NY 10016

Transferred to Digital Printing 2006

British Library Cataloguing-in-Publication Data
A CIP catalogue record for this book is available from the British Library.

Library of Congress Cataloging-in-Publication Data are available

ISBN: 1-85728-692-8 HB
1-85728-693-6 PB

Typeset by Best-set Typesetter Ltd., Hong Kong

Contents

1. What is Policing? 1
   Introduction 1
   What Officers Do – An Anecdote 1
   The Same the Whole World Over? 3
   Crime-Fighters? 4
   Peacekeeping and Service? 12
   Monopolists of Force? 15
   Exercising Authority 20
   Policing, Citizens and the State 20
   Policing Non-Citizens: The Colonial Example 24
   Continental and Other Forms of Policing 26
   Contesting Citizenship 28
   Conclusion 30

2. Keeping People in Their Place 31
   Introduction 31
   Discretion in Policing 31
   A Flawed Perspective 38
   Policing Subordination and Exclusion 45
   Citizenship and Resistance 61
   Negotiating Respectability 62
   Keeping People in Their Place 63

3. Keeping Dissent in Its Place 64
   Introduction 64
   Criminals, Citizens and the State 64
   Creating a Duopoly of Force 69
   Control through Inclusion 70
   "Ordinary Decent Protesters" 73
   A Common Democratic Solution 74
   Civil Rights: Contesting Citizenship 75
   Reversing Inclusion 78

Policing Divided Societies 84
The Resurgence of Militarization 87
Conclusion 95

4. Thought, Talk and Action 97
Introduction 97
Are Police Officers Born or Made? 97
Continuities in Explanations of Police Behaviour 102
Appreciating the "Oral Tradition" of Policing 109
Conclusion 120

5. Abusing Authority 121
Introduction 121
Bribery and Corruption 121
The Invitational *Edges* of Corruption 125
"Bending" and "Breaking the Rules" 127
Excessive Force 149
Conclusion 158

6. Controlling Police Officers 159
Introduction 159
Regulating Police Wrongdoing 159
Conclusion 183

7. Controlling Police Organizations 184
Introduction 184
Independence and Control 184
Impartiality, Discretion and Law 191
Accommodating Constitutional Tensions 195
Abuses of Power 196
A Mechanism for Restraint? 197
Making a Difference 201
Constructing Constitutionalism 204

8. Reform and Change 206
Introduction 206
Community Policing 206
Police Management 226
Privatization 243
Conclusion 249

Bibliography 251

Index 296

For Diane, for everything

CHAPTER 1

What is Policing?

Introduction

The simple answer to the question "What is policing?" is that policing is what police officers do. There is much sense in this response, but it is typical of the sociologist to make life complex by showing that there is much more to the subject under examination than meets the eye. This can be frustrating for the reader, because before we can examine our subject we need to stand back from it and assess *why* it needs examining and *what* needs examination. However, I will try and temper your frustration by eschewing general conceptual issues – at least for the moment – and concentrate instead on what real-life police officers actually do or rather did during one evening's duty in Chicago.

What Officers Do – An Anecdote

I met the two officers I was to accompany for the Friday evening's patrol at the police station. Pete had seven years' experience, having spent a few years in the military. He was white, married, had a couple of kids, lived in the suburbs and was soon hoping for posting to the detective branch. Al was a rookie, having graduated from the police academy just a few months previously. He was much younger than Pete, an unmarried African–American and was attached to his more experienced partner so as to learn how the job should be done in practice – a relationship that is common in police forces throughout the world and goes by a variety of official designations, such as "Field Training Officer" (van Maanen 1973) or "Tutor Constable" (Fielding 1988). The attitudes of the two men were also quite typical of their respective roles and experience: Al was enthusiastic at the prospect of getting out on the street and talked excitedly about his work. Pete was more laconic and not a little cynical – his was a job to be done and a period to survive.

I climbed into the rear of the blue and white patrol car and with Pete driving we pulled out into the early evening traffic which had obligingly stopped to allow us onto the road. For a while we drove around the area for which these officers were responsible. Similar to a wild animal establishing its territory we cruised the area to see that everything was as it should be. As we did so my companions pointed to various housing projects containing low-cost accommodation and from where we might expect to receive calls. There was quite a bit of personal domestic chatter between Pete and Al and gossip about colleagues and events within the police bureaucracy.

It took about an hour of patrolling before Al reached for the radio handset and acknowledged receipt of a dispatch. He explained that there was a drunk causing a nuisance in a bar near the city centre. We drove directly but without undue haste to the bar. As the officers walked into the dimly lit interior the angry exchanges from a group of people standing near the bar suddenly hushed. Pete asked what the problem was and the smartly dressed manager told of how the dishevelled man had become drunk and refused to leave when asked to do so by the bartender, who was also standing in the group. The man was clearly very intoxicated, unable to stand without swaying and his speech was slurred. Pete turned to him and asked whether he was going to leave or would he prefer to be arrested. The man lurched unsteadily towards the door onto the street with Pete and Al in close attendance. Outside the man slumped against the display window of a neighbouring shop as Pete warned him that if there was any recurrence of trouble he would arrested. Just then another patrol car turned up and Pete ambled over to tell them that there was nothing to worry about and thanked them for stopping by; they left with a wave. Pete returned to the man and told him to go on his way.

As we climbed back in the car Pete suggested that we cruise down to the entertainment district which was not far away. People were now thronging the streets and the patrol car had some difficulty nosing its way through the heavy traffic. It was noticeable that we became the centre of attention for many pedestrians and Al took obvious but quiet delight in returning the smiles and waves of the many small groups of scantily clad young women. Having woven our way through the crowds we resumed our general patrol and then had a break for a meal.

The second half of the shift was dominated by a single incident to which we were sent immediately after the meal break. An African–American man had reported a robbery. We pulled up at the address to which the dispatcher had sent us to find the man waiting on the footpath. The story he told was this: he had been in business with another man for a couple of years, but they had begun to experience financial problems and could not pay their small group of employees. His partner had proposed selling the personal computer that was used in the office, but the complainant had refused to permit this. He had been in the office during the evening, trying to find alternative ways of saving the business, when two nephews of his partner turned up to take the computer. He had resisted and they had beaten him before removing the computer. Pete shone his flashlight onto the man's face and inspected the cut and bruising around his left eye; meanwhile Al was taking notes. The complainant did not know where the nephews might be found, but he gave an address for his business partner. He said that he would remain in the office for a while and the officers went in search of the partner at what turned out to be a surprisingly swanky apartment building. The officers enquired of the concierge who used the internal phone to call the partner. He refused to see the officers, but agreed to talk on the phone. He alleged that he was not a "partner" but had merely loaned the complainant money to start his business. The computer had been repossessed when the complainant had failed to repay the loan. His nephews had acted in self-defence when the complainant had pulled a gun on them and they had disarmed him. He did not know where his nephews were at that moment because they were trying to sell the computer and recoup his loss.

The officers returned to the complainant who again met us in the street – a habit the officers found disconcerting. Why did he not invite them into his office? It was now very dark and so all four of us climbed into the patrol car. The business partner's account was relayed to the complainant who, of course, disputed much of it. "What about the gun?", asked the officers. Well yes, the man conceded, he was in possession of a gun, but he had not pulled it on his assailants, they had simply stolen it along with the computer. Where was his licence for the gun? Well, he did not have a licence, it was a war trophy from Vietnam. Pete and Al climbed out of the car and had a brief conversation about what to do next. Pete then summoned the complainant. Look, he told him, they would take no action about the gun, but so far as they were concerned this was a civil dispute between business partners and he had better see a lawyer first thing Monday morning. With that we returned to the car and the complainant returned disgruntled to his office. Pulling up in a convenient place Al now started to write up a report. Turning to Pete he asked how he should report a stolen computer, unregistered gun, and so forth. Pete took the form from him and tore it into small pieces. Picking up the radio handset he broadcast to the dispatcher that they had investigated the incident but it turned out not to be a police matter.

We then cruised our area for the remainder of the shift and returned to the police station in the early hours of the morning. As I thanked Pete and Al for their hospitality, they apologized for the lack of action during the shift; it was an unusually quiet evening, they explained. Having bidden farewell to my hosts I stood waiting in the main foyer of the station for a taxi. Suddenly the doors burst open and two officers entered struggling to control a man – the man who Al and Pete had earlier ejected from the bar. As they passed near me, the man spat blood on the floor and I could see that in the midst of the saliva and blood lay a tooth.

The Same the Whole World Over?

I do not relate this anecdote to prove that I survived the mean streets of Chicago, quite the contrary: what is remarkable about this anecdote is that it is wholly unremarkable. At the time that the Chicago Police Department allowed me to accompany Pete and Al on patrol I was in the midst of three years' observation of police patrol in my home town of Reading, England, and I had witnessed comparable events many times before. True, complainants in Reading do not usually have guns and neither do the police, but police officers share the experience of finding themselves enmeshed in complex quarrels as well as ejecting unruly drunks from bars. My experience is far from exceptional, indeed it is the norm. Many writers on the police describe essentially similar events to those related above. In various American police departments things seem to be much the same as in Chicago (Bittner 1967a, ibid. b; Wilson 1969; Rubenstein 1973; Muir 1977; Sykes & Brent 1983); Ericson (1982) found that policing was essentially similar in a municipal police force in Ontario during the 1970s; Cain (1973), Manning (1977); Chatterton (1983), Holdaway (1983), McClure (1980), Young (1991), Smith & Gray (1983) and Kemp *et al.* (1992a) depict similar scenes in various English police forces over a thirty-year period; and Punch (1979a) revealed that policing in Amsterdam conformed to this general picture. Even in those societies that appear to be very distinct from North America and Europe we still find clear echoes of police engaged in the kind of work I have described. Thus, despite the enormously difficult and dangerous security situation in Northern Ireland, members of the Royal Ulster Constabulary perform much the same tasks, at least away from areas where terrorism flourishes, as do police elsewhere (Brewer 1990a). Things are much the same in such socially, culturally and economically distinctive societies as India in the 1960s (Bayley 1969) and contemporary Japan (Bayley 1976, ibid. 1991a; Ames 1981). Even the People's Police of Soviet-dominated East Germany, as distinct from the infamous Stasis, shared much in common with their counterparts in the liberal democracies (Wolfe 1992). Likewise, the militia of the Soviet Union concerned itself mainly with such tasks, albeit armed with far more formidable powers (Shelley 1990, 1996). Historically, we find a remarkably similar picture of policing in Oregon (Websdale 1991, ibid. 1994, ibid. 1995), Kentucky (Websdale & Johnson 1997), Merseyside (Brogden 1991) and elsewhere in Britain (Weinberger 1995).

Social scientists have become so familiar with amalgamating research from such a broad diversity of social, economic, political, cultural and historical conditions that there is the danger that we lose sight of the genuinely remarkable consistency midst diversity that research reveals. When Banton compared the police in Edinburgh in Scotland with a police department in North Carolina it was the *similarities* between them that allowed him to discuss *generally* what policing entailed (Banton 1964). We need to keep this consistency across apparently diverse conditions firmly in mind lest we slide into parochial and particular explanations for why policing takes the form it does.

Crime-Fighters?

So what is the consistent core of policing? The obvious answer is that the police enforce the law and by so doing ensure that the "bad guys" get their just desserts and the rest of us remain safe in our beds. This traditional image of policing, to which the police themselves tenaciously hold and fictional portrayal re-affirms, is that of the proverbial "thin blue line" protecting society from lawlessness. Patrolling officers prevent crime by their presence and the possibility that they will stumble across an offence in progress or use their supposed "sixth sense" to recognize that something is amiss with a person or situation. Alternatively, once a crime has been committed the patrol car speeding to the scene of a crime may catch the criminal red-handed probably after a struggle. If neither prevention nor immediate apprehension succeed then the third line of defence lies in detection: the superior intellectual powers and dogged persistence of the sleuth concludes with the assemblage of evidence that brings the guilty to justice. The problem of crime in modern societies, from this perspective, is simply that there are not enough police. As an officer quoted in the magazine of the Police Federation of England and Wales would have us believe: "With more officers the crime rate would tumble in dramatic fashion and the entire community would feel safer. It would ease the biggest fear in the minds of the public which currently is that one day they will become a victim of crime" (*Police* magazine, May 1997: 6). Popular as these image are, successive generations of researchers have found that they have little substance.

There are two principal grounds that police researchers have relied upon for denying that law enforcement is not the defining characteristic of policing: first, law enforcement is neither what the police do nor what the public ask the police to do; and secondly the police are not very effective crime-fighters. There are also two subsidiary arguments that might additionally be employed: that police are not, and never have been, *organized* to fight crime; and there are many more enforcement agencies than the police.

Non-Crime-Fighting

Under-Enforcing the Law

Pete and Al epitomize one of the most dominant characteristics of the police – the *non*-enforcement of the law. As Reiss noted, "No tour of duty is typical except in the sense that *the modal tour of duty does not involve an arrest* of any person. . . . This is not to say that arrests could not have been made on many tours of duty, but often they are not because the officer exercises his discretion not to make such arrests" (Reiss 1971: 19). Pete and Al *could* have arrested the drunk in the bar who was clearly committing offences, yet they were content to escort him outside and let him go with a warning. The dispute over the computer involved a whole range of possible offences including assault, possession of an unregistered firearm, and theft, but the officers concluded that it was better dealt with as a civil dispute. The characteristic feature of policing is *under enforcement of the law* – not its enforcement. It is instructive to note that when police unions in the United States wish to bring industrial pressure to bear, one tactic they employ is the "ticket blizzard" when they do rigorously enforce the law and usually succeed in bringing the police organization and much of local society to a halt. Most of the time, discretion is exercised in favour of non-enforcement.

Public Demand

A substantial proportion of the public in the advanced economies call upon the police for assistance during the period of a year, but only a minority do so to report crime. Estimates vary according to the precise definitions used by the researcher (an issue to which we will return shortly), but there is widespread agreement that complaints of crime comprise between only a quarter and a third of the problems that the public ask the police to assist with (see for example: Comrie & Kings 1975; Antunes & Scott 1981; Ekblom & Heal 1982; Shapland & Vagg 1988). In my own research, I found that only just over a quarter of calls were reports of crimes and these resulted overwhelmingly in one of two outcomes: a crime complaint form was completed or no action was taken usually because the alarm turned out to be false (Waddington 1993a). Only rarely was an arrest made and if it was then it arose mainly because the suspect was handed over to the police by store detectives who had detained the person on suspicion of shoplifting. Not only was the media image of the police rushing to the scene of a crime and apprehending criminals extremely rare in actuality, the most likely outcome of any instant mobile response was that by the time the police arrived at the scene there was nothing for them to do. Indeed, I incidentally discovered while doing other research (1985), that most arrests were made inside the police station – officers routinely made appointments, which suspects kept, in order to make an arrest at a mutually convenient time! Perhaps most surprising of all is that victim satisfaction with the police does not seem to rely upon whether the culprit is arrested and prosecuted. What victims seem to want most (but do not always get) is sympathetic and considerate treatment by the police (Mayhew *et al.* 1993, ibid. 1994).

Ineffective Crime-Fighters

Police need not spend a great deal of time on crime-fighting in order to deter criminals and respond effectively on those occasions when crime occurs. One might imagine police officers, as they often imagine themselves, as crime-fighters that are either filling in time doing other tasks while they await the next crime, or actually being deflected from their prime task by all the incidental "rubbish" or "bullshit" that the police organization and public heaps upon them. Certainly, the clear implication of the 1996 British Government White Paper was that it took the latter view, complaining that "In a typical day, only 18 per cent of calls to the police are about crime and only about 40 per cent of police officers' time is spent dealing directly with crime" (Home Office 1993: para 2.3).

In so far as the police devote themselves to crime-fighting, they do so through patrolling with the aim of preventing crime and detecting criminals after the event.

Patrolling

The traditional weapon in the police armoury designed to prevent crime is patrolling. Bayley estimates that in 28 separate forces the proportions of total personnel devoted to patrol work are: 65 per cent in the US, 64 per cent in Canada, 56 per cent in Britain, 54 per cent in Australia, and 40 per cent in Japan (Bayley 1994). The justification for this considerable investment of resources is that it enables police to deter offenders by their presence and swiftly intervene when crime occurs and thus capture offenders. A neat idea, but unfortunately not one that corresponds to reality. The classic study on preventative patrol was an experiment conducted in Kansas City in which levels of motor patrol were systematically varied and the impact on crime assessed (Kelling *et al.* 1974; Pate *et al.* 1976). The outcome was that it did not matter much whether police patrolled as normal, intensively or did not patrol at all and only reacted to calls for assistance. Larson criticized the implementation of the experiment, since it proved difficult to ensure that police complied with the experimental conditions. For example, patrolling officers seemed to find compelling reasons to drive through those areas that were supposed have no preventative patrol (Larson 1976). Even so, Kansas City provides strong evidence for doubting the effectiveness of visible patrolling as a crime control strategy. Do foot patrols fair any better? Well, not according to the Newark Foot Patrol Experiment where a similar assessment was conducted by systematically varying the allocation of foot patrols without any discernible impact on crime rates, albeit that there were other payoffs from foot patrolling (Wilson & Kelling 1982). In Britain the authoritative Audit Commission concludes that traditional styles of patrol are grossly inefficient as a means of crime control (Audit Commission 1996).

There is, in sum, surprisingly wide agreement among academic commentators that police patrol is a peculiarly ineffective method of crime prevention (Hough, J.M. &

Clarke 1980; Morris & Heal 1981; Wycoff 1982; Heal & Morris 1985; Audit Commission 1996; Hough, M. 1996)

"Sleuthing"

If routine patrol has little preventative impact, do police fight crime effectively once it has occurred? Again, the answer seems to be that they do not. The notion that the police catch offenders red-handed at the scene of a crime has little to support it, mainly because whatever the police do to reduce the time it takes them to respond to the complaint that a crime has been committed, they can do nothing to shrink the much longer delay between the crime occurring and it being brought to their attention (Bieck 1977; but see also Cordner *et al.* 1983). It is now widely accepted that such reactive policing has had little, if any, payoff in terms of detecting criminals at possibly considerable cost in police–public relations. Nor do detectives live up to their media image as persistent sleuths. Greenwood's major study of detective work in police forces throughout the United States found that uniformed officers made most arrests and that, "Only about 3 per cent of all index arrests appeared to result from special investigative efforts where organization, training or skill could make any conceivable difference" (Greenwood 1980: 36). This estimate is remarkably similar to a British study by Steer who found that most detections were straightforward (Steer 1980). As an anonymous British detective remarked, "Criminal investigation work is the sort of work that any good Prudential insurance man could do" (McClure cited in Bayley 1994a: 28).

Also contrary to its popular image, forensic science has little impact on detection. Maguire found that fingerprint evidence was responsible for less than half of one per cent of detections of household burglars (Maguire 1982). Greater investment in investigative resources have very little impact on the amount of crime detected, since for the most part evidence that is not immediately apparent to the police (such as eyewitnesses who identify the offender) is unlikely to come to light later (see Loveday 1995a for a review of this literature). Nor does it seem that future developments hold much hope of transforming this situation. As Morgan and Newburn point out, the current fashion for "intelligence-led policing" has failed to appreciate just how numerous are the persistent repeat offenders who are responsible for a disproportionate amount of crime and on whom "intelligence-led policing" is supposed to concentrate. They estimate that this "hard core" numbers at least 300,000 in Britain – more than enough to swamp police resources (Morgan & Newburn 1997). Research on British detectives found that much of their time was consumed on routine administration rather than anything that could be described as investigation (Tarling & Burrows 1984). Rather than investigating crime and detecting criminals, detectives spend most of their time engaged in the "legalization" of cases; that is, ensuring that the case file satisfies legal requirements so as to secure conviction (Dixon 1997).

Differences do exist between police forces in their "clear-up rates'; however this seems to owe more to administrative arrangements than to the detection of offenders. For example, Burrows found that substantial differences between forces in the number of burglaries cleared up was not due to differential success in arresting burglars, but to procedures whereby individual convicted burglars were encouraged to admit to burglaries they had committed but for which they had not yet been charged (Burrows

1986). Cicourel argued that differences in rates of juvenile delinquency between two similar American cities were almost entirely attributable to divergent recording and prosecuting practices (Cicourel 1968). In a similar vein, Farrington and Dowds found that the reason why one police force had a much higher crime rate than its neighbours was almost entirely due to differences in recording practices (Farrington & Dowds 1985).

If the police play such a small role in the detection of offenders, how do criminals get caught? The short answer is that the main "players" in clearing up crimes are the public: in the main it is they who discover offences and detect offenders. For instance, Mawby found that contrary to his initial expectations, the differences in crime rates between areas of a large industrial city were not attributable to police action, but to the public's willingness to report offences and identify offenders (Mawby 1979). Contrary to the prevailing criminological orthodoxy of the time, the police seemed to have little idea of crime patterns in the city and took few steps to target particular districts. Likewise, Steer concluded that all but a tiny minority of detections were straightforward because unless a witness identified a suspect, the likelihood of detection was remote indeed (Steer 1980). Police may exercise some skills in convincing suspects to confess and incriminate others, but the notion that investigation amounts to the painstaking assemblage of evidence to reveal a previously unidentified criminal is largely without foundation.

More recently, an avalanche of victim surveys have demonstrated the extent to which the police are reliant upon the public for knowledge of crime in their area (US Department of Justice 1976–1998; Hindelang & Gottfredson 1976; Hough, M. & Mayhew 1983, ibid. 1985; Skogan 1984; Mirrlees-Black *et al.* 1996; Gottfredson 1986; Mayhew *et al.* 1989, ibid. 1993). Criminologists have long suspected that there is a vast number of offences that go unrecorded in the criminal statistics – what they call the "dark figure" of crime. What victim surveys have demonstrated is that it is the public who have the greatest influence on the size of this "dark figure" by not *reporting* offences. Moreover, this pattern of non-reporting varies between types of offence and is often susceptible to arbitrary influences such as the need to comply with insurance company procedures before claims can be made. This largely explains why virtually all thefts of and from motor vehicles are reported, but only a third to a quarter of legally more serious offences of violence are brought to the attention of the police.

Perhaps if there were more police they would prove more effective. However, such a relationship is evident neither from international comparisons, nor from comparing different police forces within particular countries, nor from comparing the effects of fluctuating police strength over time. Bayley found that it was difficult to make international comparisons for want of good evidence, but in so far as it possible it seems that there is little correlation between police numbers and levels of crime (Bayley 1985). There is much better evidence for crime patterns within countries; but the problems of analysis are formidable, since social and economic conditions might vary and so might the particular mix of crimes between areas. However, it is clear that per capita expenditure on policing in Britain is not correlated with low crime rates nor with an ability to clear up those offences that are committed (Audit Commission 1993). When the year-long strike by coal miners led to a significant shift in police officers from the streets of non-mining areas to the coalfields, there was little discernible impact on crime levels (Waddington 1985). Carr-Hill and Stern even suggest that the more police there are in an area the more likely it is that offences will be reported to them, thus offsetting any deterrent impact that their presence might otherwise have had (Carr-Hill & Stern 1979). Perhaps even more dramatically, since the election of Mrs Thatcher's government in 1979 until the early 1990s expenditure on policing increased by 75 per cent in real terms but this did not prevent crime rates doubling (Cassels 1996; see also Audit Commission 1993). There is, in short, precious little evidence that spending money on policing has any discernible payoff in reducing crime.

In conclusion, the general consensus among researchers is that the police have, and could only have, limited impact upon crime rates (Manning 1980a). This has recently, and vigorously, been challenged by Sherman who argues that it is too defeatist (Sherman 1986; ibid. 1992a). He points to the success that has been achieved in focusing police effort on crime "hot spots" as a means for the police to make a significant impact on crime. However, not even Sherman suggests that such ventures would radically transform policing to the extent that would be necessary in order for the police to justify their public image as society's principal bulwark against crime (Sherman 1993). The most that one can claim is that the police have only a marginal impact on crime rates, but that the size of that margin might be capable of expansion.

Not a Crime-Fighting Organization

Just because the police are ineffective as crime-fighters does not mean that crime-fighting is not their main *raison d'être*. Various critics have suggested ways in which crime-fighting might be improved. We have seen that Sherman prescribes the rational targeting of "hot spots", while others promote "community policing", "zero tolerance", and the like. We will consider these prescriptions later in this book, but for the moment just note that critics are *agreed* that policing needs radical change if it is to become more effective in crime control. The way that policing has traditionally been performed is simply not good enough. Now, this raises an intriguing question: why, if this is the case, are police in so many jurisdictions organized as they are? Has there been a world-wide conspiracy among police officers stretching over a century or more to foist ineffective crime control on the public? Have succeeding generations of police administrators been so catastrophically inept that it has taken a bunch of late twentieth-century academic reformers to point out that policing methods must change?

It is difficult to imagine that when in 1829 Robert Peel dispersed his "New Police" throughout London in highly visible attire he imagined that they would capture many criminals. Surely, it was apparent from the beginning that if crime-fighting was the principal goal (as Peel insisted it was), then penetration of the criminal "underworld" by police acting *in cognito* or through the employment of police spies would have a much greater likelihood of success. There was a model for such an efficient crime control organization in Fouche's police in Revolutionary France, but Peel and his cronies recoiled from the idea. The addition of a detective arm to the London Metropolitan Police had to wait for over a generation – a delay that indicates a lack of political will. Yet, it was precisely the fact that Peel's "New Police" were so visible that encouraged others, especially in the United States, to model their own police forces along these lines (Miller 1977a). Despite climbing crime rates for much of the twentieth century and their escalation since the Second World War, there has been little demand for a radical re-structuring of policing. True, police forces have invested increasingly in technology, such as radio and motorized patrol, but policing remains very largely the same as it did a hundred years ago, with patrol the principal investment of resources. Despite its singular failure to control escalating crime levels, patrolling continues to be practised in ways that seem designed to perpetuate ineffectiveness. For instance, police patrolling is almost entirely restricted to public places, such as streets, whereas much crime is committed in private (Stinchcombe 1963). If the task of the police was genuinely to fight crime why does the police organization continue to be shackled by this private/public distinction? Why does this organization continue to survive almost entirely unchanged when it consistently, universally and spectacularly fails to achieve its avowedly prime goal?

If policing was genuinely devoted to crime-fighting police priorities would be radically altered. Instead of searching for thieves, rapists and murderers, police would concentrate upon those areas of social life where criminal activity is rife. Lawlessness is endemic on our highways as motorists defy speed restrictions and commit a multitude of actions that amount to violations of the criminal law. Nor are these minor transgressions, as the toll of deaths and injuries, not to mention the cost of damage to property, attests. Yet, traffic policing is regarded by police and public alike as a marginal police responsibility, almost a distraction from "real police work" (a judgement that social scientists tacitly endorse by the lack of attention given to this aspect of policing). As many radical, and not-so-radical, critics have been eager to point out, the criminality to be found on the streets is pretty low-level compared to that perpetrated by corporate executives and other "white collar" criminals (Nelken 1994). One only needs to consider the injury and death caused by unsafe industrial processes and the vast sums misappropriated by various corporate scams to appreciate the seriousness of "white collar crime". Yet, such crime is not only something to which the police pay little attention, it is an area of criminality from which they are all but excluded institutionally in favour of various regulatory mechanisms, including self-regulation (Braithwaite & Fisse 1987). Now, it is certainly arguable that so-called "compliance" strategies are more effective than enforcement strategies (Reiss 1983, ibid. 1984). However, the significance for us in seeking a definition of policing is that corporate crime represents a whole swathe of criminality that hardly touches policing. Policing, as we normally understand it, concentrates on "crime on the streets" not "crime in the suites". If the police were genuinely a crime-fighting organization, they would not be so marginalized.

Just One Law Enforcer Among Many

Even if the police do not spend all, or even most, of their time engaged in law enforcement, are not very good at it, and do not deploy their resources to most effect, crime-fighting might still be their defining characteristic if they alone had responsibility for it. However, that is very far from being the case, for there is, in virtually all jurisdictions, a plethora of other law enforcers, arguably more effective than the police (Rock 1995a). First, there are those officials responsible for detecting breaches of particular laws, such as those concerning immigration, customs and excise, trading standards, tax and television licence evasion, social security fraud, abusive or obscene telephone calls, and much more besides. Secondly, there is the army of inspectors who enforce the law on such things as weights and measures, the construction of buildings, health and safety at work, environmental health, pollution, and the safety of public transport (Carson 1970; Hutter 1989). Thirdly, there are private individuals who acquire enforcement responsibilities by virtue of their employment, such as company auditors who must report any breach of company law to the authorities. Finally, there are, in addition, private commercial and voluntary organizations who, while not mandated to enforce the law, do so none the less, such as officers of the Royal Society for the Prevention of Cruelty to Animals, Royal Society for the Protection of Birds and National Society for the Prevention of Cruelty to Children. Research for the Royal Commission on Criminal Procedure found that around 20 per cent of all prosecutions were brought by public bodies other than the police (Lidstone *et al.* 1980), a figure that excludes private individuals and organizations. It is at least arguably the case that many of these organizations are devoted much more exclusively to law enforcement than are the police. To this list should be added others, like investigative journalists, whose actions have a determining influence on law enforcement agencies. In some cases, journalists expose wrongdoing and then merely hand over their dossiers of evidence to prosecuting authorities in much the same way that the police do.

Moreover, if we take seriously the notion that it is the *prevention* of crime that defines policing, then we need to acknowledge the vast contribution that *non*-police organizations and individuals make to the achievement of this goal. Local authorities that install crime prevention devices in premises on high-crime public housing estates seem to have a considerable impact on rates of residential burglary (Allatt 1984). Teachers might not see their task as preventing their charges from committing crimes, but undoubtedly one of the measures that reduced crime in the second half of the nineteenth century was the introduction of compulsory education that swept large numbers of children from the street and into the classroom. Indeed, the whole "disciplined" style of industrialized production that evolved in the second half of the nineteenth century was probably responsible for the reduction in crime that occurred during this period (Lane 1992). The explanation for the growth of crime during the second half of the twentieth century seems readily explicable in terms of how these "disciplines" have atrophied in the face of much greater social and geographical mobility, public anonymity and privatized style of living. Central government, through its manipulation of economic policy, seems to have a profound effect on not only the overall level of crime, but also the types of crime committed. Field's impressive econometric analysis of British crime rates over the twentieth century found that when the economic cycle moved into recession acquisitive crimes increased, presumably as individuals substituted illicit for legal means of satisfying their material aspirations. When, on the other hand, the economy began to improve then crimes of violence showed a distinct increase, probably for the simple reason that people with money in their pockets want to enjoy themselves in the company of others whom they then attack (Field 1990). In other words, the police cannot lay claim to be society's "thin blue line" against disorder and lawlessness, for they are supplemented by a host of social controls which, if absent, would leave the police virtually powerless.

Crime? Not the Task of the Police

Police have largely been castigated for their failure to stem the soaring crime rate. An alternative approach is to question whether crime-fighting is the actual goal of policing at all. In his historical analysis of the British Prison Service, Thomas (1972) distinguishes between goals that are stated and those to which the organization actually aspires. The latter can be determined, he argues, from what constitutes a "disaster" for the organization. Thus, in the case of prisons, the true disaster was not failing to rehabilitate prisoners – the notional top priority – but the occurrence of riots and escapes. Applied to policing this suggests that accelerating crime rates throughout most of the western world have not precipitated the "disaster" that would have occurred if their task was genuinely that of crime-fighting. Whatever the pretence to the contrary, the conclusion seems quite clear: policing is not primarily concerned with crime-fighting.

Peacekeeping and Service?

If policing cannot convincingly be defined in terms of law enforcement and crime-fighting, can it be accommodated by a definition that acknowledges the breadth of the police role? There is merit in this approach, but it too ultimately fails to explain what is distinctive about policing.

We have already seen how the notion of policing as law enforcement fails to explain the chronic under-enforcement of the law practised by officers. This was recognized by Banton in his pioneering comparison of Scottish and American police when he drew a distinction between the police as "law officers" and "peace officers" (Banton 1964). The essential difference lies in the goals that the police are seeking to achieve. The goal of a "law officer" is to enforce the law as an end in itself, but the "peace officer" seeks to maintain order and uses a variety of resources to do so. Hence, Reiss's observation, quoted above, that the police only rarely make arrests despite plentiful opportunities to do so. If Pete and Al can escort the drunk out of the bar, then order is restored without the necessity of arresting him. Much routine police work consists of quelling various forms of "trouble" that the public draw to officers' attention. Thus, troublesome passengers find themselves ejected from buses, customers are removed from shops and places of entertainment, and boisterous youngsters are "moved on" from the streetcorners on which they gather. Frequently, the mere act of reporting the problem to the police is sufficient for the troublesome people to depart the scene, leaving the police little to do upon arrival but report to the dispatcher that everything was now "all quiet". In doing so, police maintain order in an understated and largely unacknowledged fashion.

Much of this order maintenance work involves disputes that erupt between people in some kind of relationship, usually members of the same family. A staple of policing is intervening in "domestic" disputes between spouses, lovers, parents and children and so forth. Officers typically quell the ferocity of the quarrel and then try and discover what the dispute is about, what alternatives are open to the parties to resolve it or at least prevent its re-eruption into a disturbance, and then to persuade, cajole, coerce and ultimately force compliance with their preferred solution (Kemp *et al.* 1992a). On some occasions their task may be passively to stand guard and provide reassurance as when, for instance, one person returns to premises they have shared with an estranged partner to retrieve personal possessions. Such disputes range across the spectrum from civilized disagreement to violent struggles, and can involve individuals or groups.

Much of this is routine and free from danger, but police can find that "peacekeeping" exposes them to serious threat of violence such as on an occasion that I witnessed during observations in Reading. In the midst of the miners' strike of 1984 to 1985, when a large proportion of the available manpower (and it was exclusively male) had been deployed to the coalfields, I accompanied Dave and a handful of newly trained recruits in a personnel carrier as they patrolled the town during a Saturday evening. They had been requested to pay special attention to a particular pub that was the favoured meeting place of a local gang of skinheads. It had lost its licence to sell alcohol and this was its last day of operation before going out of business. Rumour had it that to "celebrate" the occasion a gang of skinheads from a neighbouring town would visit the pub in order to stage a fight. On one of our repeated passes by the pub trouble erupted right in front of us. A crowd was gathered outside the pub and suddenly one young man reeled away from it, blood pouring from a wound that had nearly severed his ear. Jumping from the personnel carrier officers pushed their way between the two factions who had already commenced a general brawl, while others administered first aid and Dave summoned an ambulance. The two groups of skinheads squared up to each other just a few yards apart, with the line of new police recruits between them becoming increasingly anxious. Dave had asked over the radio for reinforcements, but had been told that it would take at least twenty minutes for them to arrive. So he began walking casually between the two, now separated, groups and engaging individuals in conversation. He recognized one as the brother of someone he had recently arrested and said to another "Don't I know you? You live in Whitley." Eventually, a couple of vans with dogs and handlers arrived and then more uniformed officers. The visiting group of skinheads was escorted to the railway station a brief walk away and the incident was over. As we resumed our patrol I congratulated Dave on his skill in handling the confrontation. He confirmed my impression that his tactic had been to deny anonymity to members of the gang. "'We might lose it tonight'", he explained, "'but they know I know who they are and we'll be around in the morning'". Although he had smiled broadly throughout the episode he confessed that he had been enormously anxious, or as he put it, "I was shitting myself!". It is noteworthy that apart from my field notes the only account of this incident lies in the brief records of radio transmissions and the eventual "write off" – once the visitors had been escorted to their train – that all was now quiet. No one was arrested and no formal action of any kind resulted.

It is in taking a wide variety of actions, many of them informal, that the craft of "peacekeeping" is manifested (Muir 1977; Bittner 1983; Bayley & Bittner 1984, ibid. 1985). For example, Kemp *et al.* describe an episode in which a police officer tries to arbitrate in a dispute between householders and a demolition firm who have dropped rubble into the former's garden. The aim of the officer is to have the dispute resolved informally by apology from the site manager and the payment of a small amount of money as compensation for the modest damage caused (Kemp *et al.* 1992a: 57–59). On other occasions less orthodox methods might be employed:

> An elderly gentleman presented himself at East Ham police station. Proffering a piece of paper, he said to the inquiry officer: "I've done my lines". The paper contained the words "I must not drive in the No Entry zone" 50 times. Further investigation revealed that an officer had indeed pulled him up for a minor transgression, but added as a joke: "If you do 50 lines, I'll let you off this time." ("Dogberry", *Police* magazine, January 1996: 9)

However, it is clear that while the police often resort to informal means of restoring some semblance of order, the *potential* of invoking the law remains salient. The skinheads did not consummate their confrontation because of Dave's charm, but because they feared that they would be recognized and vulnerable to arrest on a future occasion. When Pete and Al escorted the drunk from the bar the drunk knew that any resistance would result in arrest and outside they used the prospect of arrest as a threat. Thus, the maintenance of order is quite definitely conducted within the "shadow of the law".

Help and Assistance

It is not only through sub-criminal disorder that "the peace" is disturbed and police intervene to restore it. Another common task that police perform is to apprehend the mentally ill for their own safety and that of others. Here too, the police have available a range of options from which they select to deal with a given problem (Bittner 1967a). Writing of policing in the "red light" district of Amsterdam, Punch records two incidents that display the range of police action. In the first, police are called to an elderly woman on a bus who is clearly deranged and was returned to the old people's home where she resided wearing a police officer's hat and "waving regally out of the window" of the police car (Punch 1979a: 136). A much less savoury incident concerned an elderly man who lived in indescribable filth and had apparently tried to set fire to the couch on which he sat in his apartment. The police discovered that neighbours had tried to persuade him to seek help, but that he had attacked one of them with knife. "Tired of the almost overpowering smell, two patrolmen grabbed the old man, pulled him unwillingly down the stairs and shoved him, with his two yapping dogs, complaining into the back of the van", later charging him with attempted murder (Punch 1979a: 138). Thus, while the police may or may not use the law, it is clear that in the case of the mentally ill their intervention is intended to help everyone concerned, not least the mentally ill person who might – like the man sat on the couch – be a danger to themselves (Bittner 1967a).

While both order maintenance and apprehending the mentally ill both involve the use of legal powers, the involvement of the police in helping people in distress extends far beyond anything that could remotely be described as law enforcement. As Bittner remarks, "no human problem exists, or is imaginable, about which it could be said with finality that this certainly could not become the proper business of the police" (Bittner 1974: 30). Amongst the calls made to a divisional control room were the routine, tragic and bizarre (Waddington 1993a). Callers informed the police that elderly people had not been seen for some time during very cold weather and officers invariably visited to assure themselves that the person was safe, breaking into their homes where necessary to render assistance to those in distress or confirm death. Police are asked to seek missing people, especially children, and while most return home safely, this sometimes involves police in acute personal tragedies unconnected with crime. On the other hand, police humour often celebrates the sometimes bizarre incidents in which they become involved:

> Police in Kent didn't know whether to laugh or cry about the very sad fate that befell two young women who set out on a day trip to France with the intention of picking up cheap wine and other bargains. Their van ran out of diesel on the M20. Instead of using a nearby motorway telephone they hitched a lift with a lorry driver who took them 20 miles to a filling station near the Dartford Tunnel. Here they filled up a can with fuel and hired a taxi to return to the van, paying the

> driver £50 in advance. Unfortunately they could not remember where they had left their vehicle and, after a fruitless search, returned to the filling station and dialled 999 to report it stolen. Meanwhile the taxi drove off, with their fuel still inside. Police helped them locate the van, which by now had a flat battery because the hazard lights had been left on. A garage had to be called out to tow it, at a cost of £130. And they never did get that wine. ('Dogberry", *Police* magazine, February 1996: 26)

So diverse is the police role that some commentators have suggested that they should be considered a social service (Punch & Naylor 1973; Punch 1979b), while Cumming *et al.* describe the police officer as a "philosopher, guide and friend". This extended role is not restricted to modern societies characterized by anonymity. Bayley remarks of India:

> Policemen are continually called upon to perform a host of services for members of the public that have nothing at all to do with maintaining order and preventing crime. . . . The Indian police are not unique in the extent to which they are loaded with duties extraneous to their primary functions. Policemen around the world complain of this, and with good reason. (Bayley 1969)

The same author describes how in Japan police render an enormously wide range of services to local residents, including assistance with the completion of bureaucratic forms (Bayley 1976).

Yet it would misleading to divorce these aspects of the role from that of narrow law enforcement or to seek a definition of policing as either exclusively concerned with law enforcement (Lea & Young 1984) or "care" rather than "control" (Stephens & Becker 1994a, ibid. b). As Punch, himself an advocate of the "social service" aspects of policing, reminds us:

> A benign and experienced constable, polished at handling "domestics", still brings to the situation a uniform, weaponry and a battery of resource charges which can be called upon if he fails to negotiate a satisfactory outcome. (Punch 1979a: 147)

Alice Hills equally points out that in responding to civil disasters, such as fires, train and air crashes, and crowd stampedes, no simple distinction can be drawn between "care" and "control", since controlling the scene becomes the *sine qua non* for care to be administered (Hills 1997). It was the failure of the police to control the situation at the Hillsborough soccer stadium that both led to the disaster itself and impeded an effective response by the emergency services (Taylor 1989). Moreover, Shapland and Vagg point to the fluidity of most incidents in which the police become involved. In many instances, it is initially far from clear whether or not police are dealing with a criminal matter. Clarity tends to dawn slowly during the course of the encounter as a result of the construction that is placed upon events by the various parties – most notably, but not exclusively, the police themselves (Shapland & Vagg 1988: 36–39).

Monopolists of Force?

In searching for some underlying unity midst the apparent diversity of police activity a consensus has emerged in police research that the essence of policing lies not in what police *do* but in their *potential*, specifically their potential to use legitimate force. As Shapland and Hobbs note:

> The problem is that most of the so-called "service" jobs of the police (which, indeed, were sometimes seen by officers as not "police work") have a potential emergency element which may involve the need for coercion or legally sanctioned violence against persons or property. (1989: 22)

Pete and Al might have dealt with the troublesome drunk informally, but, for whatever reason, their colleagues who burst through the door of the police station struggling with him later that night, opted for an alternative course of action. It is the availability of recourse to force that, according to Bittner, distinguishes police from others (Bittner 1970, ibid. 1974). While some occupations and individuals are entitled to use force in specific circumstances or towards particular individuals, the remit of the police entails a *general* capacity to use forceful means. This allows police authoritatively to intervene in a wide range of situations, impose provisional solutions and "brook no opposition": when they instruct troublesome individuals to "move on" this is accompanied by the unspoken qualification "or else". Even when providing help to those in distress, the capacity to use force is a valuable resource. Thus, if an elderly person does not answer their door, the police can, and not infrequently do, *break-in* to administer first aid or confirm death. People report such things as dangerously icy road conditions to the police, so that the latter can *close* the road, not simply advise road-users of the danger. In searching for a missing child the police may enter, by force if necessary, property from which others are excluded. Because of this general capacity to use force, the police become the repository for dealing with any situation that involves "something-that-ought-not-to-be-happening-and-about-which-someone-had-better-do-something-now!" (Bittner 1974: 30).

Bittner's formulation, to which most researchers now subscribe, is tremendously insightful and instructive. Not only does it encompass the diversity of law enforcement and routine peacekeeping, but other tasks that the police perform such as public order and traffic control. A line of police officers can act as a cordon preventing access to a location by a crowd far more numerous than themselves, not because they physically prevent the crowd pushing them aside, but because they symbolically demarcate what is permissible from impermissible – breach the cordon and there will be trouble. Likewise, a traffic officer is unable forcibly to stop a speeding motorist, but if the signal to pull over is ignored then the driver is inviting serious trouble. This was fictitiously, but powerfully, illustrated in the film *Vanishing Point* in which the driver of a high-powered car defeats all attempts to halt his progress until he is killed at an unsurpassable road block. However, there remain objections and difficulties even with this concept.

Non-Forceful Encounters

Sykes and Brent object to the emphasis given to force on the grounds that police only rarely make recourse to force, the vast majority of police–public encounters being conducted perfectly cordially (Sykes & Brent 1983). Certainly, their observations that most encounters are civil have been confirmed by victim surveys and other observers (Smith 1983a; Moxon & Jones 1984; Southgate & Ekblom 1984; ibid. 1986; Southgate & Crisp 1993; Skogan 1994). They also receive support from Kleinig (Kleinig 1996) who doubts the wisdom, on ethical grounds, of defining policing in terms of a largely unrealized potential. He fears that if police come to accept that policing is defined by their monopoly of force, they might be tempted towards greater use of forceful means. However, Sykes and Brent's own meticulously collected and analyzed data undermines their critique of Bittner, for it demonstrates two things: first, that police intervention is authoritative and, second, that on those rare occasions when their authority is questioned coercion follows – usually pretty speedily. Their analysis shows that encounters with members of the public are suffused with authority: exchanges between police and others can be reduced to a simple pairing of action and reaction in which the police almost invariably lead. Hence, police ask questions and members of the public provide answers; police make allegations to which the accused should respond with admission or denial, but not a question or silence. Anyone breaking such an "adjacency pair" – for example, by replying to a question with question ("What's going on here?", "Who wants to know?") – can expect to receive short shrift from the police. Such minor incivility is regarded as a challenge to police authority that provokes a coercive response. Thus, what Sykes and Brent's data demonstrates is just how thin is the veneer of civility in police–public encounters and that the maintenance of civility relies on *members of the public* deferring to the authority of the police (Sykes & Clark 1975); if they refuse, then the coercive underpinnings of that authority are clearly revealed, especially when police authority is publicly and visibly challenged (Worden 1996).

Care

A less explicit objection can be extrapolated from the observation that a substantial slice of police work entails, not *control*, but *care* (Stephens & Becker 1994a, ibid. b). How, one might ask is the "monopoly of force" related to helping those in distress? Bittner was acutely aware of this, since he himself had analyzed how police deal with the mentally ill (Bittner 1967a). This analysis showed how police tried to avoid having the person committed to a psychiatric hospital, an approach that might seem "caring" but which also had considerable elements of expediency. However, it also demonstrates *inter alia* that the final recourse is the *forcible* apprehension of the deranged person. In other apparently "caring" aspects of their role, the capacity ultimately to use force can be detected. When elderly people are thought by neighbours to be ill (or worse) it is the monopoly of force that enables the police to *break in*. At road accidents it is this monopoly that enables police to *direct* traffic and *control* crowds. The realization that the "monopoly of force" is compatible with administering "care" as well as "control" is a useful corrective to those analyzes of policing that seek to impose such facile dichotomies. Yet, it is difficult to understand what role, however latent, the "monopoly of force" plays in informing relatives of the sudden death of loved ones, or the reassurance that victims of crimes such as burglary feel by the arrival of the police (Maguire 1982). One answer is that the police simply acquire residual tasks because they are readily available around the clock to respond to emergencies (Punch & Naylor 1973; Punch 1979b). If so, then it needs to be explained why police acquire only particular residual functions and not others. Police do not feed the poor or house the homeless; they do not provide foster parents for orphaned children; they do not repair broken-down cars, even when occupants are far from home; nor do they awaken students who have overslept on the morning of vital examinations.

Patrol Force

Defining the police task in terms of the potential to use force is problematic for other reasons too. These all arise from the tendency of researchers to treat policing as a series of discrete episodes. When ethnographers describe "police work" they invariably do so by describing a series of *encounters*. Likewise, non-participant observation counts discrete contacts between particular police officers and identifiable members of the public. This leaves much of policing ignored. First, routine patrolling is hardly ever mentioned: it is wandering aimlessly "waiting for something to happen" (Bayley 1994: 23). Yet, most of the time of most police personnel is actually consumed in wandering aimlessly as did Pete and Al for most the time that I accompanied them. If this is simply making oneself available for mobilization, then it is a strangely universal method of doing so. There are alternatives: the fire and ambulance services do not wander aimlessly, but deploy from fixed locations. It has already been established that there is little crime-fighting payoff from patrolling and yet police in hundreds of jurisdictions throughout the western world feel compelled to wander the streets. Although the Japanese police are noted for the mini-police stations that are situated in most localities (the koban), and to which local residents go for a wide range of police services, the police share the compulsion of their western counterparts to use it as a base from which to patrol the area (Bayley 1976). It is a compulsion that equally afflicted the colonial police in the days of empire, when they rode out in armed columns "to show the flag" (Anderson & Killingray 1991). The more difficult such aimless wandering becomes, the more resources are devoted to ensuring that it continues unimpeded. In South Africa, during the period that the ANC were making the townships "ungovernable" as part of the liberation struggle, the South African Police continued to patrol albeit in armoured personnel carriers bristling with weapons, or in squads of eight or more walking gingerly, with one officer on "point" scouting for danger and another walking backwards protecting the rear from attack. A similar scene has been common in Northern Ireland: a military platoon accompanied by one or more helicopters, deployed to escort a "community constable" through an area where terrorism flourished. As Weitzer comments:

> The patrols play little role in the control of ordinary crime or insurgent activities. . . . Rather, the goal appears to be more symbolic: the RUC can claim it does community policing in every neighbourhood and the patrols are another way of demonstrating, with officers on foot as well as in landrovers, that the authorities remain "in control" of the area or at least have not been driven out by insurgents. It is yet another display of the police presence in an area, preventing the establishment of "no-go" areas, like those that appeared during the disturbances of the early 1970s when Catholics erected barricades blocking entry to their neighbourhoods. (Weitzer 1995: 245)

Any suggestion that an area has become "no go" to the police is stoutly resisted and on occasion massive resources are deployed to "take back" those locations from which police have been excluded. Hence, in 1989 I accompanied officers of the London Metropolitan Police who, in their hundreds and backed by armed squads, raided a "symbolic location" on the Broadwater Farm housing estate on the pretext that it had become a centre for drug dealing. The raid was conceived in the utmost secrecy and officers were summoned to the force training centre at Hendon under the subterfuge that they would be participating in an "exercise". After a morning briefing, officers moved to a forward holding area, from which the "first wave", clad in riot-gear and body armour, embarked into furniture vans that entered the estate without disclosing the nature of their "cargo". Officers leapt from the vans and stormed the citadel from every direction simultaneously, arresting those who were wanted for drug-trafficking or who obstructed the operation. Later, I was allowed to watch covertly collected video evidence that showed the area as a brazen market place for supplying drugs. Twenty-seven suspects were eventually arrested and convicted for offences of supplying drugs, but the drugs found and the sentences handed down were hardly commensurate with the scale of the operation. The extent of the operation made no sense as a mere drugs-raid, but made perfect sense in terms of re-asserting police authority over territory. In order to establish the area as a drug market, dealers had made it a "no-go" area for the police: intimidating and harassing patrolling officers so that they avoided the area for fear of attack. This massive operation was intended to "take back" the erstwhile public space and assert that the police had the capacity to occupy it, even if it took an operation of this magnitude. All this indicates that there is more – much more – to patrolling than simply being available for mobilization. Patrolling is a symbolic affirmation of authority (Walker 1996).

Secondly, even the most fleeting contact between police officers is invested with a significance that seems only tenuously connected to the capacity to use force. One only needs to observe the change in driving behaviour in the vicinity of a police patrol car to appreciate that the mere presence of the police often has a profound impact upon those around them. One might imagine that such attentiveness is merely prudent, lest one inadvertently commits some offence. However, the police rarely pass by without the close attention of all those who see them. For example, when Pete and Al drove through the entertainment district, they became the centre of attention for many of those who caught sight of them. There seems little that could be prudential in such behaviour; indeed it might draw unwanted police attention to those who display it.

Thirdly, police routinely breach rules of common courtesy and casual contact. Overtly watching what others do and returning their gaze is a wholesale violation of norms of non-verbal behaviour in which police routinely engage (Rubenstein 1973). A shouted conversation with a pedestrian or other motorist from the window of a police car is normally thought of as aggressive, but is habitual amongst motorized police (Southgate & Ekblom 1986). Approaching a fellow citizen in a public place and requiring them, however politely, to account for themselves, is an intrusion into personal privacy of which the police think nothing (Southgate & Ekblom 1986). Instructing others how to behave in a public place, as when police direct traffic, is a denial of individual autonomy that few would impose. Denying access to public places, such as a road closed because of some emergency, is a restriction on the freedom of movement that would evoke public protest if imposed by anyone other than the police. Parking a police car in a "no parking" zone amounts to an immunity to legal restriction that is shared by few others. In short, police officers *routinely* act, in the performance of their duty, in ways that would otherwise be exceptional or downright illegal if done by anyone else.

Exercising Authority

What the police *do*, as opposed to have the potential to do, is *exercise authority*. They do so not only when they intervene in some incident, but also when they wander aimlessly about asserting their right not only to pass through public space, but also to *command* it by watching whoever they choose and tacitly granting permission to others to go about their business. This is illustrated daily in the vicinity of the famous Duomo in Florence where the pedestrian area is populated by dozens of street-traders and artists plying their wares to hordes of tourists. The area is safe and orderly: traders seem to have established "pitches" from which to do business and when my wife bought a painting from a street artist the transaction was conducted through the use of a credit card and the aid of a local shopkeeper with whom the artist had an arrangement. Periodically, however, this orderly scene is disrupted: artists quickly fold away their paintings and earnestly attend to capturing on canvas the scene before them; street-traders grasp the blankets on which their wares have been displayed and step into the shadows; musicians suddenly cease playing. The cause of this disruption is invariably a pair of patrolling police officers. When they have passed normality resumes and street-life recommences. This intervention by the police has neither a crime-fighting nor order-maintenance rationale, but it does assert police *command* of this area. It symbolizes to street-traders that they operate under a police dispensation that can be instantly and arbitrarily revoked. Patrolling might be disruptive of the order that normally prevails in the vicinity of the Duomo, but it is an assertion of police authority. When police intervene in some situation they do so *authoritatively: they* structure conversations around *their* concerns (Glauser & Tullar 1985); *they* are expected to display certainty and not equivocate (Holdaway 1983); *they* find it difficult to apologize, since that is tantamount to demeaning themselves (Southgate & Ekblom 1986); and most of all *they demand deference* (Sykes & Clark 1975). This is no less true when they offer help and assistance as opposed to imposing control. The reason that the police inform relatives of a sudden death is because they have the *authority* to do so. Now, this is no more than a quibble with Bittner's formulation, for the authority that police exercise is undoubtedly founded upon the monopoly of legitimate force, that is, it is essentially *coercive*. However, it remains an important quibble, because we must be aware that such authority is not exercised episodically when police become involved in some incident, but imbues *everything* that the police do.

Policing, Citizens and the State

Not only does the notion of policing as the ubiquitous exercise of coercive authority lend coherence to police activity (and apparent inactivity), but it links this level of analysis with that of the police role in wider society. For the authority that police officers exercise is granted by the state: they are the *custodians* of the state's monopoly of legitimate force. The police do not intervene is *any* emergency – for entirely private matters remain largely outside their responsibility. They intervene when an emergency is or threatens to become *public*: thus assisting someone locked out of premises or a vehicle *authorizes* otherwise illegal behaviour. In the next chapter it will be argued that responding to victims with care and consideration *authoritatively* confirms their victimhood. This recognition that the authority the police wield is that of the state draws our attention to two crucial issues: *who* is policed and how policing is organized.

If policing is the exercise of authority, then we must consider those over whom that authority is exercised. I do not refer here to the particular individuals whom they coerce, but the generality of the population. In authoritarian societies this poses little problem, since the police are unambiguously the arm of those who wield power. However, in those societies claiming democratic status, it poses an enormous problem for, as Klockars notes, installing a police force entails that the general population licenses certain of their fellows to coerce the rest of them (Klockars 1985). In other words, policing lies at the hub of the conundrum that has occupied political philosophers for centuries – the role of the state as both a guarantor of, and most powerful threat to, liberty. The irony is that the "police idea" takes hold and develops during the same period and in the same place that the notion of "citizenship" is also taking root.

According to Marshall's classic thesis, citizenship has three elements that developed more or less in succession in the eighteenth, nineteenth and twentieth centuries (Marshall 1950). Initially, during the eighteenth century, the population was granted civil rights "necessary for individual freedom – liberty of the person, freedom of speech, thought and faith, the right to own property and to conclude valid contracts, and the right to justice" (Marshall 1950: 10). This was followed, in the nineteenth century, by the extension of political rights "to participate in the exercise of political power, as a member of a body invested with political authority or as an elector of the members of such a body" (p. 11). More contentiously, Marshall asserts that the twentieth century has seen the development of a range of social rights "from the right to a modicum of economic welfare and security to the right to share to the full in the social heritage and to live the life of a civilized being according to the standards prevailing in the society" (p. 11). It has been the last of these elements, and particularly its relationship to social class, that has been the focus of much of the debate that has recently been awakened by the rediscovery of Marshall's thesis (Turner 1990, ibid. 1993a, ibid. 1993b). However, it is Marshall's less contentious observations on the development of civil and political citizenship that command our attention.

The development of civil and political elements of citizenship are crucial to understanding policing, since it is the police whose exercise of authority threatens to curtail those liberties; for example by stopping and searching a suspect or re-routing a potentially disorderly protest march. It is in the contested terrain between statehood and citizenship that we find the explanation for Peel's abstinence from following the undoubtedly successful French model of policing. For the degree of resistance that greeted Peel's proposals to institute his "New Police" pays ample testimony to the extent to which the civil element of citizenship had taken root in England by the end of the eighteenth century (Stead 1977; Critchley 1978; ibid. 1985a; Emsley 1991). "Policing" was repugnant to the English because it was equated with the autocratic power of the French monarchy, with its militarized forms of police patrol and ubiquitous spying, both of which were regarded as inimical to liberty. For instance, Emsley quotes the *Daily Universal Register* (that was later to become the august *Times*) as rejecting a proposal to introduce a police force in London in 1785: "Our constitution can admit nothing like a French police; and many foreigners have declared that they would rather lose their money to an English thief, than their liberty to a *Lieutenant de Police*." (Emsley 1983: 28)

Palmer points out that opposition to the installation of a police in London was common across the social spectrum and founded upon a strong attachment to the notion of the "free born Englishman" that had emerged from the ruins of the feudal system (Palmer 1988). Yet, paradoxically and despite appearances, once established, the police in Britain quickly acquired responsibilities for regulating a broad, indeed indefinite, spectrum of routine activity not very different to that of their counterparts on the continent. Legislation gave them omnibus powers to control the burning of bonfires, shaking of floor-coverings, flying of kites and many more everyday occurrences. They became responsible for the licensing of dogs, public houses, places of entertainment, aliens, guns and prisoners released on "ticket of leave". Despite the long-standing antipathy to a "standing army", this is exactly what Peel's reforms produced, albeit disguised as a "police", rather than military, force.

The police idea was established in the face of widespread opposition and so the question arises: why was it able to prevail? Historians have given various answers to that question. The principal division of opinion is between, on the one hand, "Whig historians", who see in the police an institution that "preserved society from 'uncontrollable crime and mob violence' " (Emsley 1983: 4) and who attribute opposition to the police idea as a form of perversity. Their interpretation of history is opposed, on the other, by "revisionists" (Reiner 1985a) who – not to put too fine a point on it – see the police as an instrument of ruling class oppression (for example, Harring 1983). A secondary division exists between those who argue that traditional systems of maintaining order had collapsed under the weight of urbanization and industrialization, and those who argue that traditional institutions remained viable and were gratuitously swept aside. Yet another argument is between those who insist that the New Police were intended to address problems of crime, whereas others give greater prominence to the threat of mob violence and the general disorder of the streets as a motivator.

It is unnecessary for our purposes to delve too deeply into these debates, for what seems beyond dispute is that the police, at least in England, was a product of the massive growth of the state during the last half of the eighteenth and first half of the nineteenth centuries. Beside this singular fact these various disagreements seem to pale into insignificance. The police, and the state they served, was *both* oppressive *and* benign. Policing reflected this dual role: the "street life" of the lower classes was repressed while a blind eye was turned to other transgressions (Cohen 1979). Equally, there seems no compelling reason to believe that the prime motivation for installing a police was to control crime *or* disorder, since either of them presented a threat to the hegemony of state power that would need to be contained. Finally, revisionists might well be correct in arguing that traditional systems of crime control and dispute resolution had not broken down, but even where those systems continued to operate effectively they did so in an essentially *local* manner beyond the control of the state. As the state grew throughout the nineteenth century, it absorbed and transformed alternative systems of power and control. In its vanguard was the police, who in England became the "domestic missionary" promoting the "gospel" of social discipline (Storch 1976).

At the same time, the state could not ride roughshod in imposing its power on the civil population, for as it was developing, so too was the concept of citizenship. Indeed, it is tempting to regard the installation of Peel's professional police as itself an *expression* of citizenship, since it bifurcated the state's monopoly of force into civil and military realms. We will return to this issue later, but suffice it to note for now that state authority had been entrusted to military custodians long before the police were installed. Throughout the eighteenth century military intervention had been increasing

(Emsley 1983); the question is why it was thought necessary or prudent to remove military control of the civil population? The answer cannot be found in the inability of the military to perform policing duties for, as we will shortly see, the military continued its policing role throughout the empire. Indeed, it is something of a paradox that as the capacity of the military to subjugate the civil population by force became increasingly feasible and used throughout the colonies, so they increasingly retreated from doing so with regard to the domestic civil population (Vogler 1991). In other words, a sharp distinction came to be drawn between exercising coercive authority over one's own citizens and others whose claim to citizenship was non-existent or rejected. The distinction between the police and the military is that military violence is directed *away* from the state and its citizens. Those upon whom military violence may be inflicted are not "us", but "them", and therefore "we" need have no fear of military might. Indeed, the military, unlike the police, are valorized precisely because of their association with violence, which is used to protect or promote the interests of the state and its citizens.

This leaves the police in a curiously ambivalent position: as Bittner (Bittner 1970) notes, policing is a "tainted" occupation, which he attributes to the association of the police with crime, disorder, general unpleasantness, but most of all to the police use of violence. However, as the military parallel illustrates, it is not association with violence *per se* that taints policing, but the fact that police may use violence against "us" and therefore they present a threat – a threat that is recognized every time a driver checks his speed in the presence of a police car. What this has meant for policing, at least in England (and later, America), was that its authority would need careful legitimation. Thus, from the outset Peel's New Police trod cautiously in their dealings with the civil population, as indicated in the General Instructions issued to the infant London Metropolitan Police:

> He will be civil and attentive to all persons of every rank and class; insolence or incivility will not be passed over.
>
> . . . He must be particularly cautious, not to interfere idly or unnecessarily; when required to act, he will do so with decision and boldness; on all occasions he may expect to receive the fullest support in the execution of his authority.
>
> He must remember, that there is no qualification more indispensable to a Police Officer, than a perfect command of temper, never suffering himself to be moved in the slightest degree, by any language or threats that may be used; if he do his duty in a quiet and determined manner, such conduct will probably induce well-disposed by-standers to assist him, should he require it. (Quoted in Stead 1985a: 41)

Central to the process of legitimation was the promulgation of crime-fighting as the *raison d'être* of policing. Again, it is instructive to quote the General Instructions to the London Metropolitan Police:

> It should be understood, at the outset, that the principal object to be attained is "*the Prevention of Crime*". (Quoted in Stead 1985a: 40)

The appeal of crime-fighting as a legitimating symbol is compelling: criminals exclude themselves from the moral community of citizens by their actions. Moreover criminals represent a threat to other citizens and hence coercive authority can be justified as necessary to protect the innocent from the depredations of the lawless and disorderly. Thus, the police become depicted as heroic: the "thin blue line" that protects the citizenry from the depredations of the criminally inclined. Of course, reality repeatedly bursts through this ideological construction exposing both that the police role is not confined to crime-fighting and that they are not particularly effective crime-fighters. Policing is, therefore, precarious: its "cover" can be "blown" at any time and the coercive power of the state exposed. Hence, the police expend considerable rhetorical resources in an unrelenting effort to perpetuate and restore faith in the mythology of crime-fighting.

The precariousness of the police institution is reflected in the distinctive "Anglo–Saxon" approach to policing.

> Anglo–Saxon police are deployed largely for emergency response, not for routine, low-visibility interaction with the public. . . . In large measure their deployment is conditioned by the suspicion with which they are viewed by the public. . . . The public questions police authority, argues about police intrusion, and is prepared to fend off police action through legal means. . . . It wants to keep the police at bay, is resentful of contact, and fearful of pervasive police intrusion into community life. But the public does not want to share responsibility for social control with the police either. Crime is a police matter. (Bayley 1982a: 5).

The danger in this discussion is that it is too parochial, indeed the reason for Bayley's designation of "Anglo–Saxon" policing is to differentiate it from "authoritarian" and "oriental" styles. In authoritarian systems:

> Police do not exist to help citizens, they exist to service the state. They do not placate the public, they direct it; they are not pressured by the public, they bully it. . . . Authoritarian police stress control through deterrence, not prevention through amelioration. . . . A sign of this is the martial appearance of Authoritarian police, with weapons displayed prominently. Authoritarian police try to overawe, and they easily do so having so many controls on their side. (Bayley 1982a: 2)

The more cynical reader might doubt the extent of the difference: police in all jurisdictions "exist to service the state". And can it really be maintained that police in Britain and America do not "bully" or "overawe"? However, what Bayley captures is a difference of general style that reflects a relationship between police and, on the one hand, citizens and on the other, non-citizens.

Policing Non-Citizens: The Colonial Example

Those differences of style come into clearer focus when we compare policing in very different socio–political contexts. One such context that proves particularly instructive is that of colonial policing.

Police research has paid relatively little attention to colonial policing (but see Mawby 1990), which is ironic since Robert Peel contrived to be founder of not only the epitome of civil policing – the London "bobby" – but also its antithesis the Royal Irish Constabulary – that became the model for a very different style of policing throughout the British Empire. Within the British Isles, Ireland was the first laboratory chosen for the policing experiment (Palmer 1988). As was to be repeated later on the mainland, opposition to the installation of professional police was fierce with the threat to liberty, coupled to anxieties about cost, to the forefront of objections. As was to happen in London, policing was established first in the capital city – Dublin – and only later extended to the rest of the province. However, it is the differences that are instructive: first, policing was introduced in Ireland much earlier than in mainland Britain, the first Dublin Police Act being passed in 1786. This was introduced against considerable public turmoil throughout Ireland as both Protestants and Catholics wrung concessions from the government in London. But London too was in turmoil in this period: it was, after all, the immediate aftermath of the Gordon Riots, when an anti-Catholic mob had rampaged through the heart of the capital for almost a week leaving hundreds dead and buildings ruined (Critchley 1970), as well as the earlier agitation of John Wilkes that was in many ways more serious since it promoted the movement that would result in the franchise being extended and aristocratic privilege undermined. Yet, in London the response of the ruling class was muted, whereas in Ireland it provoked the installation of a professional police for Dublin, at first armed and centrally controlled. The second difference is that as the idea of policing took hold in Ireland and it was spread throughout the rural hinterland, it remained centrally controlled. Whereas on the mainland, policing became an organizational patchwork of different types of police force operating in towns, counties and the capital. Thirdly, and most significantly, the police of all-Ireland (at first called the Peace Preservation Force and only later the Royal Irish Constabulary) very quickly evolved into an armed gendarmerie. Officers were housed in barracks segregated from the local population and patrolled in armed quasi-military columns (Palmer 1988). It was a style of policing that would culminate in a police force out of control and the massacre by the "Black and Tans" at Croker Park (Townshend 1992).

What explains the divergent paths that policing took from such similar origins in Ireland and England? An indication of the answer to this question lies in the fact that Ireland became the model for policing throughout the British empire: colonial police were trained in Dublin, and later Belfast; and the RIC (and later RUC) became a fertile recruiting ground for commissioned and non-commissioned officers in colonial police forces. The common policing problems that colonial police shared arose from their task in imposing an alien authority upon rebellious native populations (Anderson & Killingray 1991, ibid. 1992). Since those native populations did not comprise citizens, the colonial police were free to impose their authority without trepidation. Hence, the chiefs of rebellious tribes were summarily executed and villages burned as a form of collective punishment (Ahire 1991). The police themselves were often literally paramilitary (Hills 1995), a pattern continued by the South African Police who not only controlled the townships of apartheid South Africa like an occupying army, but ventured into bordering states to attack insurgents (Cawthra 1993). Police were housed in barracks from which they patrolled the surrounding territory in heavily armed columns (sometimes accompanied by artillery).

However, such a style of policing was not intrinsic to the police force *per se*, for paramilitary forces could and did transmute into civil police. The most notable examples were the Canadian North-West Mounted Police (the "Mounties") and the New Zealand Police. Initially, the "Mounties" were a quintessential paramilitary force, as is still evident from the red tunics and black riding breeches worn for ceremonial purposes and evocative of the traditional "red coats" of the nineteenth-century British army. The task of the Mounties was to pacify the frontier ahead of the settlers, a quasi-military operation that was accomplished by quasi-military means. Thereafter, once pacified, the Mounties adopted the style of civil police towards settlers and thus earned the affection that makes them still symbolic of Canadian nationhood (Morrison 1975, ibid. 1991). The New Zealand Police performed a similar role, taking a prominent part in the Maori wars, before disarming and transforming themselves into a civil police modelled explicitly on the London Metropolitan force when the task became one of policing the influx of immigrants from Britain (Hill 1986, ibid. 1991). The transformation of the RIC into the Garda Siochana after British rule ceased in the south of Ireland took a different route to the same conclusion: former members of the RIC were literally hounded from the country and an unarmed civil police was created as one of the most obvious tokens not only of independent statehood, but of the citizenship of the civil population (Ryder 1989). However not even colonial police forces were indiscriminately oppressive: Seegers points out that the apartheid South African Police were authoritarian and even totalitarian towards the black African population, but liberal in their dealings with whites (Seegers 1991). This suggests strongly that *how* a society is policed depends upon *who* is policed. When it is citizens with civil and political rights, then policing is approached with caution; but when the recipients of police authority are not citizens, then police are free to exercise naked coercive force.

Continental and Other Forms of Policing

The stark differences between metropolitan and colonial styles of policing, not least within the British Isles themselves, illustrate a wider implication of the fact that the police are the custodians of state authority: *how* that authority is exercised reflects the relationship between the state and the citizen.

> In sum, police structures are determined by political settlements and the traditions thus engendered. It follows that police structures are not affected by crime in general but only by one kind of crime: violent offences perceived to threaten the political order. The more frequent they are and the more threatening they seem, the more likely it is that a country's police system will be centralized. Challenges to the political legitimacy of government are the most powerful facilitators of police centralization. (Bayley 1985: 72)

Citizenship was nowhere won without bloodshed, but Bayley's observation alerts us to the fact that in some states it was achieved with greater difficulty than in the Anglo–Saxon world. This chimes with Mann's corrective to Marshall's exclusively English perspective on the growth of citizenship, drawing attention to the diverse routes through which citizenship has emerged. He argues that in "France, Spain and Italy reactionaries (usually monarchist and clerical) and secular liberals struggled over political citizenship for most of the nineteenth and twentieth centuries, with many violent changes of regime" (Mann 1996: 132). On the other hand, states such as Germany, Austria, Russia and Japan evolved in the direction of incorporating limited citizenship rights within authoritarian regimes, to which one might add that, in the case of Germany and Japan, democratic regimes were imposed following the Second World War while some elements of the previous political culture remained. These differences of political tradition continue to influence the structure of policing in continental Europe.

The monarchical centralism of France was evident in its early embrace of centralized militaristic policing designed to protect the ruling élite. Indeed, as has been noted above, the French system was, to late eighteenth- and early nineteenth-century English, the epitome of everything that was objectionable in the notion of policing *per se*. The reason for this being that the French then, as now, conceived policing unequivocally as the protection of the state. The guard of Paris and the *marechaussée* who policed the rural areas were both highly militarized and centrally directed (Emsley 1983). The political turmoil of, and following, the French Revolution, did not usher in a more civil style of policing; on the contrary, "one of the consequences of the Revolution was to inspire subsequent régimes to create a police apparatus which would protect them from revolution" (Roach 1985: 109). Yet, whilst the contemporary French police system still bears these hallmarks of its centralized, militaristic and authoritarian origins, it also reflects the pressure for citizenship. The paramilitary *Gendarmerie* is paralleled by the *Police Nationale*, a civil force responsible for the large cities. Central influence remains strong since both forces are under the direct control of government ministers: the *Police Nationale* are responsible to the Minister of the Interior, while the *Gendarmerie* are accountable to the Minister of Defence and retain a military role in time of war. However, as Monjardet is anxious to point out, there is a remarkable convergence in policing between the Anglo–Saxon nations and France, with the latter emphasising the need to achieve closer police–public relations, consistent with a developed democracy (Monjardet 1995). Similar struggles to shake off an oppressive past can be seen in several other police systems that have emerged from authoritarian traditions, most notably Spain and Italy, where the police remain tainted by their association with Fascist regimes (Collin 1985; MacDonald 1985; Jaime-Jimenez and Reinares 1998). Attesting to Mann's argument about the relative success of the authoritarian tradition in Germany, policing in that country continues to be unequivocally regarded as the arm of the executive (Funk 1995).

Tradition weighs heavily on the police, for not only does the state have a vested interest in the organization and function of the custodians of its monopoly of legitimate force over its own citizens, there is little incentive to disturb the political settlement between state and citizens embodied in its police. The apparently remarkable tenacity of policing structures is, perhaps, less surprising on reflection. Even when colonial and other oppressive regimes are overthrown, those structures of policing tend to remain. Thus, Bayley remarks how, during the Allied occupation of West Germany, the American, British and French sectors were policed in ways reflecting the respective national traditions of the occupying powers. However, once responsibility for policing was transferred to the re-constructed Federal Republic, traditional patterns of policing soon re-emerged (Bayley 1985). Weitzer wryly points out that in Zimbabwe the colonial policing system was retained virtually unaltered by the post-colonial regime (Weitzer 1990).

Internal Variations on a Theme

There seems, therefore, ample justification for Bayley's remark that "National structures of policing reflect decisions about the geographical distribution of political power" (Bayley 1992: 531). However, this is true not only between states, but also within them. Policing typically spreads from the centre of power to the periphery. In France, Ireland and Britain, it was the capital city that first acquired a professional police force directly controlled by the central government. Moreover, the policing of the capital typically remains distinct from the remainder of the police structure: the

Dublin City police long remained distinct from policing in the rest of Ireland; it was not until 1966 that the police of Paris were incorporated into the *Police Nationale* (Horton 1995); and the London Metropolitan Police continues to occupy a unique position in Britain. In the United States professional policing was first introduced in the *de facto* seats of political and economic power – New York and Boston.

From the centre of political and economic power policing was diffused according to the strategic interests of the state. London was the site for Peel's experiment that then spread, with more or less enthusiasm, to centres of industrial production where economic power lay. In doing so, local municipal power was expressed through the insistence that police be controlled by city councils, and not by central government. The rural counties were slower and more reluctant to embrace professional policing (probably because landed interests could be effectively safeguarded through private means) and when they did install a professional police the pattern of governance reflected neither that of the cities nor central government. As political power shifted towards the centre throughout the late nineteenth and the twentieth centuries, so policing has become progressively more uniform in Britain.

Even under French centralism, the diffusion of the "police idea" reflected the distribution of political and economic power. The *marechaussée* safeguarded the lines of communication via the road system; however, it was not until 1941 that wartime conditions enabled the incorporation of diverse municipal police into the national police structure (Horton 1995). Policing in the United States, by contrast, was and remains an intensely local affair in which every tier of government lays claim to its own police force. This is true not only of municipalities, but of different agencies within government at almost any level. Large cities are often policed by state and city forces, supplemented by the police of the transport authority, museums and art galleries, universities, hospitals and sundry other such organizations, including in Washington, DC, the Cathedral Police, who have the distinction of not carrying sidearms (presumably relying on thunderbolts when forceful intervention is required!). As individual state government became increasingly important, this was reflected in the growth of state police forces with a major responsibility for policing the expanding system of highways. The fragmentation of policing in America reflects traditional scepticism towards central government, but as central government has grown since the 1930s, so too have police establishments, but in ways that reflect traditional concerns at the concentration of political power. Thus at the Federal level too there is a plethora of police agencies: in addition to the Federal Bureau of Investigation, there is the Secret Service (that apart from guarding the President, is the enforcement arm of the Treasury), Border Patrol, Department of Alcohol, Tobacco and Firearms, Drug Enforcement Administration and many more besides. A similar pattern of local fragmentation was to be found in the Netherlands, reflecting traditional power relationships based upon the notion of "pillarization", in which conflicts between deeply divided social groups were avoided by each living largely separate lives under a liberal state umbrella (Jones 1995).

Contesting Citizenship

To the extent that the civil population are regarded as citizens with rights, the exercise of state authority by the police is restrained. However, policing is not simply restrained or unrestrained *per se*, but tends to be restrained when dealing with *some* members of the civil population and less so when dealing with others. This draws our attention to how citizenship develops unevenly amongst the civil population and is contested by those seeking or denying this status.

Even in England, where the Anglo-Saxon model of citizenship took root, the status of citizen was extended unevenly; for example, voting rights in Britain were granted to property owners, and then to adult males, before women received them. But granting constitutional rights does not ensure that those to whom they apply are accorded the status of full citizens. The history of the United States illustrates this point vividly: slaves were emancipated following the Civil War, but this did not mean that they and their descendants acquired the full status of citizens. They had a constitutional right to vote, but that was worth little if they were subjected to segregation, discrimination and intimidation that inhibited or prevented them from voter registration. Despite democratic rhetoric, citizenship is far from uniform throughout the civil population: some have full citizenship, while that of others is partial, qualified or, in some cases, almost entirely absent. Thus, while Marshall was correct in appreciating that citizenship could extend beyond the legal and political spheres, to encompass social and economic rights, he was less attentive to the other side of the coin – that legal and political rights could in practice be subverted by social and economic action.

If citizenship is unevenly distributed, the civil population are not merely passive recipients of rights: they assert their citizenship and contest its denial. Again, the United States exemplifies this well. The Civil Rights Movement of the 1950s and 60s was just such an assertion of citizenship hitherto denied by policies of segregation and discrimination (McAdam 1982, ibid. 1988). It was resisted by dominant white interests whose control of the state apparatus meant that the instruments of resistance were the police, whose batons, birdshot and snarling dogs were unleashed upon non-violent protesters. As the Civil Rights Movement began to prevail, so policing became increasingly restrained, albeit that discrimination and abuse remain persistent features of police–race relations.

Civil Rights and Citizenship

The effects of the Civil Rights Movement were felt well beyond the borders of the United States. Its relative success in extending citizenship to African–Americans became a beacon that others began to follow. Racial, ethnic and religious minorities began to emulate the aspirations and methods of the Civil Rights Movement and demand full citizenship; students, both within America and beyond, also demanded the rights of citizens; and so too did women and more recently gay men and lesbians. In some cases, this brought protesters into direct confrontation with the police (see Chapter 3), but more generally it re-defined the police as the oppressive arm of the state. Amongst the intellectual youth that had been at the forefront of civil rights mobilization, the police were no longer "bobbies" or "cops", but became "pigs" and "the fuzz". Their presence was far from re-assurring, it was offensive; their actions were invariably construed as malign and often brutal.

This perception of the police and policing was not confined to the slogans and chants of protesters, but was disseminated throughout the wider movement. That movement drew particular strength from liberal intellectuals, including lawyers who pursued civil rights in the courts. It has had a profound influence upon the development of academic thinking about the police, which has incorporated a fundamental normative scepticism of policing to which liberal sentiment in the Anglo–Saxon tradition was in any case disposed. Research on policing has not been exclusively the province of disinterested scholarship, but covers a broad spectrum, much of which adheres to a liberal commitment to police reform. The outbreaks of serious rioting in the American ghettos during the 1960s and the British inner-cities fifteen years later (Reiner 1989a) gave a further impetus to that approach which has been dominated by a normative concern for those "below" (Jefferson 1993) – the disadvantaged, dispossessed and discriminated against. Advocacy of the grievances of those who are "below" has prompted a version of *exposé* research, designed to reveal – and thereby condemn – the police for departing from standards of proper conduct. In doing so it has contributed enormously and positively to public awareness and police policy.

However, this political role has also contributed to obscurantism, for proponents of civil rights have systematically denied their own effectiveness. Instead of celebrating their achievements, they continue to portray civil liberties as few and imperilled, and citizens, especially those amongst such marginal groups as ethnic minorities, as the oppressed victims of the police. The police are represented as a powerful institution, replete with legal powers and coercive technology. For the purposes of political mobilization this stance commends itself, since it promotes vigilance and rallies support for otherwise unpopular causes and groups. Yet, it is an analytical distortion that fails to appreciate how policing is shaped by the relationship between the police and citizens. It refuses to recognize how influential is the status of citizenship and the notion of rights. It fails to appreciate how *restrained* is the application of police authority to those who enjoy citizenship. It is to the analysis of this relationship that the remainder of this book is devoted.

Conclusion

What is policing? It is the exercise of the authority of state over the civil population. That authority is based on the monopoly of legitimate coercion – cops usually ask or command people to do something and those people normally comply; but if they do not then the cops will *force* them into compliance. The indeterminable scope of the police role arises from this exercise of authority: they intervene in any situation where someone in authority is required to "take charge". This might involve assisting someone to gain entry into premises from which they have locked themselves out to confronting armed terrorists. Most of the time it involves mere presence: watching those around them and abstaining from intervention. How this is done and the way that policing is organized reflects the relationship between the civil population and the state. To the extent that police exercise authority over *citizens* then policing is hesitant and cautious because citizens have rights, but where the police impose alien authority on a rebellious subject population then coercive power is exercised with little restraint. It is in this relationship between police and citizens that many of the issues that have pre-occupied police research lie.

CHAPTER 2

Keeping People in Their Place

Introduction

Recognizing that the police are custodians of the state's ultimate monopoly of legitimate coercion leads us to consider another abiding concern of police researchers – the issue of discretion. Police officers do not mechanically enforce the law: they pay attention to some incidents and not to others; they invoke their formal powers against some suspects while allowing others to go with a warning; they pay more attention to some people than to others. In other words, discretion is the pivot upon which the exercise of authority revolves. However, for all its centrality and the prolonged deliberation that it has received, discretion is still poorly understood. In the first half of this chapter I will try to present the current understanding of discretion, and then, in the second half, develop that understanding to consider the social organization of discretion.

Discretion in Policing

One of the earliest contributions of serious academic study of policing was the "discovery" of discretion. Prior to the revisionism of the 1960s, the prevailing assumption had been that policing was little more than the application of the law. Criminals committed crimes and the police captured the criminals who were tried and convicted by the courts. In the United States, with its constitutional commitment to the doctrine of the "separation of powers", the police belong to the executive and have no business making quasi-judicial decisions. If the police have good grounds for believing that a crime has been committed, then their constitutional duty is to record it and conduct an investigation. If that investigation leads them to believe that a particular person committed the offence, then their constitutional task is to bring that person before a court. Ignoring offences and allowing suspects to go free is no part of their constitutionally mandated function. This constitutional fiction was revealed as such by Joseph Goldstein, who pointed to the plentiful opportunity the police have to invoke the criminal law or abstain from doing so because they operate in conditions of "low visibility" (Goldstein 1960). That is, decisions taken on the street or in the privacy of the patrol car or police station *not* to invoke the law were essentially unreviewable; because the only people likely to know that such a decision had been taken were the cop and the suspect. Thus, a great tide of invisible crime might exist because of police inaction; and worse still, police may be usurping the role of the legislature by failing to enforce enacted laws and also the courts by presuming to adjudicate on guilt and impose a penalty. For example, if a legislature outlaws the possession of drugs, the police should not allow offenders to escape prosecution in return for information about suppliers of drugs, even if this results in the "big fish" continuing to supply. Their task is to arrest drug-users and drug-suppliers as and when they discover their existence. The police may or may not be correct in believing that the best way to reduce illicit drug-taking is by arresting major suppliers, but they are constitutionally incompetent to make such a decision – that is for the legislature to decide. The police should enforce the law so that its consequences become apparent and the legislature can evaluate it and amend it as they choose. Goldstein's critique was quickly joined by LaFave who produced a massive tome on behalf of the American Bar Association that documented the enormous variety of purposes that arresting suspects actually served, and which extended well beyond that of enforcing the law (LaFave 1962a, ibid. b, ibid. 1965). Much later, Kenneth Culp Davis argued that the exercise of discretion by police officials injected arbitrariness into the criminal justice system that amounted to a usurpation of the rule of law (Davis 1975, see also Fletcher 1984).

It is not just the privacy of police decision-making that renders the exercise of discretion unreviewable. The actions of control room operatives may be quite obvious, even captured on audio-tape for later scrutiny, but they still exercise extensive discretion that insinuates itself into the practices of police officers and civilian employees alike. In Canada, Shearing found that instead of complying with the policy of the force to dispatch patrol cars as rapidly as possible, operatives employed their own priorities in ways that seemed to disadvantage callers whose demeanour was deemed inappropriate by operatives, and they also discriminated against those from ethnic-minority groups (Shearing 1974). Meanwhile, McCabe and Sutcliffe were pointing to the prevalence of "talking out" – convincing callers that their call was not police business (McCabe & Sutcliffe 1978). I also discovered that operatives in an English divisional control room applied their own intuitive gradations to calls instead of the rather crude distinction between "immediate" and "delayed" response imposed by official instructions. One of the reasons for this was that the policy, although having the appearance of clarity, left a great deal to interpretation. For example, an immediate response was to be made if "a serious offence is in progress"; but this obliged operatives to make a decision about whether this was so in any given instance. Many callers *claimed* that offences were in progress, but the credibility of their claims needed to be evaluated, as did the relative seriousness of the offences being committed (Waddington 1993a). Indeed, Manning (1988) argues that it is necessary for operatives to read between the lines of a conversation with a caller to reconstruct what is actually going on; a process that is essentially and irreducibly context-specific (taking into account the caller's tone of voice, ambient sounds, background knowledge and much more). Discretion, therefore, lurks in the process of *translating* a unique conversation with a particular caller into the organisational language of the police (Scott & Percy 1983) – a subjective process that is irrecoverable despite the technological paraphernalia of the control room. If discretion can thrive in this environment, imagine how rampant it must be on the street where supervision is virtually non-existent!

If police routinely exercise discretion then an important task for research is to identify the criteria they employ in arriving at a decision. In answering this question the legal constitutional origins of the debate continue to set the terms for research, for the issue has become one of apportioning influence on police discretion between legal and *extra*-legal factors (see Brooks 1993 for a detailed review). Research has amassed evidence that clearly points to the vast extent of police discretion and the influence of extra-legal considerations. Gardiner, for example, compared different police departments in Massachusetts and concluded that those departments with a specialist traffic division were more inclined to issue tickets for traffic violations (Gardiner 1969). This conclusion received support from British research that indicated, amongst other things, that specialist traffic police were simply much more knowledgeable about traffic offences and regarded them more seriously than their non-specialist colleagues (Layzell 1985). These and other researchers also pointed to the influence of internal quotas designed to motivate officers to issue tickets. The quota system encouraged officers to issue more tickets as the end of the quota period approached, and to concentrate their attention on those vehicles and drivers that offered the greatest prospects of finding violations – a practice that tended to discriminate against the less affluent, whose elderly vehicles were likely to be less well maintained (Pepinsky 1971; Lundman 1979). Such practices do not extend only to traffic enforcement; as we saw in the previous chapter, patterns of crime are often attributed to how police enforce and under-enforce the law.

Defining Crime

The discovery of police discretion and the influence of extra-legal considerations upon it have ramifications that are much wider than legal theory and constitutional propriety. For criminologists the assumption that police mechanically enforced the law tacitly justified research that uncritically accepted the veracity of official statistics. If the convicted criminal population consisted of predominantly lower-class males, then the explanation for this was to be found in the psychology and social experiences of lower-class males; if official crime rates remorselessly increased, then it indicated a flaw within the social fabric; if one country had higher crime rates than another, then this revealed a malaise in the social organization of the former; and so on. To discover that police did not simply enforce the law, but were selective in how they did so, created intellectual turmoil. Now it had to be recognized that official crime statistics were a construction that incorporated the definitions, priorities and possibly the vested interests of officials (Bottomley 1973; Wiles 1971).

Crime surveys have consistently revealed a gap between offences reported by the public and those recorded by the police, the size of gap varying according to type of offence, but amounting overall to about 40 per cent in Britain (Hough & Mayhew 1983, ibid. 1985; Mayhew *et al.* 1989, ibid. 1993; Mirrlees-Black *et al.* 1996). Research in two English police forces drew attention to the widespread habit of "cuffing" – that is, failing to record undoubtedly criminal offences – that effectively distorted the patterns revealed in criminal statistics (McCabe & Sutcliffe 1978). Even if reported offences are initially accepted as genuinely criminal, subsequent investigation may lead to this judgement being retrospectively altered and the offence "no crimed" – a fate that befalls around 10 per cent of cases (Coleman & Bottomley 1976).

Police discretion is not limited to failing or refusing to record offences brought to their attention by the public, but extends to deciding *how* to record those offences, a process that allows considerable latitude. For example, damage to an exterior window might indicate an attempted burglary or simply criminal damage. In Britain, the former is a "notifiable offence" that is included in the criminal statistics, whereas the latter is not. If there is pressure to give the appearance of reduced crime, there is scope for the creative categorization of such an offence, so that it does not appear in the criminal statistics (see Young, M. 1991 for an account of some of creative practices in which detectives indulge in reporting offences). In the novel the *Glitter Dome*, former detective-turned-author, Joseph Wambaugh, captures just how "creative" officers can be, when detectives Al Mackey and Martin Welborn "clear-up" what seemed like an unsolvable murder, by demonstrating how the victim "actually" committed "suicide"!

> Through a videotaped demonstration, Al Mackey, using the "suicide" weapon, performed convincingly for the camera and persuaded the ever-persuadable Captain Woofer that a man of average strength like the cocaine dealer Dilly O'Rourke, given utter dedication to self-destruction, could actually strike a fatal blow to the front of the skull. It took some doing, including expert opinion from a pathologist regarding the fragility of the human skull at the point of violent contact with the hatchet.
>
> The mushy hole in the *back* of his skull was another story. Martin Welborn, in his youth a Jesuit seminarian, had suggested wryly after three weeks of fruitless investigation that it was time to *pray* for the answer. And lo, within the hour their prayers were answered, not by the God of failed seminarians, but by Lord Buddha.
>
> While they were going over Dilly's former digs for the thirteenth time, a sandwich vendor with her hair full of dandelions came tripping in from Hollywood Boulevard carrying a thirty-pound brass Buddha in her track-marked, tattooed little arms. She apologized for having removed it the night Dilly O'Rourke was taken off to become part of the Eternal Force. Someone said she might get in trouble and should bring it back.
>
> She was startled right out of her place in space when the two detectives, with grins a yard wide, grabbed her and sat her down and pumped her shallow well of memories until she recalled that Lord Buddha had always rested over by the Ouija board where Dilly's dead body was visited by every coked-out tenant of the building before someone stopped chanting mantras and called the cops.
>
> Al Mackey's performance was spectacular. The videotape showed him miming the self-inflicted blow to the front of the skull after which he dropped the hatchet, held the back of his wrist to his forehead like a damsel on the train track, and staggered exactly nine feet five inches across the room, keeling over and feigning a bone-popping collision with the unyielding brass bean of the chubby Chinese deity. (Wambaugh 1981: 41–42)

The "law of gravity" does not apply to the recording of crime, so not all incidents are reduced in seriousness. Blom-Cooper and Drabble suggest that the anomalously high incidence of "muggings" in the Lambeth district of London in the early 1980s arose from a tendency to *increase* the seriousness of incidents of street crime (Blom-Cooper & Drabble 1982). This then justified aggressive stop-and-search operations in this area of high ethnic-minority settlement that in turn eventually provoked the riot of 1981.

Whatever its other consequences, one result of these and other practices is to provide a potentially distorted image of crime (see Bottomley & Pease 1993 for a review of the validity of criminal statistics).

Defining Criminals

If the police can use their extensive discretion to define crime, they can use that same discretion to concentrate attention on vulnerable sections of the population and cast them in the role of "criminals". In his pioneering study of policing in two California cities, Skolnick points to how police officers decide whether or not to prosecute traffic ticket violators, prostitutes and drug informants. Traffic violators who have failed to pay their fine are visited by the Enforcement Officer who can arrest them or allow time to pay. In deciding one way or the other, Enforcement Officers are influenced by the character and social circumstances of the violator. Those who are employed and residentially stable tend not to be arrested, whereas their unemployed and rootless counterparts are more likely to wind up in jail. Prostitutes are given latitude by vice cops in order to secure their services as informants and minor drug offenders likewise are offered immunity to prosecution in return for informing on suppliers (Skolnick 1966). Thus, instead of equality before the law, different groups receive different treatment according to wholly extra-legal considerations.

Two consequences arise from this selective exercise of discretion: first, those who offend the prejudices, or whose arrest serves the interests of the police are subjected to routine harassment. The Policy Studies Institute found that in London young black men were much more likely to be stopped, especially if they were driving an old-model Ford that officers had come to associate with the disreputable. The report points out: "The proportion of all adults who have been stopped in a vehicle in the past twelve months is 14 per cent; the proportion of young West Indians who own or have the use of a vehicle who have been stopped in a vehicle is 49 per cent." (Smith 1983a: 97.) According to recent internal police figures, little seems to have changed with black men still much more likely to be stopped and searched (*Police Review*, 26 January 1995). Secondly, by concentrating on particular types of people in particular areas – usually inhabitants of the inner-cities and ghettos – the police selectively discover the criminal acts committed therein, leaving equivalent criminality elsewhere undiscovered (Armstrong & Wilson 1973; Damer 1974). Not only does this distort the criminal statistics by leading to the arbitrary over-representation of people with particular characteristics, such as the lower classes and ethnic minorities (Wiles 1971; Hartjen 1972), it can make matters worse. Wilkins showed how the labelling of a group as deviant can lead to the exaggeration of those characteristics that make them deviant (Wilkins 1964; see also Matza 1969). Young claims that this is precisely what occurred in the case of users of soft drugs who came increasingly to define themselves as drug-users because of the oppressive attentions of the police (Young 1971). According to Gilroy, it is processes such as these that are responsible for the over-representation of young black men in the convicted criminal population (Gilroy 1987).

Moral Panics

The distortion of criminal statistics can, with the assistance of the mass media, go far beyond the over-representation of vulnerable groups to include the virtual creation of more or less artificial "crime waves". The phenomenon was identified by Medalia and Larsen (1958) who demonstrated that a mysterious "epidemic" of windscreen shattering in Seattle, that had enjoyed brief national notoriety, was actually baseless. Windscreens in the Seattle area had been no more prone to shatter than elsewhere. It was due to entirely fortuitous circumstances that the media had concentrated on what purportedly was a rash of shattered windscreens and this had sparked a self-reinforcing spiral of selective attention and reportage of otherwise innocuous events until the media tired of the story and it disappeared from view.

Cohen argued that much the same process accounted for the sudden upsurge of apparently new and threatening forms of lawlessness, such as that which infected many seaside resorts in Britain during the early 1960s during public holiday weekends. The innocent fun of the seaside was destroyed as adherents of the "mod" or "rocker" teenage life-styles battled with each other. The popular press fumed with indignation, experts pontificated upon the reasons for it, and religious spokespeople saw in it portents of moral degeneration. And then, as suddenly as it appeared, it faded from sight. It was, argued Cohen, a "moral panic" – a term that has now entered the general lexicon. In such a moral panic media attention is captured by some particular event, fears are aroused, the apparatus of social control is mobilized, tolerance is reduced so that incidents that would otherwise have gone unnoticed are now subjected to formal action which serves to fuel the appearance that something new and threatening is growing; and so it continues until the media tire of the story and it fades like shattered windscreens (Cohen 1972). In similar vein, Taylor argued that the succession of juvenile delinquency crime waves that had afflicted Britain in the post-World War Two era were attributable, not to a growth in youthful criminality, but to the expansion of an army of professionals who had a vested interest in perceiving that a problem existed for them to address (Taylor 1981). Likewise, Hall and his colleagues argued influentially that the apparent growth of the crime of "mugging" in Britain during the early 1970s had been a virtual figment of the imagination of what they dubbed the "control culture" – police, judiciary, and mass media. The sudden growth in public alarm at this crime disclosed more about capitalism's "crisis of legitimacy" and the need to deflect attention by invoking racist imagery, than it did about crime patterns (Hall *et al.* 1978). (See Goode & Ben-Yehuda 1994 for a contemporary review of research on moral panics.)

Justice Without Trial

Because the police exercise discretion *not* to arrest in most instances, these decisions remain beyond the scrutiny of the courts. For most potential offenders justice is dispensed not in court, but on the streetcorner; not by a judge, but by a police officer. The criminal justice system is not characterized by the processing of crimes from their commission to the sentencing of the offender, but by the selective exclusion of cases long before they get to trial. The President's Commission on Law Enforcement and Administration of Justice (1967) accurately depicted the criminal justice system as a funnel with a very wide neck tapering to a very narrow spout. A great many crimes are committed, but few enter the formal processes of criminal justice and of those that do only a small minority are concluded with the conviction of an offender. Crime survey data has confirmed the existence of a huge reservoir of unreported crime, but once reported discretionary judgements by criminal justice officials – not least of whom are the police – results in progressive attrition as the case moves through the system. In the United States only 50 per cent of arrests result in conviction and Petersilia *et al.* found that amongst the various police departments in the Los Angeles area there was a wide diversity of attrition rates (Petersilia *et al.* 1990). In Scotland only eight per cent of cases of sexual assault resulted in the conviction of an offender (Chambers & Millar 1983).

The growth of alternative means of dealing with offenders, especially juveniles, has also meant that discretion must be exercised in selecting those who will be dealt with through these means. In Britain the formal cautioning of juvenile offenders has developed throughout the post-World War Two period in a haphazard and for much of the time unlegislated fashion. Differences in force policy have meant that juveniles in some areas have had a much higher likelihood of being cautioned than their counterparts elsewhere (Laycock & Tarling 1985), differences paralleled in Australia (Tait 1994). Procedural safeguards that exist in court are attenuated or entirely absent in these circumstances, as illustrated by the tendency of police to use the offer of a caution in cases, where insufficient evidence exists to bring a case before the court (Steer 1970). As Tait remarks about the use of cautions in Australia: "The assumption of guilt underlies the practice of cautioning young persons . . . Formal cautions are in effect an extreme form of charge-bargaining: 'All charges will be dropped if you admit your guilt.'" (Tait 1994: 61–62.) Although they are intended to act as a diversion from prosecution, it seems that these alternative methods of disposal are employed in cases that would not otherwise have been prosecuted at all, resulting in the "net" of the criminal justice system catching more offenders than previously (Ditchfield 1976).

In sum, what passes for justice is dispensed, not in the public forum of the criminal court with all its safeguards, but by officials, such as the police, on the street. Thus, for civil libertarians, the exercise of discretion is often equated with the abuse of civil liberties (Hewitt 1982).

Discretion and Discrimination

It seems that the exercise of police discretion is not only an intrinsic usurpation of the law, but is also discriminatory against the poor, ill-educated, young and often ethnic minority residents of deprived neighbourhoods, and contributes to the distortion of our understanding of crime causing the false over-representation of particular groups and the occurrence of mythical "crime waves". This manifests itself across a wide range of policing activity and criminal justice procedures and is targeted mainly at the powerless and dispossessed (Galliher 1971; Hagan & Morden 1981; Rudovsky 1982). In recent years most attention has focused on discrimination shown towards black people who are likely to be stopped and searched, arrested and treated more harshly by the police in a wide variety of jurisdictions (Gould 1969; Ferdinand & Luchterhand 1970; Thornberry 1973, ibid. 1979; Hepburn 1978; Pope 1978; Liska & Tausig 1979; Institute of Race Relations 1981; Ogletree *et al.* 1995).

A Flawed Perspective

The "discovery" of discretion usefully drew attention to the fact that the police did not merely enforce the law, but exercised some choice about whether to do so; choices that have a significant impact upon the criminal justice system as a whole. What has been less helpful is the normative insistence that the police *should* merely enforce the law, and its corollary that exercising discretion was a usurpation of the judicial function, for this has narrowed the debate.

First, it is far from clear that the police (or any other official) *could* strictly enforce the law, even in principle. As Pepinsky argues, rules of any kind require interpretation, as he illustrates in relation to the *Miranda* rules that govern the detention and interrogation of suspects in the United States. At numerous critical junctures the wording of the rules gives rise to ambiguities of meaning, such as "whether a suspect who responds to a police request to come to the stationhouse to answer questions is 'in custody'" (Pepinsky 1984: 259). He adds that it took several years for many of these ambiguities to be resolved by the courts, but equally many more remain. As Wilkinson and Evans point out, when rules stipulate that cautions are to be administered in all except serious cases, it is in the various interpretations of what is "serious" that differing practices in different police forces occurs (Wilkinson & Evans 1990). Moreover, few crimes are based on "strict liability", but instead require some criminal intent to accompany the act, and gauging intent depends on inference of a subjective state. Thus, a police officer would need to decide whether a person deliberately or accidentally damaged the property of another in order to determine whether a crime had or had not been committed. Because of the uncertainties that inevitably accompany rules it is virtually unimaginable that police action *could* be anything other than discretionary.

Secondly, the desirability of the police acting in strict accordance with the law is highly questionable. There is the obvious difficulty that the law is so extensive that no criminal justice system could process all the cases that the strict enforcement of those laws would generate (Goldstein 1964). In addition, the law applied without discretion would be a very blunt instrument. It is, for instance, doubtful if the ends of justice are served by the prosecution of a parent whose careless driving has resulted in the death of their own child (Finnegan 1978). Indeed, to prescribe that police officers should enforce the law without regard to the ends of justice is to substitute means for ends – a social malaise that Merton described as "ritualism", a species of normative decay (Merton 1957). According to these criteria, as Bittner remarks "an incompetent, ineffective, and injudicious officer could remain in good standing in his department provided it cannot be shown by any accepted method of proof that he has violated some expressly formulated norm of conduct" (Bittner 1983: 5). It is noteworthy, for example, that in Wilson's comparative examination of eight American police departments it was those characterized as "legalistic" that had the highest rates both of arrest of ethnic minorities and for complaints of misconduct (Wilson 1969).

Thirdly, establishing that police officers' decision-making is not dictated by legal precept does not establish thereby that they are acting in a discriminatory fashion. True discretion involves considering any decision on its merits, taking all relevant factors into consideration, weighing available options, and arriving at the most appropriate conclusion. Of course, discretion can become a cloak under which prejudice and discrimination hides, but that does not make discretion itself offensive. Equally, the fact that discretionary decisions are patterned by age, class and race does not establish that discretion is cloaking prejudice. The officers whom Piliavin and Briar observed had a specialist responsibility for dealing with juveniles and were required "to justify their juvenile disposition decisions not simply by evidence proving a youth had committed a crime . . . but in (sic) the *character* of the youth" (Piliavin & Briar 1964: 209). In judging character, paying attention to the fact that some young men adopt the style of "tough guys" who refuse to defer to police officers may be entirely defensible. The over-representation of lower-class ethnic-minority youth among those arrested may simply reflect the higher proportion of youngsters "at risk" in those sections of the population. This possibility has fuelled an extensive and inconclusive debate about whether the delinquency and criminality is *actually* concentrated among certain sections of the population, or whether it arises from discriminatory practices throughout the criminal justice system.

Law As the Servant of Order

I do not propose to get into that debate here, because it is unnecessary to do so. The connection between discretion and discrimination can be established more directly, albeit by a different route. Paradoxically, discrimination results from the entirely proper and ethical exercise of discretion. As Kleinig insists, discretion can only be properly exercised if it serves ends *superior* to those of the law, which he suggests should be basic communal values (Kleinig 1996). Now, whatever the normative merits of this position, it raises crucial empirical and analytical issues. First, if the exercise of discretion is guided by reference to basic communal values, this implies that law is subordinate to these values; for if there was a clash between the two then we would expect communal values to prevail. One corollary of this is that the oft-drawn distinction between "law enforcement" and "order maintenance" cannot be sustained because conceptually the former is subsumed by the latter. In maintaining order a police officer might invoke the law, but it is inconceivable that the officer could enforce the law by invoking an order-maintenance tactic; for example issuing a warning to a thief (although it is conceivable that crime might be prevented by these means). This is consistent with the view of some researchers that the law is used selectively as one *resource* among others for the maintenance of order. In the previous chapter attention was drawn to how police officers selectively use "resource charges" in the fulfilment of their order-maintenance duties. They might do so expediently to remove truculent people from a scene of disorder, but also, and more importantly, to maintain the dominant *moral* order. Both Bittner (1967b) and Chatterton (1983) have drawn attention to how officers are guided by their conception of moral culpability in deciding whether and whom to arrest. Chatterton contrasts two violent domestic incidents: in one, the officer refuses to take formal action against a husband who has clearly struck his wife because, in the officer's eyes, she at least shares some culpability for the incident; in the other, an officer takes the unilateral decision to arrest a man on a dubious charge because the man so terrifies his wife and her father that they are unwilling to take action themselves (Chatterton 1983). As these examples illustrate, what guides police decision-making is not the law, but officers' conception of social values to be authoritatively imposed, if necessary, on those who are recalcitrant. Thus, in a neat reversal of the legalism of Goldstein, LaFave and Davis, the law is revealed as the servant of the police, not their master.

This interpretation is unaffected by the observation that officers appear to exercise little discretion in enforcing the law in relation to more serious offences (Sherman 1980a). For homicide, rape, assault and theft will, in all but the most exceptional circumstances, tend to be breaches of basic communal values as much as they violate the criminal code. It is amongst the legally petty offences that we find police exercising most discretion, for here there is far greater likelihood that the law and communal values will clash. However, it is precisely with regard to legally petty offences that the police are most often accused of discrimination (Carter & Clelland 1979).

Policing Subordination

This brings me to the second analytical implication of the view that discretion is the servant of basic communal values. For the issue arises as to *which* community and its values the police should and do serve. If *all* communities deserve equal consideration, then the notion of discretion being guided by communal values would serve little purpose. When police come to move rowdy youths from a streetcorner, those youths would be entitled to claim that they were a community with distinctive values to which the police should defer. This is not only patently absurd, it also draws our attention to the fact that values are felt to be compelling precisely because they claim to have *universality*. Hence Kleinig's explicit qualification that the values that should guide the police must be "*basic*" and not merely local or temporary preferences (Kleinig 1996). Empirically and analytically the issue that this raises is where are these essentially *superior* values to be found? Whose values should, or are most likely to, prevail?

In order to answer these questions we must abandon the implicit assumption of much of the debate over discretion, namely, that discretion is exercised by lone individuals on a case-by-case basis. The fact is that the police exercise their discretion within a social context of domination and subordination. Practical police officers are rarely perplexed about which values should apply, because certain values *prevail* since they are the values of dominant groups in society. The street life of the nineteenth- and early twentieth-century working class was an expression of communal values, yet the police suppressed it in the interests of "public decorum" (Stead 1977). Immigrants to America brought with them the customs and values of their native lands but these too were suppressed in pursuit of such ideals as that of abstinence and sabbatarianism (Miller 1977a, ibid. b). In other words, the exercise of police discretion is *intrinsically* discriminatory, because it imposes dominant social values upon subordinate sections of the population – it is the *imposition of respectability*.

Exclusion and Citizenship

Subordinating some sections of the population to the values of others through the exercise of police discretion also has practical value for the police. It reassures those in dominant positions that they need not fear the custodians of the state's monopoly of legitimate coercion. Abiding by respectable standards will normally ensure immunity to police intervention, and in the event that one does encounter the police then it offers the assurance that they will serve one's interests. In Wilson's study of police departments in eight American cities, those that he characterized as "service orientated" policed high-income residential neighbourhoods and saw their function as protecting residents from the depredations of outsiders (Wilson 1969). However, police cannot impose the norms of respectability upon more than a relatively small section of the general population. Hence policing is characterized by a majoritarian ethos with police regarding their task as the protection of "ordinary decent people". How is the disreputable minority defined? The obvious answer would seem to be "criminals", but our discussion of discretion leads to the conclusion that since the police do not simply enforce the law they do not restrict themselves to those who have violated it. The wider discretionary authority possessed by the police is used to protect prevailing values from those sections of society that pose a threat to those values – the marginal and dispossessed. What they are marginal to and dispossessed of is citizenship itself.

Criminalizing Exclusion

Thus, exclusion and subordination are legitimated through the process of *criminalizing* groups whose lifestyles offend prevailing respectable values. There is a tendency in some normative discussions of this process to idealize the concept of "crime" and to suggest that such criminalization is morally wrong. For example, when the law in England was extended to effectively outlaw "travellers" who camped uninvited on others' land, this was attacked as a gratuitous criminalization of a lifestyle (Malyon 1995). Now, whether the legislation was justified by the harm done by travellers to farming interests is a normative issue, but analytically there is nothing to distinguish this legislation from any other, such as that outlawing the persistent "stalking" of another person (that is, following, pestering and generally being a nuisance). Criminalization is the legal mechanism through which exclusion is achieved and the fact that it bears most heavily, indeed almost entirely, on the shoulders of the most marginal sections of society is a reflection of their marginality. "Crimes" do not exist in some Platonic universe, they are constructed through social processes of enactment and judicial interpretation. They define the outer limits of what is and is not minimally acceptable conduct.

However, it would be a mistake to equate the commission of criminal acts with *criminality*. Crimes are defined behaviourally: anyone taking the property of another without their consent and with the intention of permanently depriving them of it commits the crime of theft. Yet, that does not, by itself, constitute them as "a criminal", for "criminality" is a much broader construct than those who commit or have committed criminal acts. If it were not, then around a quarter of the adult male population in Britain would be "criminals", even on the most restrictive of definitions. Deserved as some feminists might imagine this appellation to be, it plainly does not correspond to common usage. "A criminal" is someone whose lifestyle centres around or is significantly influenced by the commission of crimes. Criminality, in other words, is the hallmark of exclusion – those who are beyond the moral boundaries of society. And police do not control the commission of crime, they contain criminality: that is, they keep the excluded in their place.

Thus, the police patrol the boundaries of citizenship: the citizenship of those who are "respectable" is secured, while those who attack the state exclude themselves from citizenship. Between these extremes are those whose claim to citizenship is insecure and needs repeatedly to be negotiated. Police are the *de facto* arbiters of their citizenship, it is they who are "police property" and this is a mark of their marginality.

Maintaining Order

A further implication of the view that discretion is the application of prevailing social values lies in the definition of policing as "social peacekeeping" (Kleinig 1996), or "order maintenance", as police researchers more commonly describe it. For it should now be clear that the police do not maintain order *per se*, but impose a particular order. The distinction is crucial, since many deviant sub-cultures could be considered to exhibit their own order; conforming to their own values and norms, and not at all behaving in an overtly disorderly manner. Their behaviour is not unordered, but ordered in ways that do not conform to prevailing notions of respectability. For example, it is common and expected practice amongst Afro-Caribbeans attending a party to purchase alcohol from their host – a "shebeen". Yet, under the guise of "order maintenance" the police might close down such a party, because the order that exists violates prevailing canons of respectability, albeit that those "canons of respectability" would tolerate party-goers buying their alcohol at a local retail outlet and bringing it with them to the party. Thus, what police do is not to maintain order by preventing or quelling disorder, but to order social relationships in conformity with prevailing notions of respectability. They do so by keeping subordinate groups "in their place" and excluding those who challenge that order.

Maintaining subordination can actually promote disorder, rather than "public tranquillity". It is widely believed that extensive use of "stop and search" by police prompted the 1981 riot in Brixton, south London. In his report Lord Scarman insisted that the maintenance of "public tranquillity" was a higher priority than "law enforcement" (Scarman 1981). If this implied allowing minor delinquencies, such as possession of cannabis, to go unpunished, then it was a small price to pay to avoid the damage to people and property occasioned by the riot. This was a useful corrective to the heavy-handed implementation of police powers that had preceded the riot. Yet, interpreted strictly it is an absurdity: the police could avoid all manner of violent confrontation by simply allowing disreputable and illegal conduct to continue unmolested. This would maintain tranquillity but not *order*: order maintenance is the imposition of a particular order upon those who deviate from it.

Harassment

Thus, policing offers protection to citizens from the internal threat posed by those on the margins of citizenship. However, the *means* employed for this purpose are only relatively rarely that of arrest, for the law is grossly *under*-enforced. Prevailing social values are imposed by routine *harassment and intimidation*. It is among those who are excluded that we find what Lee calls "police property" (Lee 1981), upon whom police authority is imposed by such means. This is the dark side of order maintenance and "peacekeeping": costermongers being chased from the streets of nineteenth-century London (Cohen 1979); coolies being harassed in Dehli (Bayley 1969); and young people expelled from streetcorners the world over.

Civility, the "Quality of Life" and "Zero Tolerance"

A revised normative light has recently been shed on police harassment of marginal sections of the population: in the name of ensuring "civility", police in the United States, Britain and elsewhere, are being encouraged to pay more attention to "quality of life" issues and show "zero tolerance" to such minor depredations as street begging, offering unwanted windscreen washing to motorists waiting at traffic lights, and creating noise that irritates neighbours. The justification for this is that such minor incivilities increase fear of crime (Maxfield 1984, ibid. 1987; Hough 1995); and this, in turn, causes people to retreat from public spaces, creating conditions conducive to increased criminal activity. This is, in essence, the "broken windows" hypothesis (Wilson & Kelling 1982), for which strong empirical support undoubtedly exists (Skogan 1990) and to which we will return in the final chapter.

What I want to draw attention to here is not whether so-called "zero tolerance" is justified or not, but what it means. People who are associated with incivilities are those on the margins of respectability: beggars, alcoholics, "derelicts", the homeless, rowdy youngsters, vandals who damage property and daub slogans, those who create litter, and those who hold noisy parties late into the night. Who suffers incivilities? It is "ordinary respectable people":

> There are always 13 and 14-year-olds pretending to be thugs. There will be a group blocking the street, and an old lady will walk around them. She probably has arthritis, which makes it hard for her to handle the curb, but she has to endure the indignity of it as well as the pain so that she can get around those kids without getting into any trouble. (Skogan 1990: 27)

Women of all ages are among the most vulnerable to such incivilities:

> Our urban area was not an inner-city area, or part of a very large city. Yet individuals clearly did not go out at night and this was a response, not to "something good on the telly", but to their fear of crime. In particular, many women had already curtailed their lives to exclude the possibility of going out. The habit had been infectious. The streets were empty of women at night. (Shapland & Vagg 1988: 127)

However, some women are also part of the problem, for prostitutes hardly count as "women" for the purposes of this discussion: it is they who take advantage of the streets that have been vacated by *ordinary* women; it is their trade that gives another turn to the spiral of decline. On the other hand, homeless people who in Britain sell the magazine *The Big Issue* are not seen as a source of incivility. Why? Because despite standing in public places selling their magazine (an activity that legally amounts to "peddling"), they are not like "squeegee merchants" who stand at traffic lights trying to sell their dubious services to motorists. Selling *The Big Issue* represents an attempt to climb out of homelessness and poverty and regain respectability – it is, by the standards of the respectable, commendable.

How are the police to restore civility? They do so by harassing those whose behaviour offends against civility: gangs of young people hanging out on streetcorners, alcoholics and derelicts, the homeless, and prostitutes. Wilson and Kelling's describe this role in a pen-portrait:

> The people on the street were primarily black: the officer who walked the street was white. The people were made up of "regulars" and "strangers". Regulars included both "decent folk" and some drunks and derelicts who were always there but who "knew their place". Strangers were, well, strangers, and viewed suspiciously, sometimes apprehensively. The officer – call him Kelly – knew who the regulars were, and they knew him. As he saw his job, he was to keep an eye on strangers, and make certain that the disreputable regulars observed some informal but widely understood rules. Drunks and addicts could sit on the stoops, but could not lie down. People could drink on side streets, but not at the main intersection. Bottles had to be in paper bags. Talking to, bothering, or begging from people waiting at the bus stop was strictly forbidden. If a dispute erupted between a businessman and a customer, the business man was assumed to be right, especially if the customer was a stranger. (Wilson & Kelling 1982: 30)

Let me make it clear: normatively I support the "broken windows" hypothesis. I favour the promotion of civility in public places. Yet, analytically what "civility" amounts to is the assertion of respectable values and the role of the police is to harass sub-criminal nuisances associated with subordinate and excluded sections of the population. As Choongh (1997) puts it, policing is a process of imposing "social discipline" upon "the dross".

Community Values

The objection to the perspective on policing being presented here is that the police do not impose a single notion of respectability on all, but are sensitive to the local community in which they operate. Thus, Bittner argues that on "skid row" officers will find it expedient to operate in terms of a value system that deviates from strict respectability (Bittner 1967b). In the "red light" district of Amsterdam much the same applies:

> One evening a respectable, middle-aged man approached a foot-patrol in the Oudezijds Achterburgwal and said that he had been cheated out of 25 guilders by a prostitute. He was a Dutch American who listened to the girl's come-on chat to prospective clients in which 25 guilders was mentioned. He went up to her, spoke in English, and followed her into her room without discussing the price. Shortly afterwards he left not only dissatisfied but with only 50 guilders change from a 100-guilder note. He was claiming a further 25 guilders back, while complaining that he had received nothing for his money. We entered the premises of the young Black prostitute who was wearing the briefest of mini-skirts and a revealing blouse. In reply to the accusation she began a vehement tirade. In short she said, "He followed me in and started talking English so I automatically doubled the price like I do for every foreigner. Then I got his prick out and he wanted to fuck me with my clothes off. Look, nobody fucks me with my clothes off for 25 guilders, nobody. Then the silly old fool couldn't get a proper hard-on and when he couldn't come after ten minutes I shoved him out. Then the bastard starts talking Dutch." The policemen listened to this and then turned to the man. Paul said, "Did she hold your prick", and the man replied sheepishly, "Well, yes she did". Paul went on, "You didn't tell us that did you? Anyway, you gave her the money, you didn't agree a price but she did hold your prick, so you got something for your money, and ten minutes *is the rule around here*. Then that business of

> pretending not to understand Dutch, well, I think you tried to be a bit of a smart Alec. But we can't do anything more for you." (Punch 1979a: 146–7, emphasis added)

This suggests that it is local, rather than general, values that prevail. However, respectable order is maintained *provided skid-row bums and prostitutes remain in their territorial place*. As Skogan remarks:

> Peddlers and street musicians, sidewalk drinking, and dense late-night foot traffic can be tolerated in the *right places*, just as the antics long associated with Mardi Gras and Halloween are appropriate at the right time. (Skogan 1990: 9)

Thus, it comes as no surprise to discover that the likelihood of a black person being stopped and searched by the London Metropolitan Police is *higher* in areas of *low* ethnic-minority settlement than it is in areas of high ethnic-minority settlement, for in the former black people are *out of place* and in the latter they are *in their place*. (Smith 1983a).

"Commonsense"

One final implication of the notion that the police enforce prevailing notions of respectability is that the police do not impose their *own* values but those of dominant groups. Police officers often refer to their command of "commonsense" and researchers just as commonly disparage this claim, preferring to see police actions as an expression of police values – the so-called "police sub-culture" that will be discussed at length in Chapter 4. Suffice it to note here, on the one hand, that there is indeed a considerable gap between police values and those of the average person. Research conducted for the British police noted that the police put a much higher premium on crime-fighting than do the public (Joint Consultative Committee 1990). On the other hand, there is a very *close* correspondence between the tasks the public value and what police actually *do*. For the one complaint that seems common across many jurisdictions is that routine policing involves officers in "rubbish" or "bullshit" work; that is, non-crime-fighting order maintenance. When they are engaged in such "rubbish" they apply not their narrow police perspective, nor the law, but a *commonsense* of what is acceptable.

Policing Subordination and Exclusion

It is the imposition of prevailing standards of respectability upon those who are subordinated or excluded that gives policing its general shape. Policing is distributed so that it adversely affects the young, the lower class, and racial minorities – and especially the combination of all three.

Juveniles

It may at first seem odd to regard juveniles as "excluded", but that is precisely what they are – "not-yet-citizens". Their lack of citizenship rights is apparent in their exclusion from normal criminal trial procedures that embody citizenship. Formal cautions administered by the police are an extra-legal form of penalty devised with youth in mind and applied almost exclusively to young offenders. Ostensibly, it is intended to prevent young people entering the criminal justice system, but in actuality it serves to reinforce the subordinate status of the young; for, as noted above, guilt is often assumed and the "net" of the criminal justice system widened. However, the rhetoric of "welfare" that surrounds the control of young serves to negate any claims they might have to citizenship and leaves them vulnerable to authoritative intervention that can be quite oppressive (James 1994), but is presented as serving *their* longer-term interests. In Australia legislation on truancy and child neglect licensed the police to exercise control that went far beyond crime prevention or detection.

> ... historically police were given responsibilities for surveilling the lives of children and young people in ways that extended well beyond the notion of criminal offence or its prevention. Police policies and concerns, which were much more interventionist than those considered acceptable for adults, were developed in the context of monitoring and controlling the social life of young people. (Finnane 1994: 8)

Likewise, juveniles in many American jurisdictions are subject to curfew laws that do not apply to their elders because young people must not be allowed to roam unsupervised during the hours of darkness, but remain under domestic control. Because welfarist assumptions maintain that adolescents need extensive surveillance and control "for their *own* good", police are encouraged to collaborate with other agencies normally dedicated to the care and protection of young people, residents in the neighbourhood and even the parents of those concerned to extend surveillance and control (Factor & Stenson 1989; Thorpe 1994; Morgan 1997). By a curious twist of logic, those children who are deemed to be "at risk" of embarking on a criminal career are subject to interventions that seem calculated precisely to enhance that risk.

As Bittner has pointed out juveniles are subject to almost continual surveillance and are accountable to adults for virtually everything they do. They not only cause trouble, they are trouble (Bittner 1976). Children and young people are marginal and represent a threat to adult conceptions of order and propriety. Among adults, rowdiness by young people is a major cause of complaint (Shapland & Vagg 1988), and the experience of youthful incivility is closely associated with fear of crime (Maxfield 1987). Nor is this a development of the late twentieth century, for as Pearson reminds us, concern about youth crime and disorder has been a topic of social and political concern since the mid-nineteenth century at least (Pearson 1983). Moral panics may be prompted by a wide range of incidents, but youth has a particular potency for stimulating such panics because they are already society's "folk devils" (Cohen 1972). The association of the words "juvenile" and "delinquency" is one to which sociologists and criminologists have long subscribed when they focused on "youth cultures", delinquent sub-cultures and educational underachievement.

Since the division of youth and adulthood is the most fundamental boundary of citizenship, it is no surprise to find that most policing involves the control and containment of youth, much of it being direct authoritative intervention that often amounts to harassment. Thus, "younger people are much more likely to be stopped than older people, by a factor of about 11 to 1 in terms of the proportion of people stopped or about 30 to 1 in terms of the mean number of stops per person". (Smith 1983a: 95). Frequently, police intervene to impose adult conceptions of proper behaviour over public space. Youngsters want to "hang out", but adults find such behaviour intrusive and threatening (Werthman & Piliavin 1967; Edwards *et al.* 1987).

> While the police could argue that they are simply "doing their job" by stopping and questioning young people on the street, the reverse perception is usually quite different. The "street" represents for many young people a place to express themselves without close parental or "adult" control, at little or no cost in commercial or financial terms. It is also a sphere or domain where "things happen", where there are people to see, and where one can be seen by others. In short, for many young people the street is an important site for social activity. And the intrusion of "authority" into one's social affairs can and does create resentment and resistance, especially if this is done in a heavy-handed fashion. (White 1994: 109)

Such "heavy-handedness" can become heavy indeed, as when police in some southern English towns responded to a perceived increase in drunken rowdiness – so-called "lager louts" – by an intimidatory presence of large numbers of officers and early intervention in any incident that they suspected might get out of hand (Tuck 1989). Thus, the relationship between young people and the police is structurally adversarial, the police use wide, often arbitrary, powers to maintain adherence to adult conceptions of appropriate behaviour.

When they intervene, police officers expect to receive deference not only because of their uniform, but also because they are themselves adults and those with whom they are interacting are "*only* kids". Failure to display overt respect not only challenges the authority of the officer, but is also taken as symptomatic of youthful rebellion against adult norms and values *per se* – a "tough guy" – that justifies the assertion of power through formal action. Conversely, the young person who shows due, but not exaggerated, deference indicates that he or, less commonly, she knows his or her place (Piliavin & Briar 1964; Black & Reiss 1970; Lundman *et al.* 1978). It is little wonder, therefore, that attitudes of young people towards the police are consistently less positive than those of adults (Shaw & Williamson 1972; Belson 1975; "Which?" 1990; O'Connor 1994; Wortley *et al.* 1996).

However, it is not only young people themselves who must defer to prevailing adult values, but also their parents. When predominantly white middle-class parents express concern at their child's delinquency and the child also expresses contrition, the police are reassured that the family adheres to prevailing adult norms and that any lapse is an aberration (Bennett 1979; Fisher & Mawby 1982). On the other hand, ethnic-minority children from single-parent families living in ghetto neighbourhoods who display anti-authority attitudes merely confirm that they are beyond the bounds of respectability and are treated more harshly as a result (Ferdinand & Luchterhand 1970). Thus, the rhetoric of welfare facilitates discriminatory practices, privileging those who can convince the authorities that they accept prevailing values and punishing those who challenge those values.

One aspect of the relationship between young people and the police that has escaped attention until recently concerns their victimization. Research in Edinburgh has revealed just how immersed young people are in crime irrespective of their social class. They both perpetrate a good many minor offences, but also suffer considerable victimization, not least from adults who exploit their vulnerability. Police, however, are inclined to dismiss their victimization as "kids stuff" and unworthy of official attention.

This leaves young people feeling perplexed about, and resentful at, police priorities that result in their being given "hassle" for minor nuisances, but no support when they are victims of more serious crimes (Anderson *et al.* 1994; Loader 1996).

> It seems that young people experience a marked imbalance in the dimensions of police force and service that they receive. As users of public space, they encounter levels of routine police supervision that for the most part bear little relation to the problems they actually occasion. Young people are in this respect over-controlled. In stark contrast, young people remain under-protected by the police in relation to the degree of victimization they encounter while out in public. This disproportionate balance of force and service signifies, perhaps above all else, that young people in public spaces are the effective property of the police: acted upon at the bequest of others, yet unable to articulate their own concerns and demands. (Loader 1996: 28)

It is little surprise, therefore, to find that as victims young people are much less satisfied with the police response than other groups, indeed "differences between age groups are much more marked than those between ethnic groups" (Smith 1983a: 82).

However, youth is a transitional status and the ambiguity of their status is reflected in the ambivalence shown to police intervention. As Loader notes, once schooling is finished, patterns of use of space and other facilities and relations with the police change: for the majority – disciplined by work – there is little contact; for the minority – who remain excluded from full citizenship – relations are conditioned by attributes that are not so easily shed; class and race are not a "stage" one "passes through" (Loader 1996).

Class

Policing is mainly an urban phenomenon, and what we know about it is based on not just urban policing, but on the policing of the most disadvantaged neighbourhoods – where the "action" is – and the "action" is the policing of class.

The Marxist view is that the police simply serve the interests of the ruling class (Chambliss 1975, ibid. 1982; Carter & Clelland 1979; Rudovsky 1982; Harring 1983). However, even as some Marxists acknowledge, this is much too simplistic since crime and disorder can harm other members of the working class as much as they do the bourgeoisie. In any event, attempting to impose bourgeois values upon the working class by coercion would simply be beyond the capacity of most police forces; especially in industrialized economies that require minimum compliance even from subordinate classes. The historical task for the police, therefore, was to identify a minority who posed a threat to the majority and this meant exploiting fissures *within* the traditional working class. In the industrial city of Liverpool, as Brogden explains:

> The expansion of police powers at the end of the 1860s narrowly focussed on a specific group, a focus which in Liverpool, as elsewhere, seems to have had the assent of both working class and bourgeoisie. Organizational factors within the police institution contributed to an easier relation with the respectable working class, and to the institutionalized exclusion of the lower classes. The antagonistic milieu of the street for patrolling police officers resulted in practical compro-

> mises. If police officers as individuals wished to survive, and if the police institution as a corporate body aimed to gain a measure of consent, tolerance was necessary. Discretionary law enforcement led to a truce with one class at the cost of joint criminalization of the lower orders. (Brogden 1982: 190–191)

Thus, as the police institution took shape in the nineteenth century the growing "demand for order" was exploited to identify and exclude the "dangerous classes" (Silver 1967). "Police property" was not to be found among the *respectable* middle and working classes, but among the disreputable section of society whom Marx himself dismissed as the "lumpenproletariat" (Jefferson 1991). Whereas patrolling officers found it expedient to ignore minor infractions by, and offer assistance to, the respectable working class in the interests of establishing a workable "truce" (Cohen 1979), no such accommodation was extended to "low life" (Brogden 1985). As Miller points out, the police of nineteenth-century London literally patrolled the boundary between respectability and disreputability; for most arrests were made, not in the "rookeries" that cradled the "dangerous classes", but at the margins between these areas and their more respectable neighbours (Miller 1977a).

The pattern established during the last century continues to be felt in contemporary society. As the Policy Studies Institute discovered in their survey of Londoners, it is with the most disadvantaged and deprived that the police have the most intense relationship (Smith 1983a). However, increasingly in Britain, as elsewhere in the world, this section of the population is defined more by race rather than class.

Race

The policing of racial minorities has attracted enormous attention from police researchers virtually from the inception of serious academic study of policing. However, it is less clear that attention has paid explanatory dividends. There is ample evidence that racial minorities are over-represented in criminal justice systems throughout the industrialized world, but why this is so still remains clouded in controversy. Clarification depends upon shedding assumptions that have their origins in the emphasis given to discretionary enforcement of the law by isolated police officers and recognizing instead that policing is inextricably tied to social exclusion.

The terms of the debate about police–race relations has focused on the issue of whether and how far police *officers* are racially prejudiced and act in a discriminatory fashion to racial minorities. There is an extensive literature, to which we will return in a later chapter, documenting the attitudes of police officers and drawing attention to the racism of the sub-culture of the lower ranks. But whether it stems from deep psychological causes or the sub-culture of the occupational group, racial prejudice is assumed to lie *within* individual police officers and infect their exercise of discretion, resulting in discrimination. Certainly, it is easy to recognize the malign influence of racism in acts of apparent discrimination of which members of racial minorities complain (Humphry 1972; Institute of Race Relations 1987; Pulle 1973). However, systematic research remains divided: there are many studies that find black people treated unduly harshly by the police and other agencies of criminal justice (Gould 1969; Thornberry 1973, ibid. 1979; Hepburn 1978; Pope 1978; Liska & Tausig 1979; Dannefer & Schutt 1982; Mhlanga 1993); but even this research is not unequivocal and many studies suffer from methodological problems that call their conclusions into question.

Moreover, these studies are offset by others that simply fail to find that the police discriminate. In other words, the over-representation of lower-class and racial-minority groups is attributable (or, at least, *mainly* attributable) to differences in actual levels of offending (Shannon 1963; McEachern & Bauzer 1967; Terry 1967; Hindelang 1969, ibid. 1978; Hohenstein 1969; MacDonald 1969; Green 1970; Weiner & Willie 1971; Cohen & Kluegel 1979; Mawby 1979; Pratt 1980; Landau 1981; Smith *et al.* 1984). Stevens and Willis (1979) conclude that the amount of police discrimination needed to account for race differences is simply too incredible to merit serious consideration. Smith's recent review of the evidence would seem to suggest that actual differences do exist between racial groups in contemporary Britain explicable in terms of their exposure to conditions long associated with criminality among lower-class sections of the population (Smith 1994).

Equally, while there seems little doubt that racial minorities receive harsher treatment from the police, it is not at all clear that this is attributable to their race as opposed to their predominantly lower-class social status. Tuck and Southgate found that in a deprived district of a British northern industrial city, there was little difference between lower-class white and black people in their experience of and attitudes towards the police (Tuck & Southgate 1981). As Jefferson remarks, black people occupy a social niche previously occupied by costermongers (Jefferson 1991). Like generations of working-class adolescents before them (Brogden 1985), young blacks in contemporary Britain experience the full brunt of police order maintenance with the possibly important qualification that it is now accompanied by racist taunts, slurs and insults (Reiner 1985b).

Stop and Search

To give this discussion some substance, let us consider the particularly vexed issue of stop and search. Not only is this a controversial practice, it also epitomizes the exercise of police discretion and the issues associated with it. The authority given to police officers to stop people in public places, question and search them is justified in principle as a weapon in crime-fighting. The modest intrusion into the lives of citizens can reveal criminals in possession of contraband and uncover other evidence of criminality. For instance, Moore (1980) has argued that stop and search has proven an effective means of reducing the carrying of firearms on American streets. However, its effectiveness against crime in general is more equivocal. American research found that field-interrogation strategies did genuinely suppress robberies (Wilson & Boland 1978a) although this has been challenged (Wilson & Boland 1978b; Jacob & Rich 1980, ibid. 1981). Nevertheless, Sherman argues that if properly targeted, stop and search is a police strategy that works (Sherman 1986, ibid. 1990, ibid. 1992a). Research in London concluded:

> Some population groups are many times more likely to be stopped than others. This shows that, by and large, police officers do not make stops randomly, and to the extent that the groups that are likely to be stopped are ones that contain a high proportion of offenders it shows that they are using their powers intelligently. (Smith 1983a: 92)

However, the authors hastily add that belonging to a section of the population that harbours a disproportionate number of offenders does not justify stopping and searching any particular individual. On the other hand, another British research study concluded that stop and search led to arrests on only around 10 per cent of occasions and that many of these arrests were for public-order offences arising from antagonism to the stop itself (Willis 1983). Recent research in London showed that when police were required to hand a leaflet to all those stopped explaining their rights, the number of stops markedly declined without any adverse effect on the overall crime or detection rates when compared to another division that did not operate this scheme (Gibbons 1997a).

As this last piece of research incidentally confirms, stop and search continues to be used much more frequently against racial minorities, earning the predictable accusation that it is an expression of racism common among officers (Gibbons 1997). Other research in London confirms that black people particularly are more likely to be stopped (*Police Review*, 26 January 1995), while Norris *et al.*, found not only that young blacks were stopped very much more frequently than other racial groups, but that these stops were made on a more speculative basis, albeit that few differences emerged in the treatment of people after they had been stopped (Norris *et al.* 1992). However, even this picture needs some qualification for the PSI report found no significant difference in the proportions of different racial groups that were stopped. Where the difference lay was in the likelihood of any *particular individual* being stopped; for a minority of black people are stopped repeatedly – the likelihood of their being stopped while on foot was four times higher than for white people (Smith 1983a: 95). Moreover, the "strike rate" of around 12 per cent does not differ between racial groups.

> The latter result is important. It shows that the tendency for the police to stop a higher proportion of West Indians than of white people is justified in the sense that an equal proportion of stops of the two groups produces a "result". However, this is a justification only in a narrow sense. The great majority both of white people and of West Indians who are stopped are not shown to have committed an offence. (Smith 1983a: 116)

One problem with research on police–race relations is the broad categories of race that are employed: the problem is stated crudely as a police–"*black*" issue. Yet, it is repeatedly observed that whereas Afro-Caribbeans *are* stopped very disproportionately to their numbers in the population at large, Asians from the Indian sub-continent are stopped much less than would be expected, given their proportion of the population; indeed their contact with the police is typically as victims and campaigners demanding *more vigorous* policing. Jefferson and Walker found that in their sample drawn from an area of high racial minority settlement, Asians had much less contact with the police – especially of an unpleasant variety – and were generally favourably disposed to the police compared to black and white people (Jefferson & Walker 1993). Once the definition of race is refined even more, it emerges that it is the Irish who are *most* likely to be stopped and black Africans who are *least* likely. Moreover, Greeks, Turks and Cypriots also experience police stops at a rate almost as high as Afro-Caribbeans. As Young wryly notes "whatever the basis of the accusation of police racism, it is obviously not a matter of a knee-jerk reaction to the colour of a person's skin" (Young 1994: 65). However, it also seems from this research that differences cannot be attributed to class: being working class does increase the likelihood of young white men being stopped, but class has no effect on the likelihood that young black men will be stopped. Considering the weight of evidence, we are left with a complex picture in which stop and search is undoubtedly employed disproportionately against young Afro–Caribbean men, but not exclusively so; and there is some justification for this in the likelihood that a crime will be detected.

The problem with this approach is that it embodies the atomized individualism of the discretion debate. Because individual police officers decide to stop and search individual members of the public, it is imagined that the explanation for their conduct is to be found *within* this exercise of discretion. Although Skogan found that the person's attitude to being stopped was strongly influenced by the particular behaviour of the officer(s) (Skogan 1994), that behaviour would always need to be interpreted. One might draw an analogy here with the experience of racial harassment: Bowling argues that the experience of harassment cannot be captured by the "event-based" assumptions of the criminal justice system. Individual acts of harassment acquire their meaning and significance from being embedded within a context of intimidation (Bowling 1993). Likewise, the significance of being stopped by the police is not considered in isolation, but against wider experiences of being stopped repeatedly and knowing that one's friends and acquaintances are also frequently stopped. Those experiences are refracted through a culture that attributes meaning and significance and contains oppositional components. Such opposition is most pronounced among the young homeless, such as those Small (1983) observed, and Rastafarians who have contrived a culture of resistance (Cashmore & Troyna 1982). While such an oppositional culture effectively accounts for experience it also serves to de-couple discrete police actions and reactions to them. Thus, apparently innocuous behaviour on the part of the police can still elicit a negative reaction since its cultural meaning might be anything but innocuous. Hence, black people are more critical of police even when objective grounds for dissatisfaction are statistically controlled (Bayley & Mendelsohn 1969; Furstenberg & Wellford 1973). Despite there being little difference between how racial groups encounter the police, black people are still more hostile, reflecting their generalized hostility to the police (Tuck & Southgate 1981; Skogan 1994; see also Field 1984; Waddington & Braddock 1991). Hence, it is methodologically unsound to treat accusations of racial prejudice and discrimination as *evidence* of it, as some researchers are prone to do (see, for example, Choongh 1997).

If this is so for one party to such encounters – black people, especially young black men – it is equally true for the other party – the police. Their experience is no less partial and no less subject to interpretation. One of the first researchers to take police–race relations seriously in Britain, John Lambert (Lambert 1970), pointed to the paradox that whereas the Irish were 16 times over-represented among those arrested in the police division he studied, officers saw the then still modest black population as more troublesome. He attributed this to what he called the "ecological fallacy": because new immigrants disproportionately resided in high-crime areas, they were perceived as criminal even though they were not disproportionately involved in crime. In addition, he observed that the police did have extensive contact with immigrants through the occurrence of non-criminal problems in which the police became involved in their "peacekeeping" capacity – such as disputes between landlords and tenants – that officers tended to dislike and consider irksome. Thus, police perceptions were based on their very partial experience of immigrants: from afar they were equated with high-crime areas, whereas what little contact there was tended to be adversarial. Young offers a similar interpretation for the targeting of Afro–Caribbeans for stop and search: the one offence with which young black men are associated is "mugging" – an offence distinguished by the fact that while victim and offender do not usually know each other, they do come face-to-face. Hence, victims are usually able to report the racial identity of their attacker. However, burglary and drug-dealing are, for different reasons, hidden from view either because the public cannot or will not identify the race of the offender. Denied information about the racial identity of burglars and drug-dealers, the police generalize from what they know about mugging to what they imagine about crime *per se*; which thereby justifies targeting this group of "known" offenders (Young 1994).

In other words, into any encounter between police and black people – especially young black men – both parties bring cultural presuppositions that enhance the likelihood of conflict. Conflict is not inevitable, since one or other party may take deliberate steps to avoid it. For example, the PSI researchers found:

> . . . where the victim was a West Indian, the police were more likely to take some action, to make a full investigation, to move quickly and to catch the offender than where the victim was white or Asian. The differences shown are quite large. . . . In a broader context it does seem likely that the police make greater efforts on behalf of West Indian than other victims because they are conscious of criticisms by West Indians as a group, and concerned about the general quality of relations with them. (Smith 1983a: 84–85)

However, while conflict might be avoided, at least on these occasions, the relationship between police and citizen has, at least for the police, become *racialized* (Holdaway 1996). That is, the relationship is defined in racial terms even when police behaviour is exemplary, as described above by Smith. One might imagine a hypothetical officer saying to him- or herself "This is a black person; police–black relations are sensitive; therefore, I had better over-compensate"; or in other words, "I had better be on my guard". No wonder that officers claim that they do not know how to relate to black people (Southgate & Ekblom 1986). However, the problem with Holdaway's analysis is that racialization is attributed only to the police – there is no *relationship* in police–black "relations". Yet, racial minorities are also actively engaged in the racialization of policing, for they too construe encounters with the police in racial terms.

> Young Rastafarians gather on street corners. Young thieves gather on street corners. Some marginalised men gather on street corners. Some Rastas are thieves and marginalised men. Some young Rastas are simply lawfully and peacefully going about their business. But the police, in the task of preventing crime (in the literal sense of pre-venting), stop, question and harass the most visible of those on the street corners – the Rastas. The police station itself comes to be called Babylon and the whole recurrent theme of the captivity is enacted and dramatised once again. (Rex 1982: 70)

Vilified as "Babylon" police find that they confront hostility in their relationships with Afro–Caribbeans, especially the young whom Gilroy regards as being in the vanguard of the struggle against oppression (Gilroy 1982). Fielding describes one such encounter when a patrolling officer sought to have a group of Rastafarians remove from the footpath the cars that they were repairing. He describes in vivid detail how the officer's request was interpreted as a challenge and responded to, not only with resistance, but intimidation. In this case, the officer skilfully succeeded in achieving his goal without invoking the law (Fielding 1995), but other officers might be less skilled or otherwise constrained to invoke legal powers. Hence, recent research on the use of the newly introduced offence of "disorderly conduct" found an over-representation of Afro-Caribbeans among those arrested for this offence. In a substantial proportion of cases reviewed there was an explicit racial element that seemed to arise from exception being taken by Afro-Caribbean men to routine police action, such as stop and search, which they perceived to be racially motivated. Such hostile encounters seem to rest on a pervasive hostility to the police that initiates a cycle of escalation terminating in arrest for disorderly conduct. (Brown & Ellis 1994; see also Maung & Mirrlees-Black 1994). Whether justified or not, such a turn of events seems likely to reinforce *mutually* negative stereotypes.

However, these encounters also take place in a wider context, one in which Afro-Caribbeans predominantly occupy economically and socially marginal positions. The gap between the well-off and the poor has been increasing in most industrial societies – not least in Britain – and this has affected the non-white population particularly adversely. For example, "unemployment rates for Black Caribbeans are approximately double the British national average, for Black Africans three times as high, and higher still for Pakistanis and Bangladeshis" (Morgan & Newburn 1997: 23). Racial minorities are also concentrated in areas of severe urban decline manifested not only in rotting housing, but also disproportionate numbers of single-parent families and, of course, criminal victimization. It seems now to be widely accepted that young Afro-Caribbeans are disproportionately involved in street crime – "mugging" (Pratt 1980) – which some commentators interpret as a form of resistance to deprivation and discrimination (Lea & Young 1984). All of this seems designed to bring police into contact – and into conflict – with racial minorities, especially Afro-Caribbeans.

There is a still wider context that reinforces these conflictual tendencies; that is institutional racism. This is a term that has been trivialized in much of the debate about police–race relations, seemingly equated with widespread and unthinking racism within institutions like the police or society as a whole (see Scraton 1982). This is certainly a factor, but there is a more profound sense in which institutional racism infects modern life and that lies in social organization itself. A society like apartheid South Africa was institutionally racist, so too were (perhaps still are) the southern states of the United States and Australia. What characterizes these societies is that principal social divisions run along racial lines. Whether one is white or black (or in the South African case, "coloured") has an overwhelmingly determinant influence upon one's life experiences and life chances. Traditionally, that has not been the case in Britain, in which social division has been organized along *class* lines. Other societies, such as the northern United States conflate both systems of subordination and exclusion, with class inequalities and ethnic divisions (which extended well beyond the black–white divide to encompass the various waves of European and now third-world immigration) overlaid upon each other in a complex patchwork. But in the last half-century Britain has been transformed from a society divided in terms of class to one increasingly riven by race. More than that, racial minorities in Britain have been increasingly denied full citizenship, being subject to discriminatory laws designed to restrict racial minority immigration and much more besides (Gordon 1981, ibid. 1983). Racial minorities are also politically marginalized in a political process still dominated by traditional class divisions (Lea & Young 1982; see also Crewe 1983), and in a policy context that has persistently interpreted "race" as a problem for over thirty years (Fisher & Joshua 1982; Keith 1991; Solomos 1993).

This has profound implications for policing. When Banton wrote his pioneering comparison of policing in Scotland and the southern United States, he drew attention to the advantages of policing an integrated and "homogeneous" society, compared to the "heterogeneity" of the southern states (Banton 1964). With the benefit of hindsight this description of post-World War Two Britain is perhaps unduly flattering: a society characterized by deep class divisions hardly epitomizes "homogeneity". As studies of working-class culture reminded us, there were significant cultural differences between social classes, including great distrust of the police in working-class neighbourhoods where policing could be a pretty robust business (Whittaker 1964, ibid. 1979; Brogden 1991; Weinberger 1995). However, what is characteristic of class division is its permeability: there is the opportunity for social mobility however difficult it is to achieve. While subordinate classes may be denied full citizenship, citizenship can in principle be acquired. Societies divided by race (and to a lesser extent religion) are much less permeable and the denial of citizenship far starker, earning their description as truly "divided societies" (Weitzer 1990; Brewer 1991a, ibid. 1994; Mapstone 1992). Whereas "police property" in a class-divided society needs to be *constructed* from internal divisions among the mass of the working class, in racially divided societies race defines unambiguously who is "police property". Hence, racism in the police is commonplace: in the United States police have antagonistic relations with African–Americans and to a lesser extent Latinos; in Canada eastern Europeans occupy a similar niche; in Holland police come into conflict with Surinamers; Australian police have a long history of oppressing Aborginals; the Japanese enjoy poor relations with Koreans; Germany has long experienced conflict between the police and Turkish migrant labour; in France Algerians are the despised minority; and in Finland the gypsies are discriminated against. These patterns of exclusion are not simply the product of prejudicial attitudes, but are deeply woven into the social structure and not easily removed. In the United States the emergence of African–American mayors and chiefs of police responsible for predominantly African–American-dominated police departments has not eradicated the structural racism of policing the urban ghettos, save perhaps to lend legitimacy to oppressive strategies (Skolnick & Bayley 1986; Cashmore & McLaughlin 1991). Considered in this context, there is nothing unusual in the antagonism that exists in Britain between Afro–Caribbeans and the police, nor the selective use of oppressive authoritative intervention. Whatever the reason for any particular stop and search, it has the latent function of asserting police authority and reminding those on the receiving end of their effective non-citizenship (Choongh 1997). Nor is this new: the Vagrancy Act was *defined* as a means of harassing marginal sections of the population – what the Act describes as "rogues, vagabonds and incorrigible thieves" (Brogden 1985).

Policing Inclusion

Patrolling the boundary of inclusion and exclusion does not just involve excluding the disreputable minority, it also entails *including* the "respectable" majority within the ambit of full citizenship. Where Lee's description of marginal groups as "police property" (Lee 1981) is misleading is in its failure to recognize that complainants and victims are also "police property". In fact, police "proprietorship" extends to the entire civil population – the "included" as well as the "excluded".

Complainants and Victims

A stock response to the argument that police act as an agency of exclusion is to point to the extent to which policing is *reactive*; that is a large slice of police work is initiated by complaints from members of the public. Indeed, this is true: as noted in the previous chapter, the public, not the police, are the principal agents of discovering offences and detecting offenders. Even when the arrest is for a so-called "victimless" crime – such as public order offences and prostitution – police action resulting in the arrest is often initiated by a member of the public (Chatterton 1976a). Moreover, as Black (1970) indicated long ago, complainants are also instrumental in whether an arrest is made or not through their explicit preference – arrest is much more likely if the victim expressly demands it. All this significantly tempers the scope for the exercise of discretion by the police and explains, it is argued, many of the patterns of apparent discrimination. Those people who act as "watchers" over public space rely upon stereotypes in deciding whether the police should be called and thus direct the police towards certain types of people in particular situations (Shapland & Vagg 1988).

What this argument fails to recognize is that by reacting to calls from the public and being influenced by the wishes of victims the police act to reinforce patterns of domination and subordination, exclusion and inclusion. The act of summoning the police is itself indicative of citizenship: one is claiming one's right to state protection from actual or potential victimization. The often-observed fact that working-class people in high-crime neighbourhoods are among the most frequent complainants only undermines the crudest class-analyses, wherein it is imagined that the police simply suppress the working class who, in turn, oppose and resist police intervention. By responding to the frequent complaints of working-class people, the police confirm their identity as "respectable" and differentiate them from those who are "rough". In doing so, the police help to keep both in their respective places: the "respectable" remain allied with prevailing norms of respectability, while the "roughs" feel the weight of state repression.

However, once the police have arrived, the complainant finds that control over the encounter is immediately ceded to the police: the police ask the questions and determine the adequacy of the answers they receive. The citizen might *mobilize* police intervention, but that does not mean that the police act on the complainant's behalf (Reiss & Bordua 1967). As Ericson (1982) observes, to invoke the police involves "handing over" the problem to them. Once they have taken charge of the incident, their authority to define the situation and their expert knowledge of likely consequences means that even though complainants might be given a choice over which course of action should be taken, it is, in actuality, largely notional. Members of the public are aware of this loss of control over events once the incident is handed over to the police and the fear that they may "go too far" in dealing with minor problems acts as a disincentive to invoking police intervention (Shapland & Vagg 1987a, ibid. b, ibid. 1988). On the other hand, part of the re-assurance that victims of crimes like burglary obtain from the arrival of the police is that they *do* take charge of the incident and treat it as a crime (Maguire 1982). Police usually "do something" and rarely tell complainants there is nothing they can do or to sort the problem out for themselves (Southgate & Ekblom 1986). Indeed, public satisfaction with the police relies much more upon the care and attention that is offered, than upon whether the offender is captured. In doing so, the police confirm the victimhood of the citizen and the interest of the state in their plight.

Marginal Victims

However, this confirmation of victimhood is far from automatic. The strict demarcation between "the innocent" and "the guilty" – as if they were wholly separate groups of people – cannot be sustained, since those who occupy the statuses of "victim" and "perpetrator" frequently overlap.

> People who have been repeatedly the victims of crime in the past year are at least twice as likely to have been arrested in the past five years as people who have not repeatedly been the victims of crime. . . . These findings powerfully suggest that while everyone has a certain chance of being the victim of crime, there is a group of people who have a much higher than average chance of being victims, and these people, who tend to be repeatedly victims, also have a much higher than average chance of being arrested. This supports the hypothesis that to a considerable extent the police deal with a limited clientele of people who tend to be in trouble both as victims and as offenders . . ." (Smith 1983a: 124)

In a study of 60 disputes, Kemp *et al.* (1992a) found that police were likely to marginalize or even criminalize the complainant in order to secure their own short-term goals. Victims of racial harassment and racially motivated crime also find that the police often refuse to treat the offence as a crime and thus deny them legitimate victimhood (Jefferson & Grimshaw 1984a). Nowhere is the negotiation of victimhood more apparent than in the policing of domestic violence.

"Domestics"

"Domestics" have a particular poignancy among both police officers and those who research policing. For the former they epitomize "rubbish": inconclusive, low-status order-maintenance work that is regarded as a distraction from "real police work". By the same token researchers have long regarded domestics as epitomizing the wider role of the police and the discretion that necessarily accompanies it. Dealing with domestics was the hidden, but valuable, work that the police did (Parnas 1967; ibid. 1970). In recent years feminist writers have placed an entirely different construction on the policing of domestics that has transformed, at least, official police policy (Hanmer & Maynard 1987; Hanmer *et al.* 1989; Hanmer & Saunders 1988; Police Monitoring and Research Group 1987a; for a general review of the literature on domestic violence see Smith 1989).

There can be little doubt that for many women the home – far from being a haven of security in a hostile world – is the site of violence, intimidation and brutality. Nearly half of all violence against women in Britain is "domestic" and over ten per cent of women report that they have suffered physical violence from their partner during the course of their relationship; with working-class, separated and divorced women, and those under 30 years of age being most at risk (Mirrlees-Black 1995). Yet, victims of such non-stranger violence are disinclined to report the matter to the police, even though they suffer injury (Skogan 1994). Nevertheless, sufficient victims *do* report their victimization to make "domestics" a staple of policing in almost all jurisdictions. Horton and Smith found that officers in the forces they observed on average attended domestic disputes once every five tours of duty (Horton & Smith 1988).

Yet, despite the scale of the problem, and the fact that domestic violence tends to be committed by repeat offenders, arrests are rare (Horton & Smith 1988; Yearnshire 1996). Typically, officers attempt to resolve the problem by calming the parties to the dispute and suggesting or imposing a practical short-term solution (such as the temporary removal of one of the parties) sometimes accompanied by threats of harsher action if the police are called to the address in the near future. In terms of maintaining order, this is often reasonably successful (Horton & Smith 1988). Whether or not violence has ceased before the police arrive, in most cases the determinants of arrest lie in what happens once the police are on the scene. If violence continues or erupts while the officers are present, the offender is likely to be arrested because he threatens the control that officers seek to maintain. Equally, if the offender is disrespectful to the police or non-compliant, then he is likely to be arrested. Even if an arrest is made, it is more likely that it will be justified by the use of a "resource charge", such as drunkenness, than for assault. It is very rare that the police make an arrest on the basis of the violence that the offender has inflicted upon his victim (Buzawa & Buzawa 1993). Typically, the police avoid the legal implications of what has taken place by placing a particular construction on events that strips them of their obvious criminal characteristics. A brutal beating is thus diminished and transformed into a "civil dispute" in relation to which the officer provides "advice" (Kemp *et al.* 1992a, ibid. b). Frequently, the victim will be recorded as not supporting the arrest of the offender; but this is a fine illustration of how the desires of the complainant can be manipulated by authoritative police officers. Officers may take the victim aside and point out that if they arrest the male partner he will be kept in the cells overnight, appear in court next morning, possibly be remanded for a future hearing, and either receive a fine or short period of imprisonment – all of which means that the family income will suffer. Thus, officers exploit the economic vulnerability of most women to persuade them not to "press charges". Practices such as these are, according to Radford, the reason why women report only a small minority of episodes of domestic violence (Radford, J. 1978).

It is, of course, this avoidance of arresting men who have clearly committed serious criminal assaults that has been the main topic of controversy surrounding the policing of domestic violence (Edwards 1989a). As McCabe and Sutcliffe noted long ago, the term "domestic" is an informal category referring to often serious assaults that both diminishes the importance of the crime and leaves women vulnerable to future violence. The question then is why police officers do not arrest violent men in *these* circumstances when they would almost certainly arrest them for a comparable assault committed in a non-domestic context. Police officers tend to justify their decisions on the grounds that the victims themselves are disinclined to support prosecution, thus making an arrest a waste of time. Horror stories are told by police officers of their arresting men for serious physical abuse only to find that the victim declines to give evidence and withdraws statements after the case has been prepared. These stories receive some support from a Vera Institute report that found that more than half the assault charges brought in the context of "communal" (i.e. domestic) violence are dismissed by prosecutors for want of victim co-operation (Wilson 1980). Hence, police resist making arrests in the first instance and invest little effort in preparing the prosecution in the event that an arrest is made. Thus, one way or another, police officers regard "domestics" as troublesome, difficult and inconclusive.

Feminist writers have regarded this kind of justification with scepticism, not to say downright cynicism, seeing instead the brutal hand of patriarchy at work. A nice illustration of how patriarchal assumptions become embedded in the exercise of police discretion is to be found in Edward's critique of what Chatterton considers an illustration of "good coppering" (Chatterton 1983; Edwards 1989b). As described above, Chatterton mentioned how an officer, whom he considers epitomizes the "good copper", dealt with a case of domestic violence: there was little doubt that the woman complainant had indeed been assaulted – her face was bruised and her husband did not deny striking her. However, the husband explains to the officer how he had returned home to find the house dishevelled (breakfast crockery unwashed), the coal fire unlit, the two young children left alone and unfed after returning from school, and then how his wife had returned home apparently in the company of another man. During the course of the ensuing quarrel he had struck her and said that he would do so again unless his wife changed her behaviour. Chatterton describes how throughout the period when the husband is giving his version of events, the children stood either side of him forming a group, whereas the wife, sitting in the opposite corner, makes frequent hostile interjections. The officer warned the man not to strike his wife in future and persuades the woman not to "press charges". Chatterton remarks:

> The status of the woman as a "good mother" was undermined by the contextual features of the stage on which she made her pitch to be seen as a person legitimately claiming victim status. (Chatterton 1983: 213)

Now, it is precisely on these grounds that Edwards is critical: by persuading the victim not to "press charges", the officer reinforces the notion that violence is an acceptable means of keeping women within traditional gender definitions. Why is it assumed that it is the *woman's* responsibility to wash the breakfast dishes, light the fire and care for the children? The assumption that "a woman's place is in the home" is a reflection of the fact that policing is traditionally a *male* occupation that discriminates against women (Benn 1985). Websdale chronicles how in Eugene, Oregon, and Kentucky, police have historically colluded with men in ignoring domestic violence to women. This is particularly so in rural areas where officers are more embedded in the local community and reflect dominant communal values towards women (Websdale 1995; Websdale & Johnson 1997)

It is tempting at this point to draw the simple conclusion – both convenient for my thesis and likely to win feminist support – that just as the police exercise their discretion to subordinate and exclude youth, the lower classes and racial minorities, so too they perform the same function in relation to women. A strong case can readily be assembled to support such a conclusion; for the policing of domestic violence does not occur in a social vacuum, any more than does the policing of age, class and race. The dominant values that are likely to guide officers in taking discretionary action are patriarchal: women are regarded as subordinate chattels of men. Women who fail to comply with their subordinate status receive little sympathy (Alder 1994) and those who actively challenge it – feminist campaigners, lesbians and others – are likely to be actively suppressed (Benn 1985; Saunders & Taylor 1987). One of the weapons used to maintain male dominance is the threat of violence and sexual violation reflected not only in a tolerance of domestic violence, but also the unsympathetic response to sexual victimization (Chambers & Millar 1983; Edwards 1990). Police attitudes to women are reinforced by the courts that apply discriminatory law to women. Thus, Edwards draws attention to the invidious comparison between how victims of rape have been accused of provoking their attacker through their attire and demeanour; while, on the other hand, women who kill abusive husbands are deemed not to have been provoked by years of violence (Edwards 1989b). Likewise, Radford argues that close examination of the discourse used in courts diminishes the victimization of women (Radford, L. 1978; but see also Hedderman & Hough 1994). In the United States and Britain the law has traditionally been couched in terms that actually impede police officers from making arrests in cases of domestic violence (Buzawa & Buzawa 1993; Conway 1996; Sanders 1988). "French law bars the police from entering the 'sacred place' (*sacré lieu*) of a private home between the hours of 9 pm and 6 am – unless they are asked to do so by someone inside the home, or unless there is a 'person in danger'" and this has dissuaded police from intervening in cases of domestic violence (Horton 1995: 147–8).

Unfortunately, there is sufficient evidence that fails to fit this interpretation as to demand at least some qualification. First, "domestic" violence should not be confused with male violence towards women, for one-in-eight victims of domestic violence are men (Mirrlees-Black 1995); and there is no evidence that they receive any better treatment from the police than do women victims. Secondly, "domestics" not only involve violence, but embrace a much wider spectrum of disputes. Thus, an allegation of theft made by one member of a estranged couple against the other, is still regarded as a "domestic" and no more likely to result in arrest and/or prosecution than accusations of violence made in similar circumstances. Thirdly, "domestics" do not refer only to disputes occurring within the home or between individuals who are intimately related, but extend to disputes between neighbours, landlords and tenants, and so forth, for whom patriarchal values would have little relevance, but are still dismissed as "rubbish" by officers (Waddington 1993a). Fourthly, there is some doubt about the extent to which police officers impose patriarchal values on unwilling female victims. Horton and Smith concluded that in only a very small minority of the domestic incidents they observed did the victim want the man arrested. Instead, it seemed to the observers that most victims wanted the police to take their side in the dispute and resolve the matter informally (Horton & Smith 1988). Ethnographic research of a small number of abused women living on a public housing estate revealed that women generally, including victims, regarded male abuse as normal and often provoked by the woman herself (Bush & Hood-Williams 1995). Now, this might be regarded as paying handsome testimony to the hegemony of patriarchal values, but it also means that it is not only the police who exercise discretion on the basis of such values – these values might be commonly shared by all those involved. Finally, the policing of "domestics", especially domestic violence, is not simply the policing of gender, but also of class. As Buzawa and Buzawa (1993) point out, while domestic violence seems to be as common among middle-class couples as it is in the working class, middle-class women do not turn to the police nearly so frequently, preferring instead to use alternatives like the family physician, priest or counsellor. Consequently, police action (and inaction) is concentrated upon domestic violence among predominantly deprived sections of the population and it is noticeable how often researchers comment upon the dirty and dishevelled homes in which such incidents occur (Horton & Smith 1988).

This evidence, taken together, suggests that it is not gender *per se* that the police impose, but respectability. Of course, respectability is gendered: respectable women are sexually faithful wives and caring mothers who do not challenge the boundaries of femininity. But respectability contains elements that go beyond gender, to include concepts of *privacy*. Stinchcombe argued that the private–public divide conditions policing, with police breaching private space only if invited (Stinchcombe 1963). This has been criticized for its failure to recognize that police will transgress privacy if criminal activity is thought likely to occur, as when surveillance is mounted in public lavatories to detect homosexual activities. However, while private *space* may not be as inviolate as Stinchcombe thought, private *relationships* are. Consider the following distinction: when a disturbance occurs within the private space of a shop or place of entertainment, the police have little compunction about ejecting those causing a nuisance; but a disturbance in a family home is highly unlikely to occasion such a response (Kemp *et al.* 1992b). Both are disturbances in private places, but the former is a public relationship whereas the latter is personal, perhaps intimately so. It is this personal sphere that respectability dictates should remain private and not stray into the public domain. Hence, as Horton and Smith note, officers are often critical of the parties for involving the police in their private quarrel: couples should sort out their relationship themselves and to do otherwise is a confession of failure (Horton & Smith 1988). Moreover, respectability implies *innocence*; but the complexities of any relationship are such as to leave all parties culpable to some degree or other. This is why police complain that domestics are "messy", "grief" and "weary"– whether they entail allegations of violence or not.

Citizenship and Resistance

From everything written above it would seem that police exercise their discretion to keep people "in their place"; not only the young, members of lower class and racial minorities, and women, but also victims and members of the public whose respectability is affirmed by the care and attention they receive from the police. But this is not the whole story, at least not in western liberal democracies. For citizenship is not an attribute that is granted or withheld *per se*, but a status that is continually negotiated and renegotiated. This means that historically groups at the margins of citizenship can negotiate themselves into or be negotiated out of full citizenship. The shifting sands of respectability make policing itself rather precarious; for it cannot be guaranteed that those upon whom "respectable" values are imposed are, at the time of the encounter, on one or the other side of the citizenship line; or that later their citizenship will not be redefined and police conduct regarded as impermissible.

The policing of women is a conspicuous example of this process: while gender equality has not been fully achieved, the feminist movement has successfully negotiated women into more complete citizenship. From establishing female suffrage through to the achievement of equal employment rights the demand for gender equality has been felt in criminal justice system no less than elsewhere. In the police it has been reflected in a significant shift in the treatment of women victims of sexual offences and domestic violence (Albertson Fineman & Mykitiuk 1994; Jones *et al.* 1994). Many police forces in Britain now have "Sexual Offences Squads" and "Domestic Violence Units" staffed by officers specially trained to treat victims with the care and sensitivity that is required (Bourlet 1990; Farrell & Buckley 1993; Edwards 1994). In France, legal changes have been made and police practice amended through policy changes that reflect the same pressures as elsewhere (Horton 1995). Moreover, the policy of "presumptive arrest" in domestic violence cases – pioneered in the United States – has been enthusiastically embraced on both sides of the Atlantic (Sherman 1992b; Sherman *et al.* 1992). The reasons for this are complex and not simply attributable to the obvious effectiveness of arresting abusive husbands (Sheptycki 1993). The driving force has been the imperative to accord women that most basic right of a citizen – the protection of the state.

Likewise, the movement to extend civil rights (that is, full citizenship) to African-Americans has offered a model of resistance to black minorities throughout the western world. While few would pretend that racism in the police, or elsewhere, has been eradicated, the police have been repeatedly and publicly embarrassed by the apparent racial bias in rates of stop and search, and arrest, as well as allegations that they do not take racial harassment and violence seriously enough (Home Affairs Select Committee 1980; ibid. 1986). Official inquiries that have followed such conspicuous events as riots (Kerner 1968; Scarman 1981) and the use of excessive violence (as in the Rodney King beating [Christopher 1991]) have often lent support (to put it no higher), to allegations of racial discrimination in policing. However, the fate of black people illustrates the reversibility of this process: as concern about crime in general, and drugs in particular, has escalated, so public concern about racial bias has become more muted and the policing of the ghettos in America and inner-cities in Britain has become more aggressive (Cashmore & McLaughlin 1991).

Policing has become more precarious since the 1960s because respectability is less clearly defined. When social relationships were more clearly ordered, for example by class, then the police knew who was and was not respectable – who was their "property" and where they were to be found. How the police treated their "property" then was probably more oppressive than how they treat anyone now (Brogden 1991; Weinberger 1995). Yet, the 1950s are looked upon as a "Golden Age" of consent. It was because the oppressive actions of the police towards predominantly lower-class men were taken in pursuit of clearly prevailing standards of respectability – the "respectable" expressed no dissent at what the police did. Police actions have not changed, except to become more accommodating; but notions of respectability have become less clear and more actively contested, making the exercise of discretionary coercion more precarious.

Negotiating Respectability

Structural variables explain much of the patterning of police activity on the grand scale. The "policed" population are overwhelmingly young, lower class and members of racial minorities. However, it would be mistaken to imagine that police officers are simply dictated to by these structural considerations; for there is ample scope for individual officers to interpret what and who is "respectable". The fact that they intervene *authoritatively* also means that their interpretations tend to prevail. Police action in any encounter tends to be very context-specific, but it is still respectability that is frequently at issue. This is nicely illustrated by an anecdote told by a friend of mine.

Many years ago he spent his summer holiday in Monte Carlo where, predictably, he lost most of his money in the casino. Arriving back in his home town late at night, somewhat dishevelled after a long journey and being short of funds, he decided to walk home rather than take a taxi. Nearing his home he was stopped by a patrolling police officer who inquired where he had been. "Monte Carlo", replied my friend wearily. "Okay, smart arse", came the response, "open the case". The officer got it wrong: here was a respectable law-abiding person who did not display the normal signs of respectability. Once the officer realized that indeed my friend was a respectable citizen who had just returned from Monte Carlo, his attitude abruptly changed. Who precisely the police are dealing with, and particularly their respectability, is often in doubt even in the most deprived neighbourhoods. Police are often at pains to remind the inquisitive researcher that many of those living in such places are "good as gold" and "salt of the earth" – respectable people who deserve their protection.

The negotiability of respectable status affords police officers a considerable measure of "relative autonomy" (Marenin 1982) within which they can pursue their own occupational interests. The principal interest of the police is the maintenance of their authority; for that is the principal resource that they deploy when dealing with incidents. Deferring to police authority is also a token of respectability that is quickly established. Some commentators make the mistake of imagining that authority is merely a means to an end and that if alternatives are available they can (and should) be used (Southgate & Ekblom 1986). What this fails to appreciate is that the police do not seek solutions to problems, they *authoritatively intervene*; and without that authority their intervention has no more influence than that of any other person.

Keeping People in Their Place

The police do not enforce the law because they cannot. Laws must be interpreted and that interpretation is always context-specific. Therefore, discretion is unavoidable. However, discretion is also discriminatory, since it inevitably depends on imposing the prevailing values of dominant social groups who set the standards of respectability. Police patrol the boundaries of "respectability" and thereby subordinate and exclude those whose claims to full citizenship are, at least, doubtful – youth, lower social classes, and racial minorities. Of course, where these statuses overlap claims to citizenship are most insecure and it is, therefore, no surprise that most police attention is concentrated on lower class, racial-minority youth – particularly young men. Yet, the police not only exclude, they also include: by reacting to calls from the public, allowing complainants to influence their decisions and treating victims with care and attention, they confirm that their task is to "serve and protect" respectable people. Even here the boundary of respectability is repeatedly drawn by decisions to accept or reject claims to victimhood as commonly occurs in cases of domestic violence.

CHAPTER 3

Keeping Dissent in Its Place

Introduction

Patrolling the boundaries of respectability – and thus reproducing patterns of domination and subordination, and inclusion and exclusion – is the exercise of largely invisible state power. Individual officers selectively exercise their discretion on the street under the guise of neutrally enforcing the law and keeping the peace. But the police "keep people in their place" in quite another, and much more visible, manner when they suppress overt dissent against prevailing social, political and economic conditions. Here the notion of the police as neutral and impartial enforcers of the law is exposed for the myth that it is; since their first duty becomes transparent – to protect the state, whose coercive arm they are. This exposure of the fundamental role of the police as custodians of the state's monopoly of legitimate coercion can be revelatory: it was the riots in the American ghettos in the 1960s that prompted broad academic interest in the police; and then the riots in Britain's inner-cities almost two decades later that stimulated comparable interest on the other side of the Atlantic (Reiner 1989a). Not surprisingly, the debates that ensued were dominated by normative considerations: were the police "guilty" of the various abuses that had been alleged? What has received much less attention is the way that the policing of public order exposes the tensions between state power on the one hand, and citizenship on the other. It is to exploring this issue that this chapter will be devoted.

Criminals, Citizens and the State

The distinctive feature of the criminal justice system is that the state claims a vested interest in what might otherwise be considered a dispute between individuals: a murder, rape, or theft clearly involves a wrong to a specific victim, but the prosecution is brought (in all but exceptional circumstances) by and on behalf of the state. The state claims a vested interest in such disputes because the maintenance of order is the basis upon which state authority rests: the ultimate threat to the state is anarchy. Now, clearly if the civil population engages in rampant murder, rape and pillage (not to mention parking in no-parking zones), society would have descended into a Hobbesian "state of nature" in which state authority had collapsed. This, of course, is not only a hypothetical possibility – as the fate of countries like Somalia, Sierra Leone and Lebanon demonstrate. Nevertheless, crime would need to reach astronomical proportions before the integrity of the state is seriously jeopardized. What places the state more directly in jeopardy is mass dissent. As Dahrendorf comments, rioting is serious not just because people might be injured or killed, and property damaged or destroyed; its seriousness lies in the conspicuous refusal of citizens to accept the authority of the state (Dahrendorf 1985). This is not hypothetical either, indeed it is very real: the apartheid regime in South Africa was fundamentally weakened by the African Nationalist Congress campaign to make the townships "ungovernable"; the Palestinian "Intifada" has done more to wring concessions from the Israeli government than several wars; the Berlin wall collapsed after the authority of the communist regime was undermined by protesters in Leipzig who gathered with lighted candles and refused to disperse; the Marcos regime in the Philippines was brought down by the mass civil disobedience of "people power"; the Shah of Iran was defeated by the mass mobilization of the civil population by Ayatollah Khomeini and his followers; the American war effort in Vietnam was fatally undermined by widespread civil disobedience and rioting on college campuses; the student protests in Paris during May 1968 caused the regime of President de Gaulle to totter. Mobilized mass dissent is undoubtedly dangerous to the health of the state; indeed insurrection and rebellion must rank second only to enemy invasion as the primary threat to the continued existence of state power.

States, therefore, have a fundamental interest in suppressing mass dissent that threatens insurrection; but democratic states face obstacles that do not hinder their authoritarian neighbours when it comes to suppressing dissent – the fact that their civil population consists of citizens with rights. When, in 1989, Chinese students gathered in Tiananmen Square, the regime of Deng Xiaoping correctly estimated that it posed a serious threat to the continuation of communist rule in China. They responded to this threat as authoritarian regimes (unencumbered by the patronage of democratic states) are wont to respond to threats to their survival: they suppressed the students with overwhelming force with the loss of hundreds, if not thousands, of lives. They are not alone: the Burmese military regime was almost as ruthless in its suppression of the pro-democracy movement headed by Aung San Suu Kyi; Indonesian security forces have been no less savage in East Timor; and, of course, the Soviet military uncompromisingly crushed periodic uprisings in East Germany, Hungary and Czechoslovakia during its post-war occupation of eastern Europe. The willingness to suppress by force is not simply a reflection of the intrinsic brutality of the regime (although doubtless that helps), but reflects the relationship between state and civil population.

On Sunday, 13 April 1919, in the Punjab city of Amritsar, a crowd estimated at 25,000 strong, at least, gathered on a large piece of enclosed ground in defiance of a ban issued by the British army. General Dyer and a force of 90 Gurka soldiers entered the enclosure and, without warning, opened fire on the unarmed and unresisting crowd. After the first volley was fired high, the infantrymen were instructed to fire directly at the crowd. Then, as the crowd tried desperately to escape through the narrow exits, fire was directed to where congestion was most acute. Those who tried to scale the walls were picked-off. The soldiers were instructed to "sweep the ground" in order to hit those who were lying prone to avoid the bullets. After between ten and fifteen minutes of continuous rifle fire and the expenditure of 1,650 rounds of high-velocity ammunition the soldiers left the square without offering assistance to the dying and wounded.

It is officially estimated that 379 people – men, women and children – died in that onslaught and 1,200 others were wounded; but this is almost certainly a gross underestimate of the carnage. Dyer was perfectly open about his purpose: it was to "produce the necessary moral and widespread effect – not only on those who were present, but more especially throughout the Punjab" (Furneaux 1963: 13).

Dyer was eventually censured by an official inquiry and relieved of his command, but that censure was hesitant and equivocal. The initial response of his superiors was to commend his actions and propose him for promotion; he was toasted by the colonial élite as having saved India from a second Mutiny; while he was eventually required to retire on half salary, his military colleagues resisted pressure to censure him more severely; a majority of the House of Lords backed him, as did a substantial minority of the governing Conservative Party in the House of Commons; a national newspaper in England established a fund to which subscribers gave a huge amount; and a civil court indirectly exonerated him. Although castigated as the perpetrator of a "monstrous act" by Winston Churchill, it was never suggested that Dyer was a criminal and the general opinion was that, at worst, he had committed an "error of judgement". Just as telling were the other contemporaneous military operations designed to suppress incipient rebellion throughout the Punjab that escaped censure – indeed were hardly noticed. These included the use of aircraft to bomb and machine-gun disorderly and riotous gatherings (Furneaux 1963). What the massacre at Amritsar teaches us is that when the civil population is denied citizenship, even otherwise democratic regimes are uninhibited in slaughtering dissenters.

How does citizenship act as an obstacle to forceful state suppression of dissent? It is not simply a question of citizens having rights; for criminals also have rights and yet the state has much less compunction about using even lethal force against criminals than against rioters, despite the fact that criminals pose less threat to state interests and survival than do rioters (Waddington 1995; see also ibid. 1990). Whereas an armed robber who is shot and killed by police during a robbery is unlikely to receive public sympathy, a furore followed the use of non-lethal batons and Mace sprays to disperse violent protesters outside the Democratic Party Convention in Chicago in 1968 (Walker 1968). So, what is it that distinguishes the criminal from the rioter? Certainly, it is not that one commits criminal offences, whereas the other does not. Protesters and pickets might, and rioters certainly do, commit criminal offences – some of them serious. What distinguishes them is that the criminal places him or herself beyond the moral community of citizens by using unacceptable means to achieve illicit goals. The bank robber is almost invariably seeking personal gain by threatening fellow citizens with illegal violence. In doing so, the robber abrogates some (though not all) rights of citizenship and the police are entitled to use as much force as is necessary to prevent the commission of the crime or make an arrest. This is not the case with protesters and rioters who, far from abnegating their citizenship by their illegal conduct, are conspicuously and directly participating in the political process – a right *reserved* for citizens.

Protesters who meekly assemble to hear speeches protesting at some grievance are not only acting lawfully; they are acting *virtuously* for they are actively engaged in the political process – the right peacefully to protest or mobilize political opinion is the quintessence of citizenship. The virtue that attaches to active participation in the political process even extends to those whose form of participation involves illegality. Minor criminal transgressions committed in the context of a demonstration – such as obstruction of the highway are unlikely to detract from the virtue that attaches to protest. Even the commission of more serious offences is unlikely to be viewed with the same degree of opprobrium as would otherwise accrue. Those who engage in passive civil disobedience by, for example, staging a "sit-in", may be undoubtedly breaching the law, but their unwillingness to use violence and readiness to accept arrest and imprisonment for their actions serve only to reinforce their virtue as citizens willing to suffer in the interests of ideals. Even significant acts of violence committed in the course of protest may be regarded as less contemptible than would otherwise be the case, because it is endowed with the dignity that comes from pursuing political motives. Even when protesters are treated as pariahs, posterity may prove more forgiving. Hence, those who engaged in violent protests in pursuit of universal adult suffrage, trade union rights and civil rights for minorities are now regarded as heroes. Protest is *principled* action and acquires moral dignity as a result (Waddington 1995).

The dignity of protest is not assured, but ambiguous. Those who profess odious beliefs, however legally, are likely to receive opprobrium. Their demonstrations are likely to be tolerated, rather than celebrated by anyone other than themselves. They might even be regarded as provocative, as when neo-fascists staged legal marches through areas of high ethnic-minority settlement – a practice quite common during the 1970s in Britain (Clutterbuck 1980). Thus, it was not the opponents of neo-fascist organizations that received the weight of public condemnation, but those who provoked them by what was ostensibly lawful and peaceful political activity. As soon as protesters act illegally, and more so when they act with violence, the ambiguity of their status becomes acute. Riots staged against religious, racial and ethnic minorities – of which there have been many in Britain (Panayi 1993b) and America (Janowitz 1970) rarely receive public sympathy. In recent years, Ulster loyalists who have rioted in protest at the Anglo–Irish agreement, resurgent neo-fascists in continental Europe and the Afrikaner "resistance" in South Africa have enjoyed the public status of little more than violent thugs. However, as these examples illustrate, even such pariah groups receive the sympathy if not the active support of at least some audiences and that support may change over time. This is not just something that happens, but is actively pursued by protesters whose protests are part of, or can be assimilated into, a wider social movement – that is, they are either *political* or amenable to *politicization*. It is this political dimension that makes public disorder ambiguous: any crowd activity could be an assertion of political rectitude, an understandable albeit mistaken response to provocation, or an orgy of mindless violence, depending upon which interpretation ultimately prevails.

As Turner has argued, the aim of rioters and their sympathizers is to legitimate their violence and present it, not as criminal activity, but as a politically communicative act (see also Ball-Rokeach 1972):

> Looting is not primarily a means of acquiring property, as it is normally viewed in disaster situations; breaking store windows and burning buildings is not merely a perverted form of amusement or immoral vengeance like the usual vandalism and arson; threats of violence and injury to persons are not simply criminal actions. All are expressions of outrage against injustice of sufficient magnitude and duration to render the resort to such exceptional means of communication understandable to the observer. (Turner 1969: 816)

To the extent that this venture is successful rioters retain the status as full citizens, engaged in the political process, and police action is likely to be viewed as of, at least, questionable legitimacy. If the venture fails then rioters become the "enemy within" whom the police can suppress with virtual impunity. Thus, policing public order shares with other policing tasks the patrolling of the boundaries of respectability; the difference lies in the visibility and politically contested terrain over which those boundaries are drawn.

Now, the ambiguous status of those who engage in illegal protest places the police in an equally ambiguous position. Confronting an unambiguous criminal, like the hypothetical armed robber, is morally straightforward: the police wear the proverbial white hat and the robber is the "bad guy" in the black hat – police use coercive force, possibly lethal, so as to protect the rest of us. However, if police intervene against protesters who are acting illegally then they might find themselves wearing the "black hat". A nice illustration of this difficulty arose in the mid-1990s when protests were held at several British seaports against the export of live animals to continental Europe (Critcher 1996). There was almost universal agreement that the conditions that these animals would suffer at their destination was morally indefensible; indeed had been illegal in Britain since 1990. By enabling exporters to continue their trade, despite the opposition of protesters, the police effectively ensured that morally indefensible treatment of animals could continue. It was implausible for the police to shield behind the justification that they were merely enforcing the law, since in this case the law that sanctioned the suffering of animals was widely regarded as itself unjust (an alien imposition of the European Union). Thus, by enforcing the law against protesters who were clearly acting illegally, the police found themselves "defending injustice" by coercing those who were upholding moral virtue.

The police face a comparable dilemma to that faced by protesters; if they act with overt force the ambiguity of their moral status becomes acute. Even when protesters resort to violence it is not at all clear that this confers moral superiority upon the police. For just as protesters might use violence for the achievement of what they perceive to be higher ideals, so too the police use violent methods in pursuit of a common good – that is, law and order. There is, therefore, little moral distinction between police and disorderly crowds in the means that each employs in pursuit of its goal. In consequence, public order policing can readily become a battle of moral equals in which the legitimacy (and hence authority) of police action is open to question, if not undermined entirely.

The status of police action is ambiguous because it does not rest solely upon what they do, but upon the status of those to whom they do it. Very few (but still not few enough) regard the Ku Klux Klan as anything other than a morally and political degenerate movement. Police suppression of groups such as this can be taken pretty safely on the assumption that the "white hat" will remain securely in place. However, in many other instances it is far from clear whether the grievance and the methods of protest employed is sufficiently odious to prevailing political opinion to enable suppression to proceed with impunity. This is obviously the case with organized campaigns; for example, the protests of militant "eco-warriors" such as "Earth First" occur within a context of a favourable climate of public opinion generated by more moderate environmental protest groups (Short 1991). Police repression of even such extreme groups can easily rebound if repression is perceived to be a heavy handed over-reaction. Indeed, the provocation of state repression is itself a means of mobilizing support for militant action. Thus, quite apart from any "battle" that might occur on the streets (or elsewhere) between police and protesters, the police can find themselves engaged in a political debate with protesters and their sympathizers over the propriety of their respective conduct, the outcome of which is decidedly uncertain. This is essentially a zero-sum game: to the extent that one party can portray themselves in a favourable light to relevant audiences, they do so at the expense of the other party – if one side wins, the other must lose.

There is a distinct similarity between the policing of public order and routine police work – both involve patrolling the boundary between inclusion and exclusion, domination and subordination. Coercion may be used to exclude and subordinate. In both cases the precise boundary is ambiguous, changing and negotiable lending a measure of precariousness to police action. Where they differ is in their visibility and the overtly political dimension of public order policing. Historically, this has been the central problematic to which the police of liberal democracies have had to adapt. Central to this has been the relationship of the police and the military.

Creating a Duopoly of Force

On Monday, 16 August 1819, some 80,000 people gathered illegally on St Peter's Fields near the industrial city of Manchester to listen to the radical orator, Henry Hunt, espouse the case for parliamentary reform. Magistrates read the Riot Act ordering the crowd to disperse and then instructed troops to arrest Hunt. The Manchester Yeomanry – a part-time militia force comprising members of the petite bourgeoisie – charged into the crowd and were followed by a troop of Hussars dispatched to rescue their volunteer comrades when it appeared that the latter might be overwhelmed. The resulting carnage left eleven people dead and four-hundred wounded, including around one-hundred women. Critchley concludes his account of these events: "The shock to the nation was intense" (Critchley 1970: 115–17). That shock became one of the most persuasive arguments for the installation of a civil police. But it has a more profound significance than that.

"Peterloo", as it came to be known, did not occur in isolation: it came after a century when policing had very largely, albeit sporadically – been undertaken by the military. As noted in Chapter 1, it followed the anti-Catholic Gordon Riots that left 400 dead, agitation of John Wilkes for liberal political reform, and the epidemic of machine-smashing by "Luddites" fearful of the threat of industrial production to their livelihoods. The first quarter of the nineteenth century was a period of the most intense political, social and economic turmoil, not only in Britain but elsewhere. The American and French Revolutions had not only successfully swept away monarchical rule and installed republics, but fuelled radicalism throughout Europe that left many regimes in peril. If the Magistrates who surveyed the scene on St Peter's Field had a sense of foreboding then it was both justified and prescient, for in just 13 years the Great Reform Act would be passed and within 50 years universal male suffrage would be established – democracy threatened and aristocratic privilege was on the wane. There was, in short, precious little to lose and everything to gain by suppressing by force this illegal and potentially rebellious gathering. The situation they faced was no less perilous than that confronting General Dyer exactly a hundred years later. Why, then, were they so timid? Why did they not act with the brutal decisiveness shown by Dyer? Why deploy a troop of ill-disciplined yeomen when artillery was available? What point was there in killing only eleven and injuring a few hundred, when the capacity to kill hundreds and maim thousands was readily to hand? Imagine what carnage a fusillade of grape-shot would have wreaked amongst that crowd gathered in the summer sunshine. It would have sent a clear message that the political elite was prepared to defend their power and privileges with the utmost resolve. It would have sent a chill throughout the country equivalent to that which pacified the Punjab in 1919. True, it might just have sparked a revolution along the lines of the American and French insurrections; but then so might the relatively minor use of force for which the authorities opted. The Counting House massacre in Boston, 1770, claimed many fewer lives than "Peterloo", yet contributed to revolutionary sentiments throughout the American colonies. And why did such a relatively small "body count" so traumatize the nation?

We can, of course, only speculate about the answers to these questions, but what is indisputable is that "Peterloo" marks the inception of a process of the demilitarization of controlling public disorder in Britain. It crystallized the perceived necessity for a nonmilitary alternative of crowd control and thus contributed to demands for the installation of a civil police. Once established, the civil police acquired primary responsibility for subduing "the mob"; and doing so *without* recourse to military weapons. Thus, paradoxically, at the very time that democratic agitation was reaching a crescendo, the aristocratic state withdrew its most potent coercive arm and substituted a less forceful alternative – *and lost!* True, for the remainder of the nineteenth century and into the first quarter of the twentieth, the military remained as a potentially lethal long-stop to be called upon as a last resort; but it was a *last* resort, the use of which remained shrouded in controversy. Moreover, despite their lack of coercive "muscle", the police won the historic three-way tussle with the military and the magistracy over supremacy in public order management (Vogler 1991). As Amritsar illustrates, this was in stark contrast to the policing of the Empire, which was brutal and repressive (Bowden 1975; Brogden 1989; Ahire 1991; Anderson & Killingray 1991, ibid. 1992).

The fact that the political élite abstained from using its military might against its own civil population in Britain, pays ample testimony to the influence of the idea of "citizenship" upon those who wielded political power. "The shock to the nation was intense", not because a few people had been killed, but because "freeborn Englishmen" had been cut down like an enemy. The reason that the military retreated from controlling the civil population was not because its weaponry was ineffective – on the contrary, developments in military weapons technology massively enhanced the coercive power at the disposal of the state. A hand-grenade lobbed into the midst of a crowd would, in all probability, disperse survivors very quickly. Yet, it is virtually inconceivable that police would use such a weapon. Why? Because the very characteristics that make hand-grenades suitable for military conflict – its *indiscriminate lethality* – render them inappropriate for controlling citizens with rights.[1]

Control through Inclusion

Getting rid of the military did not get rid of the problem: crowds continued to be disorderly and police use of force to quell them continued to be surrounded

[1] Another reason for excluding the military from domestic affairs was the fear of *coup d'état*. However, it is difficult to understand why this should have been so worrying to an aristocratic élite that also held the levers of military power. A standing army barracked in central London posed more threat to democratic government than to the aristocratic hegemony that continued throughout much of the nineteenth century.

with controversy. When Constable Culley was stabbed to death at the "Battle of Coldbath Field" in 1833, the coroner's jury initially returned a verdict of "justifiable homicide", apparently in protest at the violence shown by the police (Brogden 1983). Treading the line between effective suppression of disorder and the avoidance of excessive repression proved a perilous one, and during the nineteenth century several Commissioners of the London Metropolitan Police were dismissed for straying from the path (Critchley 1970). There was ample incentive for discovering alternative means of controlling dissent to that of naked suppression by either military or police; and ironically it was to develop in that cauldron of class conflict – industrial disputes.

According to Roger Geary (whose history of the policing of industrial disputes ranks amongst the few standard works on the subject), the hundred years from the mid-nineteenth to the mid-twentieth centuries would see the transition from "stoning and shooting" to "pushing and shoving" (Geary 1985). Industrial conflict in the mid-nineteenth century had become a pretty bloody affair – although less bloody than it might have been. Strikers sought physically to incapacitate their employers with whom they were in dispute by smashing plant and machinery, and preventing the employment of "blackleg" labour by violence and intimidation. They were opposed, often haphazardly, by detachments of troops summoned by local magistrates, who were, of course, closely allied with employers. This was the situation at the small coalmining village of Featherstone in 1893 when, amongst the confusion that tended to accompany these events, the troops opened fire on strikers killing two of their number and two more bystanders. What is significant about the Featherstone shooting was that it was the last time that troops would open fire on strikers in Britain. A series of events began the transformation from these bloody confrontations to a situation in the mid-twentieth century when picketing had become a more or less symbolic protest. It was the unlikely couplet of Winston Churchill and an army general that was to play the most significant role in the early years of the twentieth century.

South Wales was racked by industrial turmoil in the coalmines and the authorities called for troops to assist the police in maintaining order. Churchill, who was then Home Secretary, rejected the request and dispatched instead a detachment of Metropolitan Police – an action that was blatantly illegal, since he had no authority to intervene (Vogler 1991). Moreover, he placed the Metropolitan Police and troops (that were kept on standby) under the command, not of the local magistracy who were allied with manufacturing interests, but of General Macready to ensure their impartiality. While neither Churchill nor the Metropolitan Police acquired many friends amongst the strikers of South Wales – for the strike was eventually broken amid scenes of serious rioting and violence by the police – this intervention was notable as a major de-escalation in the cycle of violence that had accompanied industrial disruption hitherto. It established that the maintenance of public order was a *police* responsibility into which the military would stray only in the most extreme circumstances. Despite the rioting with which the mining village of Tonypandy is associated, it also established that order was more effectively secured in the absence of overtly violent suppression. Even during the General Strike of 1927 major confrontation was avoided. Policing of industrial disputes increasingly sought a *modus vivendi* between police and pickets in which "ground rules" were agreed. This developed over the next few decades into the practice whereby a handful of pickets posted at factory gates relied on the equally token police presence to stop vehicles entering strike-bound premises so that pickets could attempt to persuade drivers not to cross the picket-line. When there was a confrontation between police and pickets it usually took the form of pre-arranged desultory "pushing and shoving". This is, of course, a simplistic gloss on complex historical events that did not evolve nearly so smoothly; but it captures the clear trend during the first half of the twentieth century towards significant de-escalation in violence.

Why did this transformation occur? Geary's answer is that it arose out of a tacit conspiracy between the ruling élite and the Labour Movement to "cool it" on the picket-line. This conspiracy was founded on a mutuality of interest that evolved from the very institution of citizenship that had posed the dilemma in the first instance. The enfranchisement of the adult male working class had prompted the development of a parliamentary arm to the Labour Movement which was destined to evolve into the Labour Party with a realistic prospect of being elected to government. Violent suppression of strikes by the military or the police would serve only to provoke sympathy for strikers and the wider Labour Movement that might be turned to the electoral advantage of the Labour Party. On the other hand, violent prosecution of a strike would reciprocally risk sacrificing public sympathy to the electoral disadvantage of the Labour Party. So, by opening the constitutional route to power for the industrial masses – by granting them not only civil but also political citizenship – violent conflict was contained – what is described sociologically as the "incorporation of the working class".

This incorporation was not restricted to industrial disputes alone. A similarly marked decline took place in public disorder generally (Dunning *et al.* 1987). Some of this arose from the same root as the decline in industrial violence: disorder accompanying elections showed a precipitate decline from the early years of this century to its current level of conformity – one is tempted to say "apathy". However, similar declines in disorder associated with sporting events and entertainment suggests a wider explanation. Lane has argued that the apparent decline in crime, observable in several western societies, from around 1850 to the outbreak of the First World War was due to the growth of "disciplines" associated with industrial and urban life (Lane 1992). This is a compelling argument and one that is not restricted to crime, for by opening the constitutional route to political power, the Labour Movement was constrained by its accompanying parliamentary disciplines. Moreover, sport and leisure also became increasingly disciplined. The creation of spectator sport was itself the imposition of significant discipline as supporters of rival teams were increasingly corralled into more or less passive observation of the "battle" being done on their behalf by their respective teams. The commercialization of spectator sport has served to further strengthen the incentives for soccer clubs to ensure that spectator violence does not mar the profitability of the business; hence spectators are screened on entry, penned-in, seated and kept under surveillance lest they disturb the "family" entertainment provided for them. Likewise, the commercialization of fairs, following the success of Barnham and Bailey in the United States, transformed occasions associated with mayhem into relatively tranquil forms of entertainment (Cunningham 1977). The consumption of alcohol was gradually contained, not by overt suppression, but through the introduction of a licensing regime that reduced the strength of the product and encouraged the development of that icon of English civilization – the country pub! The working class of Britain was, if this argument is correct, not only incorporated into established political and economic institutions, but into the wider institutions of urban life which acted to contain and constrain behaviour.

"Ordinary Decent Protesters"

Once conduct is institutionalized, it can be policed with a more or less light touch. So it is with the policing of political protest. Most protest consists of demonstrators assembling and then marching to a rally carrying placards and shouting slogans, before listening to speeches and departing. My observations of the policing of political protest in London showed that in the vast majority of instances most control was exercised by the demonstrators themselves, with police exercising influence through their facilitation of minimally disruptive protest activity (Waddington 1993c, ibid. 1994a, ibid. b, ibid. 1996a). Thus, protest organizers notified the police well in advance, complied readily with police guidance, and were anxious not only to remain within the law but within the parameters of constitutional protest. This allowed the police to influence the course of events without exercising overt authority, still less using coercion. Pre-protest negotiations were concluded within an aura of amicability reminiscent of business people arranging a mutually beneficial deal, with police offerng help and guidance, as well doing the occasional favour, so as to "win over" protesters. They exerted control through their use of their knowledge and expertise upon which protesters were invited to depend; upon bureaucratic mechanisms that induced protesters to supply more information than was required by law and enter into legally unenforceable "contracts"; and if persuasion became necessary it was not the force of legality that was appealed to, but the self-interests of the protesters – their safety and the need to avoid antagonizing bystanders. Physical control over marches was mainly in the hands of traffic police who orchestrated the flow of traffic around marchers so as to keep them contained within a "moving wall of steel" – reserves of riot-police were kept safely out of sight and only rarely deployed.

Thus, the norms of democratic protest are reproduced sustaining expectations of what acceptable protest entails. Provided that protesters "play the (democratic) game" they can expect not only that the police will abstain from exercising overt coercion, but also offer them protection. This extends even to protesters who challenge fundamental state interests, provided they do so through constitutionally acceptable means. For example, the annual march to commemorate the "Bloody Sunday" shootings in Londonderry in 1972 and demand British disengagement from Northern Ireland, is routinely accompanied by a police operation to prevent attacks upon marchers from their neo-fascist opponents.

The role of citizenship in restraining the policing of "ordinary decent protesters" is quite clear. First, senior police officers do exhibit an unreflexive, but nonetheless profound belief in the right of peaceful protest. This occasionally led them to resist the attempts of government to stifle protests that were regarded as politically inconvenient. This extended to showing considerable tolerance for protesters who committed even relatively serious breaches of the law. Secondly, police feel restrained in taking any action that is likely to provoke allegations of "provocation", "heavy-handedness" or "brutality". Throughout the planning of contentious events, police were very aware of the likelihood that, if disorder ensued, there might be an inquiry or action in the civil or criminal courts that might result in criticisms of their actions. Hence, there was the utmost sensitivity shown about the deployment of riot-control police: the assumption being that they should be kept out of sight even of bystanders until needed and could only be deployed once disorder had become sufficiently serious that no other course of action remained open.

Like the officer on the street, those engaged in public order operations patrol the boundaries of respectability: "playing the constitutional game" being the hallmark of respectable political involvement.

A Common Democratic Solution?

A remarkably similar account could be given of the United States, albeit that the historical timing would be shifted towards the more recent past. Industrial conflict during the nineteenth and early twentieth centuries was associated with serious violence; indeed battles between strikers and company police, sometimes backed by troops, were often bloody in the extreme with many lives lost and injuries caused (Center for Research on Criminal Justice 1977; Taft & Ross 1979). The transformation came with Roosevelt's New Deal and specifically the Wagner Act of 1935, supplemented by the Taft-Hartley Act of 1947, that conferred rights upon the labour unions but also served to incorporate them into the capitalist economy and democratic institutions. America also has a history of violent political protest and agitation. As Gamson has documented, the use of violence in the United States has been historically associated with the successful achievement of political aims (Gamson 1975). This tradition was continued until relatively recently – for example, during the campus unrest to the Vietnam War. However, despite the continuation of many active social movements, there has been a marked decline in violent protest in the United States, especially in Washington, DC. McPhail *et al.* have documented this decline and attribute it to a shift in police tactics from what they describe as "escalated force" to "negotiated management" (McPhail *et al.* 1998). The latter gives much greater and a more positive emphasis to the civil rights of protesters, tolerance of disruption and contact and communication between protesters and police, while giving less emphasis to making arrests and using force to quell disorder than did its predecessor. This shift reflects a wider change in the political climate emanating from Supreme Court decisions and Presidential Commissions of Inquiry. The development of a system of issuing permits to protest in areas like those under the jurisdiction of the National Park Service in Washington, DC, has become the vehicle for police and protesters to negotiate mutually acceptable arrangements.

Let me illustrate how the process works: I am assured by the Special Operations Division of the Washington Metropolitan Police that both police and protesters know that the aim of staging a protest is for it to be broadcast on the 6 pm evening news and that this is unlikely in the absence of disorder and arrests. So police negotiate with protesters an agreed "outbreak" of violence to be staged for the attending news media. Those who are to engage in this "outbreak" are clearly identified and as much of the paperwork connected with their arrest as possible is completed beforehand. The incident is staged at around 4 pm – the most convenient time for it to reach the airwaves in the evening news. The police have constructed a special "paddy wagon" equipped with doors at the front and rear allowing those arrested to enter at one end, complete formalities as they proceed along its length and exit at the other – a process lasting only a few minutes. What happens if protesters refused to stage a pre-arranged incident and actually became violent? Well, they are be arrested at 4.30 and thus miss the evening news! (I cannot attest to the accuracy of this account, but it makes a good story and illustrates the shift to which McPhail *et al.* draw attention.)

It is not just in Britain and America that the benefits accruing from negotiated styles of public order policing have been recognized. Della Porta has described how, in both Germany and Italy, the policing of political demonstrations has become less violent over the past quarter of a century and how police now view their task as no longer one of confrontation and use of force, but containment through co-operation (della Porta 1994b, ibid. 1998) – an interpretation supported by Winter's research on the historical development of policing in West Germany (Winter 1998). A similar picture emerges from France where Fillieule and Jobard have obtained access to the substantial archive of the formidable *Compagnies Républicaines de Sécurité* (CRS). They conclude:

> . . . the usual image of the police battling with demonstrators is nowadays quite misleading. Disorder is quite rare, even in the biggest and most problematic protest events. By and large, demonstrators co-operate with the police, assemble at a previously agreed location, proceed along an agreed route and disperse peacefully, regardless of the perceived results of their actions. (Fillieule & Jobard 1998: 1)

It is tempting to perceive these developments as an international democratic "conquest of violence" (Critchley 1970), but that would be misleading. Protest continues to pose acute problems for policing because the boundaries of political "respectability" are always uncertain and shifting. Indeed, the relative quiescence of contemporary western democracies is the product of a period of turmoil and struggle during the 1960s and 70s over the issue of civil rights (della Porta 1994a).

Civil Rights: Contesting Citizenship

The Civil Rights Movement as we now understand it, began with the Montgomery bus boycott in 1955 that rapidly spread throughout the southern states, followed by lunch counter sit-ins, "freedom rides", the march on Washington, and eventually concluded with the "long hot summers" of ghetto riots that continued until the end of the 1960s. It prompted civil rights movements throughout the liberal democracies, not least in Northern Ireland where demands for civil rights for Catholics initiated a series of events that developed into the current "troubles". On the continent of Europe it sparked student protests in France, Germany and Italy that spawned the "civil rights coalition" which eventually had a liberalizing effect on the state, especially the police. It is not my intention here to analyze the Civil Rights Movement in the United States or elsewhere: there is insufficient space and others have done so much better than I could aspire to achieve (McAdam 1982, ibid. 1983, ibid. 1988; Killian 1984). My intention here is to examine the public order policing of sections of the population whose citizenship is highly contested.

From the abolition of slavery until the Second World War the citizenship of African–Americans was only notional, especially in the southern states. Denied full voting rights, receiving segregated and inadequate education, ghetto-ized, poverty-stricken and suffering persistent discrimination in all walks of life, their "emancipation" was not even skin deep. Not surprisingly, therefore, the policing of African–Americans was neo-colonial: brutal oppression by white officers was endemic.

"Race riots" in the first half of this century invariably involved the violent suppression of African–Americans irrespective of their culpability. Inevitably, perhaps, the response to the civil disobedience of Civil Rights protesters was a continuation of this style of policing: participants in lunch counter sit-ins and freedom rides were arrested, usually for quite serious charges, such as "inciting a riot" (Killian 1984); and demonstrations were dispersed with tear-gas, buckshot and snarling dogs, as in the infamous case of the Selma march. However, the political climate had changed following the Supreme Court decision on segregated education. The dignity with which many Civil Rights protests were conducted and the eloquence with which leaders, like Martin Luther King, Jnr, articulated grievances – contrasting the high ideals of the American Constitution with the squalid reality of the lives of African–Americans – made the espousal of white supremacist views increasingly disreputable. Thus, when the ghetto riots erupted in the mid- to late-1960s, African–Americans were no longer a section of the population excluded from full citizenship: they were in the midst of a transition. That transition might reasonably be thought to have been compromised by the ghetto riots; certainly rioters were disowned by the Civil Rights leadership. However, the Kerner Commission (1968) and weight of articulate opinion came to regard the rioters as victims of oppression that, at least, provoked their actions, even if it did not justify them (Fogelson 1971). This was in stark contrast to the conclusions of the McCone Commssion (1965) just a few years previously, that largely dismissed the Los Angeles, Watts, riot as an orgy of criminal hooliganism. This transformation in official thinking was no mean intellectual achievement for the Civil Rights Movement, for it amounted to the articulation of "theory of riots" that purported to explain these events to the advantage of rioters (see Skolnick 1969). Part of the legacy of the Civil Rights Movement has been to bestow this theory upon, and thereby dignify as "political", later episodes of disorder elsewhere in the world such as the inner-city riots of the 1980s in Britain (Scarman 1981).

Explaining Riots: The Normative Dimension

Taylor has argued that there are three "theories" that tend to circulate in the aftermath of serious disorder: the conservative, liberal and radical (Taylor 1984). Each of these "theories" draws support from academic thought and commentary and so the line between disinterested scholarship and political partisanship is frequently blurred or disappears entirely. The "conservative" theory is favoured by the political establishment, including the police. It maintains, more or less implicitly, that existing social, political and economic arrangements are satisfactory; or if not, that change is possible through constitutional means, and therefore that violent protest is certainly unnecessary – it is criminal hooliganism masquerading as political action (Anderton 1981; Metropolitan Police 1981, ibid. 1985; Oxford 1981; Dear 1986; Richards 1986; Flanders 1991; Metcalfe 1991; Kendrick 1995). By effectively seeking to criminalize those engaged in disorder it confers moral superiority on the police and their use of force to suppress disorder. The "liberal" theory regards riot and disorder as symptomatic of social injustices that cannot be resolved through mere suppression, but through social, political and economic reform. The "radical" view agrees with the liberal analysis that riots and disorder are symptomatic of social injustices, but regards the origins of this injustice as lying in the fundamental structure of society and thus not amenable to reform; injustices will only be removed by the transformation of society. The Kerner and Scarman reports can clearly be located in the "liberal" category: conceding that African–Americans and black British people suffer deprivation, discrimination and police harassment and making recommendations intended to ameliorate social and economic conditions, and reform the police. The "liberal" theory has received widespread academic support and come to acquire the status of an orthodoxy,[2] albeit one that has not gone entirely uncontested.[3]

So effective has been the dominance of the liberal–radical view (that I have elsewhere described as the "critical consensus" [Waddington 1991]) that it is worth considering the force of this argument. Its central contention is that the actions of rioters are rational and that their complaints should be taken seriously (Bachrach & Baratz 1970; Kettle & Hodges 1982; Benyon 1984a, ibid. 1987a, ibid. b; Benyon & Solomos 1987a, ibid. b). The political basis of this view is clearly revealed in the grounds offered for rejecting previous, allegedly "conservative", theories. These grounds lie not in the inability of previous theories to explain the occurrence of disorder, but in their failure to accept rioters' own reasons for action. For example, Currie and Skolnick (1972) reject Smelser's highly influential "value-added" theory of collective behaviour (Smelser 1962) on the grounds that it treats rioters' beliefs as contingently related to underlying structural change – beliefs need not be true or accurately identify the reasons for grievances in order to work effectively as mobilizers of opinion. This, they argue "allows Smelser to discredit the beliefs of the participants in collective action on *a priori* grounds" (Currie & Skolnick 1972: 67 emphasis added). The imperative to avoid *discrediting* participants is clearly normative, for if rioters are motivated by something other than the grievances they avow, there is no compulsion to remedy those grievances; for doing so will not ameliorate or eradicate unrest. Thus, as Benyon and Solomos (1987a) insist, the "central factor" is injustice and it is this that must be corrected.

There are, however, serious difficulties with this notion that participants in collective action should be taken seriously. Foremost amongst them is that it is selectively applied: not all rioters are credited with rational beliefs. Indeed, Skolnick himself dismisses white racist violence as a mere "backlash" (Skolnick 1969) and many other commentators seek to distance rioters whom they favour from those who they do not. Hence, liberal and radical writers dismiss out of hand any equation of inner-city riots with such discreditable forms of collective behaviour as soccer hooliganism (Murdock 1984; Benyon 1987a). *Ad hoc* distinctions of this kind are transparently political, but Marx (1972) has sought to impose intellectual coherence by distinguishing between

[2] (Allen & Adair 1969; Skolnick 1969; Stark 1972; Gilbert 1975; Rogaly 1977; Gutzmore 1978; Wright 1978; Viorst 1979; Rosenhead 1981; Venner 1981; Hall 1982; Kettle & Hodges 1982; Gilroy 1983; Manwaring-White 1983; Coulter *et al.* 1984; National Council for Civil Liberties 1984, ibid. 1986, ibid. 1987; de Friend & Uglow 1985; Fine & Millar 1985; Northam 1985, ibid. 1988; Reed & Adamson 1985; Gifford 1986; Scraton 1985, ibid. 1987b; Edgar 1988; Jackson 1989; Green 1990; Bowes 1966; Rainwater 1967; Fogelson 1970; Hahn & Feagin 1973; Heirich 1976; Ackroyd *et al.* 1977; Hall 1979; Worpole 1979; Bergesen 1980; Cohen 1980; State Research 1981a; Cowell *et al.* 1982; British Society for Social Responsibility in Science 1983; Joshua *et al.* 1983; Benyon 1984b; Reicher 1984; Beynon 1985; East *et al.* 1985a, ibid. 1985b; Independent Inquiry Panel 1985; Jackson, B. & with Wardle 1986; Benyon & Solomos 1987b; The Police Monitoring and Research Group 1987; McCabe *et al.* 1988; Northam 1988; Stephens 1988; Uglow 1988; Cashmore & McLaughlin 1991; Hawkins & Thomas 1991; Solomos & Rackett 1991; Rose 1992; Roseneil 1995)

[3] (Clutterbuck 1973, ibid. 1980; Banfield 1974; Deane-Drummond 1975; Button 1978)

"issue-oriented" and "issueless" riots; but this only serves to highlight the difficulties of making such a distinction. On the one hand, there is often as much reason to suppose that disfavoured groups are ideologically motivated as there is to attribute political motive to those who are favoured. For example, odious though their beliefs may be, there can be little doubt that fascists are ideologically motivated (Fielding 1981a; Thurlow 1987; Drechon & Mitra 1992). On the other hand, there are the methodological problems associated with discovering what, if any, issues a more or less violent crowd are pursuing. As Berk points out, it becomes a little hazardous in the midst of a riot to inquire too closely why rioters are rioting (Berk 1972). In fact, the connection between the existence of issues and riotous or disorderly behaviour is rarely established, but merely speculatively inferred. Some inferences are more plausible than others: the outbreak of rioting in south-central Los Angeles in 1992 can plausibly be attributed to the acquittal of four police officers for the beating of Rodney King because of the close proximity of the events and the growing tension that had accompanied the jury's deliberations (Webster & Williams 1992). However, the attribution of issue-orientation in other events seems more problematic. For example, David Waddington *et al.* credit rowdy youths congregating in a shopping precinct with pursuing issues on the unsupported grounds that in this instance "territory is at stake" (Waddington *et al.* 1989). More commonly, analysts simply point to the deprivation, discrimination and harassment suffered by rioters and assert that these background conditions are causally related to their riotous behaviour. The possibility that they may be unconnected is suggested by research that compares riot-afflicted and riot-free areas, which shows that riot-free areas suffer no less from socio-economic injustices than their riot-afflicted counterparts (Horowitz 1983; Sherman 1983a; Parry *et al.* 1987). Thus, the concept of "issue-orientation" does not assist us in distinguishing validly and reliably between different types of disorder.

Political Success Rising from Explanatory Ashes

No matter how implausible the liberal–radical theory of riot is as an explanation of why riots occur where and when they do, it is a political fact that some outbreaks of disorder are treated by the authorities as the expression of a political grievance. This was the achievement of the "liberal" theory of riots and political mobilization of the Civil Rights Movement (McAdam 1983): it dignified what was hitherto otiose and incorporated those who by their actions threatened to exclude themselves. However, in both America and Britain it did not prevent the increased reliance on methods of overt suppression to contain future rioting – an issue to which we will return shortly. But first we must consider how the political process of inclusion can be variable.

Reversing Inclusion

The influence of the "liberal" theory of rights has extended citizenship even to ethnic-minority rioters. Normatively, this can be seen as a genuine triumph for the idea of civil rights; sociologically it amounts to the incorporation of previously excluded groups within the ambit of citizenship. But just as the individual officer on the street patrols the boundary between inclusion and exclusion, so too do officers engaged in public order policing. Della Porta observes that the Italian police share with the police of London that I studied the distinction between "the opposition" and "ordinary genuine protesters" (della Porta 1998; Waddington 1994). This is consistent with changes in the wider discourse over the past three decades in Italy and West Germany which have seen an increasing differentiation of "good" and "bad" demonstrators (della Porta 1994a). Repression continues; it is just that – like the "community constables" that Fielding studied (Fielding 1995) – the police have learned to make more refined and sensitive distinctions, and eschew the belief that all protest is a fundamental threat to the state.

Thus, while the notion of citizenship and its extension to previously excluded groups has been the engine that has driven public-order policing in liberal democracies towards the accommodation of protest and control through negotiation, the boundary between citizens and non-citizens continues to be drawn and enforced. This is the other side of the historical coin; for while the dominant tendency in Britain throughout this century has been to defuse class conflict by incorporating the working class – particularly the Labour Movement – there have been parallel developments in the opposite direction. The principal development being the covert preparations made by successive British governments of all political persuasions to defeat strikes that threatened the national interest and which culminated in the policing of the year-long coalminers' strike of 1984 to 1985.

Preparing for Class War

The immediate aftermath of the First World War found Britain in turmoil: the demobilization of the wartime army was imposing massive economic strain that was being felt in increasing industrial unrest. The major trade unions in coalmining, railways and the docks had formed themselves into the "Triple Alliance" which threatened a stranglehold on the economy. In addition to which the fear of Bolshevism among the ruling élite had reached levels of hysteria. The response of government was to begin contingency planning for the confrontation that seemed inevitable. Despite changes of governing party during the inter-war period, a national system of contingency planning to defeat strikes that threatened the national interest was progressively developed, albeit in fits and starts (Jeffery & Hennessy 1983).

The police were to play a central role in this process, despite the fact that there was no national police organization, and the government had no direct control over policing outside of London – local councils being responsible for the policing of larger towns and cities, and committees comprising councillors and magistrates having responsibility for the rural counties. So, central government set about covertly creating the framework for a national police organization to be implemented should it become necessary. Some elements of this framework already existed in constitutional arrangements stretching back to the nineteenth century, whereby central government paid some of the costs of policing in return for the right to inspect and adjudicate upon the efficiency of local forces. In addition, rudimentary arrangements existed for forces to offer assistance to each other; but these were *ad hoc* and the procedures for obtaining financial compensation unsatisfactory. There was an even more pressing problem: the loyalty of the police could not be relied upon. Disaffection was as rife among police officers as it was among other workers and there had been a police strike in 1918

(Reynolds & Judge 1969) and another in 1919. It was necessary, therefore, to ensure the reliability of the police. The Desborough Committee of 1919, resulting in the Police Act in the same year, played a crucial role in both respects. It was convened ostensibly to review the terms and conditions of employment of police officers as a response to the 1918 strike. In the short term it bought off all but the most militant officers, but at the price of de-unionizing the police. Officers would henceforth be represented by the Police Federation and subject to nationally agreed terms and conditions of employment. A further recommendation of the Committee was for central government to pay half the cost of the police, and the creation of a department of the Home Office dedicated to police matters. It also ushered in greater consultation among and co-ordination between chief constables throughout the land. Incidental to its main purpose, the Committee also recommended that the Home Secretary should be able to require any police force to send officers to support others that were in need. It also initiated a frenetic period of centralization of a wide range of police functions. Summing up this period, Critchley remarks:

> The importance of the Desborough Committee, in introducing a new era for the police service, can hardly be exaggerated. The current of change ran deep, and its course was permanent. . . . By 1939 . . . the Home Office had built up a position of quite remarkable influence in police affairs, when it is remembered how detached the department had been before the First World War . . . (Critchley 1978: 219)

During this same period the concept of "constabulary independence" emerged, which, according to Lustgarten, was intended to distance senior officers from the control of increasingly common radical Labour-controlled town and city councils sympathetic to strikers (Lustgarten 1986). Now tamed and under effective central direction, the police came to be integrated into the national system of civil contingency planning that by the outbreak of the Second World War amounted, in the estimation of Morgan (1987), to a shadow national police force in all but name.

The history of civil contingency planning between the World Wars is significant in two quite different respects. First, it testifies to the fragility of the "truce" that had emerged between the state and the organized working class: incorporation was conditional upon not challenging too directly the fundamental interests of the state. If such a challenge had occurred, then the state was willing and able vigorously to prosecute a class war against organized labour. It was only because trade union leaders, most notably members of the Triple Alliance, did not fully pursue their radical aims that such a class war was avoided (Weinberger 1991). Secondly, the creation of this almost entirely covert system of civil contingency planning did not prevent the continued development of the transition from "stoning and shooting" to "pushing and shoving" that reached its zenith in the immediate post-Second World War period. These were genuinely parallel developments: the British state pursued peace while preparing for class war.

The "Enemy Within"

The incorporation of the working class had always been conditional and less than universal. Those members of the working class who remained outside union organization were much more vulnerable to state repression. The clearest illustration of this being the fate of the communist-inspired National Unemployed Workers Movement that organized "hunger marches" in protest at suffering caused in the 1930s by the Great Depression (Geary 1985; Morgan 1987). Independent of the Trade Union Congress, this organization and its protests benefited from none of the tacit understandings concluded between police and pickets. On the contrary, its communist connections made its attempt to mobilize the unemployed appear to the authorities as a threat to state power. Hunger marches were, therefore, subject to infiltration by police and security service spies and marchers were dispersed with considerable violence by the police. It was outrage at the treatment meted out to such hunger marchers that prompted a coterie of left-wing intellectuals to found the National Council of Civil Liberties in the mid-1930s (Bowes 1966). However, once the Trade Union Congress took responsibility for campaigning on behalf of the unemployed, policing of hunger marches became much more accommodating.

The fate of the unemployed did not, in itself, represent a major threat to the historical settlement that had incorporated the organized working class into political, social and economic institutions. The historical settlement between the state and organized labour, expressed in the transformation from "stoning and shooting" to "pushing and shoving", began to unravel during the post-Second World War era as the British economy faltered in delivering a prosperous welfare state. There is much with which I would disagree in Hall *et al.*'s account of the "mugging" scare of the early 1970s (Hall *et al.* 1978; Waddington 1986a), but there can be little doubt that their description of this period as a "crisis of legitimacy" is entirely warranted. Despite a Labour Government being in power from 1964 to 1970, this period was marked by labour disruption often related to governmental attempts to regulate prices and incomes. So seriously did the Labour government view industrial relations that it established a Royal Commission under Lord Donovan to make recommendations (Donovan 1968) and published a White Paper entitled "In Place of Strife" that proposed a number of reforms, including restrictions on union power (Department of Employment 1969). In the event, the Labour Party lost the 1970 election and the incoming Conservative administration was pledged to introduce strict controls over the unions, pledges that were almost immediately redeemed by the establishment of the Industrial Relations Court. This framework of law, together with continuing attempts to implement state controls over prices and incomes, led to repeated conflicts between the trade unions and government. At the forefront of these conflicts were Britain's coalminers, who were destined to play a central and ultimately tragic role in the events of the succeeding two decades. In 1972 the National Union of Mineworkers called a national strike that severely hampered electricity generation and, thereby, industrial production. The strike also witnessed the development of a novel form of picketing: the mobilization of huge numbers of "flying pickets" who would forcibly close premises by their sheer weight of numbers. This tactic proved dramatically successful in closing the Saltley coke works in the industrial Midlands city of Birmingham where the local police were first exhausted and then defeated in their attempts to keep the coke works open. Unable to defeat the miners, the government fabricated a face-saving formula. However, in 1974 the miners again went on strike and although its solidarity meant that there was little confrontation with the police, the outcome was even more ominous for the state: the government called an election on the theme of "Who rules Britain?" and lost narrowly – union power had prevailed (Clutterbuck 1980).

At this juncture there was a revealing overlap between civil contingency planning and civil defence that illustrates just how far both are concerned with protecting the state against attack. Plans that were developed during the Cold War for policing cities following nuclear bombardment were now adapted to meet a new, more immediate and domestic threat – crippling strikes. Police were central to civil defence because in the event of war they had responsibility for restoring civil authority after any nuclear detonation on the mainland. Incidentally, it is commonly believed that no one would have survived a full-scale nuclear exchange, but the planning assumption was that up to 11 million people would survive, at least initially, even a 200-megaton attack. There would be, if the worst came to worst, still a major policing task to be performed under the most hazardous circumstances. This would be achieved by mobilizing self-sufficient squads of officers who would await the nuclear bombardment in the relative safety of the countryside and return to the cities once the bombardment was completed. Their task would be to restore and maintain civil authority and they would be armed for the purpose.

These "mobile columns", became the template for Police Support Units that could be mobilized to counter "flying pickets". Henceforth, police would be mobilized for, and deployed during, public order operations as squads. Using a model long employed by the London Metropolitan Police, these were initially composed of one inspector, two sergeants and 20 constables, but was later revised to one inspector, three sergeants and 18 constables. The mutual aid arrangements that had so conspicuously failed at Saltley were also augmented by the establishment of a "clearing house" at New Scotland Yard. This "National Reporting Centre" served to match requests for aid to the supply of officers. However, while industrial disruption continued (Rogaly 1977), the election of the Labour Party committed to pursuing a "Social Contract" with the unions meant that these arrangements were not employed in the context of industrial disputes. Industrial disruption was again credited with defeating an elected government when, following the so-called "Winter of Discontent", the Conservatives were returned to power under the premiership of Mrs Thatcher in 1979. Her government's uncompromising dedication to market economics virtually ensured that there would be an eventual confrontation with the unions in which the police would take a leading part.

The rehearsal for the major battle was in the small northern industrial town of Warrington, where an entrepreneurial newspaper publisher installed new technology that rendered redundant the traditional skills of members of the powerful print unions. The unions resisted and used the hitherto successful tactic of mass "flying" pickets, but were defeated by police officers – some equipped with newly acquired riot-gear – who had been mobilized nationally. After this "curtain raiser" the main show began in 1984 when the miners again held a strike. However, this time it was far from solid; for internal tactical reasons the national leadership did not call a national strike for which they would need the authority of a ballot. Instead, each of the semi-autonomous coalmining areas went on strike with the more militant coalfields leading the way in an attempt to build sufficient momentum to persuade their more moderate colleagues to join them. The tactic failed as some areas were split and others – most notably Nottinghamshire – refusing to strike. "Flying pickets" were mobilized from areas neighbouring Nottinghamshire in an attempt to impose the strike and violence flared, with one picket being killed at Ollerton colliery in Nottinghamshire (*Sunday Times* Insight Team 1985). There then commenced the largest peacetime police operation in British history, with up to 14,000 officers being deployed to the coalfields via the National Reporting

Centre amid accusations of telephone-tapping and infiltration by the security services (Kettle 1985; Milne 1994). Initially, most police effort was devoted to keeping Nottinghamshire and other "working" areas free from "flying pickets", and this was achieved by the introduction of a novel "interception" policy. The roads to the Nottinghamshire collieries were blocked by police and vehicles carrying pickets were turned away – a tactic that was extended throughout the coalfields (East & Thomas 1985). This policy was challenged in the courts (Moss v McLaughlin) but the *de facto* extension of police powers was upheld. In addition, miners arrested at picket-lines found themselves subjected to bail conditions that effectively prevented them from continued participation in picketing (Christian 1985; McMullen 1985). Sympathetic local Labour-controlled councils found themselves unable to influence how the strike was policed despite their representation on Police Authorities notionally responsible for policing in their area (Okojie 1985; Spencer 1985a; Loveday 1986). As the strike eventually began to crumble police became involved in protecting individuals who returned to work at otherwise strike-bound collieries. The strike eventually collapsed after a year; the union was split; the industry continued its decline with the loss of an enormous number of jobs and the eventual elimination of coalmining in areas like South Wales, where it had been a staple of the economy; and it was eventually sold to private companies.

There was a final encore of industrial militancy when the print unions became involved in a dispute with News International – publishers of *The Times* and other titles – over the introduction of new technology at a printing plant in London's East End. For much of 1986 print unions picketed the site and there were periodic occasions of serious disorder between pickets and riot-clad police; but eventually the unions were defeated and where News International had led, the rest of Britain's national newspapers quickly followed.

The significance of these events lies not in the complaints of police brutality and abuse of civil liberties that are the almost inevitable accompaniment of such confrontations[4], but how they illustrate how state authority can be exercised through the velvet glove and the steel fist. The historical settlement between labour and the British state was premised upon the tacit understanding that national interests would not be fundamentally challenged. So long as the economy expanded to meet the aspirations of most members of the working class, this was an arrangement that the unions could accept. However, once the economy faltered, and technological change began to threaten the existence of jobs and whole industries, then the unions no longer had much to gain and little to lose by challenging the state. Faced with this challenge the British state did what all states tend to do: it responded by mobilizing sufficient coercive might to defeat the challenge. What is remarkable is that it was so restrained. The consequence was nevertheless to push trade unions in general, and strikers in particular, towards the margins of citizenship. They became, in Mrs Thatcher's felicitous phrase, the "enemy within", against whom state power could be used with relative impunity.

However, resort to overtly coercive state authority is not reserved for strikers: it is an ever-present potential in the policing of public order. For while "ordinary decent protesters" will be accommodated so long as they "play the (democratic) game", the

[4] (Coulter *et al.* 1984; National Council for Civil Liberties 1984; de Friend & Uglow 1985; Masterman 1985; Reed & Adamson 1985; Jackson, B. & Wardle 1986; Hillyard & Percy-Smith 1988; McCabe *et al.* 1988; Ewing & Gearty 1990; Green 1990)

riot-squads remain kept in readiness should protesters cease being so obliging. Senior officers in London regarded the availability of riot-squads as "insurance" and the capacity of the police to act coercively is, in turn, "insurance" for the state as a whole. This is a universal; what distinguishes states is their willingness to resort to this "insurance". Apart from authoritarian states founded on coercion, it is in divided societies that we find police habitually resorting to coercive methods of maintaining public order.

Policing Divided Societies

All societies are divided – Britain has traditionally been divided by class, whereas other societies have been based upon divisions of race, ethnicity, caste and religion – but the depth of those divisions varies. Brewer suggests that when divisions are fundamental, they can have the following impact on policing:

1. Selective enforcement of the law in favour of the dominant group.
2. Discriminatory practices which limit the exercise of the rights of the minority.
3. Political partisanship in upholding and enforcing the distribution of political power by allowing unequal rights to political protest; the use of repression to inhibit the forces of political change and opposition; and direct police involvement in the political process.
4. Lack of autonomy from the political system.
5. Absence of effective mechanisms of public accountability.
6. Relatively unrestrained use of force.
7. A dual role which arises from responsibilities for ordinary crime and internal security.
8. Polarization of attitudes towards the police and their conduct.
9. Social composition [of the police] biased towards the dominant groups.
10. Chronic and endemic manpower shortage.
11. Diffusion of policing functions throughout the dominant group, as volunteer groups and other compatible agencies are drawn into a policing role.
12. Close operational links between the police and the military (Brewer 1991a: 181–83).

Weitzer argues that Northern Ireland is a classic illustration of a divided society and its impact on policing (Weitzer 1990, ibid. 1995). Certainly, Northern Ireland is a deeply divided society, and those divisions have a dramatic and sometimes devastating impact on the policing of public order. Indeed the "troubles" that have afflicted that province since 1968 were triggered by fierce clashes between mobs representing Loyalist Protestants and Nationalist Catholics (Ryder 1989). During the so-called "marching season" that occupies most of the summer months, the two sides confront one another as each marches to affirm its separate identity (Jarman & Bryan 1996; North 1997). The "zero-sum game" that is played by each side in this divided society leaves no room for the compromise upon which police elsewhere rely to achieve "negotiated management" (McPhail *et al.* 1998). If a march by one side is facilitated, then the other feels defeated and humiliated. Thus, the police present themselves as the hapless meat in the sandwich, squeezed by the intransigence of the two parties and compelled to use force to implement whatever decision they take. Thus, in 1996, the RUC initially rerouted a highly contentious parade by the Orange Order from its usual route from Drumcree parish church along the predominantly Catholic Garvaghy Road in the mainly Protestant town of Portadown. Marchers refused to follow the alternative route and remained in the vicinity of the church; and after an increasingly violent "stand-off" of several days (and with loyalist violence and disruption erupting elsewhere in the province), the police reversed their decision and forced the march through. This action then prompted equal and opposite violence – not only from the enraged residents of the Garvaghy Road, but in the Catholic enclaves of other towns and cities throughout Northern Ireland (North 1997).

While such confrontations are undoubtedly symptomatic of the fundamental divisions in Northern Ireland, it is not clear that the notion of a "*divided* society" is a useful one for analyzing policing. Divisions of such intensity erupt elsewhere and prompt similar policing tactics without the wider implications experienced in Northern Ireland. In the United States a major constitutional issue arose when neo-fascists tried to march through the Chicago suburb of Skokie which was home to a large Jewish population, but were prevented from doing so by the town council. The issue was taken to the Supreme Court and eventually the right to march was upheld and it took place, fortunately without violence (Sherr 1989, ibid. 1993). Violence is not so easily avoided: for example, during my observations in London, I witnessed two marches over a single weekend that were virtually the mirror image of each other. The first was a march to protest about racist violence, following the racist murder of an Afro–Caribbean youth; while the second was an annual parade by a neo-fascist organization notionally held to commemorate Britain's war-dead. Each was opposed by hostile counter-demonstrators willing to use violence. Each was protected with equal vigour by the police who deployed massive resources to keep the two groups apart and on each occasion corralled the counter-demonstrators until their opponents were safely out of reach (Waddington 1994a). Considered in isolation, the police are inevitably exposed to charges of partisanship. Counter-demonstrators at both the marches mentioned immediately above were vocal in the condemnation of the police and allegations of police impropriety in detaining them.

In some ways, being sandwiched between contending parties is comforting for the police, since it is manifestly a position of neutrality – rather like a referee at a boxing match. Thus, feelings run very deep in the United States over the issue of abortion, but the police have been able to separate the sides to this dispute without falling into partisanship. For instance, Skolnick and Fyfe point to how the Los Angeles police violently broke up a protest by conservative anti-abortionists, who are normally supportive of the police, using "nunchakus" (martial arts weapons) causing many injuries (Skolnick & Fyfe 1993). In recent years the RUC has sought to shed its traditional partisan role in favour of that as impartial guardian of the peace and its officers have suffered as a result. When the RUC confronted loyalist demonstrators opposed to the Anglo–Irish Agreement in the mid-1980s, the families of some individual officers were driven from their homes by loyalist mobs. More recently, a police officer was kicked to death by a loyalist mob allegedly angered at the protection afforded to worshippers in a nearby Catholic church, that was regularly besieged by loyalist demonstrators, protesting at restrictions imposed on their marching activities (*Police Review*, 6 June 1997). The price of neutrality might be to earn the hostility of both sides of the divide and while, perhaps, this is uncomfortable for the officers concerned, it seems a feasible possibility – akin to the role performed by the United Nations peacekeepers in the former Yugoslavia and other international troublespots.

Yet, impartiality has eluded the RUC, despite dedicated attempts to pursue it; just as it has eluded the security forces as a whole. When the British Army were originally deployed in 1969, they were welcomed by Catholics as saviours from the ravages of loyalist mobs; but this did not prevent a gulf rapidly opening between the Army and the Catholic population. This disaffection did not result from *division*, but from relations of *domination and subordination*: the characteristic common to Northern Ireland, South Africa and Israel is that these respective states directly embody the domination of one section of their population over another. Northern Ireland was created as a *Protestant* state; South Africa was the *volkstaat* for Afrikaners; and Israel is the home of the *Jews*. Moreover, each state faces or has faced a fundamental challenge to its *raison d'être*. The extent of that threat was made manifest in South Africa by the eventual overthrow of the apartheid regime and the installation of a president and government elected through universal adult suffrage. Until recently, Israel's existence was challenged by many of its neighbours in the Middle East and the Palestinian population in the refugee camps and occupied territories. Northern Ireland too has been subject to continuous threat since its foundation in the partition of Ireland: the Republic of Ireland laid constitutional claim to the territory of what it regarded as the "six counties" under British occupation. When the state itself is under threat, the police – as custodians of civil authority – are inevitably drawn towards its defence. By contrast, the significant religious and ethnic divisions experienced throughout the nineteenth and first half of the twentieth centuries in mainland Britain, that periodically erupted in serious rioting (Panayi 1993a), did not challenge the state; for these fault-lines did not coincide with the politically relevant divisions of social class. Thus, police intervention could be impartial – keeping opponents apart.

While there is little doubt that police officers in the SAP, Israeli Police and RUC exhibited allegiance to one side of a communal divide and, therefore, pursued their partisan duties with vigour and enthusiasm, it is doubtful whether an impartial force would have proven any more successful. For the imposition of civil authority is the routine affirmation of state power and it is the very existence of the state – at least as constituted at the time – that is rejected by the subordinated population. Hence, the discrimination to which Brewer refers is not some gratuitous infliction, but inherent to the police function, which earns inevitable opposition. Given the threat under which these states operate, policing is much too important to be left to the police alone and tends to be politicized and fused with the military (the partner in the custodianship of state force). As both Brewer (1993) and Weitzer (1985) both separately acknowledge, police reform in Northern Ireland is hampered by its security role; and that role can only change with a fundamental transformation of the state that the police serve. The same fate befell colonial police forces throughout the British Empire that often sought to shift towards a model based on that of the metropolitan British "bobby"; but were thwarted by the demands of their security role in the face of insurgency (Anderson & Killingray 1992; see also Bowden 1975). Even when oppressed populations achieve independence, the political compromises may continue to divide them and encourage internal opposition to the infant state that may result in the police suppressing that opposition and thus becoming aligned with the dominant section (Milton-Edwards 1997).

In other words, when the fate of the state is unalterably aligned with that of the dominant group in a zero-sum game, the police role simultaneously becomes that of defending the interests of both the state and the dominant group. The importance of deep social and ideological division is that it affords little or no opportunity for incorporation.

The Resurgence of Militarization

Among the lengths to which states like Ireland, Israel and South Africa will go in their own defence is the fusion of the military and police function: the state is felt to be under threat from an "enemy within" – the subordinate population. In these countries the military have taken a direct role in policing with troops patrolling areas in which the subordinate population reside and the police have acquired military equipment and tactics. However, revealing differences can be detected between the policing of different "settler states': Weitzer (1990) argues that Northern Ireland has been characterized by much greater restraint than that found in Rhodesia during its lengthy internal war with African insurgents. This he attributes to the direct involvement of the British state in Northern Ireland. Rhodesia was internationally regarded as a pariah fighting for its survival against strong, persistent and eventually successful insurgent movements. Like the apartheid state in South Africa, it had little to lose and everything to gain from using whatever methods they could to secure their survival. Thus, it is as unsurprising as it is deplorable that in South Africa demonstrators were shot down with callous indifference in Sharpeville, Sebokeng (Goldstone 1990), Uitenhage (Kannenmeyer 1985), and many more occasions. The infamous "Operation Trojan Horse" – when in response to the stoning of municipal vehicles in the townships, police officers hid in trucks and then opened fire upon children who stoned them – is merely symptomatic of policing without restraint (Brogden & Shearing 1993; Cawthra 1993). The security services supported and financed the Inkata Freedom Party, and engaged in the assassination of opponents of the regime in exile as well as in South Africa. Indeed, so blurred had the lines between police and military become in the final days of the apartheid regime that the police were equipped and acted as a light infantry division in neighbouring border states (Cawthra 1993; see also Nathan 1989).

It is tempting to see a unity between this experience and that in Northern Ireland. Certainly there are significant similarities: unlike the police of the Republic, or those of mainland Britain, the RUC have had a tradition of carrying firearms and since 1969 they have received the support of an overt military presence. There have also been allegations of excessive use of force: the so-called "shoot to kill" policy. Yet, there are also significant differences ranging from the cosmetic to the tactical. Cosmetically, the police have avoided assimilation into the military: the policy of "police primacy" that has operated since the mid-1970s is an explicit insistence that this is a civil – not military – conflict. This has been accompanied by the avoidance of a militaristic appearance by the police who, instead of simply adopting perfectly serviceable military vehicles, have customized civilian Land Rovers to act as armoured cars; instead of acquiring military weapons, RUC officers have been equipped with revolvers and non-automatic carbines and rifles. For their part, the military have adopted rules of engagement more consistent with policing than with war: although equipped with automatic weapons, soldiers have been instructed to fire only single-shots when necessary. Neither police nor soldiers have any immunity to the criminal law, so that force deemed not to have been "reasonable in the circumstances" is punishable – as the prosecution and imprisonment of several soldiers testifies. This is in stark contrast to the SAP during the last days of apartheid: they patrolled townships in Caspirs – military vehicles equipped with belt-fed .30-inch general-purpose machine guns; standard equipment included automatic assault rifles and semi-automatic "battle" shotguns; and officers were offered immunity to prosecution if they used force "in good faith".

Perhaps the best illustration of restraint is to be found in the most controversial weapon used in Northern Ireland – the plastic baton round. This weapon originated in Hong Kong where the police fired short pieces of hardwood from the barrels of shotguns at the legs of rioting crowds. The wooden baton was intended to bounce at shin height among the crowd, inflicting minor injuries, and intended to act as an encouragement to disperse. When the current "troubles" erupted in Northern Ireland the authorities were anxious to find a suitable dispersal weapon. It is not clear why the staple weapons, used successfully in other colonial contexts – CS tear-smoke and water canon – were deemed to be unsuitable, save possibly for the fact that they had been used by the RUC in the "Battle of the Bogside" which left the police as a discredited force (Scarman *et al.* 1972; Ryder 1989). In any event, it was decided to adopt the "baton round"; but the hardwood variant proved unsuitable because of the likelihood that it could break and rioters suffer wounds from the resulting splinters. Thus, the rubber variant of the baton round was born: fired from a converted military signal pistol, the tactic was to bounce the baton among the crowd. Unfortunately, three people were killed by this weapon, albeit that the fatality rate was less than one per 18,000 firings. There were also allegations that troops had doctored the batons and inserted objects like touch batteries to increase the weight and thus impact energy of the baton and even razor blades to lacerate those struck. The weapon then underwent a fundamental transformation in the form of the plastic baton round: this too was fired from a converted signal pistol, but was intended to be aimed directly at a particular individual who was committing some act that would justify the infliction of an incapacitating sub-lethal injury. The irony is that this later weapon has a rather higher fatality rate at around one per 4,000 firings. Yet, despite the vigorous campaign to ban the weapon (Wright 1978; Rosenhead 1985; British Society for Social Responsibility in Science 1983; Northam 1985; Information on Ireland 1987), including a reference to the European Commission on Human Rights, it not only continues to be used, but has been exported to police forces in many countries, including some in Europe (for a detail discussion of this weapon, see Waddington 1991). More recently the converted signal pistol has been replaced by a specially designed launcher to enhance accuracy.

Quite apart from the merits or otherwise of this weapon, the nature of its development and deployment is instructive. First, it is noteworthy that a weapon that had long been used by the Royal Hong Kong Police was considered too injurious to use in Ireland. Secondly, although the fatality rate of the rubber baton round was much lower than that of its plastic successor, it too was deemed to be unacceptable. Finally, although police forces on the mainland of Britain maintain stocks of these weapons, they have yet to be used, despite the occurrence of serious rioting. This reflects how the tension between state security and citizenship actually affects internal security strategy and tactics. The wooden baton round was used pretty freely in Hong Kong, because those injured by it were a subject native population under colonial rule. When imported into Northern Ireland the injuries inflicted on colonial subjects were no longer acceptable and a less injurious alternative required. Then why exchange the rubber version for a weapon with a higher fatality rate? The answer lies in the *indiscriminate* exposure of rioters to risk of death from the rubber baton round. Indiscriminate use of force is characteristic of military tactics and the weapons they use. Police weapons, on the other hand, are intended to be used with discrimination, that is, against specific individuals acting in particular ways that justify the use of such force. The latest innovations have ensured that the weapon is fired more accurately; but it is instructive that an alternative design of baton round has not been adopted, even though it would increase accuracy even more. This type of baton round – often referred to as a "tadpole" because of its appearance – has a bulbous nose and a stabilizing tail. However, the authorities have been concerned that if the round should miss its target, ricochet off a hard surface and thus become unstable, the baton round might strike bystanders "tail" first, causing significant injury. Thus, because of this eventuality, this particular weapon has not been deployed in Northern Ireland. This is what differentiates citizens from a subject population – they cannot be injured with impunity – and even the subordinate population of Northern Ireland enjoy sufficient citizenship to benefit from such restraint. Yet the police on the mainland of Britain have abstained from the use of plastic baton rounds, and this testifies to the threat under which the Northern Ireland state is thought to exist.

Diffusing Militarism

The discussion of baton rounds in Northern Ireland leads to consideration of two related matters: terrorism and the diffusion of riot-control technology. A persistent theme in much of the critical literature on policing over the past twenty years has been the adoption, by police on the mainland of Britain, of coercive technology and methods developed or applied in Northern Ireland. This extends beyond baton rounds to include the use of armoured Land Rovers for riot-control and firearms units; protective riot-gear, including the acquisition (although not yet the use) of CS smoke; and the general development of an armed capability never previously available to what has hitherto been a distinctively unarmed police force. Of course, police learn from each other: McCarthy *et al.* document the diffusion of what they call "public order management systems" through various networks (McCarthy *et al.* 1995). The "Irish model" was diffused throughout the British empire; American public order policing was transformed from "escalating force" to "negotiated management" through the SEADOC documents and training regimes; methods of handling soccer hooligans have been diffused throughout Europe; and China has recently adopted a permit system modelled on that in use in the United States. However, as the authors note, methods are adapted as well as diffused according to the circumstances in which they are employed and I would maintain that the citizenship status of those against whom the methods are intended to be used is a major factor encouraging or inhibiting their use. This has been crucial in what has been correctly seen as a militarization of policing, not only in Northern Ireland and Britain, but also throughout liberal democracies world-wide.

Policing Terrorists

The "terrorist" enjoys a very peculiar, possibly unique, status: on the one hand, terrorists both reject and are rejected by the state whom they oppose – terrorists are genuinely and self-consciously the "enemy within". In this regard terrorism closes the gap between the police and military; for example, on the mainland of Britain military intervention against terrorists is politically acceptable, but not against civilian criminals, even if the latter act in ways indistinguishable from the former. On the other hand, states seek to deny to terrorists the legitimacy of combatants in a war by criminalizing their acts. This imposes the contrary imperative: namely to arrest and prosecute, rather than attack and eliminate. This contradiction has been felt not only in Northern

Ireland, but also in mainland Britain. For example, when the Special Air Service (SAS) – who have a specialist role in counter-terrorism – attacked the Iranian embassy in 1980 and freed the hostages that had been seized, they killed all but one of the terrorists. At the subsequent inquest the question arose as to whether all such killings were lawful, for one terrorist had been overpowered once the assault had commenced by a police officer who had been taken hostage and was under arrest. When the troopers encountered the arrested man they shot him dead. The coroner explicitly invited the jury to consider carefully the implications for the wider state interest in returning their verdicts; the jury obliged by returning verdicts of "lawful killing" in each case.

On the mainland of Britain military intervention against terrorists has been restricted to such occasional operations. In Northern Ireland, where the Provisional IRA have conducted a terrorist campaign during the past quarter of a century, the SAS have played a more extensive role that has, at times, treated terrorists as an enemy force rather than as citizens of the state. An illustration of this was the ambush at the Loughgall police station in 1987: according to Urban's account, this operation literally involved hundreds of troops and police and the discharge of possibly as many as 1,200 rounds of automatic fire. All the terrorists were gunned down, some of them while still in the van that brought them to the scene; but not before they were able to detonate the bomb that partially demolished the police station. Two wholly innocent bystanders, mistaken for members of the terrorist unit, were also shot – one fatally (Urban 1992). This was a typical military ambush: a field of fire was created designed to eliminate the enemy. While this was an extreme example it is not entirely unique: several deaths of alleged terrorists have followed confrontations with members of the security forces, often allegedly members of the SAS, in which a great many shots were fired. For instance, Michael Devine was hit by a total of 28 bullets when he and two other IRA terrorists "on active service" (who were also killed) were confronted by a military unit who fired a total of 117 rounds (Amnesty International 1988; see also Asmal 1985). It is hardly surprising that when deployed against heavily armed terrorists the military revert to methods normally employed against an enemy – but it remains the case that terrorists are treated as an enemy.

However, a further concern has been expressed about the development within the police of a similar style of engagement. The use of Headquarters Mobile Support Units comprising heavily armed and specially trained officers to engage terrorist suspects have been involved in a series of contentious shootings and led to the infamous "Stalker inquiry" conducted by a senior officer from a mainland British police force. Stalker alleged that his team of investigators uncovered evidence that had not been considered by any court, some of it contradicting the official version of events (Stalker 1988; Amnesty International 1988). He also claimed that his investigation was obstructed and that other agencies of the state, including the British Secret Intelligence Service had played an undisclosed role. Stalker was eventually removed from the inquiry amid controversial circumstances and the inquiry was concluded by Colin Sampson who recommended reforms of some structures and procedures.

There can be little doubt that, in the circumstances of Northern Ireland, the gap between police and military styles of operation have been narrowed. This is hardly surprising given the context of an insurrectionary war that threatens the continued existence of the state. Indeed, what is remarkable is that police officers and soldiers are prosecuted and sometimes imprisoned for actions taken in defence of the state. However, the narrowing of the police–military gap has been much more widespread than

Northern Ireland. In 1966 the Los Angeles Police developed Special Weapons and Tactics (SWAT), a development that was enthusiastically emulated throughout the United States (Beck 1972). At around the same time, the otherwise unarmed London Metropolitan Police introduced a dedicated firearms branch successively designated "D11", "PT17" and "SO19", and the gendarmaries of Europe have also developed a similar capacity (Roach & Thomaneck 1985). Prepared for combat these units are indistinguishable: dressed in black or dark blue one-piece hooded coveralls, equipped with respirators, ballistic helmets and body armour (including ceramic plates for protection against high-velocity ammunition); armed with the Heckler and Koch MP5 sub-machine gun and 9mm side-arms; and trained in techniques of "dynamic entry". Not only are they indistinguishable from each other, but also from élite military units, like the SAS, who have a similar task to perform. There are compelling tactical reasons for such equipment; for example, the hooded coverall and respirator is necessary to protect the wearer from contamination by CS irritant and the colour and lack of insignia on the coverall avoids presenting an adversary with a clear target. The Heckler and Koch MP5 has acquired an awesome reputation for reliability and accuracy, and devices like distraction grenades and tactics such as abseiling are needed to enter premises safely (for details see Waddington 1991). The question that arises, however, is whether these tactics reflect a *strategic* shift in policing.

As Kraska and his collaborators have pointed out (Kraska & Cubellis 1997; Kraska & Kappeler 1997) there has been a rapid expansion of SWAT-like police squads. Their surveys of American police forces large and small reveal that almost all had such a unit and that having been introduced to deal with occasional *reactive* tasks, such as hostage-taking, the remit of these squads had generally expanded to include *pro-active* interventions, particularly drug raids. Moreover, in some cities, these squads had been deployed pro-actively to present a formidable armed presence on the streets of high-crime neighbourhoods, especially those suffering from gang warfare. Although evidence is, by contrast, only anecdotal, the same pattern can be seen elsewhere. In Britain, specialist armed units have increasingly been used to execute drug raids, as in the United States. Also, the police at international airports, having been covertly armed from the 1970s onwards, were allowed to carry Heckler and Koch MP5s overtly from the mid-1980s, and then to carry side-arms openly from the 1990s. Armed response vehicles have been deployed on routine patrol in many police forces since the end of 1980s and recently crews have carried side-arms openly (Waddington & Hamilton 1997). In the city of Liverpool, following a series of gang-related shootings, the police mounted an overt armed presence as a deterrent. After a series of high-profile murders of unarmed police officers, the Police Federation balloted its members on the routine arming of the police. Although routine arming was soundly defeated, there was much more support for it among younger officers – especially in urban areas. To the growth of specialist armed squads should be added the parallel development of riot-control squads such as Special Patrol Groups since the 1970s and the recent adoption by many forces of overtly carried long batons and incapacitant sprays (Kock *et al.* 1993; Kock & Rix 1997). Throughout Europe the terrorist movements of the 1970s – Baarder-Meinhoff, Action Direct, ETA, Red Brigades, *et al.* – prompted an escalation in armed police capacity. For instance, Italy's Caribinieri formed a specialist unit that successfully hunted down the Red Brigades in the 1980s. Likewise, in Australia, areas of Aborginal settlement have been subjected to heavy-handed raids, such as "Operation Sue" in the Redfern district of Sydney (Chan 1997).

As Kraska and Kappeler argue, the use of such "heavy" policing is concentrated in particular neighbourhoods: poor, high-crime areas in which ethnic and racial minorities are over-represented (Kraska & Kappeler 1997). They point to how the rhetoric of the "war on drugs" has combined with notions of "community policing" and "zero tolerance" to legitimate such activities. Indeed, it is an irony that leading advocates of "community policing" have praised American police departments, commanded by African–Americans policing cities whose mayors are also African–Americans, who have used such aggressive tactics as closing off areas and searching everyone found therein (Skolnick & Bayley 1986). As some critics have noted, the transformation of the racial composition of American police forces over the past twenty years that more nearly reflect the people that they police has not had the hoped-for impact on policing styles (Cashmore & McLaughlin 1991). Indeed, the evidence seems to be that African–American officers are no less, and may be even more, inclined to shoot non-white suspects than the previous generation of predominantly white officers did – an inclination attributed to the characteristics of the areas policed (Milton *et al.* 1977; Fyfe 1981; Goldkamp 1982; Meyer 1982; Takagi 1982; Liska & Yu 1992). This is not restricted to the United States by any means: in Britain the doctrine of "early resolution" has legitimated aggressive response to any semblance of disorder by dedicated squads of riot-police.

We see in this process of diffusion two patterns: first, the development of more heavily armed, militaristic styles of policing emerge in the mid-1960s. This was a period of political turmoil: the Civil Rights Movement had successfully challenged white hegemony in the United States and was being emulated around the world by other subordinated groups; the war in Vietnam had prompted campus riots; similar riots had erupted throughout Europe; labour unrest became acute, especially in Britain; terrorist activity reached a pinnacle; political assassination claimed the lives of President Kennedy, Senator Robert Kennedy, and Martin Luther King, and Presidents Reagan and Ford narrowly escaped assassination attempts; spree killings by deranged gunmen occurred periodically on a world-wide basis; and violent crime showed a persistent increase. The "crisis of legitimacy" that Hall *et al.*, detected in Britain at the beginning of the 1970s (Hall *et al.* 1978), seems to have infected much of the industrial liberal democratic world and the response to this threat was to increase reliance on the state's ultimate resource – its monopoly of the legitimate force. The second pattern is that the recourse to forceful methods is concentrated upon those who do not enjoy the full rights of citizenship. In the United States, the irony of the Civil Rights Movement is that the fruits of citizenship that it harvested have been allowed to rot in high-crime, drug-infested ghettos – a pattern that is repeated throughout the inner-cities and public housing estates of European cities. Thus, we have the combination of a perceived threat to the state associated with a section of the population denied full citizenship producing a *de facto* style of policing that is akin to that employed against colonial peoples.

The Irony of Militarization

It would appear that very little can be said in favour of the growth of militarization, but although this development betokens the relative exclusion of sections of the population likely to be treated coercively by the police, the picture is not entirely bleak. Of course, the police themselves are obliged, very largely, to deal with the situation as they find it. The RUC might very well mean it when they profess that they would dearly like to dispense with plastic baton rounds; however to do so unilaterally in conditions where violent rioting is likely to erupt might prove more dangerous to all concerned than to continue the use of this weapon. For to cease the use of plastic baton rounds would deny the security forces an option between hand-to-hand fighting and the use of lethal ammunition. Indeed, I have argued in the past that weapons such as plastic baton rounds, CS smoke and water canon are more consistent with the doctrine of "minimum use of force" than relying on traditional methods, such as the baton or mounted charge (Waddington 1991). Those who oppose the introduction of these weapons do so, not only because they are allegedly more injurious, but also because they are more *effective* than their alternatives in suppressing riot. The danger that critics see in these weapons is that the state will rely upon suppression rather than incorporation and compromise (Ackroyd *et al.* 1977; Rosenhead 1981, ibid. 1985; British Society for Social Responsibility in Science 1983; Manwaring-White 1983). This is, of course, a danger, but ultimately the state will resort to any force to ensure its survival or it will succumb. Normatively, one might wish that some states did succumb, but if the recent history of South Africa is any guide, the level of force that the state will resort to in its death-throes is likely to far exceed anything that falls within the spectrum of riot-control technology. Indeed, the measure of restraint that weapons such as CS smoke, water canon and even plastic baton rounds represent indicate that those against whom they used are not thought either to pose a serious threat to the state and/or to fall within the ambit of citizenship.

Apart from the development of less than lethal weaponry, another aspect of militarization has been the development of command and control. Jefferson and I have conducted a protracted debate regarding the merits or otherwise of this and related developments (Jefferson 1987, ibid. 1990, ibid. 1993; Waddington 1987a, ibid. 1993b). Although approaching the issues from diametrically opposite directions, there appears to be considerable agreement on crucial empirical issues. Jefferson consistently argues that when officers are engaged in manoeuvres, such as "clearing the street", or when deployed in personnel carriers with minimal supervision, they can and do become needlessly aggressive. Indeed, this is precisely why close quarter contact between police officers and those engaged in disorder is best avoided (and, hence, alternative weapons used to distance the crowd from police cordons) or, if unavoidable, conducted by officers who are properly trained and adequately supervised (Reiner 1985c). Traditionally, poorly trained and largely unsupervised officers conducted such manoeuvres to the probable detriment of all concerned. Certainly, traditional methods left many with broken heads (Dunning *et al.* 1987; Morgan, J. 1987; Weinberger 1991; Emsley 1996). It is, perhaps, instructive that the yeomanry that so disastrously charged into the crowd at "Peterloo" were a part-time, drunken bunch of incompetents (Critchley 1970).

Disagreement focuses on Jefferson's assertion that the use of "paramilitary"[5] methods predisposes towards escalation of violence. Little evidence is adduced in support of this contention and it is contradicted by my observations of public-order operations over a three-year period in London (it is also inconsistent with more recently published evidence from several European countries with far more developed paramilitary police systems [della Porta 1994a, ibid. 1998; Fillieule & Jobard 1998; Jaime-Jimenez 1998; Winter 1998; Wisler & Kriesi 1998]). Jefferson justifies this contention on the grounds

[5] Both of us were correctly chastised by Hills for sloppy use of the term "paramilitary" (Hills 1995). For that reason I have abstained from using the term throughout this chapter.

that he is adopting a "bottom up" perspective (Jefferson 1993), which seems to amount to articulating the opposition felt by members of a crowd to coercive police tactics. If so, there is no dispute between us, since few would imagine that coercive tactics of any description are likely to win the active endorsement of those against whom they are used. In evaluating police methods surely the appropriate standard to apply is that which achieves the lawful aim with minimal infliction of injury. "Bad" consequences do not always follow from "bad" methods: the highly militarized force firearms unit of the Metropolitan Police conduct an average of three or more operations each day and only rarely have they fired shots. This is matched by the unwritten irony in Kraska and Kappeler's analysis of the development of militarized policing in the United States (Kraska & Kappeler 1997); for the period during which this militarization has developed corresponds to a significant decline in suspects shot and killed by the police (Fyfe 1978; Sherman 1983b). It is also instructive that in France it is the quintessentially paramilitary Gendarmarie that is regarded as exhibiting disciplined restraint, rather than its civil counterpart the riot-control arm of which is the *Compagnies Républicaines de Sécurité* (the *CRS*) notorious for its use of robust methods of riot-control. According to Horton, it is the very militarism of the Gendarmarie that ensures relative restraint through its strong sense of professionalism and close supervision by superiors (Horton 1995).

Concentrating on police methods confuses the symptoms and the disease: modern liberal societies have suffered a growth in crime, disorder and dissent in the post-Second World War era; that has prompted the police into adopting an increasingly overt coercive role; the adoption of militarized methods of public order policing ironically represent a measure of restraint in responding to the challenges that the police face.

Militarization and Professionalism

One might conclude from this discussion that if force must be used it is better that it be used militaristically, for that ensures restraint. Well, not entirely. The disciplined application of force *is* the hallmark of the military, but not all military operations are characterized by discipline or restraint (Kraska, personal communication 1998). A good illustration of this was to be found in the apartheid South African Police – an undoubtedly militaristic force. I had the dubious privilege of inquiring into the operations of the SAP on the occasion of the massacre at Boipatong a township in the Vaal Triangle around Johannesburg (Waddington 1992, ibid. 1994c). This inquiry incidentally revealed that an abortive visit to the township by the State President, Mr de Klerk, was not pre-planned and the township (that was known to be hostile) was not secured; a disorderly crowd was allowed to encircle the State President's limousine endangering him; he was extricated from this perilous situation by an impromptu breakout by escorting vehicles along an unplanned route, the safety of which could not be guaranteed. If this litany of incompetence in protecting the Head of State is not enough, in the clash with rioters that followed, police shot and killed a rioter; a mortuary van containing just two officers was dispatched to retrieve the body from the midst of the riot; and when rioters attacked the van, one of officers opened fire with his assault rifle killing several more rioters. Nor was this an isolated incident; other official reports have testified to the rampant indiscipline and lack of restraint manifested in how the SAP responded to actual or threatened disorder (Kannenmeyer 1985; Goldstone 1990).

It was no accident that the SAP displayed the face of incompetent and undisciplined militarism, for there was no incentive to be disciplined or competent. Their task was to keep the non-white population in its place (and their place was in the townships) by *whatever means were necessary, or even expedient.* They could afford to deploy Caspirs to potentially riotous conditions without a functioning radio, as happened at Uitenhage (Kannenmeyer 1985), because if the situation demanded it they could always shoot their way out. Since the victims of their incompetence and indiscipline were literally non-citizens, no adverse consequences would be suffered by such action. Indeed, the SAP suffered such comprehensive incompetence that it could not protect even the State President when the need arose. General Dyer and his Gurkas were not incompetent, nor indisciplined, but they nevertheless slaughtered unarmed and unresisting protesters. Those Punjabi protesters shared with their counterparts in apartheid South Africa the status of non-citizens. The application of military force to non-citizens (who, of course, are usually enemy combatants) is to eliminate them. The Amritsar massacre was a "monstrous act", but Dyer was not a monster – he was a soldier behaving like a soldier.

What distinguishes the soldier from the police officer is that policing involves the possible application of force to *citizens*, and that is a crucial qualification for it transforms the ends that military-style tactics are intended to achieve. Thus, although SWAT units are heavily armed (SWAT is allegedly an acronym for "Several Weirdoes Armed to the Teeth!" [Bayley 1994a: 31]), their tactics remained restrained, at least compared to comparable military units. The great danger is that contemporary industrial societies are developing in the direction of greater exclusion and in so doing are defining sections of their populations as beyond citizenship and hence beyond restraint.

Conclusion

The so-called doctrine of "policing by consent" has been allowed to operate in Britain not because of policing strategy *per se*, but because the incorporation of the working class into mainstream social, political and economic institutions negated any serious threat that class conflict might pose. When it seemed that such a threat could materialize, the state covertly prepared for class war; and when it eventually materialized during the 1960s, 70s and 80s, police used a measure of coercion not previously witnessed to defeat it. This historical example illustrates a much a wider pattern: the state is restrained in using coercion against those sections of its population it deems to be citizens, but shows much less restraint in suppressing dissent from those on the margins of citizenship and even less those beyond those margins. The widespread militarization of policing witnessed since the 1960s reflects the "crisis of legitimacy" faced by democratic states and the increasing exclusion of substantial sections of their population. The other side of the coin (and a side often ignored by "committed" advocates of disorderly marginalized groups) is that the margins themselves are unclear, subject to change and negotiable. This surrounds outbreaks of disorder involving those groups in controversy and injects caution into the policing of groups that are marginal.

Thus, while on the face of it, routine and public-order policing appear to be quite distinct functions that the police perform, they share a common underlying *rationale*: to maintain the prevailing order of social relations. This does not inevitably mean being lackeys of powerful interests, for those in positions might occasionally over-reach themselves. However, those interests will tend to be served because those in positions of power have greater influence over the definition of what is and is not "acceptable".

CHAPTER 4

Thought, Talk and Action

Introduction

The debate surrounding police discretion, and particularly its normative tone, has led to a pre-occupation among researchers with police *officers* – not the work they do, but the kind of people they are. If police activity is not determined by the law, then what standards do police enforce and from where do they obtain them? The lurking suspicion is that the exercise of discretion is merely a cloak for the expression of prejudice. Moreover, reforms of policing have been repeatedly thwarted by resistance from the lower ranks and this reinforces attempts to understand the motives and attitudes of those officers. Typically, researchers have sought the source of police discretion either in officers' psyche or in their sub-culture. This is a fundamentally flawed perspective driven more by a desire to apportion blame than to explain.

Are Police Officers Born or Made?

Psychologists and sociologists largely agree on the characteristics of the police – and they are none-too-savoury – but disagree about their origins. Psychologists look to the character of police *officers*, whereas sociologists seek depravity in the police *sub-culture*.

Born Coppers

The most obvious place to start searching for reasons for action is within individuals. Are police officers particular kinds of people? Are those with particular psychological dispositions attracted to the work of policing? And what impact does police experience have on those recruited? One of the earliest contributions to this approach (Niederhoffer 1967), suggested that policing was particularly attractive to working-class authoritarians and that subsequent experience exacerbates cynicism and isolation. McNamara suggested that police officers were also isolated and insecure, attracted by the structure of a disciplined hierarchical organization (McNamara 1967; see also Hahn 1971). In Britain Colman and Gorman claimed that police recruits were more authoritarian, dogmatic and conservative than the general population (Colman & Gorman 1982).

The widespread acceptance of the view that policing attracts people with unsavoury attitudes has led to policy changes designed to exclude or change those exhibiting inappropriate personal characteristics. Lord Scarman concluded his highly influential report into the British inner-city riots of 1981 with a recommendation that recruitment procedures should include measures to identify and exclude those with racist attitudes (Scarman 1981) as did the Christopher Commission that inquired into the LAPD following the beating of Rodney King (Christopher 1991). Almost fifteen years before Scarman, following the riots in the urban ghettos of America, emphasis was given to improving the educational level of police recruits in the hope that this would inject greater liberalism into the police (President's Commission on Law Enforcement and Administration of Justice 1967). However, subsequent experience of screening out officers with undesirable traits has not been encouraging, since officers continue to exhibit unwanted psychological traits despite efforts to eradicate them (Grant & Grant 1996).

Police Sub-Culture

Sociologists generally are suspicious of explanations based on personality characteristics and prefer to look to culture as the explanation for behaviour. In this case they can marshal a considerable amount of evidence in support; for even psychologically based research tends to find that attitudes such as authoritarianism, conservatism and racism become, at least, much more marked once recruits have been assimilated into the police role and its associated sub-culture (Butler & Cochrane 1977; Colman & Gorman 1982; Brown, L. & Willis 1985). Like any culture, the police sub-culture is an extensive set of belief, values, and practices. It includes the particular argot and humour of the occupation; the way the social and physical environment is perceived; relationships between officers and those outside the police force; and much more besides. However, there are certain aspects of the police sub-culture to which researchers and commentators repeatedly return: the sense of mission; the desire for action and excitement, especially the glorification of violence; an "Us/Them" division of the social world with its in-group isolation and solidarity, on the one hand, and racist components, on the other; its authoritarian conservatism; and its suspicion and cynicism, especially towards the law and legal procedures (Reiner 1992).

Mission

In their own estimation the police are the proverbial "thin blue line" that stands between anarchy and order (Reiner 1992; Fielding 1994a). It is through their efforts that crime and disorder is prevented and that which does occur is detected. For example, the Operational Policing Review found that officers questioned in a survey strongly endorsed responding to emergencies, detecting and arresting offenders, and investigating crimes as far more important than any other task (Joint Consultative Committee 1990 sect. 6, p 8). This is a vision that is repeatedly reaffirmed in the police press, especially those written by serving and retired officers. However, as we have seen in Chapter 1, it is singularly at variance with reality – the police are not society's crime-fighters and officers who believe otherwise are simply deluding themselves. Yet, delusion is rife: it is the common experience of researchers who accompany officers during hours of boring patrol to be told – as I was told by Al and Pete – at its conclusion that the tour of duty was unduly quiet and one should have been present a week previously when it was so busy!

Action and Excitement

Aimlessly wandering the streets is hardly the epitome of an exciting life, yet canteen conversation continues to perpetuate the myth that policing is centrally concerned with "search, chase and arrest" and officers relish telling "war stories" that glorify violent encounters (van Maanen 1980; Holdaway 1983; Smith & Gray 1983; Fielding 1994a). Police also take every opportunity to participate in anything that offers the promise of, or excuse for, excitement. Hence, patrol car drivers will speed to calls that do not require an urgent response just for the thrill of driving at high speed (Holdaway 1983; Smith & Gray 1983).

This preoccupation with action, excitement and violence can be subsumed within what Smith and Gray (1983) refer to as the "cult of masculinity" (see also Fielding 1994a). Police officers are expected to be physically and emotionally tough, aggressive, engage in traditionally masculine pastimes of heavy drinking and predatory heterosexuality. This creates a particularly difficult working environment for female officers who find themselves habitually despised because of their lack of physical strength and supposed emotional "weakness" (Smith & Gray 1983; Jones 1986; Heidensohn 1992; Brown *et al.* 1995), even though objective research has found little difference between the effectiveness of male and female officers (Bloch & Anderson 1974; Sherman 1975; Grennan 1987; Noaks & Christopher 1990; Brown, B. 1994; Neville & Brown 1996). Women officers find themselves faced with the dilemma of defining their occupational role as either "policeWOMEN", who retain their femininity at the expense of their police role, or "POLICEwomen" who conform with their male colleagues' "cult of masculinity" by sacrificing their femininity (Martin 1979; Brewer 1990a, ibid. 1991b). It perhaps goes without saying that this "cult of masculinity" is intolerant of homosexuality (Smith & Gray 1983).

"Us/Them"

The exclusion of, and discrimination towards, female officers is indicative of another feature of the police sub-culture – the rigid distinction between "Us" (the police) and "Them" (the rest of the population).

The police are a notoriously insular occupational group (Clark 1965). As van Maanen remarks, the uniform symbolizes for the police their separateness from the rest of the population (van Maanen 1973) who, in Britain, are dismissively referred to as, at best, "civies". The orientation to "Us" is one of intense peer solidarity and loyalty that is expressed in practice through the eagerness with which officers support colleagues who call for help. As Smith and Gray remark, after the officers they were observing arrived at the scene of one such call along with a half a dozen vehicles, it was perceived as a "good response" despite there being no need for such a deluge (Smith & Gray 1983). Van Maanen notes that the rookie officer is accepted into the group only after his (or less commonly her) metal is tested by the way they respond to a "hot" or "heavy" call (van Maanen 1973). Group loyalty is also expressed through the willingness of officers to protect colleagues from disciplinary or criminal investigation or penalty (Westley 1956; Stoddard 1968; Holdaway 1983; Smith & Gray 1983; Kappeler *et al.* 1994). This routine feature of policing was dramatically brought to public attention by an incident in the mid-1980s when officers savagely assaulted three youths in the London district of Holloway, the investigation into which was effectively thwarted by the refusal of their peers to give evidence against them (Holdaway 1986). Officers who join the work group find that their loyalty is tested by being exposed to minor deviancy to evaluate their trustworthiness in safeguarding the secrets of policing (a fate that can also befall the academic ethnographer seeking to establish rapport [Smith & Gray 1983]). Malcolm Young recounts how, having spend several years away from the police obtaining a degree in anthropology, he was posted to the "Bridewell" (that is, the central cell complex) in order for him to win his spurs again (Young 1991). Police officers who fail the test are regarded as dangerous and subjected to ritual humiliation, such as when officers presented Simon Holdaway (still a police sergeant, but covertly conducting an ethnography of policing and unwilling to compromise the rights of prisoners) with a yellow tea mug "Because you're scared" (Holdaway 1983: 8).

However, loyalty is not undifferentiated, for there is a complex pattern of vertical and horizontal divisions within the police organization that qualifies the loyalty that the officer is expected to show. At one extreme, police officers are notoriously unwilling to share information about anything with anyone. In this way they try to maintain control over the information that is the life-blood of the organization (Manning 1977) and prevent any "comeback" that might arise from actions they have taken (Chatterton 1979, ibid. 1983). Thus, incidents are "written off" to the control room in cryptic and stereotyped formats, such as "all quiet on arrival", "parties advised, no need for police action", and so forth (Waddington 1993a). Beyond the jealously guarded information of an individual kind, officers owe most loyalty to their partners with whom they crew a police vehicle. Loyalty also extends to the shift or "relief" with whom they routinely work and a police support unit or "serial" convened for the purposes of a public-order operation. There is something of a gulf between "reliefs" and specialist officers. For example, Fielding notes that community constables tend become detached from the culture of the reliefs (Fielding 1994a, ibid. 1995) by whom they are despised as less than "real police officers" (Fielding 1994b). There is an even greater gulf between the lower ranks and their superiors who are widely regarded as remote and untrustworthy (Holdaway 1983; Punch 1983; Reuss-Ianni 1983; Reuss-Ianni & Ianni 1983). So the temptation to regard the police sub-culture as monolithic must be avoided (Shapland & Vagg 1988), although there are elements common to the whole occupation. It is the culture of the lower ranks, and especially those engaged on routine patrol, to which most descriptions of the police sub-culture apply.

Just as the notion of "Us" is differentiated, so too is "Them". The police regard themselves as protecting "ordinary decent people" from the depredations of the disorderly, lawless and criminal. "Ordinary decent people" are equated with the "respectable working class" and middle class (Cain 1973; Smith & Gray 1983). However, apart from occasional criminal investigations, officers have little contact with this section of the population. Their attention is directed towards those from whose predations "ordinary decent people" must be protected. This is most obviously the case in relation to criminals, but while the police will seek to arrest such criminals they also have high regard for the "good class villain" who knows the game and commits crimes worthy of police attention (Hobbs 1988). Indeed, one of the components of a "good arrest" is that the suspect is of this high quality (Smith & Gray 1983). However, the paths of the lower ranks, especially those engaged on routine patrol, and "good class villains" rarely cross. Most police work involves contact with "police property" (Lee 1981): the young, marginalized working-class, ethnic-minority men who live in urban ghettos. Police typically despise such people, referring to them by such derogatory terms as "scumbags", "slag", "toe-rags", "scrotes", "sprigs", "pukers" and many more besides.

Racism is endemic: Skolnick suggests that for American police officers the African–American constitutes a "symbolic assailant" (Skolnick 1966; see also Kappeler *et al.* 1994), a view that Holdaway qualifies slightly, suggesting that in Britain black people represent the threat of incipient disorder rather than actual danger (Holdaway 1983). Certainly, there is a wealth of ethnographic observation testifying to the deep hostility shown by police officers towards members of racial and ethnic minorities (Lambert 1970; Punch 1979a; Holdaway 1983, ibid. 1995; Smith & Gray 1983; Graef 1989). In sum, whether at the level of individual attitudes, common beliefs and stereotypes, there is compelling evidence to support the view that the police – especially the lower ranks – are hostile to racial and ethnic minorities.

Authoritarian Conservativism

Consistent with the rigidity of this "Us/Them" view of the world, and especially its racist connotations, is the evidence of widespread authoritarian conservative attitudes among police officers. While evidence of authoritarianism is equivocal, there is less doubt that the police are decidedly conservative in their views (Bayley & Mendelsohn 1969; Lipset 1969, ibid. 1971; Fielding & Fielding 1991), reflected not least in the political stances of their representative associations (Reiner 1978a, ibid. b, ibid. 1980). All this combines into a view that is predictably "tough-minded" on issues of crime control, as the Operational Policing Review confirmed:

> Police officers generally feel that strong positive policing; arrest and prosecution and stricter laws and fines have been more effective in reducing crime than areas of soft policing such as prevention, community liaison and a caring approach to policing. (Joint Consultative Committee 1990 sect 6, p. 23)

Suspicion and Cynicism

Police officers have a distinctively jaundiced view of the world. According to Rubenstein (Rubenstein 1973), cops will discount most of what "ordinary people" tell them. Thus, an apparently clear description of a suspect car, including its make and colour, will be treated as referring to almost any vehicle that looks at all suspicious. Likewise, police control-room staff display a strong imperative to send an officer to the scene of almost any incident in order to provide an authoritative version of events, because they do not trust what "civies" tell them, however well-intentioned (Waddington 1993a). Police view the world through a perceptual lens that is selectively attuned to incongruities that would escape the rest of us, but might be indicative of something amiss. Bayley and Mendelsohn describe how officers monitor the reflection of their car headlights in the windows of business premises as a means of detecting whether any have been broken (Bayley & Mendelsohn 1969). It is this attention to incongruity that directs attention to suspicious people – the wrong people in the wrong place. Skolnick describes how plainclothes officers driving unmarked cars pay attention to the behaviour of pedestrians. If they show signs of recognizing that the vehicle is a police car by abruptly changing their behaviour, they will become vulnerable to a search (Skolnick 1966). Likewise, the Policy Studies Institute research into the London Metropolitan Police suggests that ethnic minorities were more vulnerable to being stopped by the police in areas of relatively low ethnic-minority settlement where, the authors suggested, their presence was regarded by police as incongruous (Smith 1983a).

This general suspicion tends to take the form of hard-bitten cynicism, of the kind frequently portrayed by novelists and dramatists. It is expressed in the distinctively black humour of the police towards normally distressing events such as sudden death (Young 1995). Cynicism is also directed towards the police organization whose policies and procedures are often dismissed as unnecessary obstacles to the successful achievement of the task. Police the world over echo the view that policing cannot be done "according to the book". Needless to say, such cynicism is also expressed in opposition to police reforms. It has, for example, been widely noted that community policing initiatives have had to contend with subversion and outright opposition by the lower ranks (Irving *et al.* 1989; Guyot 1991; Dixon & Stanko 1993; ibid. 1995; Bennett 1994a; Fielding 1994b; Lurigio & Skogan 1994; Pate & Shtull 1994; Rosenbaum 1994; Skogan *et al.* 1994; Seagrave 1996). Such cynicism takes a more sinister turn when it is directed towards the criminal justice process. Being unable to perform their task "according to the book", justifies endemic lying (Manning 1974) – not least to ensure that actual practice is presented as conforming to legal precept and ensuring that the officer's "back" (or other part of the anatomy) is "covered" (van Maanen 1974, ibid. 1975; Manning & van Maanen 1977). Police often disregard or try to circumnavigate legal safeguards designed to protect suspects from abuse of police power. Thus, searches may be conducted illegally or on dubious grounds (Skolnick 1966; Smith 1983a, ibid. b; Smith & Gray 1983; Willis 1983; Dixon *et al.* 1990); and suspects may be detained improperly (McKenzie *et al.* 1990; Evans & Rawstorne 1995). (For further discussion, see Chapter 5)

In sum, the "underlife" of policing is very different from the public portrayal of the heroic "thin blue line" prompted by the highest motives to protect society from anarchy.

Continuities in Explanations of Police Behaviour

Despite the differences of perspective and emphasis of psychological and sociological explanations of police behaviour, there are, none the less, themes and issues that transcend disciplinary boundaries.

"Citizens in Uniform"?

Police, it is claimed, are a distinctive bunch: they behave differently to the rest of us because they are either particular types of individual, or subscribe to a peculiar subculture. However, it is by no means clear that the police are, in fact, so different. As psychological evidence has accumulated so the portrayal of police officers as *distinctively* conservative, racist, cynical, authoritarians has become more difficult to sustain. Bayley and Mendelsohn found few differences between Denver police officers and their white peers (Bayley & Mendelsohn 1969). Belson discovered that his sample of police officers in London were not distinctly cynical (Belson 1975). Lefkowitz also found police officers not exceptionally cynical, dogmatic or racist (Lefkowitz 1973). Some researchers actually discover that police are less racist and *more* tolerant than other groups in the population. Rafky found that, with one exception, "Lake City" officers "when compared to Whites in general, . . . are either more sympathetic or as sympathetic in their recognition of civil rights" (Rafky 1973: 75). Nor does it seem that increased exposure to policing ingrains particular attitudes ever more firmly. Genz and Lester found no increase in authoritarianism among officers with greater experience, but did find statistically significant differences between state and municipal police (Genz & Lester 1976). Likewise, Scripture found little or no differences in social and political attitudes between officers serving in contrasting areas of London and recently recruited trainees (Scripture 1997). Comparisons between police officers with only modest educational attainment and those with college degrees have failed to find the expected higher levels of liberalism and tolerance in the latter (Dalley 1975; Miller & Fry 1976; Roberg 1978). Even when researchers trawl through a battery of possible psychological traits that might be influenced by education, the best they come up with are modest correlations (Cascio 1977).

Perhaps the most telling evidence against the view that police officers are somehow psychologically fitted for policing is anecdotal. George Kirkham was a college professor teaching criminology and human relations who accepted the challenge of some of his police officer-students to do their job and spent six months as a sworn officer in the Jacksonville Sheriff's Department. What he documents is the transformation he underwent as he confronted the realities of police work (Kirkham 1974)

> For the first time in my life, I encountered individuals who interpreted kindness as weakness, as an invitation to disrespect or violence. I encountered men, women, and children who, in fear, desperation, or excitement looked to the person behind my blue uniform and shield for guidance, control and direction. As someone who had always condemned the exercise of authority, the acceptance of myself as an unavoidable symbol of authority came as a bitter lesson. (p. 129)

The extent of his transformation is captured in the following recollection:

> My tour of duty had been a hard one . . . As we checked off duty, I was vaguely aware of feeling tired and tense. My partner and I were headed for a restaurant and a bite of breakfast when we both heard the unmistakable sound of breaking glass coming from a church, and we spotted two long-haired, teenaged boys running from the area. We confronted them and I asked one for identification, displaying my own police identification. He sneered at me, cursed, turned, and started to walk away. The next thing I knew I had grabbed the youth by his shirt and spun him around, shouting, "I'm talking to you, punk!" I felt my partner's arm on my shoulder and heard his reassuring voice behind me, "Take it easy, Doc!". . . . My mind flashed back to a lecture during which I had told my students, "Any man who is not able to maintain absolute control of his emotions at all times has no business being a police officer". (p. 136)

Kirkham might justifiably be described as having "gone native", as anthropologists put it; like the new recruit, he was seduced by the sub-culture. Well, it is not clear that the police culture that seduces generations of recruits actually differs from wider social norms as markedly as is often supposed. For example, widespread discrimination against women in the police is often thought to be explained by the "macho" sub-culture of the lower ranks. However, discrimination against women is by no means restricted to the police (see, for example, Bucke 1994); indeed it seems endemic throughout the workforce generally. If so, invoking the *macho* police sub-culture has no explanatory force, for whatever it is that encourages discrimination has a much wider reach than a particular occupational sub-culture and must be found presumably in more widely held cultural values. There is, in short, nothing *distinctive* about the experience of *police* women to be explained; they suffer the same fate as women in many fields of employment. This lack of distinctiveness is not restricted to sexism, but extends to other attributes that are regarded as central to the police psyche and sub-culture. Brodsky and Williamson found that when they presented police and fire officers with scenarios in which police used excessive force, police were *more* censorious than their fire-service counterparts (cited in Lester 1996). Perhaps most surprising of all is that when compared to social workers – normally thought of as representing the opposite psychological profile to the police – the police officer emerges as "slightly lower than the social worker on the Move Against Aggressors scale, indicating that he was no more likely than the average individual in the norm group to counter-attack when someone acted toward him in a belligerent or aggressive manner" (Trojanowicz 1971: 558–559).

This data poses a particular knotty conundrum: if police officers do not exhibit distinctive patterns of attitudes, how can their sub-culture be as distinctive as ethnographers consistently describe it as being? There seem to be two possible answers to this: first, that ethnographers consistently err by assuming that what they observe *is* distinctive. Rarely, if ever, do ethnographers engage in explicitly comparative analysis of a range of occupational groups. Hence, when they report that police are conservative, racist, "macho", or whatever, it is difficult to establish on what criteria such conclusions are reached. There is ample scope here for the injection of normative bias: are ethnographers simply indulging their own revulsion at what might, for all we know, be virtually universal cultural characteristics? Canteens beyond the common rooms of academe may generally buzz with conservative, racist and "macho" banter indistinguishable from that of the police, albeit no less odious. This must be considered a possibility, for it is likely that only ethnographers with a "tale to tell" are going to be heard – who wants to know that cops are just like everyone else?

An alternative answer is that while cops are more or less like their fellow citizens in their *general* attitudes, these psychological traits acquire a distinctive flavour from being expressed in a particular context. Here the balance of methodological advantage is reversed, for psychometric measures need to be pitched at a sufficient level of generality to be applicable to a wide spectrum of individuals. What the ethnographer detects is not the attitudinal genotype, but its phenotype as expressed in shared beliefs and particular practices. Thus, the "cult of masculinity" might be widespread among fire-fighters, coastguards, military personnel, fishermen and a host of other occupations; but in each it is expressed in a different way. The "bottle-tester" for a police officer might be to confront a violent adversary, whereas for a fire-fighter it is to place oneself in danger of a quite different kind.

Detecting Sub-Culture

The distinction between generic and specific levels of analysis raises another awkward issue for the notion of a police sub-culture: does it actually exist? As noted above, researchers have increasingly warned of the dangers of seeing the police sub-culture as homogenous and monolithic. Individual police organizations are accused of developing their own distinctive culture. For example, in the wake of the Rodney King beating, it has been suggested that the Los Angeles Police Department had acquired a particularly aggressive law enforcement ethos tolerant of excessive force (Christopher 1991; Skolnick & Fyfe 1993; Chevigny 1995). Others have drawn distinctions between urban and rural police, suggesting that the latter are more detached from the public they serve and inward looking (Cain 1973; Websdale & Johnson 1997). Several writers have drawn attention to the hierarchical divisions within the police sub-culture, between "management cops" and "street cops" (Holdaway 1983; Punch 1983; Reuss-Ianni & Ianni 1983). Chan quotes Manning as claiming that the police contains a three-fold hierarchical division at command, middle-management and lower participants (Chan 1997). Fielding argues that among the lower echelons there are distinct sub-cultures among officers engaged in routine patrol, on the one hand, and "community constables", on the other (Fielding 1995). Jefferson (1990) hints that "paramilitary" units, like the Special Patrol Group, have a particular and aggressive variant of the police sub-culture (see also Kraska & Paulsen 1997). According to Hobbes (1988) and Young (1991) detectives too have their distinctive sub-culture that incorporates peculiar regional characteristics. Analogously, one might expect there to be divisions between traffic officers, dog handlers, and others engaged in various specialist tasks. Divisions also emerge between officers of different sexes (Martin 1979; Fielding 1994a) and races (Holdaway 1996, ibid. 1997), and even combinations of both (Martin 1995). Indeed, in his research on the socialization of police recruits, Fielding suggests that individual officers select from among the various aspects of the culture those elements that they find acceptable (Fielding 1988). However, faced with all this diversity, it seems that culture – as a set of shared artefacts – almost disappears entirely and the monolith crumbles into a pile of rubble.

Fielding has suggested that the notion of a sub-culture is an analytical device that enables researchers to focus on different levels of aggregation (Fielding, personal communication 1998). Just as astronomers can choose to gaze at super-clusters of galaxies hundreds of millions of light years across, or individual stars, so too the concept of a sub-culture enables social researchers to perceive patterns at the more or less macro level that disappear once the focus narrows. There is a difference, however, between astronomers and social researchers, and that is that stars and galaxies are objective entities, but the concept of a sub-culture is an interpretative device used by the social researcher to lend coherence to often disparate activities they witness. The danger, of course, is that the observer might infer coherence where none exists.

Not only does sub-culture disappear into a near-infinity of multiple sub-cultures, the static causal model is replaced by a much more dynamic process in which action and culture are imagined to influence each other. Hence, Holdaway has recently argued that the racism of police culture is embedded in routine practices such as off-duty drinking, that are not intrinsically racist, but which succeed in excluding ethnic-minority officers and reinforcing racial stereotypes. It is through such processes that the police sub-culture "lives" (Holdaway 1996). Fielding and Fielding's research on police attitudes to law and order issues found that recruits' initially strongly conservative views became increasingly subtle and equivocal in the face of experience (Fielding & Fielding 1991). However, it is difficult to reconcile the equivocation of such a process with the robust rejection of liberality with which police sub-culture is often credited.

Perhaps the most conceptually sophisticated version of this processual argument is to be found in Shearing and Ericson's analysis (Shearing & Ericson 1991). Taking issue with rule-based models of cultural influence generally, they argue that culture is conveyed metaphorically through stories, myths and anecdotes that do not dictate any particular course of action in any given situation, but enable, nonetheless, officers to act competently. While this approach elevates the study of police sub-culture above the normal diet of macho, racist, sexist thugs, it retains the assumption that the police sub-culture is the principal guide to action. This assumption can be challenged on several grounds: first, that even if their general model of "culture as figurative action" is accurate, it does not follow that police sub-culture is the exclusive or even prime source of cultural influence. Officers might be influenced more by the stories, myths and anecdotes of their wider culture, for example, "urban legends". Secondly, they accept uncritically the notion that policing is a craft containing subtlety and insight, whereas most routine police patrol is conducted by young, inexperienced officers who lack either trait. Thirdly, while the processes of which Shearing and Ericson write *may* produce the actions of officers it is difficult to imagine how this could be ascertained, for the processes are elusive. Before submitting to such analytical extravagance, perhaps simpler alternatives should first be exhausted.

Condemning Police Behaviour

What repeatedly emerges in both psychological and sociological approaches is the normative overtone of the analysis. The psychometric measure that has most consistently been applied to the police is that of "authoritarianism" and its derivatives, such as "dogmatism". At first glance this may seem entirely innocuous, for the police do exercise authority and might be expected to possess or acquire modes of thought consistent with such a calling. However, "authoritarian*ism*" is not, and never has been, conceptualized as a morally neutral trait. In Adorno *et al*'s original conceptualization it is virtually a form of psychopathology equated with fascism, indeed the principal psychometric measure is referred to as the "F-scale" (Adorno *et al.* 1950). From this perspective the authoritarian person does not rationally conclude that strong leadership is necessary for social order; such a belief issues from unresolved conflicts with one's father that are projected onto others. God knows what Adorno *et al.* would have made of Thomas Hobbes, the English political philosopher who advocated rule by "Leviathan"! Likewise, "dogmatism" is a psychological weakness and "flexibility" a sign of health (Rokeach 1960); not, one imagines, a view that would find favour in the Vatican. The apparent scientism of psychometric measurement becomes a cloak beneath which prejudice – liberal prejudice – shelters. Thus, Dalley feels able to assert that a "police officer scoring high on authoritarianism and conservatism, *it is surmised*, would demonstrate a high propensity for arrest" (Dalley 1975: 462 emphasis added). From this perspective those who hold illiberal attitudes are pathologized – the police are not merely morally degenerate, they are dangerous.

Much the same normative orientation is to be found in many sociologically inclined studies of the police sub-culture. For example, Holdaway (1983) clearly and explicitly (and no doubt morally justifiably) repudiates the sub-culture of his former colleagues that he so carefully documents, as does Young (1991). Outside observers clearly also find the police sub-culture disagreeable, or worse. The Policy Studies Institute researchers (Smith & Gray 1983) make no attempt to disguise their distaste for the sub-culture of the London Metropolitan Police, captured, for instance, in such brief asides as their likening it to a rugby club (which left me wondering who should be more offended the police or the thousands of rugby players and supporters!). These normative overtones licence even such sophisticated and sensitive observers of the police sub-culture as Fielding to indulge in wholly speculative and empirically unsupported suggestions that the "macho" sub-culture is in some way responsible for the various high-profile miscarriages of justice that occurred in Britain during the 1970s and 80s (Fielding 1994a).

Nor is this terribly surprising given the "original impulse" of research on the psychological traits and sub-culture of the police, which, as Reiner reminds us, "was a civil libertarian concern about the extent and sources of police deviation from due process of law" (Reiner 1985a: 85). The purpose of research has not been merely to describe and analyse, but to reform – as Holdaway makes clear:

> If I desire anything for this book, it is that it may make a small contribution to our search for a more loving and just society and therefore a more loving and just police. (Holdaway 1983)

As Chan notes "Police culture has become a convenient label for a range of negative values, attitudes, and practice norms among police officers" (Chan 1996: 10; see also Chan 1997), and it is to the *negativity* of the police sub-culture that attention is drawn. The "convenience" of the label, I suggest, lies in its condemnatory potential: the police are *to blame* for the injustices perpetrated in the name of the criminal justice system. Little has changed since Wilson observed:

> Explanations vary, but commonly they are some variation on the "bad men" theme. Unqualified, unintelligent, rude, brutal, intolerant, or insensitive men, so this theory goes, find their way (or are selectively recruited into) police work where they express their prejudices and crudeness under color of the law" (Wilson 1968: 409)

Apart from injecting distortion into any appraisal of policing, this normative insistence that the police sub-culture is to blame for the ills of the criminal justice system seems to have negative practical consequences. It perversely allows senior officers "off the hook", for whom voicing platitudes about "overturning police culture" (Woodcock 1991) and hand-wringing over its malign influence have become substitutes for effective action. And effective action can and has been taken to reform police practices in the areas of domestic violence (Edwards 1994) and the discharge of firearms (Fyfe 1978, ibid. 1982a; Reiss 1980; Sherman 1980b, ibid. 1983). The readiness of police officers to alter at least some of their practices should alert us to the possibility that the obstacles to implementation of other favoured policies might conceivably lie not within the ranks of the police, but the flaws in the policies themselves. Attributing policy failure to the unreasoning obstruction of those who implement it is an effective, albeit reprehensible, strategy for deflecting blame.

Attitudes and Action

Apart from its condemnatory potential, the "bad men" theory of policing unites psychological and sociological explanations of police behaviour in the assumption that its causes lie *within* police officers. According to this view, if we wish to understand why police officers express such virulently racist views, we need look no further than the officers themselves. Not only does this eliminate the necessity of grappling with the complexities of understanding the policing of a society increasingly divided principally along racial lines, it also offers the appearance of a solution – change the officers by screening recruits and introducing training and all will be well. Ironically, such a view also perversely injects into the academic analysis of policing a variant of the "rotten apple theory" that in other contexts researchers and commentators rightly seek to discredit. True, it is the "barrel", not the "apple", that is "rotten", but the "worm" is still *inside* the lower ranks.

However, do the subjective dispositions of police officers determine or influence their actual behaviour on the streets? The focus on the attitudes of officers and their sub-culture arose from attempts to explain the enormous discretion that the lower ranks exercise in the course of routine policing. It attempts to achieve this in two distinct ways. On the one hand, attitudinal variables seek to explain the variance in police behaviour; for instance, whether more authoritarian officers express their intolerance of minorities through higher arrest rates. Alternatively, "police sub-culture" might be conceptualized as a hypothetical construct that lends coherence and continuity to the broad spectrum of police thought and practice. Either way, these concepts seek to bridge what officers say and do in one context, usually the privacy of the police station or police car, with what they do elsewhere, most notably in encounters with members of the public. However, this conceptual bridge looks decidedly rickety as it spans the obvious chasm between what officers say and what they do. Observational studies of police behaviour on the street have overwhelmingly concluded that the principal explanatory variables are contextual. The pioneering research by Black and Reiss discovered that despite the undoubted racism expressed by officers in the privacy of the car and canteen, they could not detect any racial discrimination in the way those same officers dealt with incidents (Black 1970, ibid. 1971). Even Friedrich's re-analysis of the Black and Reiss data, showing that more prejudiced officers used more force than their less prejudiced colleagues, still concludes that the only variables to make a significant explanatory contribution are contextual (Friedrich 1980; see also Coates & Miller 1974; Smith *et al.* 1984; Locke 1996). Sherman's secondary analysis of the observational data available before 1980 likewise concludes that the seriousness of the offence is massively the most significant determinant of whether police decide to arrest or not (Sherman 1980a). Since then research published by Sykes and Brent, Rubin, and Cruse, and Worden have all testified to the importance of contextual variables and relative insignificance of attitudinal and related factors (Cruse & Rubin 1973; Sykes & Brent 1983; Worden 1989, ibid. 1996). Equally, ethnographers have often abstained from suggesting that talk and action are consonant. Most notably, the Police Studies Institute researchers frankly admitted that they were surprised at the discrepancy between canteen racism and actual treatment of black people, especially victims (Smith & Gray 1983). Likewise, Holdaway draws attention to the exaggeration that often accompanies the telling of stories suggesting a gap between canteen chatter and the reality it purports to depict (Holdaway 1983). Finally, we have noted above that officers regard much of what they are called upon to do as "rubbish" or "bullshit". Routine policing is not an expression of the values of police officers; on the contrary, it is its *negation*.

Part of the problem is that the concept of "police sub-culture" covers a multitude of sins (usually quite literally), but it is in practice reduced to privately expressed views and canteen banter. When researchers accompany officers in the course of their duties, they observe their routine practices, most of which are performed entirely unreflexively, but which nevertheless often display subtlety and sophistication. On the other hand, when officers reflect upon what they do, for the purposes of explaining their actions, opinions and beliefs, to researchers or their colleagues in the canteen, they appear crude. My own experience of observing the policing of public order in London illustrates the point: officers displayed tremendous social skill and tact in negotiating the conduct of protest demonstrations with a wide range of organizers, including homosexuals and representatives of far-left and anarchist groups. They even resisted pressure from local residents, councillors, members of parliament and government ministers to restrict the activities of such marginal groups. Nevertheless, privately they expressed vehemently "homophobic" opinions and described far left and anarchist groups as "the opposition" (Waddington 1994a, ibid. b, ibid. 1996a). An all-embracing concept of a "police sub-culture" hardly does justice to the fluidity and complexity of such behaviour. Still less do generalizations that rely on what police officers privately express or avow for the consumption of their colleagues.

That behaviour does not appear consistent with privately expressed opinions may, at first, seem surprising, but it is actually common. Since LaPiere's pioneering study in the early-1930s (LaPiere 1934) social psychologists have become increasingly aware of the gulf that often exists between attitudes and behaviour. LaPiere escorted a Chinese couple on a trip across the United States – a more time-consuming enterprise than it is today that required many overnight stops and mealbreaks. He telephoned hotels and restaurants *en route* to ask if they would serve the Chinese couple and many replied that they would not. Undaunted, he and his companions visited these establishments, only one of whom refused them service. LaPiere concluded from this that attitudes did not directly affect actual behaviour, a conclusion with which many social psychologists now agree (Brim 1960; Mischel 1973). Even when subjects in experiments are reminded of salient social values, their actions seem to be dominated by the exigencies imposed upon them by the task in hand (Darley & Batson 1984). This is no less true of tasks associated with the exercise of authority. Thus, Milgram famously demonstrated that experimental subjects chosen because they did *not* score highly on measures of authoritarianism none the less were willing to inflict electric shocks causing considerable suffering, amounting even to death, upon a hapless fellow subject simply because they were instructed to do so by an authoritative figure (Milgram 1974). Haney, *et al.* established a fake "prison" in which randomly selected students acted as either "guards" or "prisoners". So extreme was the behaviour of each, especially the "guards", that the experiment was prematurely concluded for ethical reasons (Haney *et al.* 1973). The lesson of several generations of social-psychological experimentation is clear: behaviour does not necessarily issue from inner dispositions, but is influenced far more by the circumstances in which it takes place. Applied to policing, it is the circumstances encountered on the street, rather than the banter of the canteen, that orchestrates the actions of officers.

Appreciating the "Oral Tradition" of Policing

It is tempting to conclude this discussion here: neither their personal characteristics nor sub-culture explains police behaviour. However, that would be premature, for we are left with the puzzle of why police talk as they do to each other. This is particularly puzzling in so far as canteen talk is so much at variance with police experience. If talk does not inform practice why do police officers invest so much effort in talking about their work? If policing is mundane and boring, why do police officers expend so much time trying to convince each other and themselves that it is action-packed? If women officers perform their police role indistinguishably from their male colleagues, why do those male colleagues insist that they do not? In sum, is talk empty of meaning?

It is intellectually perilous to conclude that talk is empty in meaning, since if we are tempted to dismiss what we find puzzling as meaningless the whole sociological enterprise would probably collapse! It is also probably unhelpful to regard the police sub-culture as free-standing – just something that cops do in the canteen, unconnected with anything else they do. Indeed, one might criticize much of the research on police sub-culture precisely on these grounds; Chan argues that studies of police culture have failed to relate that culture to the context in which it is grounded (Chan 1996, ibid. 1997). Certainly, there is a tendency to invoke police personality or sub-culture as an explanatory variable that simply exists for no good reason. Using Bourdieu's distinction of "habitus" and "field", Chan contends that organizational changes intended to affect the former without altering the latter are doomed to failure (Chan 1996, ibid. 1997). Thus, Australian police officers do not hold their racist views towards aboriginals and other ethnic minorities in splendid isolation, but reflect and refract their historical task as a colonial force and their current experience in policing a racially-divided society. Without changing the wider social context within which police operate, their culture is perpetuated and reform undermined.

Recognizing that culture does not exist in a vacuum both intensifies the sense of puzzlement and suggests a resolution of the puzzle. Puzzlement is intensified because if privately expressed views and canteen talk are no guide to action, what is the relationship between "habitus" and "field"? The resolution to this puzzle is to recognize that there is not just one "field". Police officers, to mix metaphors, "play" on two quite different "stages". On the street, they encounter members of the public alone; in the canteen, they encounter their colleagues as a group. Action on the street is largely instrumental (albeit that it has many symbolic overtones), whereas talk in the canteen is almost exclusively *expressive*. What police officers do in the canteen – and more rarely in private conversations with researchers – is to engage in *rhetoric*, that is, talk that *makes sense* of experience. Put crudely, the causal direction is the opposite of what is often imagined: street experience influences canteen talk. The canteen is the "repair shop" of policing, where otherwise isolated officers re-affirm their collective understanding of their role and the society they police.

Situational Experience and Collective Understanding

Police practice is largely governed, as we have seen in the previous two chapters, by the exigencies of exercising civil authority. As Bittner expresses it:

> The role of the police is best understood as a mechanism for the distribution of non-negotiably coercive force employed in accordance with the dictates of an *intuitive grasp of situational exigencies*. (Bittner 1970: 144 emphasis added)

Now, this intuitive and situational locus for police action poses as much of a problem for the police as it does for researchers who study them; for it means that any explanation or justification must be context-specific. As Manning and van Maanen note, police actions are *situationally justified* (Manning & van Maanen 1977). Such justification has to be given not only to superiors and external figures, but also to one's peers, for "competence" as a police officer entails knowing how to portray action to an array of audiences (Fielding 1984). The canteen is more than just an arena for displaying one's competence; it is also the setting in which events are interpreted, occupational esteem affirmed, and comprehensibility restored to the world of experience. The canteen is the arena for this activity, because it is where police are able to *share* experience and receive collective validation from their peers. Policing is typically conducted in isolation, invisible to one's colleagues, while the creation of a culture can only be achieved collectively through shared experience. Hence, in those relatively brief moments when they are together police invest enormous effort in re-creating experience through "war stories" and other accounts of events on the street. That is why, policing everywhere is accompanied by vibrant "oral tradition".

The Universality and Tenacity of Police Sub-Culture

Once we recognise the police sub-culture as rhetoric distinct from practices on the street, what emerges clearly is a remarkable similarity in the core elements of that rhetoric found across a broad spectrum of police organizations in a wide variety of jurisdictions. Throughout the United States, which contains many significant internal divisions between jurisdictions and law-enforcement agencies, the core elements of police talk remain recognizably the same. Those elements are shared throughout the various jurisdictions that constitute the United Kingdom, including Scotland and even Northern Ireland (with its very particular historical and contemporary differences from Great Britain [Brewer 1990a]). Throughout the former British empire, with its distinctive history of colonial policing, police talk remains recognizable in Canada (Ericson 1982), Australia (Finnane 1987, ibid. 1990; Bryett & Harrison 1993; White & Alder 1994; Stevens *et al.* 1995; Chan 1996) and even India with its very distinctive social structure and traditions (Bayley 1969). Nor are these similarities restricted to the Anglo–Saxon tradition of policing (Bayley 1982a), but extend to continental Europe (of which we admittedly know less). When Punch describes the views of officers in inner-city Amsterdam, he might just as easily be describing a British, American or Australian city. Even in a country as socially, politically and culturally distinctive as Japan patrol officers share many of the same prejudices as their counterparts elsewhere (Bayley 1976, ibid. 1991a; Ames 1981), while detectives act much like they do in other jurisdictions (Miyazawa 1992). True, there are also substantial differences to be observed, such as the curious religiousity that infected the culture of the South African Police under the apartheid regime captured so brilliantly by Brogden and Shearing (1993). Yet, even here police officers subscribed to many values that are found elsewhere. While differences between police operating in varying social, political, economic and legal contexts are hardly surprising, it is their common subscription to mission, macho, "Us/Them", and cynicism that deserves attention.

Significant features of the police sub-culture are not only to be found across jurisdictions, but they are also endorsed by groups who are thought to suffer adversely from them, most notably ethnic minorities and women. There has been relatively little comparative research on black and white police, or male and female officers, with regard to the beliefs and values that they hold or their working practices. However, what little evidence there is suggests that they conform to much the same pattern as their white male counterparts. For instance, one of the few comparisons of men and women found a remarkably high correlation between the tasks that each sex most valued, most notably with respect to the high value given to law enforcement (Jones 1986). Heidensohn cites a typical response from one of her American sample of women officers: "One shooting, two stabbings. Hauling bums. I love it" (Heidensohn 1992: 176). When women officers complain about sex discrimination, it usually refers to being prevented from doing "real police work", that is all those things that male officers value and try to keep for themselves (Bryant *et al.* 1985). So, it seems that cops are cops almost wherever they are and whoever they are!

Moreover, police sub-culture within societies shows remarkable tenacity. Holdaway (1983) notes how despite the enormous re-organization of patrol work that intervened between his own research and that of Cain and Chatterton that preceded it, the similarities are more apparent than the differences. The subsequent publication of the Policy Studies Institute report on the London Metropolitan Police served only to reinforce the strength of his observation (Smith & Gray 1983). Likewise, tolerance of the use of violence as a means of compelling deference identified as a component of police sub-culture in the early 1950s (Westley 1953, ibid. 1970) remains as true in the 1990s (Kappeler *et al.* 1994).

"Dirty Work"

Taken together this suggests the source of the police sub-culture lies deep within the fundamentals of policing itself; fundamentals that are relatively unaffected by the jurisdictional differences at least throughout the western liberal democracies. Skolnick's pioneering study of police in a Californian city usefully attributes the "working personality" of the police officer to the twin essentials of his role – authority and danger (Skolnick 1966). Since this widely endorsed couplet was postulated most attention has been focused on "danger", probably because Skolnick links it, through the notion of "symbolic assailants", to race. However, it is the coercive authority that officers wield that constitutes the common problematic that routinely requires comprehension and interpretation. For what unites officers across so many jurisdictions is the experience of wielding coercive authority over fellow citizens and that, as I have argued in the preceding chapters, entails taking actions that would otherwise be considered exceptional, exceptionable or illegal.

What is the experiential reality that lies behind the phrase "exceptional, exceptionable or illegal"? Let us begin at the extreme end of the spectrum – the use of force, *lethal* force. What unites police in all jurisdictions is that they will kill fellow citizens, if necessary. Of course, any of us might do so in self-defence, but it is virtually inconceivable that ordinary citizens could lie in wait, armed to the teeth, then confront those whom we suspect of being about to commit a crime, and shoot someone dead. This is exactly what police officers in any jurisdiction in the world might find themselves doing. It is not a common experience, but common enough to be a reality with which police must cope. And what is the reaction of police officers to such experience? Well, it is very different to that portrayed in fiction, where the cop holsters his gun and moves on to the next gunfight. In reality it is mental illness – post-traumatic stress disorder – that debilitates sufferers for years afterwards. An official examination of twenty-five officers who had shot suspects in Britain in the recent past, reported *inter alia* that one officer was so distressed at killing an armed robber that he personally paid for the man's son to obtain a private education (Manolias & Hyatt-Williams 1988). Why should protecting innocent citizens from the depredations of armed criminals evoke such a response? Well, the armed police officer is given exceptional licence to perform as a matter of duty actions that would otherwise be regarded as extreme depravity – they *are* "killers". By the same token, officers who fight with suspects who resist arrest engage in what is normally the behaviour of thugs and hoodlums, not respectable civilized people. Worse still, police fight not because they are enraged, deranged or intoxicated, but as part of their profession that they enter willingly and in the knowledge that they will be called upon to perform such tasks. Theirs is a morally ambiguous position: willing to perform dreadful deeds for a higher good (Klockars 1980). And moral ambiguity does not extend only to the use of force for police officers also lie, deceive and cheat for the greater good, as when undercover officers pretend to be what they are not. It is no accident that in liberal democratic societies, at least, the law adopts a sceptical stance in relation to the police seeking to draw the line between lawful force and illegal violence, the legitimate "sting" and illegitimate entrapment, and so on. One might accept Kleinig's view that the police can act both legally and ethically (Kleinig 1996), while acknowledging that the morality of policing is perpetually in doubt. Sociologically, policing is, as Kleinig observes, intrinsically an *anomic* occupation, for the norms that govern conduct are never clear and the police officer is obliged proverbially to sail perpetually and perilously close to the wind.

This sense of anomie is reinforced by the normative morass in which police officers often find themselves. Again, let us approach this from the extreme end of the spectrum. For six months I observed the work of a small squad of (at that time) exclusively female officers who dealt with crimes of indecency. I was attached to one of them, a 21-year-old, who in the time that I spent with her investigated the rape of 15-year-old; the gang-rape of 12-year-old who was already the mother of a small child and suffered hepatitis-B infection; the forcible abduction of a 17-year-old girl by a complete stranger; and the sexual exploitation a 14-year-old girl by her stepfather. Along the way she also investigated several complaints of indecent assault and indecent exposure. Now, I might be unduly sensitive about these matters (although it would come as a surprise to many who know me to learn that this was so!), but I found this the most uncomfortable period of observation I have experienced. I was pitched, along with Jan (who my wife and I came to know as a friend), into a world in which parents exploited their children for their own sexual gratification; other parents abdicated all responsibility for their children; sexual love was debased into a sordid act of brutal selfishness; and the erotic was perverted by men who preyed upon any vulnerable woman to obtain a moment's satisfaction by exposing their genitalia. The moral stench of this world seemed to cling to me long after retreating from the field, leaving me to question my own sexual feelings. My exposure was modest – one, maybe two shifts per week: how could Jan survive and become the loving mother of three children?

Although immersed in it, the officers in this squad did not suffer a monopoly of exposure to the sordid and obscene. Like others who have observed routine patrol work, I have seen my share of dead bodies, sometimes left to rot by family and neighbours too busy to care; I have accompanied young officers who have had the task of quelling violent quarrels between spouses old enough to be their parents; I have seen alcoholics lying sprawled in their own vomit, urine and faeces; I have stood in rooms so filthy that I avoided touching anything for fear of infection and breathed the air with maximum economy lest the stench caused me to vomit; I have witnessed parents so uninterested in their children's welfare that they have refused to attend the police station where the latter is being held in custody; I have been numbed by the personal tragedies that others have suffered; and I have watched my fellow citizens, devoid of any vestige of personal dignity, appealing to the police for all manner of help. And all this is but a small sample of the experience to which any police officer can expect to be exposed.

In other words, policing – like medicine and some other occupations – involves its practitioners in "dirty work" (Hughes 1962). How do the police survive it? They do so like so many other occupations whose work entails straying beyond the boundaries of "normality': they create and maintain an oral culture which (for all its morally reprehensible qualities) shields them from the implications of their work. An example of how police shield themselves can be found in Brewer's excellent study of how officers in Northern Ireland cope with the ever-present threat of violence (Brewer 1990b). The cavalier fatalism, routine accommodation and emphasis on one's skilful avoidance of danger that police officers voice are recognized by Brewer as functional strategies for coping with an ever-present threat that would otherwise prove overwhelming. Like medical staff and fire-fighters, when police officers adopt a fatalistic attitude they do so not as some wilful indulgence in a "cult of masculinity" but as a means of coping with a fearful reality (Menzies 1960; Manksch 1963; Simpson 1967; Clisby 1990). Fortunately, most police officers are not obliged to cope with such physical danger; the threat that they face is to their occupational self-esteem. In short, how do they convince themselves that their work is worthwhile?

"You've Got to Laugh . . ."

One aspect of police culture that has strangely escaped close attention by researchers is its humour, yet this is one of its most noticeable features. Police spend much time, when together, joking and participating in pranks (or "wind-ups" as they are known among British officers); the magazine of the British Police Federation and the widely read *Police Review* both feature columns telling of the absurdities of the police experience. For example, tales such as this selected from an issue taken at random:

> A motorist in North Yorkshire had a lucky escape when he went off the road into a water-filled ditch. The car overturned and he narrowly escaped drowning. Police got him out of the vehicle and took him to a police station for his clothes to be dried. The officers then gave him a lift back to the scene of the accident. On the way the motorist was most appreciative of the quality of the service and said it made a change from London where, he said, "my car is always being broken into". On returning to the car he found that some enterprising tea leaf [thief] had waded through the deep and muddy waters to pinch his radio/cassette player. ("Dogberry", *Police* magazine, October 1994)

Police humour often displays pronounced cynicism – after all there is nothing intrinsically amusing about the double tragedy suffered by the anonymous driver in the story above. But it "just goes to show" that people are as venal as the police imagine them to be. Cynicism is a good defence strategy: expect the worst and you will rarely be disappointed. It also diminishes the scale of human tragedy; as Young has recently remarked, the black humour with which the police surround their exposure to death succeeds in making light of experiences that would otherwise be utterly devastating (Young 1995; see also Alexander & Wells 1991; Mitchell 1996). Euphemisms are also means by which the full human significance of actions and experience can be diminished or eliminated. Specialist armed police do not practice "killing people", but "*take out* hostiles". Traffic police do not attend tragic deaths in road accidents, but "fatal RTAs". Now, in all these respects the police apply strategies common in other occupations that routinely deal with the tragic, gruesome and morally repugnant. Dick Clisby is a senior fire-fighter who describes how "old hands" torment rookies by, for example, eating a spaghetti meal having returned from attending a road accident where a victim's brains have been liberally displayed (Clisby 1990). The medical professions are, of course, notoriously cynical – a cynicism that Menzies attributes to the need to dissociate oneself from the pain, suffering and death that is the routine experience of doctors and nurses (Menzies 1960).

Not all threats to psychological good health reside on the street. The police are very cynical about their own organization and the criminal justice system of which it is a part. The columns of "Dogberry" are often packed with tales of incompetent, self-aggrandizing senior officers who care more about their privileges than the fate of their subordinates. However, it is the perceived idiocies and injustices perpetrated by the criminal justice system the provokes most ire among police officers. Prosecutors are incompetent, defence lawyers unscrupulous, judges unworldly and juries duped. As Bayley points out:

> Indian policemen share the view about lawyers – particularly defense lawyers – that is so common among law enforcement personnel in any country – politely put, they have little use for them. They believe they are obfuscating, querulous, unscrupulous, self-centred, parasitic, and hidebound. "Scum of the earth" is only one among several earthy phrases used by police officers to describe them. (Bayley 1969)

I once described to a police officer companion a friend of mine who was "a criminal lawyer"; his telling retort was that they all were – "criminal", that is!

Again, cynicism towards superiors and bureaucracy is hardly a unique characteristic of policing. However, the particular contempt that police officers have for the criminal justice system seems to have its origins in the gulf that exists between substantive and procedural justice. As routine exercisers of discretion, police officers see themselves as dispensing substantive justice and protecting the innocent. Criminal justice operates under almost precisely the opposite rules: justice is procedural, and it is the rights of the accused that need protection (Bell 1992). When the courts acquit those whom the police regard as obviously culpable or impose what is perceived to be a lenient sentence, the *raison d'être* of the police as servants of justice is challenged and thus their sense of occupational self-esteem undermined. Their commitment to the ideals of justice can, however, be sustained if perversity can be attributed to self-serving, corrupt and gullible lawyers. Indeed, from this perspective the police emerge (at least in their own eyes) as sole champions of the highest ideals.

Thus, surrounded by the moral ambiguity of their own role, venality of criminals, tragedy of victims of all kinds of misfortunes, and absurdities of the criminal justice system, cynicism is almost inevitable: "You've got to laugh, or else you'd cry".

Telling It Like It Is

Cynicism is a shield against the reality of experience, but many elements of the police sub-culture reflect or embrace the reality of that experience more or less directly. The most obvious, of course, is their authoritarianism, indeed a psychological scale purporting to measure this trait on which the police did not score highly would be of questionable validity. The same applies to the conservatism of most police officers, for the maintenance of order is an inherently conservative function. Thus, when officers advocate strong "law and order" politics, they are affirming the value of what they routinely do: policing is an authoritative and conservative occupation and it is no surprise that officers regard it as a necessary one.

Likewise, Holdaway's observation of how police regard themselves as having rights of ownership over "the ground" and developing a more or less detailed topography of trouble, danger and work (Holdaway 1983) is a direct reflection of their omnibus responsibilities. For the duration of their tour of duty the area they police is theirs, for they are, as Holdaway concedes, custodians of state authority on the street and anything that threatens, challenges or disturbs that authority must be subordinated or else authority itself is negated – hence, their awareness of locations associated with trouble and danger.

The Cult of the Monopoly of Force

The analysis of police sub-culture would be simple if it only reflected the realities of the occupation; but other aspects of the police sub-culture reflect less directly the fundamental realities of the police role. A notable illustration is the glorification of action and excitement, for routine police work is nothing if not boring and few encounters involve the use of force (Sykes & Brent 1983; Southgate & Ekblom 1984, ibid. 1986; Southgate & Crisp 1993; Skogan 1994). Yet, it remains the case that police intervention in the lives of others is invariably *authoritative* – an authority that is ultimately backed by force. So, when police tell exaggerated "war stories" that appear to "glorify violence" they are doing what those in other occupations do – celebrating what they and most observers recognize as the "real job" (Manning 1980b). Displaying courage in the face of threat is something that is widely valued and it is no surprise that officers dwell upon those events when their essential purpose is most clearly manifested. Police celebrate other skills and attributes, but the core of police's oral tradition lies in the glorification of violence over which they hold the monopoly of legitimacy.

Nor is it surprising that this celebration is generalized to a "cult of masculinity", for the exercise of coercive authority is not something that just anybody can do. It is traditionally the preserve of "real men" who are willing and able to fight. Confronting physical threat is widely regarded as "tough" work and such work is traditionally associated with masculinity. Indeed, it is instructive that Bem's Sex Role Inventory lists as typically (and exclusively) masculine traits: "aggressive", "assertive", "forceful", "willing to take a stand" and "willing to take risks" (Bem 1974) – all of which seem intuitively compatible with the exercise of coercive authority. The mere presence of women officers presents a *symbolic* challenge to the equation of police authority with masculinity that male officers predictably resist (Fielding & Fielding 1992). A genuinely feminized conception of policing, would, as Walklate suggests, fundamentally challenge "what counts as policework" (Walklate 1995: 203).

Marginality and Isolation

Policing is a *marginal* occupation, for officers wield authority over fellow citizens and this sets them apart. It is a marginality of which ordinary police officers are acutely, albeit inarticulately, aware. It is why police are everywhere (throughout the liberal democracies at least) so insular: they find social encounters with non-police friends, acquaintances, neighbours and others fraught with difficulty (McNamara 1967; see also Cain 1973). They feel more relaxed with fellow officers who share the same "back-stage" aspects of the role and with whom it is, therefore, unnecessary to maintain appearances. Despite the liberal democratic mythology of the police as "citizens in uniform", the reality is that they are set apart by the authority that they wield.

Policing is more than an isolated occupation, it is also a precarious one. As I have argued above, the police perform as a matter of duty, acts which if undertaken by anyone else would be considered exceptional, exceptionable or illegal. Like those who handle the dead, policing is "dirty work" (Hughes 1962) and like all "dirty workers" police devote considerable attention to normalizing, indeed dignifying, it – hence their profound sense of mission. Apart from celebrating the essential quality of the police role, glorifying violence and the general "cult of masculinity" is a means through which the exceptional and exceptionable is made heroic. The vision of a "thin blue line" not only places the police in the position of valiant protectors of society, but also of those who are knowledgeable of the dark side of society and, therefore, in a uniquely privileged position to apprehend the danger that threatens. In their own eyes, the police are the cognoscenti, whereas the remainder of the population are "know nothings" and naïve "civies" who cannot possibly understand the world and, therefore, cannot legitimately evaluate the contribution of the police to human welfare. Thus, not only is heroism secured, but also cynicism sustained; for the police *know* that the order that "civies" take for granted is always precariously teetering on the brink of chaos (Holdaway 1983).

Telling It Like It Ain't: Crime-Fighting

There is little doubt that the occupational self-image of the police is that of "crime-fighters" and this is not just a distortion of what they do, it is virtually a collective *delusion*. As we have already seen, a mountain of research evidence demonstrates that the police are not crime-fighters, so why does this delusion reign supreme in so many jurisdictions?

The belief that police are "crime-fighters" is a self-serving rhetoric, but not solely for internal consumption. The very fact that police devote so much rhetorical effort to affirming what their daily experience denies should alert us to the ideological importance that crime-fighting has to occupational self-esteem. The exercise of coercive authority over fellow citizens poses an obvious and acute challenge to the legitimacy of the police. Policing has historically been transformed from a potential threat to fellow citizens into their protection by ideologically identifying the police with crime-fighting. Criminals lie beyond the moral community of society, the suppression of whose depredations threaten law and order. Thus the police can present themselves as those who "serve and protect" (as the legend on many an American police car reminds us) the remainder of the respectable citizenry. Now, this is a myth: the police role extends far beyond crime-fighting and as an institution policing has little impact on crime.

However, it would be mistaken simply to dismiss the emphasis given by police officers to crime-fighting as an occupational delusion (Fielding 1994a). It is yet a further affirmation that policing is heroic: coercion is directed at those who deserve it and not to the "ordinary decent people" on whose behalf the police see themselves acting. In this way the intrinsically questionable exercise of coercive authority against fellow citizens is legitimated not only in the eyes of external audiences (to whom the crime-fighting image is presented in a deluge of fictional and purportedly factual media representation), but also to the police themselves.

Yet, the gulf between that daily reality and the ideology of crime-fighting also serves to strengthen further police cynicism as in the dismissal of most of the tasks they asked to undertake as "rubbish". The routine exercise of authority is regarded as a distraction from the "real job" of catching criminals.

The Rhetoric of Exclusion

Holdaway has recently argued that police racism has its origins in the occupational need for the police to speedily and authoritatively draw distinctions between people they encounter (Holdaway 1996, ibid. 1997). There is undoubtedly merit in this view, but there is more to it than this, for police not only identify their "property", they *despise* them. As the plethora of derogatory slurs testifies, police officers demonstrate both inventiveness and effort in denying human dignity to those with whom they have most contact. Most attention has focused on racial slurs, but as offensive as these are, it should not distract attention from the continuity that this has with generality of the police's derogatory lexicon – "slag", "scumbags" and "pukers" carry no racist overtones, but are designed to denigrate those to whom they are applied (Reiner 1985b).

An obvious explanation for this denigration is that police routinely come into conflict with the most marginal groups in society and like antagonists generally they demean their opponents. One can only be struck at the facility with which soldiers invent or resurrect abusive descriptions of adversaries. For instance, no sooner had the British task force set sail for the Falkland Islands in 1982 than the troops had dredged from obscurity the term "spics" to apply to Argentinean forces and as the Coalition forces gathered in the Gulf British soldiers equally quickly devised the notion of "ragheads" to demean Iraqi troops. While this undoubtedly plays a part, there is more to it than conflict alone. Some observers have complained about how the police sub-culture facilitates deviancy by offering techniques of neutralization akin to those employed by delinquent gangs (Sykes & Matza 1957; Fielding 1994a; Kappeler *et al.* 1994). What these observers fail to appreciate is that the techniques of neutralization to which they draw attention are not restricted to obviously deviant actions, but serve to neutralize the taint that would otherwise accompany the exercise of coercive authority over fellow citizens *per se* (Bittner 1970).

> . . . police believe in the goodness of maintaining order, the nobility of their occupation, and the fundamental fairness of the law and existing social order. . . . If law, authority and order were seen as fostering inequity or injustice, the police self-perception would be tainted and the "goodness" of the profession would be questioned by the public. Police could no longer see themselves as partners in justice, but rather partners in repression – a role most police neither sought nor would be willing to recognise (Kappeler *et al.* 1994: 105)

If the police can persuade themselves that those against whom coercive authority is exercised are contemptible, no moral dilemmas are experienced – those on the receiving end "deserve it".

"Let's Be Careful Out There!"

Policing is a dangerous occupation. There are other occupations that are more dangerous, but there are few where the normal expectation compels the worker to knowingly enter risky situations. Being the custodian of state authority on the street means imposing that authority in conditions where social, moral and legal order may have broken down. Because that authority is coercive, it entails a willingness to impose that authority by force, or to be less euphemistic about it, to *fight*. None of this is as frequent as police officers often claim; even in societies where violence is comparatively common (such as the USA) violent encounters are thankfully rare (Sykes & Brent 1983; Bayley & Garofalo 1989), yet it is real enough.

There is another danger facing police officers. As we shall see in the next chapter, the exercise of coercive authority over fellow citizens leaves officers intrinsically vulnerable to complaint and even prosecution. A routine arrest, if successfully challenged, can be transformed into an alleged assault and wrongful imprisonment with the officer potentially liable to criminal prosecution, a civil action for damages and/or an internal disciplinary charge that might terminate his career. Most officers are subject to complaints and although few are substantiated, the risk of a severe penalty being inflicted is a ubiquitous potential.

In response police officers do what others who face comparable risks do: first, they tend to exaggerate the risk through the telling of "cautionary tales" (Anderson *et al.* 1994). Secondly, they demand defensive solidarity from each other. They emphasize the willingness of officers to "back up" each other, whether it is in a fight or in fabricating evidence. Whether or not they would actually do either of these things may depend very much on the circumstances. There have been occasions where officers have testified against their colleagues, just as there are allegations that unpopular colleagues find "back-up" mysteriously disappears when they are in a tight corner (Gomez-Preston & Trescott 1995). Yet, the avowal of solidarity is important reassurance.

Perhaps They Know Something We Know

As one moves from the street to within the organization, so the grounds for arguing that the police sub-culture influences action become more plausible. This is not terribly surprising since unlike the lone officer exercising discretion among the public, officers can act as a group within the police organization. The actions of "street cops" is often to resist or oppose the demands of "management cops" (Reuss-Ianni & Ianni 1983; van Outrive & Fijnaut 1983). Again, this is hardly a novel pattern of behaviour in bureaucratic organizations, but it is often regarded as particularly malign when police reforms are undermined. The normative assumption made by researchers is that the lower ranks of the police should not obstruct potentially beneficial reforms like "community policing". We will consider this and other reform agendas in a later chapter, but suffice it to say for the moment that it is at least possible that police officers recognize bullshit when they see it. Just because they oppose "reform" does not mean that those intended reforms, however well-intentioned, are soundly based and in Chapter 7 I will argue that many are not.

Conclusion

The normative orientation to the police sub-culture tells us little about why the police in so many jurisdictions hold distinctive beliefs and values. Identifying the defining characteristic of policing as the exercise of coercive authority and also the central problematic with which police must come to terms enables an empathetic understanding of even the most disagreeable features of the police sub-culture. The "cult of masculinity" is the celebration of the core aspect of the role – the willingness and ability to use force; the sense of a crime-fighting mission provides ideological justification for the authority that is exercised against fellow citizens; the abusive, and often racist, denigration of "police property" is the means through which moral dilemmas are routinely neutralized; and the defensive solidarity of the lower ranks is the frank recognition of the precariousness of their position. Instead of pathologizing the police, this analysis of the police sub-culture exposes the surprising *fragility* of what appears at first sight to be a robust powerful social institution. Police work so hard at affirming what their experience denies because they occupy a *marginal* position in any society that has pretensions to liberal democracy.

CHAPTER 5

Abusing Authority

Introduction

Police officers stray from the proverbial "straight and narrow" in a host of ways: some have adulterous affairs, while others commit criminal acts like theft or murder. This is true for almost any body of people, but what we are interested in here are the ways in which police officers abuse the authority with which they are entrusted.

Understanding how and why police abuse their authority is impeded by the tendency to attribute police wrongdoing to "rotten apples" – unrepresentative individuals who blacken the name of the police by their illegal actions. Undoubtedly, "rotten apples" exist in the police force: Toch suggests that a few "violence-prone" officers are responsible for much of the brutality inflicted by the police (Toch 1969, ibid. 1996; see also Christopher 1991). However, concentrating on individual depravity obscures how police deviancy is structured, for police scandals are of three predominate varieties: corruption, such as accepting bribes; procedural abuses that pervert the course of justice; and the use of excessive force against suspects; all three of which occur under discernible organizational, socio-cultural, and political conditions. This chapter will show how this structure of abuse not only stems from the exploitation of opportunities offered by the role of the police officer, but is fed by aspects of the role itself. It is the latter that makes the control of abuse so difficult.

Bribery and Corruption

Given that the police have discretionary authority to institute proceedings that the civil population finds inconvenient or costly, there are obviously many opportunities for officers to abuse their discretion by accepting or demanding bribes to "turn a blind eye". Thus, in many societies citizens are expected to offer bribes to avoid tickets for traffic violations or to speed the processing of some administrative task for which the police are responsible. This rarely occurs in isolation: in such countries government officials commonly also demand bribes. The reason is usually pretty clear: it is that impoverished governments are unable adequately to remunerate their officials, and bribery, though illegal, is accepted as one of the means by which officials, including police officers, enhance their salary.

This form of corruption is less prevalent in liberal democratic industrialized societies where officials tend to be better remunerated. However, low-level corruption *is* prevalent in the form of "mooching", where officers receive benefits in kind from business people (McCormack 1996). For instance, in Britain the practice of arranging for certain motor recovery and repair businesses to receive preferential opportunities to attend vehicle accidents in return for servicing officers' private cars without charge seems to have been widespread until bureaucratic measures were introduced to ensure that all suitable firms received equal treatment. The Policy Studies Institute report on the London Metropolitan Police discovered that there was an informal catalogue of businesses that were "GTP" ("good to police") (Smith & Gray 1983).

However, in a refrain that will become increasingly familiar in this discussion, the boundary between corruption and propriety is not easily drawn. For example, some businesses openly solicit specifically police custom because they imagine that it is an advantageous market for them. Thus, insurance companies often offer lower premiums to police officers. It is unlikely that they do so in the expectation of receiving any corrupt advantage, not least because these and similar businesses also target the academic profession in much the same way and it is inconceivable that academics could offer corrupt services! Other businesses seek to attract police officers as customers (both on and off-duty) because they imagine that their mere presence offers some protection. Restaurants, pubs and clubs will often (and more or less openly) encourage police officers to patronize their establishments by offering discounts of one sort or another. Some businesses and individuals provide havens in which police can relax – what are often known as "tea holes" – for reasons best known to themselves, but thereby become complicit in a minor form of police deviancy described by Cain as "easing" (Cain 1973). Of course, the injection of any personal relationship can undermine the impartial provision of a service. Thus, if a local restaurant is "GTP", it is likely that officers would attend more quickly and deal more firmly than they otherwise might to, say, a call for assistance with a truculent customer. Whether such favouritism would extend to corruption by, for example, allowing the establishment illegally to serve alcoholic drinks is, of course, a possibility.

However, in the panoply of corruption "mooching" is of little significance, in western liberal democracies *serious* corruption is selectively restrictive, tending to be associated with the policing of morals offences, principally vice and drugs. In what has become the classic analysis of this form of deviancy Manning and Redlinger argue that it arises from the attempt to police illicit markets, such as those dealing in illegal drugs (Manning & Redlinger 1977). Participants in illicit markets behave much like their counterparts operating in legal equivalents; that is, they seek to create and maintain favourable market conditions. But they cannot achieve this through the usual mechanisms of political lobbying and seeking to establish a favourable regulatory regime. Their efforts become concentrated on attempts to neutralize enforcement, for the greatest threat to their market is legal suppression. For their part, enforcement agents are denied the usual source of knowledge of illegality – the complaints of victims – because those engaged in the market are willing participants. Thus, markets must be penetrated covertly, either by buying information or "going undercover" and pretending to be a participant. Either route is fraught with danger of corruption for they each involve establishing reciprocal relationships with those whom the police seek to suppress. Thus, informants need to be allowed to continue trading in the market in order that they can provide information about it. Charges against them will either not be made or dropped entirely. If the market is to be raided, they will be informed beforehand so that they can avoid detection. As Skolnick also notes, this amounts to the systematic toleration of illegality, which is questionable in itself (Skolnick 1966). Manning and Redlinger add that it invites corruption for it is but a small step from protecting an informant because of their potential future utility to the police, to protecting them for one's own material benefit. Likewise, if drugs are supplied to an informant in order to trade in the market, there is the temptation that any profit will be shared between the informant and the officer. Informants can also use the dependence of the officer on their information to exert pressure to "frame" or "set up" competitors in the market place so as to preserve a favourable market position for themselves. Where officers themselves operate undercover, the problems are even more acute, since this will involve *active* and *direct* participation in an illegal activity.

Because illicit markets and their penetration is intrinsically a secret activity, officers engaged in such work come under pressure from within the police organization to show *tangible* results. This too is an invitation to cut corners and engage in corrupt practices. Either the informant or the undercover agent can easily become an *agent provocateur* inducing others to commit offences that they would otherwise not have committed.

There is, perhaps, another feature that encourages corruption and that is that illicit markets are commonly seen – and not only within the police – as "not real crime". As Manning and Redlinger point out, the similarities between licit and illicit markets are at least as striking as their differences. One party supplies goods or services to another; there is no "victim" in the normal sense of someone who suffers direct harm and complains to the police. Of course, one might argue that there are many *indirect* victims, such as residents in those areas in which the market is located who are scandalized by what they experience around them. These depredations can range from women being harassed by men seeking the services of prostitutes to residents finding themselves caught in the midst of a "turf war" between rival drug-gangs. There is also a wider set of victims of thefts and burglaries from those compelled to sustain their drug habit by illegal means. Yet, it is far from clear whether attempts to suppress illicit markets by the police have a beneficial effect or not. Some criminologists have tried to convince us that police suppression succeeds in making matters worse and, implicitly, that tolerance or mere containment would be preferable (Young 1971). That refrain has recently been taken up by the most senior ranks in the British police who have begun advocating the de-criminalization of "soft drugs" (Grieve 1993). Indeed, this seems to have been the strategy adopted by generations of police to prostitution, illustrated most famously by the conflict between Nott Bower, Head Constable of Liverpool in the later nineteenth century, and the Watch Committee to which he was subordinate, over the policy of containing prostitution (Brogden 1982; Jefferson & Grimshaw 1984b). In other words, police might come to regard participants in illicit markets, not as "criminals", but as "business people" sharing much in common with their licit counterparts. Indeed, to the extent that those engaged in criminal enterprises may also and simultaneously be involved in legitimate businesses, then their status may be genuinely ambiguous. As the moral distance between the agent and the suspect shrinks and they become involved in reciprocal exchanges necessary to sustain any relationship, the agent becomes increasingly vulnerable to co-option and corruption.

Although each case exhibits idiosyncratic patterns, the corruption scandals in New York (Chevigny 1969, ibid. 1995; Knapp 1972; Mollen Commission 1994), London (Cox *et al.* 1973) and Amsterdam (Punch 1985) all conform to the pattern described above. Punch's vivid account of how "the wheel came off" in Amsterdam illustrates the argument perfectly. In an attempt to respond to a sudden influx of heroin trafficking by organized gangs among the Chinese community, officers became involved in corrupt deals with informants in order to get results. Their success was, at first, warmly applauded – not least by senior officers – until dubious practices were brought to light whereupon they became pariahs from which everyone shrank.

While the problems are most acute in penetrating illicit markets, inducements to become involved in corruption are endemic in *all* informant-based or undercover work. Dunnighan and Norris (1995a, ibid. b, ibid. 1996) have shown how despite recent attempts in Britain to regulate the use of informants by insisting that both they and the sums of money they receive must be officially registered, the use of unregistered informants remains the norm. They suggest that the competitive individualism of the detective culture militates against such regulation. Moreover, detectives would need to hide their involvement in tolerating or facilitating an informant's continued active participation in crime. Dunnighan and Norris also point to the conflicts that using an informant creates with others: agencies such as prosecutors who may themselves be deceived about the informant's role, other police officers such as custody officers who might find themselves being asked to circumvent legal procedures in order to protect an informant from prosecution, or fellow officers who may feel ill-used by detectives unwilling to keep them fully informed of the circumstances surrounding an arrest. The potential for such conflict itself seems to militate against registration, involving as it does some measure of disclosure that might breed conflict.

Even where it is quite clear that suspects are engaged in serious crimes with obvious victims, such as armed robbers, it is difficult for those handling informants or undercover agents to resist corruption. Deceit and deception is stressful, not only because of the unrelieved threat of exposure, but it also involves psychological dissonance that invites the agent to identify with the target(s) of his or her surveillance (Marx 1988). As Joseph Pistone discovered, after spending a number of years cultivating friendships and becoming reliant upon the favour of members of the Mafia, it is difficult to break those ties without some regret. He correctly anticipated that once he was revealed as an undercover agent, his principal sponsor within the Mafia, Sonny Black, would be murdered in revenge. It is a heavy responsibility to be even indirectly the cause of the death of a person whose friendship one has shared (Pistone with Woodley 1988).

As the stakes become higher, so the moral dilemmas and incitement to corruption become correspondingly more serious. Marx alleges that the Federal Bureau of Investigation (FBI) not only infiltrated radical groups in the 1960s and 70s in order to collect evidence of criminality, but also to de-stabilize them (Marx 1988). The very fact that such groups are vulnerable to infiltration is likely to "chill" even legitimate political activity. However, even more serious dilemmas arise when states are confronted by a terrorist threat. Few would expect terrorist organizations to be immune to infiltration and covert surveillance, however many of the same problems as those discussed above arise in these contexts. Informants and undercover agents must be allowed to continue participation in activities that might amount to very serious crimes in order that their credibility is maintained. They must also be protected and this might entail allowing serious crimes to continue unheeded so as not to alert the terrorists. Thus,

Urban alleges that in order not to jeopardize the ambush of an IRA active service unit at Loughgall, terrorists under constant surveillance were not impeded in their assassination of a part-time member of the Ulster Defence Regiment, William Graham (Urban 1992).

In other words, bribery and corruption tend not to occur through individual greed, but in particular policing contexts in which the normal distance between officers and suspects is diminished. Penetrating the otherwise closed world of organized criminal enterprises, either through informants or undercover agents, immerses officers in a web of relationships and actions that straddle the boundary between legality and illegality. As Manning and Redlinger express it, it brings officers to the "invitational edge of corruption": morally compromised, it is but a short step to criminal involvement.

The Invitational *Edges* of Corruption

The notion of the "invitational edge" is useful because it draws our attention to how policing itself is structurally conducive to illegality and breaches of rules. The implication of this being that anyone placed in the position of a police officer would be similarly tempted. This is a conclusion that undermines easy condemnation and adopts what some criminologists have called an "appreciative" stance towards other forms of deviancy (Matza 1969). The problem, of course, is that few of us who are not police officers are exposed to these structural conditions, so it is a difficult proposition to test. However, a test is at hand from what might appear to be an unlikely source – criminological research itself.

The position of the police officer covertly penetrating organized criminal activity is akin, indeed in some cases almost identical, to that of the ethnographic researcher. The literature on ethnographic fieldwork is crammed with reflections and some agonizing about the compromises one must make to secure access to, and the co-operation of, those whom one wishes to observe (see, for example, van Maanen 1978). Like any relationship, researchers rely upon the principle of reciprocity: explicit undertakings, such as guarantees of anonymity, are entered into; favours are exchanged; and friendships established. The main difference between the researcher and the police officer is that the former rarely has the funds with which to buy the co-operation of informants!

Also, like police officers, researchers commonly encounter ethical dilemmas of varying severity. For example, covert observation by those pretending to be "innocent" participants entails systematically misleading those who are researched. Hence, the police covertly observed by Holdaway (1983) and Young (1991) and drug-dealers observed by Fountain (Fountain 1993) did not have the opportunity to consent to their participation in these respective research studies. Now this breach of the consent principle is readily justified by the overriding need to extend our knowledge of otherwise hidden activities, for if asked explicitly to consent to being observed it is likely that at least some activities would remain disguised. In other words, criminologists might have to weigh competing considerations: the principle of informed consent against the likelihood that the research can be done at all. Since no one would engage in what they regard as worthless research, the principle of informed consent is almost invariably relegated to secondary importance. Like police officers, ethnographic researchers find themselves in a structured situation that obliges them to dissimulate, lie and deceive in pursuit of a higher goal.

The ethical dilemmas of ethnography might extend much further to include toleration of illegality. For example, Norris describes how he witnessed an incident in which police officers not only brutally assaulted two brothers, leaving one with a "suspected broken jaw" and the other with "suspected broken ribs", but also observed what was clearly a conspiracy to pervert the course of justice by officers covering up the assault. This posed a "serious dilemma": "To what extent did my duty as a citizen override my duty as a researcher?" (Norris 1993: 135). By remaining silent, Norris realized that not only would the perpetrators of such violence go unpunished, but the victims were likely to receive a harsher penalty than they would otherwise have done because of the accusations fabricated in order to cover up the violence. On the other hand, to have taken action would have jeopardized the research because officers would almost certainly withdraw co-peration. It would also have breached undertakings of anonymity entered into with research subjects and might have adversely affected future research on the police. Norris chose to remain silent about the specific incident, only disclosing it as part of his overall research findings, thus protecting the anonymity of those involved. Like police officers who use informants, Norris is caught in the ethical dilemma of whether or not to "turn a blind eye" to illegality that is incidental to his purpose in order to protect his sources and ensure the successful outcome of his investigative enterprise.

The greater danger, of course, is that the line between passively witnessing illegality and active participation might easily be crossed. A researcher witnessing what Norris observed does not have to participate in the beating or the manufacture of evidence to connive in the act. Suppose that afterwards the researcher is casually asked by a senior officer on a social occasion for his assessment of the subordinates he has been observing. Does saying that that they are "a fine bunch", or some other such generality, amount to collusion in the cover-up? Certainly, it gives a different impression to saying something like "Well, some of the things I've seen would make your hair stand on end"! Protecting one's sources might lead to taking steps calculated to frustrate the law. For example, Fountain took deliberate steps to avoid writing anything that could be used as evidence against active drug-dealers in the event of their or her arrest (Fountain 1993). So, like the police officer who contrives to have charges dropped against an informant or arranges for evidence to be conveniently "lost", the ethnographers might find themselves vulnerable to accusations that they have entered a corrupt relationship.

Incidentally, Fountain justifies her actions on the grounds that the drug-dealers she observed did not correspond at all to the popular stereotype of "evil pushers" with which she began her research. Thus, because participants in an illicit market are "not really criminal" and doing no harm to innocent victims, the researcher minimizes the extent of her collusion, like the officer who comes to "see no harm" in minor vice offences.

It has not been my purpose to excoriate my academic colleagues, indeed I have raised no issues here that they have not raised themselves. My aim has been to draw attention to how principled people can engage in an enterprise designed to serve an honourable purpose and yet find themselves facing acute ethical dilemmas. This seems to confirm the fundamental proposition advanced by Manning and Redlinger (1977), that certain activities bring those who engage in them to the "invitational edges of corruption", and that corruption is not simply attributable to the fallibility of individual police officers.

However, if *all* that Manning and Redlinger were arguing was that policing allows officers to become corrupt, then it would not amount to much. Many occupations do so from bread salesmen (Ditton 1977) to executives of multi-national companies. They claim more: that policing *invites* deviancy and that invitation, in undercover operations, is extended by those with a vested interest in subverting the enforcement of the law – namely the participants in the illicit activity. They actively seek to ensnare officers in a web of mutual dependence and reciprocity that compromises the integrity of the police and thus safeguards their business interests. In the remaining sections of this chapter, I will explain how this analysis can be extended to a wide range of police activity.

"Bending" and "Breaking" the Rules

Although, by its nature it is difficult to estimate how much bribery and corruption occurs, it seems to be infrequent even in those police organizations, like the New York Police Department, that have suffered a series of major scandals. Much more common, indeed endemic, is the "bending" or "breaking" of the rules that supposedly govern police behaviour. This includes routine violations of internal disciplinary regulations, such as smoking an illicit cigarette. More seriously, officers take actions strictly forbidden by law, such as stopping and searching someone without the necessary grounds for suspicion. Equally, procedures designed to safeguard the rights of suspects and other vulnerable people might be ignored or circumvented. Improper bargains are sometimes struck with some suspects, for example, by offering bail if they will admit to a charge, or concluding a *de facto* "plea bargain" in which the suspect admits to a lesser offence to that of which he or she was originally suspected. In some cases, evidence is fabricated and/or admissions obtained improperly. Sometimes the rules that are violated are internal to the bureaucracy, but often they are statutory or have their basis in common law. How can we explain this endemic level of deviancy among police officers who have a duty to uphold the law?

This seems paradoxical at first, since policing is a thoroughly bureaucratized activity governed by voluminous rules and procedures that stipulate in great detail what police should do in any situation. However, employing Manning and Redlinger's notion of how policing structurally provides "invitational edges of corruption" enables us to see that these rules, far from being part of the solution, are actually a principal cause of the problem.

Bureaucratic "Invitational Edges"

Police organizations epitomize bureaucracy: they attempt to orchestrate the behaviour of officers through a dense set of rules and procedures. Police officers, like personnel in other bureaucracies, suffer the frustrations that any such organization produces. The response of officers to these frustrations is to "work the system" by circumventing or subverting the formal rules just as their counterparts do in other bureaucracies. However, police organizations belong to a distinctive sub-set of bureaucracy, namely they are "punishment-centred" (Kelling & Kliesmet 1996). As Smith and Gray comment:

> It is important to recognise that these rules are almost purely negative in their effect: that is, police officers may be disciplined, prosecuted or otherwise get into difficulties if they are seen to break the rules, but they will not necessarily be praised, enjoy their work or achieve their career objectives if they keep to them. (Smith & Gray 1983: 169)

Or, as the former chief of Minneapolis, Tony Bouza, more forthrightly expressed it: "Police agencies are *mainly controlled through terror*, and this terror is most aimed at the one or two percent who, if left to their own devices, would set a negative tone" (cited in Kelling & Kliesmet 1996: 195), an illustration of which was the dismissal of an officer who took a stray dog home without permission (*Police Review*, 6 December 1996).

The "punishment-centred bureaucracy" of police organizations arises from the "invisible" exercise of discretionary authority, that leaves senior officers unable effectively to command their subordinates. Bordua and Reiss argue that the history of policing has been characterized by the attempts of senior officers to extend effective control over their subordinates (Bordua & Reiss 1966). The threat of penalties for transgressions is one of the few available means of achieving this and so formal rules mushroom as particular problems surface from the depths of invisibility that surrounds most police work.

> The view [among officers] is that there are so many regulations, covering so many aspects of the job, that routine work will intrinsically require violation of one or more of the rules listed in the 10,000-paragraph *General Orders*. (Manning & van Maanen 1977: 79)

Manning continues, quoting a London Metropolitan Police sergeant who "explained that the *General Orders* contained '140 years of fuck-ups. Every time something goes wrong, they make a rule about it'" (Manning & van Maanen 1977: 79).

Smith argues that police officers are subject, not to one, but three quite different kinds of rules that might conflict (Smith & Gray 1983; Smith 1986). The rules that actually govern the routine accomplishment of police tasks are "working rules", many of which are informal. These are the rules that guide officers towards cautioning contrite juveniles from respectable middle-class families, but dealing more harshly with young people who challenge their authority. To officers these rules are "commonsense" and often cannot be articulated in general terms, being instead embedded in the process of dealing with specific incidents involving particular people. Then there are "inhibitory" rules that attempt to block off particular courses of action – for example, rules that require the authorization of senior officers before a course of action can be taken, such as detaining a suspect in custody beyond a stipulated length of time. These rules are often experienced as irksome impediments to action considered legitimate under "working" rules and if they can be circumvented they will be. Finally, "presentational" rules are means by which the organization justifies itself, usually to external audiences. Thus, the detention of suspects would be presented as a sequence of actions taken with punctilious regard for procedures prescribed by statutory codes. The way these different sets of rules are selectively invoked creates what Ericson calls "organizational hypocrisy" (Ericson 1981); for officers are perfectly well aware of the gap between "working" and "presentational". They also know that provided the proverbial "wheel" does not "come off" and a scandal results, the "working" rules will continue to orchestrate their actions. However, if the "wheel comes off" presentational rules will be invoked so as to restore the appearance of propriety.

> Rule enforcement by supervisors seems to resemble a mock bureaucracy where ritualistic and punitive enforcement is applied after the fact. Since rules are surrounded with uncertainty, when disciplinary action is taken it tends to be viewed as arbitrary and the supervisors as self-serving. (Manning 1974: 244)

This is illustrated by an incident in the British police area of Northamptonshire, where a violent drunken man suffered a brain haemorrhage and almost died in custody. Five custody sergeants were subsequently disciplined for offences relating to the maintenance of custody records. However, de la Haye Davies, a police surgeon and past president of the Association of Police Surgeons, argues that this was a disaster waiting to happen because senior officers had decided to combine two custody stations into a single unit with insufficient and poorly trained staff. He accuses the police of pursuing disciplinary charges against the officers (who admitted their guilt and received relatively lenient penalties) in order to safeguard their superiors whose policy decisions and management were more culpable than they were (de la Haye Davies 1997). The chief constable has staunchly rejected these allegations (Fox 1997), but the issue remains: do rules made by superiors serve to insulate them from criticism by pushing responsibility *down* the hierarchy?

Inviting Rule-Breaking

This "punishment-centred" style has several consequences that can bring officers to the "invitational edges of corruption". First, the formal rules of the organization are regarded with almost complete contempt and for good reason.

> The prevalence of regulatory supervision, that is, control that merely measures performance against formulated norms of conduct, can only produce judgement that the assessed person did nothing wrong. Insofar as this is the case, an incompetent, ineffective, and injudicious officer could remain in good standing in his department provided it cannot be shown by any accepted method of proof that he has violated some expressly formulated norm of conduct. This comes very close to saying that an officer who shows up for work, does what he is told to do and no more, and stays out of trouble, meets the criterion of adequacy demanded of him. (Bittner 1983: 5)

Officers who limit themselves to such a specification are despised as "uniform carriers". "Real" police officers do more and in so doing risk violating "inhibitory" and "presentational" rules.

Secondly, the gap that exists between "working" and "presentational" rules fosters an occupational environment that is steeped in organizational rule-breaking – deviancy becomes the norm (McCormack 1996). A good example of this is provided by Manning who describes how a patrolling officer encountered two teenage girls who had left a party very late at night because they were being harassed by a drunken man and decided to walk home. Fearing for their safety the officer on mobile patrol gave them a lift home. When their father wrote to the officer's superiors praising his efforts, the officer was informally reprimanded because force regulations forbade the use of police vehicles for such a purpose (Manning & van Maanen 1977)! Since rule-breaking is unavoidable little significance is given to knowingly breaking other internal regulations for convenience. Cain drew attention to one aspect of such rule-breaking, namely widespread participation in "easing" in which officers take a break from the drudgery and boredom of patrol, including obtaining an illicit cup of tea at a "tea hole" and sleeping when supposedly on night duty (Cain 1973). In more recent times the radio and motor car have enabled officers to select secluded locations in which to smoke an illicit cigarette ignoring the radio (unless a call sounds "juicy" or serious) on the grounds that they are still "committed" to a task already completed or in a radio "black-spot" where reception is difficult. Such rule-breaking is so commonplace that everyone is implicated in it, denying the opportunity for objections to any particular delinquency to be made from the moral high ground.

Thirdly, while the job is not done "according to the book", this is also precarious because of the arbitrary application of the rules. There are two direct implications: on the one hand, since everyone is a rule-breaker formal rules are discredited as standards to which officers should aspire – they are regarded as "bullshit". On the other hand: "The impact of these circumstances on line officers is predictable. It is likely to make them secretive, cautious, conservative, suspicious and untrusting." (Ericson 1981: 102). Officers in a wide spectrum of jurisdictions spend much of their time "guarding their back". Chatterton argues that officers are oriented to avoiding "trouble"; and "trouble" comes in two guises – "on the job" and "in the job" (Chatterton 1979, ibid. 1983). "On-the-job trouble" is that which is experienced typically on the streets dealing with incidents and can range from preventing a successful challenge to the officer's authority to arresting a suspect. Given the discretionary nature of policing, much of this kind of trouble is dealt with informally. "In-the-job trouble" arises from the officer's relationship to the police bureaucracy, preventing "comebacks" and anything else that calls the officer's competence and propriety into question. In other words, much police action is *defensive.*

Fourthly, because the precariousness of policing is *commonly* experienced, there is a shared vested interest among officers in erecting defences against it, which creates a culture of intense peer loyalty that incorporates a "code of silence" or the "blue curtain" (Stoddard 1968). It is because the police *do not* control their working environment that they act defensively to shield all deviancy from the gaze of the bureaucracy (Fielding 1981b). For example, senior officers might make impromptu visits to police stations under their command to check that officers are behaving properly. "Improper behaviour" might amount to no more than being improperly dressed while on duty, smoking a cigarette while typing a report, grabbing a coffee in the canteen when supposedly on patrol. To prevent being caught engaging in such minor peccadilloes, colleagues who discover to which police station a senior officer is *en route* will be expected to telephone the destination and forewarn them. Hence, on arrival at the selected station, the senior officer finds officers all properly dressed and absorbed in their duties. On the other hand, officers who have violated the code of peer loyalty might find themselves excluded from such protection and left to encounter the weight of bureaucracy alone. As Cain remarks, this makes police in urban areas inward-looking; relying on each other for support rather than to members of the public (Cain 1973). This gives rise to the strong insistence upon the "no rat" rule: officers should do nothing to expose malpractice among their colleagues and are obligated to assist them in avoiding punishment (Westley 1956). The PSI researchers cite one sergeant who explained:

> If one of the boys working for me got himself into trouble, I would get all of us together and I would literally script him out of it. I would write all the parts out and if we followed them closely we couldn't be defeated. And believe me, I would do it. (Smith & Gray 1983: 72)

However, it is important to keep even this in proportion; for there is little that is unique to policing in such expressions of peer loyalty. Many occupational groups share the informal expectation that members owe a loyalty to each other, hence the hard time suffered by those who "blow the whistle" on various manifestations of "white collar crime". As Skolnick and Fyfe remark, the sub-culture of police officers consists of a normal expectation of peer loyalty in abnormal circumstances (Skolnick & Fyfe 1993).

Peer loyalty gains additional intensity among police officers from aspects of policing that have little or nothing to do with it being a punishment-centred bureaucracy. Because police work is occasionally dangerous, officers rely on peer loyalty for their sense of personal safety. Hence, if an officer calls for help, others are expected to give that first priority. The fact that this may produce an absurd over-reaction and the futile disruption to other policing tasks is less important than the re-assurance that is given by the overt display of support (Smith & Gray 1983). Equally, of course, withholding such support or being less enthusiastic in its provision represents a very severe penalty to officers who deviate from the expectations of their colleagues. Gomez-Preston describes one such incident:

> A patrol car was chasing a man who had just tried to shoot somebody while committing an armed robbery.... When the other officers began to chase the suspect on foot, I jumped out and joined them. There were about six other officers.
>
> I was concentrating so hard on catching the man, I didn't notice when we turned and ran into an alley. The alley wasn't lit, but there was light coming in from the street lamps. All of a sudden the suspect stopped and turned. I looked over my shoulder for my backup, but there was no one there....
>
> I remember knowing he was going to shoot me. He started fumbling around the waist of his pants, trying to find his gun.... I pulled my gun and fired two shots and he fell to the ground. Within 15 to 20 seconds, officers came from wherever they'd been. No one said anything: there was nothing to say. (Gomez-Preston & Trescott 1995: 401)

A fifth consequence of the "punishment-centred" mode of bureaucracy in the police is that it encourages officers to fabricate "good stories". Chatterton describes how officers coped with a system designed to constrain their autonomy: before personal radios became common, British officers on foot patrol were required to be present at particular locations at prescribed times where they could be contacted by telephone and/or meet their supervising sergeant – a system known as "fixed points". An officer who failed to attend at any such "point" was required to furnish a justification for his absence. Chatterton describes how this was routinely achieved by the telling of a "good story", which not only covered up any departure from the rules, such as having an illicit drink on duty, but was unreviewable and, if possible, testified to the commendable policing of the officer. One such "good story" was told by an experienced constable who had missed his "point": he told of how he had seen someone who looked suspicious, and so he had doubled-back and followed the man; but nothing untoward occurred and so the officer had resumed his patrol. Not only did this cover the fact that the officer had actually been consuming an illicit pint of beer, but testified to his powers of observation and clever police work in keeping the mythical person surreptitiously under observation (Chatterton 1979). More recently, Irving and Dunnighan (1993) have pointed to how the intolerance officially shown towards error in the police organization perversely encourages erring officers to "cover their tracks" by fabricating, not only a "good story", but possibly evidence as well. In other words, police are structurally invited to become consummate liars.

A final implication of "punishment-centred bureaucracy" is that it obliges senior officers to be hypocritical. They are aware that subordinates cannot police "according to the book", but they are obliged to maintain the fiction that policing is rule-governed. This creates the contradiction that police organizations are *both* "punishment-centred bureaucracies" and also notoriously indulgent; for senior officers and middle-ranking supervisors often give the "nod and a wink" to their subordinates, especially if the latter are achieving "results". This is what happened in Amsterdam where senior officers expressly avoided all knowledge about the practices of officers obtaining "results" in drugs enforcement (Punch 1985). Thus, senior officers can maintain "deniability", while allowing subordinates to flout the strict interpretation of bureaucratic and legal rules. This, of course, serves only to discredit those rules even further, for when the proverbial "wheel comes off" officers expect to be sacrificed and scapegoated for actions that were previously tacitly tolerated.

Performance

The habitual rule-bending and rule-breaking by police officers allows for more serious breaches of the rules, but what is it that entices them to step across that "invitational edge"? The answer is the organizational imperative to "perform". Again, this is not just a wilful invention of senior officers, but arises from the invisible exercise of discretion. For such invisibility poses the problem for senior officers of determining whether any particular subordinate is or is not working at all. Senior officers demand tangible evidence that the officer is not simply opting for a quiet life and that evidence comes in the form of making arrests and issuing tickets, either of which are visible to the organization. This orientation is known disparagingly among British officers as "figures" and their American counterparts as "activity". It bears particularly heavily on recruits who need to demonstrate their enthusiasm for police work and those who seek transfer to specialist roles or promotion. Equally, if an officer, through no fault of his own, has not made many arrests or issued tickets in the recent past, then he might experience some pressure from his superiors. One solution to this problem is for officers, who have an ample supply of arrests and tickets, to "give" their less well-supplied colleagues "a prisoner". This is done by pretending that an officer other than the one who actually made the arrest did so; but this single act of generosity, while it may have no impact on the substantive guilt of the suspect, can lead to perjury. For if the case comes to court, the officer will lie about his own involvement and during the course of cross-examination be forced to perjure his evidence as he extemporizes about the circumstances of the arrest. Moreover, having crossed the line, there is now little difference between this minor illegality and more serious breaches of the law, such as fabricating evidence against those believed to be guilty of offences.

Legal "Invitational Edges"

That policing cannot be "done according to the book" extends to *law* books. The police view the law with profound cynicism, both as a code they are expected to enforce upon others and as a set of constraints under which they conduct themselves.

We have already seen that discretion is an unavoidable corollary of policing: full enforcement of the law is impossible and to attempt it would be undesirable. Laws, however specific they might appear, are universal precepts that must be applied to very specific circumstances. We have also seen that the use of discretion necessarily relegates legality to a secondary status, for the law is *used* selectively to enforce prevailing notions of respectability (what some regard as inherently a violation of "democratic norms", see Hagan & Morden 1981). If the law is the servant of discretion, it follows that police officers cannot be servants of the law and this inevitably means that their relationship to it is mediated by what they (probably rightly) call "commonsense". This also means that policing in modern liberal democracies involves the police living a lie: they pretend that they *are* mere servants of the law, whereas their daily experience is that they are, if anything, its master – employing the law as and when necessary to achieve their discretionary goals. This is a situation calculated to encourage cynicism, for the ideals are not just unattainable they are actually inappropriate – to enforce the law blindly would be to perpetrate massive injustice.

Cynicism is also encouraged by legal procedures that are apprehended by officers as plain violations of commonsense, or as it is often expressed, "the law is an ass". This was one of the "bitter lessons" that Kirkham learnt during his sojourn as a Jacksonville cop – what he describes as the "depressing and at times personally crushing awareness that the toughest adversary a street cop must confront . . . is, ironically, the very law which he must struggle . . . to enforce" (1974: 131).

Using and Enforcing the Law

The paradox of the relationship of the police to law is that prior to being invoked it exists as a resource that can bolster the authoritative exercise of discretion; but once it is invoked the law is experienced as an obstacle and constraint. The *reason* for invoking the law in any situation is likely to be as specific as the situation itself, but will usually reflect an intuitive judgement of *moral* culpability. However, the law is intolerant of intuition and moral judgement, and is concerned only with whether the person committed the proscribed act with which they are charged. From the legal perspective what was relevant to the police officer in deciding to make the arrest may be wholly irrelevant to the determination of guilt. Complex and multifaceted experiences and actions must be retrospectively accommodated to legal requirements.

This has two predictable consequences: the first is that officers become practised in rendering their experiences on the street into a version suitable to legal proceedings – what Dixon describes as the production of "legalized" accounts (Dixon 1997). This need imply no impropriety. For instance, I was accompanying officers on routine patrol one Christmas Eve. Throughout the afternoon we all heard the radio dispatching other patrols to eject a persistently troublesome drunken man from various business premises in one area of the town. Eventually, our patrol was dispatched to eject him, this time from a dry-cleaners. On arrival we walked into the shop and the staff pointed him out, slumped stupefied in the corner. He was awoken and accompanied outside; he was hardly able to stand and was barely coherent. After much effort the more senior of the two officers managed to discern that the man had spent all his money getting drunk; was under the alcohol-induced impression that he was in his home town when, in fact, it was some thirty-miles distant; and had no means of getting home. Reluctantly, he was arrested and taken to the cells to sober up. The "rookie" officer was left to write up the arrest report that would accompany the man to the next sitting of the magistrates' court. The report began with an account of the patrol being dispatched to the dry-cleaners and pretty faithfully described what occurred. Upon his return from completing some administrative chore the more senior officer began reading the report; he had not read far before he wearily screwed it up and threw it away. Taking a fresh report form he dictated, "I was on duty in High Street, when I saw the defendant I now know to be John Smith. He was unsteady on his feet, his speech was slurred and his breath smelt of alcohol. I formed the impression that he was drunk. He was cautioned and arrested . . .". He explained that not only was all the surrounding context legally irrelevant, but it would create additional work, since it would probably require the officers to obtain corroborative statements from the dispatcher and the staff of the dry cleaners. Thus, what emerged was a version of events that while entirely true and which addressed all the legally relevant issues, was also wholly misleading; for it gave the impression that the police had arbitrarily picked on this hapless individual and arrested him for being drunk on Christmas Eve! Nevertheless, an account that preserved verisimilitude would only have created additional work. Thus, officers quickly learn that when they enter the legal arena they enter a strange and alien world in which events are transfigured into a "paper reality" (Manning 1974: 242). The law itself is apprehended as remote from the world of daily experience and that engenders cynicism.

The second consequence is that the legal process is experienced as threatening and frustrating. Although referring specifically to juveniles, Wheeler's account of how the police regard the courts probably applies with equal force to a much wider range of situations. He argues that the policing of juveniles is punitive; but also designed to keep youngsters out of the criminal justice system which is seen as harmful. Recourse to legal remedies tends to be taken as a last resort reserved for the most difficult and intractable individuals. The police expect, as of right, that the courts should support them in their decision. When the courts fail to convict, or hand down an inappropriately lenient sentence, officers feel that their authority is undermined (Wheeler *et al.* 1968). Thus, the law is used but it is not a reliable ally (see also Reiss & Bordua 1967).

This structural relationship to the law and the courts provides an "invitational edge to corruption" in routine policing. Founded on the knowledge that law is the servant of discretionary authority; fed by the cynical recognition of the gap between the "real world" and legal "technicalities"; and driven by the necessity to ensure the conviction of those who have provoked recourse to legal sanction, police officers are tempted to ensure the "paper reality" contains all the elements necessary to convict any person arrested. This is straightforward in many instances, for those whom the police feel compelled to arrest have usually committed several offences. Kemp *et al.* describe one of the rare occasions when the policing of a domestic dispute ended in arrest. A drunken ex-husband attacked his former wife who was pregnant at the time; but when he struggled with officers whose only aim was to eject him from his former-wife's house he was arrested and charged with being "drunk and disorderly" (Kemp *et al.* 1992a). He could also have been arrested for a breach of the peace, disorderly conduct, assault, possibly assaulting the police (which is a distinct offence) and almost certainly several other arcane offences. The selection of the particular charge was dictated by the perceived ease with which it could be legally sustained. Similar expediency is reflected in practices such as "padding" and "stacking" where officers in the United States, anticipating that charges will be reduced as part of a "plea-bargain", both inflate the initial charge in anticipatory compensation and include as many lesser offences as possible so that if more serious charges are dropped the suspect may be convicted on others (Kappeler *et al.* 1994).

However, there are occasions when police arrest people arbitrarily and then need to concoct a charge to justify their action. For example, I witnessed such an incident that arose out of a racially motivated attack upon which the police chanced almost immediately after it had occurred. The victim, still shocked and bleeding from a wound on his forehead, was asked who had done it. He waved in the general direction of a group of youths walking away. One of the officers strode off after the group and catching up with them, asked them to return to the scene so that the situation could be clarified. They objected, claiming that the incident had nothing to do with them. However, all but one eventually, albeit reluctantly, were persuaded to return. The one who refused, continued to walk away from the scene of the incident. The officer stood in his way, but the youth tried to brush past him. The officer barred his way with his outstretched hand, which the youth tried to push aside. These events were accompanied by increasingly strident warnings from the officer and obscenities from the youth. After a few inconclusive moments, the officer announced that the youth "was nicked", grabbed him and marched him to the patrol car. Meanwhile, the officer's companion had been obtaining the full story from the victim. The victim was unable to say who had assaulted him and there was, indeed, no evidence to implicate the group of youths whom the officer had accosted. They were allowed to go, but the problem remained of the arrested member of the group. There was a hasty conference among the officers at the scene which concluded that he was probably guilty of obstruction of a police officer, but there was no power of arrest for that offence. It was decided that the youth could not be allowed to "get away" with so blatantly refusing to return to the scene of the incident and challenging the officer's authority. So, he was arrested for breach of the peace and in their arrest report he was depicted as more rowdy and the situation as more volatile than it actually was. McConville *et al.* cite a similar example:

> The arresting officer was called to a party. A053 refused to turn off his "ghetto blaster". The arresting officer said to the researcher: "It would have been all right if he'd just gone away but he had to be Jack the Lad and want to be put down. So I put him down . . . I grabbed him and arrested him".
>
> Res. "On what basis?"
>
> *AO* "Well it's hard to explain. Anyone in the police would understand but you wouldn't. . . . It's a way of dealing with the situation. You get him off the street and make the residents happy. It's 'Ways and Means', just to get him away, control the situation and show the neighbours you're doing

> something. . . . It's touchy and I don't want to say any more." (McConville *et al.* 1991: 25–6)

What British police refer to as the "Ways and Means Act" is the massaging of evidence: the incident is described in such a way that recourse to arrest is legally justified.

McConville *et al.* (1991) argue that this is generalized into the practice of "case building", in which officers decide on substantive guilt prior to acquiring the evidence necessary to sustain a charge. As many of their examples illustrate, this arises from routine order maintenance, rather than the investigation of serious crime.

> The defendant was alleged to have damaged a mini-cab windscreen in the course of an argument with his girlfriend. Both had been drinking heavily and the defendant had to sleep off the effects of the drink before being fit to be interviewed. He said that, in the course of the row, he had swung his arm out "and hit the windscreen and it broke". The police then turned their attention to the question of *mens rea* [criminal intent]:
> *Police*: "Did you intend to smash the windscreen?"
> *Defendant*: "No".
> *Police*: "So you just swung your hand out in a *reckless* manner?
> *Defendant*: "Yes, that's it, just arguing".
> *Police*: "Why did you hit the window in the first place?"
> *Defendant*: "Just arguing, *reckless*, it wasn't intentional to break it . . . " (pp. 70–71)

As the authors comment, by inviting the defendant to agree that he had been reckless they establish the "mental element", without which no crime would have been committed. One might add, that they also ensure that the criminal law is employed to defend hapless mini-cab drivers from quarrelsome drunken people and thus restore prevailing norms of respectability.

It is widely agreed that police regard interrogation as a means of obtaining a confession. Not only does this provide reasonable assurance of conviction in court, but brings to a close the translation of the inevitably messy circumstances of the street into a legal "paper reality". To achieve this officers engage in various"tactics" to some of which we will shortly return when discussing procedural safeguards; but others involve tricking the suspect into a confession. I was accompanying detectives investigating a series of thefts from the unattended clothing of employees in a locker room. The manager suspected a particular employee of these thefts and the police had placed a quantity of pound notes in clothes left in the locker room as a trap. The notes in question had been treated with a chemical that was only visible under ultra-violet light. After it is was confirmed that the money had been taken, the detectives arrested the youth suspected by the manager and took him to the station. It was necessary to obtain the ultra-violent light from another station and when they arrived to pick it up they were dismayed to learn from their colleagues that it had previously failed to illuminate the chemical, even during an experiment designed to test it. Returning to the station the senior detective said to his colleague, "Whatever happens, we'll see it, right?". His colleague agreed. The suspect was taken to a darkened room, which evidently caused him some trepidation, and told to hold out his hands while the light was shone onto them. The chemical was supposed to shine bright yellow. As the suspect stood with his hands held out in the beam of the light, the two detectives started pointing at his hands and exclaiming how clear was the chemical reflection. (They certainly convinced me, but later admitted that the whole performance had been a charade!). The detectives and suspect adjourned to the interview room, where the senior detective announced that there was ample evidence to charge the suspect with the theft of the treated money. He made no further mention of it, but turned instead to the series of previous thefts. The suspect made a full written confession. He was charged with the series of thefts to which he had confessed, but no mention was made of stealing the treated money.

Lest it be imagined that these practices are a peculiarity of the British police or their counterparts in the Anglo–Saxon tradition, Miyazawa recounts equivalent tactics employed by the Japanese detectives that he observed:

> ... detectives spend much time in interrogation before they seriously search and examine physical evidence. Detectives as a policy do not collect too much evidence before the confession.... Detectives thus believe that in order to make a confession credible and voluntary, it should be obtained through long confinement, and that thereafter materials should be collected on the basis of the confession. (Miyazawa 1992: 159)

The inducement to ensure a successful prosecution by "building a case" does not rely on the unilateral decision of police officers, but reflects structural realities: the police are agents of the prosecution and defences exist to be breached. Under the inquisitorial system this structural position is openly acknowledged, for the police are usually under the direction of a public prosecutor. In the adversarial system their role is less clearly specified and prosecutors in Britain have a duty to reject cases that are unlikely to result in conviction. However, we should ask ourselves what this actually means: it is an invitation for the police to submit (that is, build) the strongest possible case against the suspect. As Lustgarten remarks:

> ... the English police take an avowedly partisan stance in a system in which partisan contest is supposed to produce truth. And the evidentiary barriers reinforce bureaucratic and resource imperatives of avoiding trials in the vast majority of cases by producing guilty pleas. This is impossible in the Continental systems, where the accused is not permitted to plead guilty. This gives the English police substantially greater incentive to seek to obtain a confession from the suspect; more generally and ominously, it would seem to be a constant pressure leading them to overstep their powers against those they "know" are guilty. (Lustgarten 1986: 2)

The "pressure" to which Lustgarten refers is akin to that which encourages less serious deviations from internal regulations, namely "performance". The police are expected routinely to ensure sufficient successful prosecutions and if they fail to do so will experience, either individually or corporately, demands to improve their performance – creating what Sharpe (1995) calls a "performance crime". Those demands become periodically more strident when particularly horrific crimes have been committed and police are thereby enticed to capture perpetrators almost "come what may". The succession of high-profile miscarriages of justices in Britain, especially those in connection with IRA terrorism, have widely been attributed to such pressure. The fact that in many of these cases forensic scientists, barristers and others involved in the prosecution were revealed as having ignored evidence inconsistent with guilt, suggests that it is not only police officers who feel this same pressure (the same applies to psychologists who allegedly have altered evidence at the behest of lawyers [Pater 1996]).

"Proper Police Procedure"

There is, however, a quite different sense in which officers believe policing cannot be done "according to the book" – the "book" in this case being the procedural rules that limit police powers. A quite remarkable, but little remarked upon, feature of modern liberal democracies is the extension of citizenship to those who have committed (or are suspected of having committed) crime. The past two-hundred years has seen a progressive extension of procedural rules and laws designed to protect suspects in criminal cases. Rules have been introduced and gradually extended limiting police intrusion into citizens' privacy by questioning, search and seizure. Based on the presumption of innocence (itself a significant token of citizenship), not only has the torture of suspects been outlawed, but what counts as torture has been extended to include any form of coercion or inducement that undermines the voluntary nature of any confession or self-incriminating statement. Criminal trial procedures are dictated by the need to be fair to the accused – as exemplified by the burden of proof resting upon the prosecution and the standard of proof being "beyond a reasonable doubt". Economic obstacles to poor defendants receiving an equally fair trial to their more affluent counterparts have been reduced by the provision of legal advice and representation at public expense. Even convicted prisoners have been granted extended rights of citizenship; for they are no longer subject to degrading and inhuman forms of treatment, such as corporal punishment, and minimum conditions of incarceration have been established along with independent review of prison conditions. Now, advocates for human rights would no doubt demand yet further improvements in the conditions to which suspects, defendants and convicted prisoners are subject, and deplore such retrograde steps as the *de facto* restoration of the death penalty in many American states. It is not my purpose to assess those arguments here; but what seems beyond empirical doubt is that one aspect of the development of citizenship over the past two centuries has been the inclusion of those who have broken even the most fundamental laws of the states of which they are citizens.

These rules have been enacted by legislatures and developed by the courts to protect suspects from oppressive treatment by police officers. However, they are apprehended by the police as obstacles to the conviction of criminals (Skolnick 1966). This is the fundamental tension at the heart of the criminal justice system between "crime control" and "due process": in the former, the goal is to convict those who are substantively guilty of the crimes with which they are charged, whereas the latter seeks to ensure that justice is dispensed in accordance with procedures that are fair to the accused (Packer 1968). The maxim that it is better that ten guilty people go free than that a single innocent person be wrongfully convicted seems to the ordinary police officer like elevating inefficiency into a design feature of the criminal justice system, and so it is. The various safeguards within the criminal justice system are designed to act as a brake against the impetus to secure convictions. The problem is that while one foot is pressed down on this brake the other is pressing ever more firmly on the accelerator. As Manning (1977) reminds us, the police are shackled to the impossible mandate of reducing crime. They (and often their political masters) are evaluated by their success in securing convictions.

It is against that background that safeguards for suspects must be viewed; for the irony is that it is police officers themselves who are responsible for implementing safeguards. The cop in the United States is required to recite the *Miranda* warning when suspects are arrested, just as their British counterparts are obliged to recite comparable warnings under statute and, before that, the "Judges Rules". It is the police who are required to *restrain themselves* when seeking to question suspects on the street, search them and seize evidence. In the police station, officers are responsible for implementing procedures designed to safeguard suspects' rights during detention and interrogation. In some jurisdictions there is some division of labour between police who patrol the streets and the "judicial police" who have responsibility for investigation and/or detention of suspects, but unfortunately we know little of their working practices. Thus, the common experience of police officers in liberal democracies is that they and/or their colleagues are responsible for impeding the success of their own goals by implementing safeguards designed to make conviction more difficult. It is, therefore, unsurprising that officers attempt to circumvent these constraints.

The irony is that the more the legal process squeezes the police to ensure propriety, the more the police are tempted to circumvent or undermine procedural restraints. Bayley describes such a chain reaction in 1960s India, but it could, just as readily, be almost anywhere else in the democratic world (Bayley 1969). Criminal procedure in India, at that time, was formally initiated by a complaint from an informant to the police who wrote down the substance of the allegation which the informant signed – the "First Information Report", or FIR. However, the courts paid increasing attention to the details contained in the FIR and their consistency with the evidence that the investigation subsequently revealed. So, the police were given an incentive to ensure that the FIR was properly completed, so as to avoid problems later on.

> Policemen have developed two strategies for handling the FIR. First, they record as little factual information as possible. Thus, they protect themselves from having the FIR used against testimony later uncovered and presented in court. They "de-fuse" the FIR. Or they may record as little information as possible initially so that they may fill in relevant details as investigation proceeds, giving the FIR maximum evidentiary weight. This practice is patently illegal. Second, police officers may demand as much factual information as possible at the outset, even to the extent of asking the informant to go away and obtain more details. In this way they protect themselves against the charge of omitting essential information so that it could be supplied later. This practice, too, is illegal. . . .
>
> The irony of the situation is that the importance attached to the FIR in courts of law is a reflection of judicial distrust of the police; but so detailed have stipulations about its use become that it is now a source of contention in itself, reinforcing the very suspicion of the police that its proper use was supposed to reduce. (Bayley 1969: 150–151)

To use an equestrian metaphor: if the jumps are too high, the horses go around them!

Street Powers

The use of powers of stop and search have been discussed at length previously in the context of police–race relations. What was omitted from that discussion is how stop and search can be formally justified by officers who use it as a harassing technique against marginal sections of the population. The principal resource here, like all street policing, is its relative invisibility: a pedestrian or motorist can be accosted on the street without anyone other than the parties directly involved knowing that the encounter has occurred. Evidence from the PSI report on the London Metropolitan Police indicated that less than half of all stops were recorded, as they were supposed to be (Smith 1983a, ibid. b; Smith & Gray 1983). Of course, if the stop produced "a result", then it would be recorded. Officers might also formally record stops to demonstrate their "activity" or because in particular circumstances it was less invisible than usual and the officers were guarding their backs.

In addition to their sheer invisibility, the exercise of police powers on the street also benefits from the latitude of interpretation. For example, a "stop" is not unambiguous: police are entitled to engage anyone in conversation and both parties may pause while they do so. Equally, anyone might allow someone else to look inside a bag that they are carrying. Even when a police officer explicitly stops and searches someone in the street, that person could perfectly well consent to them doing so – "Do you mind if I have a word with you, sir, and look in that bag you're carrying?", "Not at all, officer, go ahead" (Dixon 1989, ibid. 1997). The problem to which Dixon draws attention is how genuine is such consent? If a police officer asks to speak to someone, does the latter *genuinely* feel free to reject the request, or do they believe that they are under some compulsion, because if they refuse the police officer might use other powers to give them a "hard time"? In any case, what is the point in refusing an officer's request to search the bag one is carrying, if officers have the legal power to demand it anyway? This latitude can easily be exploited by officers if they choose to do so.

The issues are more complex than this depiction allows; for while it is true that police may "construct consent" by these means, so too might many others, especially those in positions of authority. For instance, store detectives have no power to stop and search shopping bags, but they do so routinely and "consensually". In these circumstances, consent is "constructed" by the assertion of non-existent authority and the latent threat that refusal will lead to a "scene" in a crowded shop that is likely to attract the attention of others and prove embarrassing (South 1989). Elsewhere it has been suggested that health professionals exercise *de facto* authority over others by asserting that medical needs dictate that personal information be disclosed (Abbott & Sapsford 1990). This raises the issue of whether genuine consent could ever be granted in a relationship of unequal power. On the other hand, as Porter argues (Porter 1996), there is a considerable difference between being asked for personal information by a medical professional and being manhandled by soldiers on the streets of Belfast who demand comparable private details. However much the police might request or solicit compliance, coercion is never far from the surface. The question, "Can I look in your bag?", contains the unstated clause, "but if you say no, I'll *make* you".

Even this is not the end of the story, for it may be inappropriate to assess such actions in terms of consent; for as Dixon rightly suggests, the "air of consent" may reflect an attempt to maintain civility (Dixon 1997). Both parties might tacitly understand that a police request to search is in reality a *demand* to do so, yet couched in the form of a request it avoids overtly oppressive police behaviour and allows the citizen the option of conducting the transaction on a relatively informal and even amicable basis. Ironically, conforming strictly to legal procedure might give the same encounter an air of oppressive formality. Curtis, perhaps a little tongue-in-cheek (but only a little) characterized a legally proper stop as involving an officer struggling to detain someone while uttering the following:

> My name is Police Constable 455 Algernon Nigel Arbuthnot. I am attached to Paddington Green Police Station. I am trying to detain you in order that I can search you because I suspect that you have just mugged an old lady around the corner, and I am looking for her purse. The reason I suspect you, is that you answer the description of the young man seen running away, and you were running when I stopped you. I also have to inform you that you are entitled to a copy of the record of this search which I am obliged to make straight away, but as it is raining. . . . (Curtis 1986: 97)

Police undoubtedly secure far greater compliance by the use of informal means of achieving their goals than the law would otherwise allow (see, for example, Waddington 1994a); but this still seems a more amicable way of doing business than it would otherwise be.

If, for whatever reason, the officer needs to resort to formal justification, there is ample scope do so in the rules that govern the exercise of street powers. Skolnick points out how officers become skilled in detecting suspicious behaviour that would not satisfy legal standards (Skolnick 1966). For instance, if officers in an unmarked car see someone emerge onto the street and, having caught sight of their car, give the appearance of having forgotten something and return from where they have emerged, officers become immediately suspicious. They take what might otherwise be considered innocuous behaviour (absent-mindedness) as indicating that the person recognized the unmarked car as a police vehicle and fabricated a reason to get off the street. When such people re-emerge they might find the police waiting to search them. In the event that contraband is found on their person or in their belongings, officers would have little difficulty justifying the search by referring to "furtive movements". Since no supervising authority could be present at such an encounter (for if they were, it would not occur), scrutineers are in no position to rebut the contention that the person's actions were "furtive".

Arrest

Much the same applies to the safeguarding of suspects at the point of arrest. Before being arrested an officer should have established "reasonable suspicion", "probable cause" or some other such prescribed criterion; but it is difficult to stipulate in advance what this would entail. Provided the officer can tell "a good story", then any arrest can be justified.

Similar problems arise with monitoring whether a *Miranda*-style warning was issued, since the law acknowledges some circumstances where it would be inappropriate to do so – for example, during a violent struggle. However, lawyers can still contrive to make the law look an ass. In the English case of *Director of Public Prosecutions v Hawkins* magistrates accepted that a defendant, who assaulted three officers during a violent struggle that immediately followed his being told that he was under arrest, but before he could be told what for, did *not* commit an assault on police in the execution of their duty. The case had to go to the Court of Appeal before sanity was restored and it was accepted that it was impracticable to complete the legal niceties with the suspect's foot in one's mouth! However, sometimes issuing a formal notification of rights can lead to a serious downturn in the relationship between officers and suspects. I was on patrol one Friday evening with several officers in a personnel carrier that was called to a disturbance at a pub. The sergeant decided to arrest a man and instructed one of the constables to notify him of his rights. As the constable went through the well-rehearsed recitation, the man, who had hitherto been quite compliant towards the police, became extremely agitated, screaming that he was *not* "a criminal" and struggling with the officer trying to arrest him. It took virtually the entire contingent of police to put him on board the personnel carrier!

Detention and Charge

Once a suspect has arrived at the station they are metaphorically surrounded by a web of procedural law designed to safeguard their rights, but which, many researchers argue, are systematically undermined by the very people charged with this responsibility. McKenzie *et al.* observed that police "custody officers" (sergeants with statutory responsibilities in relation to the detention and charging of suspects) very rarely applied the "necessity principle" when arrested suspects arrived at the station (McKenzie *et al.* 1990). This principle had been enacted in order to try and deter officers from habitually arresting suspects rather than issuing summonses. It envisaged the custody officer making a preliminary assessment as to whether it was appropriate to detain an arrested person or to let him or her go immediately and proceed by way of summons. This is a neat piece of legal absurdity since the suspect would need to be detained in order for the sergeant to conduct the assessment; but less arcane pressures tended to weigh against enforcing the principle. Its invocation would amount to a peremptory and public repudiation of the officer's decision to arrest in the first place. Loyalty to their colleagues tended to preclude this and if they felt the arrest was unwise or uncalled for, they would take an alternative course of action to release the suspect. Of course, what this incidentally demonstrates is the conflicting pressures under which the custody sergeant is placed, being a police officer regulating fellow officers.

Ploys

Another responsibility of the custody sergeant is to inform the suspect of their right to receive legal advice. Although since the legislation was passed in the mid-1980s the proportion of suspects receiving legal advice has increased significantly, it remains a minority. It might be thought unlikely that suspects would not avail themselves of such advice if they were properly informed of its availability, but custody officers seem reasonably scrupulous in asking whether suspects wish to receive the advice of a lawyer. The explanation for the low take-up of legal advice, according to Sanders *et al.*, lies in the "ploys" that custody officers use to dissuade suspects (Sanders *et al.* 1989). The first is to ask if legal advice is desired in the dead-pan monotone of bureaucratic form-filling. When an arrested person arrives at the "custody suite" (a euphemism referring to the cell-block in police stations!) they confront an often weary "custody officer" bureaucratically processing a succession of "prisoners". Gazing down at yet another form to be filled, he asks and writes the replies to a series of questions – name, address, age, occupation, date and time of arrest, arresting officer, etc., etc. – among which is asked whether the person wishes someone to be notified of their arrest and do they desire legal advice. If the person replies that they do not, the form is swivelled to face the person, a finger points at the places on the form that the latter has to sign. A leaflet may be given explaining the person's rights, copies of which usually adorn the walls of the "custody suite", all written in the stupefying language of bureaucratic precision. In other words, the whole encounter is a bureaucratic ritual that discourages the exercise of this safeguard.

Occasionally, a suspect will ask the custody officer or the officer who arrested them whether they should avail themselves of legal advice. They are likely to receive a reply along the lines of "Well, it depends how quickly you want to get out of here. If the lawyer bothers to come down here at all, it'll take an hour or more. In that time you'll be left waiting in the cell. It's up to you". The prospect of waiting in the cell for hours is often sufficient disincentive to invoking this safeguard, especially when the whole situation is suffused with an air of "Let's get this over as quickly as possible, shall we?". So, just as people "consent" to be stopped and searched on the street, they "consent" to abrogate rights designed to safeguard their interests (see Choongh 1997 for further discussion).

However, describing this outcome as a "ploy" perhaps imbues the police with more cunning than is justified. For as Sanders *et al.* also show *inter alia* that if suspects *do* avail themselves of their right to legal advice they are indeed likely to receive it over the telephone and, if anyone does attend the police station, they are unlikely to be legally qualified (but instead be "para-legals") and take around an hour or more to arrive (Sanders *et al.* 1989). In other words, the custody officer is usually telling no more than the truth. Furthermore, it is difficult to imagine how the custody officer might act in ways that could not be construed as a "ploy". Suppose that when asked by a suspect whether the latter should avail themselves of legal advice, the custody officer encourages them to do so. The suspect would then, at best, be led to a cell to remain there for around an hour, eventually to be taken to the interrogation room where the "para-legal" would sit, more or less mute, as the police officer asked the questions that would have been asked an hour before. The "ploy" in this case would be to ensure that the suspect had spent the hour "cooling his heals", a tactic common before the introduction of legislation. "Staring at the cell walls" for an hour or more was thought to add pressure to the suspect so that they would be eager to confess and thus avoid the claustrophobia of languishing in a cell. Whichever course the custody officer took could, therefore, be seen as "ploy" designed to disadvantage the suspect. (See also Dixon 1997)

This is not to say that police officers do not consciously engage in "ploys"; they undoubtedly do and sometimes they stray over the limits of legality. One such ploy came to light in the magazine *Police Review* where an officer wrote to complain that his superior had introduced a policy of removing shoes from suspects while they were held in custody. This was ostensibly to prevent them kicking and damaging the fabric of the "custody suite" (structures not known for their frailty!), but was actually to be used to obtain prints of patterns on soles and heals of footwear to match against similar prints left at the scenes of crime. The legal editor of *Police Review* advised that the practice was almost certainly unlawful (*Police Review*, 8 November 1996).

What the notion of "ploys" implicitly fails to recognize, however, is that rules designed to act as safeguards can easily be turned into resources. For example, it has already been mentioned that the principle of "necessity" was introduced by legislation in effort to encourage the police to use summonses, rather than arrest and charge, as a way of proceeding in less serious cases. There is good reason for doing so: arrest is a greater infringement of liberty and places the suspect in a more obviously vulnerable position – no doubt, that is why it is preferred by police officers. However, the benefits of proceeding by way of summons are less convincing than they might at first appear. Research for the Royal Commission on Criminal Procedure found that summonses took much longer to come to court and, therefore, involved a protracted period of anxiety and uncertainty for the defendant (Gemmill & Morgan-Giles 1980). Moreover, if police interrogate a person in relation to an offence in their own home – a scenario that is much more common when proceeding by way of summons – the latter cannot avail themselves of the rights of an arrested suspect: they cannot have free legal advice and the encounter is very unlikely to be tape-recorded. Now, it might be imagined that conducting the interrogation in a suspect's own home denies police much of the power available to them in the custody suite and thereby advantages the suspect. What this fails to appreciate is the capacity of the police to "take charge" of almost any encounter.

Whether the police use "ploys" or not is less important than the ubiquitous fact that in their relationships with suspects they are imbued with *power* and that power can be exercised in a myriad of ways to keep the suspect at a disadvantage (Choongh 1997).

Silence

This draws our attention to the fact that the suspect is intrinsically at a significant disadvantage whatever the circumstances and virtually all the resources lie in the hands of the police. This was the burden of Irving's evidence to the Royal Commission on Criminal Procedure (Irving & Hilgendorf 1980), in which he argued that the notion of "voluntariness" was absurd within the conditions of custodial interrogation that could not be designed better to achieve psychological dependence and compliance. The notion that by conferring some legal right or other this entire situation would be transformed is simply a legal fantasy. This is neatly illustrated by the controversy that has surrounded the so-called "right of silence" (Criminal Law Revision Committee 1972; Hurd 1987; Report of the Working Group on the Right to Silence 1989; Greer 1990; Greer & Morgan 1990; Easton 1991; Hodgson & McConville 1993; McElree & Starmer 1993; JUSTICE 1994; Morgan & Stephenson 1994; Mansfield 1995). Recent legislation in Britain has sought to curtail the exercise of this right by allowing courts the discretion to allow juries to draw an adverse inference if a person introduces into evidence something not mentioned earlier. In fact, the debate has often bordered on the bizarre with opponents and proponents appearing to argue about nothing of any significance. What is beyond dispute is that only a small minority of suspects avail themselves of the right not to answer some or all of the questions put to them during police interrogation. Moreover, a substantial proportion of those who do exercise this right are still found guilty (Baldwin & McConville 1980; Moston & Williamson 1990; Leng 1993, ibid. 1994; Brown, D. 1994). Supporters of the right argue that exercising this right is not the major obstacle to convicting offenders that their opponents claim. By the same token, of course, its removal is hardly likely to make a substantial difference to the conviction of innocent people. It is largely, in short, an irrelevance.

Nevertheless, it is an intriguing irrelevance: why do so few suspects not avail themselves of the right to remain silent? At the outset, it is worth noting that military personnel who are exposed to the likelihood of capture and interrogation (air crew, reconnaissance patrols, and the like) receive extensive training in counter-interrogation techniques. True, military personnel are likely to be treated much more harshly than civil suspects (McNab 1993), but the extent to which they need preparation testifies to the imperative that people normally feel to reply to questions. As Sykes & Brent (1983) point out, accusations normally evoke admission or denial, not silence. The "normal" reaction to being falsely accused is indignant rebuttal. Remaining silent is even more difficult when one is in custody and confronted by an authority figure upon whom one is wholly reliant. From this perspective, what is remarkable is not that so few remain silent, but that so many manage to do so. The tape or video recording of interrogations, designed to safeguard the interests of the suspect, actually contributes to the pressure on suspects to "give their side of the story". Whirring away, it is silent but stark testament to such aberrant behaviour. Weighed against these pressures, whether the police utter some mumbo-jumbo about failing to mention at the time of the interrogation something on which the suspect will later rely in court is unlikely to be of any material significance.

There is a final consideration to bear in mind, and that is that suspects may not *want* to remain silent. Smith has recently cited evidence suggesting that the majority of suspects genuinely did not want legal advice (Smith 1997). Moreover, many suspects lack the personal resources with which to exercise their rights – whatever those rights may be. Gudjonsson has estimated that a substantial *majority* of suspects suffer intellectual impairment, sufficient to prevent them resisting even relatively mild pressure (Gudjonsson *et al.* 1993; Gudjonsson 1994). Moreover, Irving found that many suspects were temporarily incapacitated through their consumption of alcohol or other drugs, or because of temporary distress (Irving & with the assistance of Linden Hilgendorf 1980; Irving 1986). In other words, police do not need to pressurize suspects very much because they are often so vulnerable that they readily succumb.

Involvement of Third Parties

Given the pressures that might be experienced by suspects in custody and their inability to resist them, an obvious safeguard is to ensure that they do not face the experience alone; hence, the provision of free legal advice, which may extend to a legal representative accompanying a suspect during interrogation. Again, the evidence is that this does little to safeguard the suspect: legal representatives are often not legally qualified, attend the station only infrequently, make few interjections during the course of interrogations, rarely advise clients to remain silent and may even persuade suspects to make admissions (Sanders *et al.* 1989; Sanders & Bridges 1993; McConville *et al.* 1994; see also Dixon 1997 for an excellent discussion of legal advisors and the right of silence). The weakness of the protection afforded by legal representatives was dramatically illustrated in the case of the "Cardiff Three", whose convictions for murder were overturned after their confessions were ruled to be inadmissible because of the oppressive interrogation to which they had been subjected – an interrogation attended by the men's solicitor who raised no objection. (See also the case of George Heron whose confession was judged to be inadmissible in almost identical circumstances.)

One of the reasons why lawyers offer such meagre protection is that few legal practices actually show any enthusiasm for representing these clients. Most lawyers regard the social detritus that flows through the custody suites of police stations as unworthy and guilty. They see it as being to everyone's advantage if they plead guilty to whatever crime they have been accused of (McConville *et al.* 1994). Sanders and Bridges go so far as to argue that police and lawyers conspire against the suspect to mislead him or her into believing "that what happens in the station is really not that important, and court is where guilt and innocence is decided" (Sanders & Bridges 1993: 41). This echoes Blumberg's earlier strictures on the United States criminal justice system as operating as a closed community of lawyers and police, to which the defendant is marginal and virtually coerced by the defence attorney to plead to whatever charge has been agreed through prior negotiation (Blumberg 1967). Hence, the long-established process of plea-bargaining works systematically to the disadvantage of most defendants, especially the poor and racial minorities (Newman 1956; *New Law Journal* 1992, ibid. 1993; McConville & Mirsky 1992). According to Dixon's excellent analysis, legal advisors throughout common law jurisdictions generally operate not in an adversarial capacity, but as a part of a negotiating process which serves the actual, but unacknowledged, goal of a criminal justice system – to secure guilty pleas (Dixon 1997).

Another reason why lawyers are not more assertive in their clients' interests is that they develop working relationships with the police. This should not be underestimated, for as Lidstone found when examining the role of magistrate acting as a constitutional restraint on the exercise of police powers, they tend to "rubber stamp" the decisions that officers have taken because they come to trust officers with whom they deal repeatedly (Lidstone 1985). Much the same relationship tends to develop between police and prosecuting agencies. Moody and Tombs (1982) found that under the Scottish system, procurators fiscal (public prosecutors) were largely reliant upon the police whom they were supposed independently to supervise. Much the same pattern of interdependence is not only occurring England since the establishment of the Crown Prosecution Service in the mid-1980s, but being actively pursued as a matter of policy (Mills 1996, ibid. 1996; Weeks 1996; see also *Police Review* [2 February 1996]). Lay visitors to police stations have also quickly become incorporated, co-opted and neutralized (Kemp & Morgan 1989; ibid. 1990).

The weak protection afforded by professional third parties also extends to parents who are supposed to safeguard their children's interests. They are not only frequently ineffective, but can be co-opted by the police into bringing pressure on their children to confess (Wilkinson & Evans 1990; Evans 1993, ibid. 1994). I witnessed a particularly dramatic example of this when I accompanied a woman officer to arrest a youth for indecent exposure; the victim being a neighbour. Upon arrival at the family home, the youth's parents welcomed the officer warmly under the mistaken impression that she had come to investigate the complaint of their daughter who had ironically been the victim of an indecent exposure just a few days previously. When the officer explained the true purpose of her visit, the parents became extremely agitated and for a while I thought we were in danger of being attacked. Eventually, the youth was arrested and taken to the police station, with his father following behind in the family car. Upon arrival, the arresting officer was obliged to find a male detective to conduct the interrogation. The detective who "took" the case read through the statement of complaint from the victim. He casually asked, "What's dad like?". The woman officer replied that he had been convicted of minor offences as a young man, but nothing recently. The detective said, "Let's talk to dad". The father was waiting in the front office and the detective invited him to a private office and suggested that before going to the custody suite the father should read the victim's statement. The father began to do so, but having read a couple of pages and becoming visibly angry as he did so, he thrust the file back into the detective's hand, saying "I've seen enough". We then adjourned to the custody suite. As his son was brought from the detention room the father launched himself at him, striking him several times before startled police officers could drag him away. The father was calmed down and accompanied his son into the interrogation room. When the son declined to answer the detective's questions (it seemed out of shame and embarrassment), his father harshly instructed him to do so. When his answers were indistinctly mumbled, his father roughly told him to speak up. The youth confessed.

The Invitational Edges of Legal Corruption

Taken together this discussion reveals what many might consider to be a disturbing chasm between law and routine police practice. However, for a "chasm" to exist there must be reasonably firm ground either side; but the law is far from firm. Contrary to the popular belief that "the law is the law", procedural limits on police practice are neither clear nor determinate. This will be discussed more fully in the next chapter; suffice it to say for the present that policing is not done "according to the book" because "the book" is simply too voluminous and incomplete. People do not conduct themselves according to rules, because it is impossible to know or retain all the rules that might govern behaviour (Shearing & Ericson 1991). It is certainly true that policing is surrounded by a plethora of rules simply too numerous to retain. Often, the rules remain in obscurity until they are chanced upon. An illustration of this is to be found in Smith's discussion of the law relating to "disturbing the public quiet" (Smith 1982). He reveals that a little-known statutory provision designed to facilitate the removal of intoxicated persons to treatment centres actually succeeds in making it an offence to be in a public place having consumed alcohol – a law of potentially draconian utility if only the police were aware of it!

The police are often depicted as continually straining at the leash of what is legally permissible – a view rightly ridiculed by Reiner as the "law of inevitable increment" (Reiner 1985a). This not only simplistically misrepresents the motivations of police officers, but also the restraining power of the law. For in reality the law is very imprecise and fluid as statutes are interpreted and common law developed by judges considering actual cases. For the police, this means that the limits of their powers are always unknown and unknowable, even when they delude themselves into believing that they do know where those limits lie. Yet the pretence is maintained that police are mere servants of the law, acting in accordance with its precepts.

It is this pretence that routinely brings police officers to the invitation edges of legal malpractice. Policing cannot be done "according to the book", but they must pretend that it can. Thus, self-conscious rule-bending and breaking is endemic in policing, as, of course, it is in many other bureaucracies. The problem, of course, is that it brings officers to the invitational edge of more serious corruption. Police are enticed over the "invitational edge" of legal corruption into practices like "verballing", that is attributing incriminating statements to the suspect that were not uttered at all, by a very potent and perverse inducement – the search for *justice*. If detectives firmly believe that suspects have committed serious crimes, they may see little difference between building the strongest possible case they can and flagrantly concocting evidence. The prospect of substantively guilty people (in the view of the police) escaping justice because of procedural impediments to securing conviction involves officers in corrupt activities that are done in the service a *higher ideal*. This is referred to in police circles as "noble cause corruption" (Gibbons 1995), because it is not self-serving but altruistic, albeit that in the long term it undermines the whole edifice of criminal justice (see also Brodeur 1981).

An example of "noble cause corruption" is provided by Wright and Irving who suggest that it epitomizes the kind of dilemma that officers routinely face.

> In this case, a young officer on plain clothes work was keeping observation near some commercial premises. They had information that the premises were to be broken-into. It was a summer night and they expected that the break-in would take place after dark. The officer was working with a colleague with whom he was in radio contact.
>
> They had been keeping watch on the premises for about three hours when he heard a disturbance behind a fence in the garden from [where] he was keeping watch. A man climbed over the fence and went towards the commercial building. The officer then lost sight of him. He called up his colleagues on the radio and told him what was happening but continued to keep watch. Shortly afterwards, there was a commotion from near the building and a person crashing through the undergrowth and fencing in the adjoining gardens, behind the fence from which the first man had come. He decided to give chase to this second person. By the time he had got over the fences, the person had got away.
>
> He then went to help his colleague and found him struggling with the first man. Together they subdued him and took him out into the adjacent road, which had street lighting. The man started to struggle again but they managed to contact the police control room for transport. When they got back to the police station, the officer who had been in the garden dealt with the prisoner, searched him and placed him in a cell. His colleagues went back to the scene of the observation with a sergeant. When they returned, they said they had found a window broken at the rear of the commercial premises. As a result, the more experienced officer charged the prisoner with burglary.
>
> This surprised the officer but he waited until he could speak to his colleague in private. He told him that he was sure he would have heard the sound of glass breaking if the man had actually got that far. Was it old damage? His

> colleague said, "You are being naïve. We are not letting him get away with that. There has to be a broken window. Just leave it at that." (Wright & Irving 1996: 208)

Lest it be imagined that only police officers are enticed into deviancy by the perverse pursuit of justice, consider this general description of social work practice:

> In its day-to-day activity on behalf of its client-misfits over matters of housing, debts, evictions, the struggle to get through this day to the next; and in its quarrelsome engagements with other professional bodies (doctors, lawyers, teachers) and the powerful agencies of government, mainstream social work takes part in "moral hustling" which defends the weak and gives them a voice against the powerful. . . . The "inside codes" of social work's occupational culture – those codes which are unwritten (or only half-written) – are filled with this rebellious spirit. A study of "industrial deviance" in social work demonstrates a wide-spread acceptance of rule-bending and rule-breaking among social workers "as part of the job". Violations of parole conditions and probation orders are ignored; "blind eyes" are turned towards welfare recipients who bend and break the rules of social-security benefit schemes. An important source of this professional deviance (if that is what it is) lies in the occupational socialisation of recruits. In education programmes they are introduced to the critical concepts of social science and to a "professional vision" of an alternative system of welfare which transcends the shortcomings of the welfare state. Faced with the realities of their working conditions, and their function within the welfare state, this industrial deviance sometimes becomes the only means by which social workers are able to exercise a measure of control over their work and realise the objectives (on behalf of their clients) which conform to the standards of the "professional vision" of welfare. It is, therefore, industrial deviance which helps them to secure the objectives for which they are led to believe they are trained and paid. (Pearson 1975: 136–7)

Excessive Force

As noted in Chapter 1, police do not often use force, but like recourse to law it is a resource that is available for the resolution of incidents. It can stretch from officers positioning their bodies in a confrontational mode ("squaring up") through to the use of lethal force. It is the ultimate expression of police authority and, like other components of that authority, it can be abused so that police become the proverbial "judge, jury and (in some cases literally) executioner". In fact, the abuse of force is remarkably structured, a pattern that remains consistent across a wide variety of jurisdictions. Like other forms of police deviancy discussed above, the abuse of force arises out of normal policing which brings officers to the "invitational edges" of this form of corruption.

Normal Force

The "invitational edge" in the case of the use of force does not arise surreptitiously from practices that are innocuous, but is intrinsic to the activity itself. On the one hand, police officers are duty-bound to use force where appropriate, but *only* where appropriate. Where force is used inappropriately it becomes *ipso facto* an assault. Officers are, therefore, invited by the police mandate to engage in activity that is inherently problematic for it hinges not on whether force is or is not used, but its appropriateness. The problem that lies at the heart of this issue is the difficulty of deciding when force is excessive. Clearly, this cannot be determined by the sheer amount of force used, because in some circumstances even the most extreme force might well be justified. Moreover, what is appropriate may be perceived differently from various perspectives, not the least important of which is the perspective of the person using force. In judging how much force is appropriate one must keep in mind the legal aphorism, "detached reflection cannot be demanded in the presence of an uplifted knife" (quoted in Ashworth 1975: 300). So a person, including a police officer, might perceive a threat where there is none and use a significant measure of force in countering it, and act entirely lawfully. Thus, in one English case, a police officer had arrested and handcuffed a man, and on arrival at the police station was seen by a superior to "drag Mr Ball from the rear of a police car and punch him to the ground, where he continued to kick and punch him, delivering 11 to 15 blows". However, the court accepted the officer's defence that "*en route to* the station, Mr Ball was aggressive and threatened him and his family, Mr Ball then tried to headbutt him when he attempted to get him out of the car.... after dragging [the suspect] from the car, they fell to the ground and he had to punch Mr Ball twice in order to restrain him after Mr Ball tried to bite him during the struggle" (*Police Review*, 1 August 1997). On the other hand, the court in another case rejected the defence that an officer struck a detained suspect across the face in order to calm him down (*Police Review*, 21 March 1997). Thus, the injunction to use force only when necessary creates an imprecise guide: the same measure of force might be deemed appropriate in some circumstances and a criminal assault in others. One implication of this is that the police may use force in the course of their work, but whether or not it was "lawful" is not decided until after the fact.

When considered more generally, perspectives on what constitutes appropriate force differ widely. For example, the term "brutality" is applied by members of the public across a wide spectrum of behaviour from the merest incivility to a brutal beating (Bayley 1996). Those with different social and political attitudes are likely to view the same actions quite differently. Thus, Portuguese research found that radical and conservative students differed in their interpretation of aggressive behaviour by suspects and police (cited in Flanagan & Vaughn 1996). On the other hand, officers do not always recognize that they have actually used force at all in certain circumstances (Adams 1996). Indeed if "force" is defined as broadly as it sometimes is, then it pervades policing; it is difficult to imagine an arrest that does not involve some measure of force, however slight. Given these ambiguities and disparities of perception, whether officers are accused of "brutality" or kindred offences is experienced by them as an arbitrary contingency and not something over which they have much control.

The use of force places police officers in an anomic situation: on the one hand they are duty-bound to do so and such action may be celebrated. On the other hand, the division between lawful and unlawful use of force is decidedly unclear and the penalties for error can be draconian.

Forcefully Terminating a Course of Action

Apart from the ambiguity that surrounds the exact location of the "invitational edge" of excessive force, officers might be brought to it, not through malign intent, but incompetence. Binder and Scharf (1980) point out that the use of lethal force by American officers is almost invariably the terminal point of a more or less protracted process of interaction in which, had other actions by the officer been taken at an earlier stage an alternative outcome may well have resulted. Unfortunately, the law does not share this breadth of perspective and only is concerned with whether the force used was justified or not in the *immediate circumstances*. Thus, to take an extreme example, officers might place themselves needlessly in jeopardy, but having done so then used no more force than was appropriate to extricate themselves from that situation. Considering the entire circumstances, the use of force could be considered unnecessary had more prudence been shown earlier in the encounter. Such a scenario is brilliantly captured in Joseph Wambaugh's fictional account of how officers Roscoe Rules and "Whaddayamean" Dean started a small riot when they were called to quell a quarrel between an African-American and his Mexican neighbour in a squalid tenement building – an incident that was beginning to peter out by the time they arrived. The officers separate the parties, both of whom are construction workers carrying "hods" containing building materials:

> "I don't want no more trouble outta you," Roscoe whispered when he got the hod carrier to a private place.
>
> "I ain't gonna give you no trouble, Officer," the black man said, looking up at the mirthless blue eyes of Roscoe Rules which were difficult to see because like most hotdogs he wore his cap tipped forward until the brim almost touched his nose.
>
> "Don't argue with me, man!" Roscoe said. His nostrils splayed as he sensed the fear on the man who stood hangdog before him.
>
> "What's you name?" Roscoe then demanded.
>
> "Charles ar–uh Henderson," the hod carrier answered, and then added impatiently, "Look, I wanna go back inside with my family. I'm tired a all this and I just wanna go to bed. I worked hard . . ."
>
> But Roscoe became enraged at the latent impudence and snarled, "Look here, Charles ar–uh Henderson, don't you be telling me what you're gonna do. I'll tell you when you can go back inside and maybe you won't be going back inside at all. Maybe you're gonna be going to the slam tonight!"
>
> "What for? I ain't done nothin. What right you got . . ."
>
> "Right? Right?" Roscoe snarled, spraying the hod carrier with saliva. "Man, one more word and I'm gonna book your ass! I'll personally lock you in the slammer! I'll set your hair on fire!"
>
> Whaddayermean Dean called down to Roscoe and suggested that they switch hod carriers. As soon as they had, he tried in vain to calm the outraged black man.
>
> A few minutes later he heard Roscoe offer some advice to the Mexican hod carrier: "If that loudmouth bitch was my old lady I'd kick her in the cunt".
>
> Twenty years ago the Mexican had broken a full bottle of beer over the head of a man for merely smiling at his woman. Twenty years ago, when she was a

lithe young girl with a smooth sensuous belly, he would have shot to death any man, cop or not, who would dare to refer to her as a bitch.

Roscoe Rules knew nothing of machismo and did not even sense the slight almost imperceptible flickering of the left eyelid of the Mexican. Nor did he notice that those burning black eyes were no longer pointed somewhere between the shield and necktie of Roscoe Rules, but were fixed on his face, at the browless blue eyes of the tall policeman.

"Now you two act like men and shake hands so we can leave," Roscoe ordered.

"Huh?" the Mexican said incredulously, and even the black hod carrier looked up in disbelief.

"I said shake hands. Let's be men about this. The fight's over and you'll feel better if you shake hands"

"I'm forty-two years old." The Mexican said softly, the eyelid flickering more noticeably. "Almost old enough to be your father. I ain't shaking hands like no kid on the playground."

"You'll do what I say or sleep in the slammer," Roscoe said, remembering how in school everyone felt better and even drank beer after a good fight.

"What charge?" demanded the Mexican, his breathing erratic now. "What fuckin' charge?"

"You both been drinking," Roscoe said, losing confidence in his constituted authority, but infuriated by the insolence which was quickly undermining what he thought was a controlled situation.

Roscoe, like most black-gloved cops, believed implicitly that if you ever backed down even for a moment in dealing with assholes and scrotes the entire structure of American law enforcement would crash to the ground in a mushroom cloud of dust.

"We ain't drunk," the Mexican said. "I had a can of beer when I got home from work. One goddamn can!" He spoke in accented Cholo English: staccato, clipped, just as he did when he was a respected gang member.

Then Roscoe Rules pushed him back into an alcove away from the eyes of those down the hall who had made their own peace by now and were preparing to go back into their apartments to fix dinner. Roscoe pulled his baton from the ring and hated this sullen Mexican and the glowering black man and even Whaddayamean Dean whose nervousness enraged Roscoe because if you ever let these scrotes think you were afraid . . .

Then Roscoe looked around, guessing there were a dozen people between them and the radio car, and started to realize that this was not the time or place. But the Mexican made Roscoe Rules forget that it was the wrong time and place when he looked at the tall policeman with the harder crueller larger body and said, "I never let a man talk to me like this. You better book me or you better let me go but don't you talk to me like this anymore or . . . or . . ."

"Or? Or?" Roscoe said, his hairless brows throbbing as he touched the small man on the chest with the tip of his stick. "You Mexicans're all alike. Think you're tough, huh? Bantam-weight champ at this garbage dump, huh? I oughtta tear that oily moustache off your face."

Then the flickering eyelid was still and the eyes glazed over. "Go ahead," the Mexican barely whispered.

And Roscoe Rules did. A second later the Mexican was standing there with a

> one inch piece of his right moustache and the skin surrounding it in Roscoe Rules' left hand, The raw flesh began to spot at once with pinpoints of blood.
>
> Then the Mexican screamed and kicked Roscoe Rules in the balls. (Wambaugh 1976: 31–34)

Well, you can probably imagine the rest, pretty soon there is complete mayhem; the hod carriers combine against their common enemy; both cops get beaten to a pulp; back-up arrives; five people are arrested; and the two hod carriers end up in jail!

While written with the licence of the novelist, like so much else of his writing, Wambaugh identifies in a single incident the patterns of police use of force and excessive force: it occurs during the course of routine "peacekeeping"; involving marginalized sections of the population; in which the assertion of authority is resisted in the presence of others; and concludes with the arrest of the abused citizen. Let us consider each of these components separately.

Routine "Peacekeeping"

Excessive force is not the preserve of special kinds of police task, but pervades all aspects of policing. Officers in Maguire and Corbett's research claimed that they had been surprised by the receipt of a complaint and that the incident was not out of the ordinary (Maguire & Corbett 1991). As we have noted already, most ordinary police work is of a diffuse "order maintenance" variety in which, as Goldsmith points out, decisions are rarely clear-cut and rely on personal judgement (Goldsmith 1991). Thus, it is no surprise that it is in connection with routine "peacekeeping" that officers are most likely to receive a complaint (Hudson 1970). These are often the kind of volatile and unpredictable circumstances that officers regard as "complaints prone" (Maguire & Corbett 1991). They are also circumstances in which officers typically resort to informal methods of "imposing provisional solutions" in ways they "brook no opposition" (Bittner 1970); which are readily experienced by those against whom they are used as the police "throwing their weight about". Maguire and Corbett found that almost all the more serious complaints of assault appeared to have resulted from "mutual antagonism [that] soon escalated into a fight or struggle in which both sides alleged violence by the other" (Maguire & Corbett 1991: 116). From there it is but a short step to goading someone into taking a swing at the officer so that force can be used in "self-defence". If an arrest is made, the non-compliant suspect might find that handcuffs are applied tightly or he is forced face down to "eat dirt".

"Contempt of Cop"

In order maintenance police are particularly reliant upon their authority to control the situation, but if that authority is denied, police in Anglo–Saxon jurisdictions have few legal powers with which to enforce it.

> English law does not recognise the continental doctrine of *rebellion* which requires a person to acquiesce in the unlawful use of official force against him, seeking such civil remedies as may be available subsequently. In this country, a person may use preventive force where a policeman wrongfully insists upon attempting to do that which is unlawful. (Smith, A.T.H. 1987: 186.)

If those present do not succumb to police authority officers are virtually obliged to use their "ability to embarrass, humiliate, and even harm the citizen" as a form of more or less illicit power (Goldsmith 1991: 17). Officers invade the personal space of others, shout at and threaten them with all manner of penalties, unless they comply. It is this coercion of deference from citizens that gives coherence to Worden's finding that the most important predictors of recourse to force are resistance by the suspect and the demeanour of the citizen/suspect (Worden 1996). This raises the question: what is "resistance" and to *what* do people resist? "Resistance" need only be symbolic: youngsters who affect the style of the "tough guy" are likely to feel the full weight of the law (Piliavin & Briar 1964; Black & Reiss 1970; Lundman *et al.* 1978); and even the breaking of an "adjacency pair" is likely to lead to the otherwise rare display of overt police coercion (Sykes & Brent 1983). In these circumstances, officers employ their battery of "resource charges" (Chatterton 1976b) in support of their authority; but that itself involves an act of force as the arrest is made and those who resist symbolically might be prone to translate that into physical resistance when faced with arrest.

Another way of "resisting" the police symbolically is to act as a "smart arse" or "wise guy". This is a form of resistance that better-educated, sometimes middle-class people are prone to. As Sykes and Clark (1975) note, apart from lower-class racial minorities, police find encounters with high-status groups equally difficult, and for the same reason – they do not defer, indeed they demand deference from the police. This may explain a distinct category of complaints against police from middle-class, middle-aged motorists who have no previous convictions and accuse officers of incivility. Maguire and Corbett (1991) conclude that these typically arise from "discussions" between police and motorists that get out of hand. Equally, the allegedly uncivil behaviour of which motorists complain, might reflect attempts by officers verbally to coerce deference in the face of resistance.

Motorists also figure in a particular form of "resistance": the failure or refusal of drivers to stop their vehicles when ordered to do so by the police. This, of course, was the spur to the most notorious act of police violence, the beating of Rodney King, about which much has been written. It is important, however, to recognize that what distinguished King was not the beating he suffered, but the fact that George Holliday made a videorecording of it. Arthur McDuffie was an African–American beaten to death by officers in Miami after he also refused to stop when commanded to do so (Kappeler *et al.* 1994). Refusing to stop when ordered to do so by the police is a direct challenge to their authority and is likely to prompt a forceful response.

"Contempt of cop" is felt most acutely when there is an audience in front of whom the police feel obliged to maintain respect. This explains Worden's finding that the use of force was *more* likely when others were present than when they were not (Worden 1996; see also Maguire & Corbett 1991), for it is more imperative for the police to retain "face" in public than it is in private. Hence, when officers acting collectively confront a group of people and assert their authority, this is more likely to result in a serious complaint (Maguire & Corbett 1991). This is so particularly if the officers are members of a Special Patrol Group who, as specialists in aggressive confrontation, are probably unwilling to back down in any such encounter. It was precisely this brew that led a highly publicized incident in recent British police history – the "Holloway Road incident" (Holdaway 1986) – when members of a District Support Unit savagely assaulted three youths who had been disrespectful towards them. However, the administration of "street justice" is no recent development: Cohen (1979) describes how police in the East End of London in the 1930s used their rolled capes to administer a stinging blow to those who denied them respect; and Brogden's (1991) and Weinberger's (1995) respective oral histories reveal routine and casual recourse to violence that only rarely erupted into scandals (Judge 1994).

There is general agreement among police in various jurisdictions that they are entitled to use force to ensure deference (Westley 1953, ibid. 1970). Kappeler *et al.* (1994) argue that just as delinquents employ what Sykes and Matza called "techniques of neutralization" (Sykes & Matza 1957), so too do the police. An example is provided by Punch quoting an Amsterdam police officer:

> If someone gets thumped here then he has earned it because no one likes to hit someone. You hear about people getting a thump that is not justified but that has not happened when I've been around. We have kicked people down the stairs but then it was someone who had tried to knife us or who had spat in our faces, and we're not accepting that. But I consider that a normal human reaction. (Punch 1979a: 81)

Through accounts such as this officers dilute or deny their own deviancy and convince themselves that those whom they abuse "deserve it". What Kappeler *et al.* overlook is, as I argued in the previous chapter, that these "techniques of neutralization" are not just deployed to deflect the implications of overtly deviant acts, but permeate normal policing. Police work entails the routine use of coercion and in order to retain their belief in their own rectitude, officers must constantly affirm that those against whom coercion is used do "deserve it". Thus, normal policing brings officers to the "invitational edge" of neutralizing their own deviancy and that of others. Added to the loyalty that is expected of peers, this produces the "blue curtain" and "code of silence" (Stoddard 1968) that impedes, if not defeats, the subsequent investigation of complaints of brutality.

Marginalized People

Reflecting the pattern of routine policing, such confrontations tend overwhelmingly to involve encounters with marginal sections of the population, especially young lower-class members of racial minority groups. Thus, in Reiss's discussion of brutality (Reiss 1968), it is a pair of alcoholics and then an African-American psychiatric patient who are roughed up, whereas respectable citizens are deferred to. In Wambaugh's story, Roscoe Rules regards the inhabitants of the cockroach-infested tenement in which the altercation described above takes place as no more than "scrotes". This is a category of person who, in police eyes, does not deserve, and only rarely receives, the respect offered to respectable people, even when the latter violate the law.

Such negative stereotyping is reciprocated by those to whom it is applied, according to Uildriks' and Mastrigt's (1991) ethnography of a deprived Scottish housing project characterized by a "toughness culture". Hence, a self-reinforcing cycle of hostility and anonymosity develops in which residents deny police legitimacy and assistance, and police assert their authority forcefully. "In certain circumstances the police may then come to regard the use of violence as a legitimate means of dealing with people, in the belief that the only language certain people understand is fear and rough treatment" (Uildriks & van Mastrigt 1991: 143).

Arrest of the Abused Citizen

Confirmation that the abused person "deserved it" can often be secured by arresting them. Here too, the gap between normal and deviant practice is less than might be imagined. For if "resource charges" can be routinely employed for expedient purposes during the course of routine policing, they can be used equally expediently for the purpose of "guarding one's back" against complaints. Russell suggests, but on the basis of precious little evidence, that this is what police do to deflect a potential complaint (Russell 1986; see also Uildriks & van Mastrigt 1991). More probably, the decision to arrest is an indistinguishable element in the whole chain of interaction that leads to arrest and complaint. Certainly, Maguire and Corbett found that a significant proportion of complaints arose from arrest situations with young men who had previous convictions

> The majority of complaints of assault followed arrest . . . in which the decision to arrest was often taken in difficult or confused circumstances. This may partly explain the fact that only about 60 per cent of those arrested were later charged with an offence. (Maguire & Corbett 1991: 44)

Lethal Force

Although recourse to potentially lethal force involves a qualitative leap in the quantum of force employed, many of the factors identified above continue to exert their influence. It is just as impossible to stipulate in advance what would amount to the improper or criminal use of firearms by police, as it is to do so for non-lethal use of force. Even when the person who is shot is found to be unarmed, the officer might have acted entirely properly, for example, fearing that they were reaching for a gun. In an armed confrontation officers are obliged to make "split-second" decisions that are inevitably prone to genuine error (Greenwood 1975; Waddington 1991).

Who gets shot, mistakenly or otherwise, is not a random occurrence however, but conforms to a clear pattern: it is marginal sections of the population who are most at risk. In the United States it is African–Americans who have traditionally been at greatest risk. This led to a protracted debate in which it was claimed that the imbalance was simply the most extreme expression of police racism (see, for example, Goldkamp 1982; Meyer 1982; Takagi 1982). As Chevigny (1995) has documented, throughout the western hemisphere a consistent pattern emerges of illicit force being used against marginal sections of the population who challenge police authority (see also Birkbeck & Gabaldon 1996). However, Fyfe (1982b) was able to show that racial differences among those whom the police shot were explicable by such factors as the greater involvement of racial minority victims in serious armed crime. Liska and Yu (1992) argue that police use of deadly force is highest where there is a large non-white local population, combined with a high homicide rate and relatively small police department. Their explanation for this is that under these circumstances officers generally have a heightened sense of threat. This suggests that while individual acts of violence by police officers may be justified, exposure to lethal force is concentrated among the most marginalized sections of the population where crime and disorder flourish.

The Invitational Edge of Assassination

A distinction needs to drawn between shootings under dubious conditions and the assassination of those whom the police decide are "bad people" who deserve to die. The latter also occurs in accordance with a pattern. Police are enticed over the invitational edge by a culture that portrays the police as engaged in a "*war* on crime", where officers are authoritatively given licence to regard the "policed" population in general, and criminal suspects in particular, as an "enemy". According to some commentators (Christopher 1991; Skolnick & Fyfe 1993; Chevigny 1995), this is what happened in Los Angeles: the LAPD had an aggressive militaristic organizational culture, the consequences of which burst onto the television screens of the world with the video-taped beating of Rodney King. Within this culture specialist squads with a penchant for apparently shooting first and asking questions later prospered. One such squad was the Special Investigation Section (SIS), whose nineteen officers had been responsible for 23 killings, wounding 23 more and shooting at and missing at least 20 others, during its first 23 years of operation. This amounts to one in 20 of this squad's arrest attempts resulting in a shooting (Skolnick & Fyfe 1993). Nor was this a peculiarity of the LAPD. Another American police department with an unenviable reputation for violence was that of Philadelphia, whose mayor, Frank Rizzo, celebrated his "tough" reputation.

> During Rizzo's eight years as Philadelphia's mayor, fatal shootings by PPD officers increased by about 20 per cent annually. In a study conducted for the US Justice Department, [it was reported that] while individual Philadephia cops were no more likely than New York cops to make arrests or to come face to face with armed people, they were *thirty-seven times* as likely as New York cops to shoot unarmed people who had threatened nobody and who were fleeing from suspected nonviolent crimes. (Skolnick & Fyfe 1993, p. 140)

Likewise, the police of Memphis have acquired a comparable reputation for shooting suspects, again fuelled by an organizational culture that emphasizes aggressive law enforcement (Fyfe 1982c). However, such encouragement to aggression is not restricted to the culture of the particular police organization, but often reflects external social, political and economic influences. For instance, the LAPD shares its trigger-happy reputation with the Los Angeles Sheriff's Department whose most senior officer is regularly re-elected, unlike the notorious Chief Gates who enjoyed civil-service protection (Chevigny 1995).

A similar pattern can be discerned internationally. As mentioned in an earlier chapter, in Northern Ireland there have been persistent allegations that the security forces have summarily executed suspected terrorists, rather than seeking to arrest them (Asmal 1985; Amnesty International 1988). In the developing countries of Latin America this even took the form of police acting as informal, but officially tolerated, "death squads" who killed homeless children on the streets and other vulnerable groups (Jakubs 1977; Bowden 1978; Huggins & Mesquita 1995; Huggins 1997). It is when the state itself is under direct and credible threat that police violence becomes most extreme. In South Africa, especially during the state of emergency that preceded the eventual collapse of apartheid, the police (along with other agencies of state security) were implicated in numerous killings (Brogden & Shearing 1993; Cawthra

1993; Weitzer & Beattie 1994). However, when states actually begin to fragment then even the depredations of apartheid pale into relative insignificance as police violence becomes genocidal (Hills 1997).

Conclusion

Policing is a scandal-prone occupation, not simply because the opportunities for illicit conduct exist, for they exist in almost any occupation (after all, even academics might corruptly ensure that high marks are awarded to certain students in return for money or favours!). Temptation is more active than that: policing places officers repeatedly at the "invitational edges of corruption" where exactly the same actions may be taken with proper or improper motives (Brodeur 1981). The reason for this is that police operate in a nether world just beyond the limits of respectability. In the fulfilment of their duties officers lie, deceive, conspire to allow illegal activities to continue, and use force. Yet, this can never be acknowledged, for the legitimacy of police authority in liberal democracy rests upon the myth that they impartially enforce the law according to "the book". This creates the "Dirty Harry problem", as Klockars has defined it (Klockars 1980): the police routinely use socially disapproved means of achieving socially desirable ends. In this condition of classic anomie, officers are repeatedly tempted to secure their purposes, which are often the same as those of the police organization itself, by exploiting the latitude that their role affords them. This might involve the accepting of bribes from, and performing corrupt services for, those with whom they are invited to establish close rapport; or it might amount to "gilding the lily" to ensure that those they believe to be guilty are convicted; or using excessive force against those who challenge or threaten them. These temptations are captured in the film "Dirty Harry" when the hero commits a string of legal violations, including excessive force, in order to extract from a psychopathic killer the whereabouts of a young girl he has kidnapped. She is dead by the time the police discover her body, but the psychopath escapes judicial penalty.

However, these are not socially indiscriminate practices, but bear hardest – like lawful routine policing itself – on those who are most socially marginal. In societies where there is a large and threatening underclass, police misconduct is endemic. In more developed societies, especially where notions of universal citizenship are firmly established, it is more restrained both quantitatively and qualitatively. Yet, the public in many societies tacitly conspire in police illegality, provided it is targeted at excluded groups and does not erupt into a public scandal.

CHAPTER 6

Controlling Police Officers

Introduction

As the preceding discussion of police deviancy highlights, without effective control the power *legitimately* to coerce fellow citizens may become corrupted into the *illegitimate* power to render the rights of citizenship nugatory. Such is the classical constitutional dilemma: who guards the guardians? It is a dilemma that arises both in relation to controlling the discretionary actions of individual officers and also in controlling the policies and procedures of the police organization. In this chapter I will consider whether and how the actions of police officers can be controlled, and what this tells us about policing as an occupation. In the next chapter the focus will be upon the control of the police *organization.*

Regulating Police Wrongdoing

A central tenet of democratic theory is that the state, through its officials, exercises only such powers over citizens as those citizens have granted to it. Unlike an autocratic state, officials cannot simply do as they wish; their powers are circumscribed by rules and they are subject to penalties if those rules are violated. In most liberal democracies the rules governing policing and their enforcement operate at two levels, internal-bureaucratic procedures and legal action. Like officials in any bureaucracy, police officers are subject to internal rules governing how they conduct themselves; for example, virtually all police forces stipulate how officers should dress, keep records of their activities and relate to superiors. In addition, police officers are usually subject to internal rules governing their relationship with citizens. Thus, in Britain, officers may not "abuse their authority" or act with "incivility" when encountering a member of the public. Suspected violations of these internal rules are investigated through internal complaints procedures, often by fellow police officers in more or less specialized departments (commonly referred to as "Internal Affairs", "Complaints and Discipline"), and adjudicated upon by superiors. Police officers might also commit criminal offences in the course of their duties, such as assault, and allegations of criminal wrongdoing will normally initiate an investigation and possible prosecution through the criminal courts. It is immediately apparent that there is enormous overlap between internal disciplinary and external criminal procedures: officers suspected of wrongdoing are usually investigated by other police officers, their guilt or innocence is adjudicated by a formal tribunal and they are subject to penalties if found guilty. In many instances, the allegations made against an officer will incorporate both internal disciplinary and criminal misconduct. For example, an officer who allegedly assaults a person is also very likely to be accused of incivility or abuse of authority. It should also be borne in mind that any criminal wrongdoing and some breaches of internal discipline will also constitute civil wrongs that might give rise to action in the civil courts. Therefore, in this section I will conflate both levels of regulation and consider how the conduct of police officers is regulated by these essentially punitive methods and assess how effective is that regulation.

Purpose?

It seems obvious that the purpose of disciplinary and legal regulation is to prevent the occurrence of wrongdoing in the first place. However, regulation might serve other functions apart from prevention.

Substantiation?

A universal feature of police regulatory mechanisms that have been studied is that only a tiny proportion of all allegations of wrongdoing are substantiated despite plentiful evidence of widespread police misconduct (Decker & Wagner 1982; Goldsmith 1991). During the 1980s of around 30,000 complaints made annually in Britain, the substantiation rate for complaints never exceeded six per cent and it was much less for allegations of assault, incivility and oppressive conduct (Maguire & Corbett 1991). The failure to substantiate more than a small proportion of allegations of wrongdoing is widely thought to bring the complaints system into disrepute. Lustgarten, commenting on the very low substantiation rate for assault and the *zero* rate for harassment, racial discrimination, giving false evidence or perjury, comments that "Either those who do bother to complain are all liars, or there is something wrong with the system" (Lustgarten 1986: 154).

While low substantiation rates appear damning at first sight, we should not uncritically view the process only from the perspective of the complainant and accept the tacit assumption that substantiation is the principle criterion of "success" (Reiner 1991b). The notion that there is some non-zero rate of substantiation that confers credibility on the regulatory process is open to the objections that, first, it is arbitrary. What rate *would* satisfy critics that the system was working satisfactorily? Secondly, it is akin to criticisms of criminal trials that fail to convict a sufficient proportion of those considered "obviously guilty". The issue is: "obvious" to *whom*? A problem of all adjudication is that while evidence may be sufficient to arouse strong suspicions of guilt, it may be insufficient to justify imposing a penalty. There may indeed be "evidence" of widespread police misconduct, without that evidence being sufficient in individual cases to establish the guilt of those against whom allegations have been made. Thirdly, like other official statistics produced within the criminal justice system, those relating to complaints against the police are not all that they seem. A proportion of those initially reported are subsequently withdrawn, not proceeded with or informally resolved.

There are, as we shall see shortly, questions that arise from this process of attrition, but if attention is paid only to complaints that are fully investigated, then the proportion of cases in which some action was taken against a police officer in Britain was eight per cent in 1990. Moreover, if the unit of measurement is cases rather than specific complaints (and one case could generate several complaints) then action is taken in over twelve per cent (Maguire & Corbett 1991). A further complication is that there can be more than one outcome to the complaints process. In the British system officers may officially be given "advice", indicating that superiors are satisfied that their actions failed to live up to expected standards while not amounting to a clear breach of the rules. Tait (1994) draws the interesting parallel between the adjudication of allegations of assault brought against police officers *and juveniles*. He argues that both escape punishment to roughly the same degree and suggests that, like juveniles, police officers benefit from "diversionary" schemes. In addition, superiors have available to them a range of informal sanctions that they can use. For example, a London Metropolitan officer was removed from consideration for promotion following an *unsubstantiated* complaint made against him (*Police Review*, 23 August 1996). Russell calculates that some action (formal or informal) is taken against an officer against whom a complaint has been made in around a quarter of cases (Russell 1986). Some researchers have suggested that one reason for complaints being withdrawn is that complainants are re-assured that informal action will indeed be taken (Maguire & Corbett 1991).

The problems of low substantiation are not restricted to internal complaints mechanisms, but also affect the trial of police officers for alleged criminal offences whose conviction rates are much lower than for other defendants. Under the Scottish system, Uildriks and Mastrigt found that the substantiation rate for officers brought before internal disciplinary hearings was much higher than for a criminal trial, so much so that:

> In terms of effectiveness and, in consequence, of deterrent value, the disciplinary procedure would thus seem to have the advantage over the criminal procedure. From such a perspective it might be tempting to consider the disciplinary rather than the criminal procedure as the main mechanism for dealing with police violence. (Uildriks & van Mastrigt 1991: 131)

Low substantiation rates are important not only because they may or may not reflect whether justice has been done in individual cases, but also for their deterrent value. Many radical critics regard low rates as indicating that police may violate the rules that supposedly govern their conduct with impunity and thus receive tacit encouragement to continue doing so. After examining the regulation of police in South Africa, Northern Ireland, England and the United States, Haysom concludes that because of the infrequency with which officers are found guilty of disciplinary or legal violations, none of the systems offers a satisfactory means of controlling police conduct (Haysom 1989). However, as Reiner points out, this is a curious inversion of normal criminological thinking.

> For years, critical criminology has pointed out the fallacies of the law-and-order deterrence equation that tougher laws plus more police power equals less crime....
>
> Shouldn't police deviance be approached in the same way? Yet in much left-wing writing it appears that sauce for the crook is not sauce for the constable. The spurned deterrence model for crime control is unreflectingly adopted for cop control. (Reiner 1985d: 126)

Strangely, perhaps, despite low substantiation rates, police officers *do* seem to experience the threat of punishment as a real and serious likelihood. Bayley and Bittner note in passing that police officers "worry a lot about repercussions from the actions they take" (Bayley & Bittner 1984: 43) and others have pointed to the general preoccupation that officers have with avoiding "trouble" (van Maanen 1974, ibid. 1975; Chatterton 1979, ibid. 1983; Norris 1989). This, of course, is not the same as avoiding actions that might prompt a complaint, for as Maguire and Corbett discovered, almost all officers receive at least one complaint during their careers and many of them view complaints as an unavoidable exigency (Maguire & Corbett 1991). The avoidance of "trouble" might even promote rule-breaking as officers engage in various tactics to "cover their back", such as perjuring themselves to ensure that the "paper reality" gives no hostages to fortune. Whether the preoccupation with "trouble" and "guarding one's back" has positive or negative consequences, what cannot be maintained is that police officers are cavalier about the prospects of complaints being made against them. This is probably due to the severity of the penalties that officers face if found guilty, however unlikely that might be. It is another expression of the anomic nature of policing in liberal democracies that officers must continually live with the prospect of suffering severe threats to their careers and/or liberty as the price of doing their duty.

Legitimacy?

Apart from any deterrent effect that they might have, regulatory mechanisms have other wider implications. As Bayley remarks, "civilian review is critical to the legitimacy of the police. Its purpose is not simply to punish erring individuals but to demonstrate to communities that the police are responsible as an institution" (Bayley 1991b: ix). Because the police wield such power over their fellow citizens, they are obliged "to reassure the public that such coercive powers are not being used excessively or repressively and to demonstrate that any specific allegations of their abuse are thoroughly and impartially investigated" (Maguire & Corbett 1991: 11). In this respect it is probably more important that "justice is *seen* to be done" than that it is actually done in practice. The Police Federation of England and Wales believe that a system in which the police investigate themselves lacks credibility and recognize a general public demand for a wholly independent system (Market & Opinion Research International Limited 1984).

A further paradox is that a legitimate system of regulation might prompt more, rather than less, complaints from the public. The long-term reduction in the number of complaints in Britain might indicate, not an improvement in police conduct, but a general and growing *lack* of confidence in the process of investigation and adjudication (Maguire & Corbett 1991). Reforms that restored confidence might reciprocally lead to an alarming rise in complaints. Goldsmith argues that the number of complaints received should be seen, not as pathological, but as "*normal* and *democratic*" (Goldsmith 1991: 18 original emphasis). Policing is, by its nature, an occupation that is likely to attract complaints and the willingness to complain should be regarded as a vote of confidence in the system for investigating wrongdoing. Goldsmith argues that it is when policing is most in need of reform that public confidence is lowest and aggrieved citizens feel least inclined to register their complaints.

Neither grievances nor confidence in complaints processes are evenly spread throughout the population. As has been repeatedly emphasized throughout this book, policing bears down most heavily upon marginalized sections of the population. This leads Goldsmith (1991) to argue that it is among such groups that the credibility of police regulation needs most crucially to be maintained. Support for this position can easily be found in the reports of various commissions of inquiry into outbreaks of urban disorder in deprived neighbourhoods over the past three decades (Kerner 1968; Cameron *et al.* 1969; Scarman 1981; Christopher 1991), which frequently draw attention to long-standing hostility to the police in such areas and lack of confidence in complaints mechanisms. On the other hand, since marginality is associated with political powerlessness, a police force that enjoys the legitimacy of the bulk of citizens regrettably can afford to lose the confidence of those on the margins of citizenship.

Satisfaction of Complainants?

Aside from these wider aims of the regulatory process, a more specific criterion of success might be its ability to satisfy complainants. By this criterion few complaints systems seem to achieve much success. Certainly, Maguire and Corbett's survey of complainants found little satisfaction with the British system (Maguire & Corbett 1991). Indeed, the picture painted by their research was strikingly similar to a previous study conducted before reforms had been introduced to enhance the complaints process (Brown 1988). A consistent theme in both studies was dissatisfaction with *procedures rather than outcomes*, and what complainants found most objectionable was that the police investigated complaints themselves. This remained a source of dissatisfaction even when complainants assessed the conduct of the investigating officer positively (as many did). In Maguire and Corbett's research, nearly twice as many complainants thought that their complaint had been "very" or "fairly thoroughly" investigated than thought to the contrary, but this did not translate into general satisfaction with the procedure. "Those who had experienced investigation of their complaints by the police were also the most adamant of our interviewees that the system should be changed to one of investigation by outsiders" (Maguire & Corbett 1991: 63). Where complaints were supervised by the independent Police Complaints Authority levels of dissatisfaction were just as high as they were for unsupervised complaints. Nor was satisfaction much greater when the complaint was substantiated. So, however hard the authorities try, they seem unable to overcome the principled objection that the police should not be seen as "judges in their own cause".

Taken together, this indicates that a system in which the police investigate alleged misconduct of other officers fails to satisfy complainants' belief in "procedural justice" (Kerstetter 1996). In order for this to be satisfied the complaints process would need to become, according to Kerstetter, more adversarial and less inquisitorial. The complainant should be allowed greater control over the process, especially being able to have their say; adjudication must be genuinely and transparently neutral giving due consideration to the complainant's views; and the decision must be explained rather than announced *ex cathedra*. As Maguire and Corbett found, the current British model (which is advanced when compared to those in other western democracies) fails pretty abysmally to satisfy these criteria. Two-thirds of complainants were dissatisfied with the lengthy investigation and lack of explanation for the decision reached. Maguire and Corbett arrive at the telling, albeit pessimistic, conclusion that:

> In sum, as long as the complaints system remains so closely interlinked with the disciplinary system – and, in serious cases, it is difficult to see how it could be uncoupled – there is limited scope for making responses more akin to those provided by other, more "consumer-oriented" organisations (where satisfaction of the complainant is accorded high priority). The position of the complainant against the police remains rather like that of the victim of crime in relation to the criminal justice system: he or she provides the initial input into a large impersonal system, which then takes over the case and processes it largely to meet organisational goals rather than in the interests of the individual. (Maguire & Corbett 1991: 197)

Obstacles and Barriers

The role of the police as investigators of police wrongdoing is felt to make complaints processes akin to that of negotiating a formidable obstacle course that is likely to end in defeat. It gives the police a "stranglehold" on the investigation of even the most serious complaints which explains why officers who have plainly killed suspects illegally still escape punishment in so many different jurisdictions (Harding 1970). A major obstacle is the notorious peer loyalty informally expected of police officers by their subculture. Their shared experience of being vulnerable to complaints breeds "defensiveness in these circumstances [that] is scarcely surprising and even natural" (Goldsmith 1991: 23). This engenders a "there but for the grace of God" attitude that discourages rigorous investigation. In addition, police officers – both investigators and those under investigation – share a common perspective towards police work *per se*. Thus, according to Lewis, the use of excessive force is thought to be a necessary aspect of police work and while officers might be judged to have gone too far on some occasion, their behaviour is not regarded as symptomatic of genuine misconduct (Lewis 1991). A further discouragement to vigorous investigation lies in the nature of much police deviance, for it is not intended to undermine the values of police organization, criminal justice system or wider society, but to uphold them – in other words, it is "noble cause corruption". Brodeur (1981) argues that this "*finis reus*" ("wilfully breaking the law to apply it efficiently") creates a weak technical offence that minimizes the perceived harm of the deviancy.

Facing such a formidably unreceptive organization, a substantial proportion of potential complainants do not bother to officially register their complaint. Citing evidence from the British Crime Survey, Maguire and Corbett point out that 10 per cent of respondents had been sufficiently annoyed by police behaviour to seriously contemplate complaining, but only a fifth of them (two per cent of the total) did so. Of those who abstained from making a complaint 31 per cent thought it would not be taken seriously or investigated properly (Maguire & Corbett 1991). Another reason is lack of knowledge about procedures, a factor that acts as a greater disincentive to working-class potential complainants (Russell 1976). Very often those who do make a complaint do so after being prompted by others more familiar with the police, including other police officers (Maguire & Corbett 1991). However, solicitors often discourage clients from making complaints because generally they do not regard it as in their clients' best interests (Uildriks & van Mastrigt 1991).

Even when the potential complainant has summoned sufficient courage to make an official complaint, it is not guaranteed to be recorded. Prior to the introduction of a formal complaints procedure in Britain, Russell found that it was common practice for officers to avoid recording complaints they regarded as "trivial" or plainly without substance – what he refers to as a "funnelling process" (Russell 1976). Twenty years after the installation of a formal procedure such "funnelling" is still to be seen in operation, with 30 per cent of Maguire and Corbett's (1991) sample feeling that they were "put off" when attempting to register their complaint. Further "funnelling" occurs even after the investigation is commenced as complaints are withdrawn. Maguire and Corbett found that in 58 per cent of cases that had been fully investigated complainants felt that they had been under pressure to withdraw their complaint and two-thirds of complainants who did withdraw their complaint did so as a result of what the investigating officer had said to them. The pressure to withdraw can be quite subtle and the decision to withdraw can even be genuinely consensual. Many complainants gained the general impression that the complaint was not worth the time and effort that investigating it would take and that the career of a dedicated officer was being unjustifiably jeopardized. Those who did withdraw tended to be convinced either that there was no need to proceed further because the registration of the complaint had had the desired effect or, more commonly, there was little prospect of substantiation (Maguire & Corbett 1991). This is remarkably reminiscent of Russell's much earlier findings that many complainants withdrew their complaint because in the light of the investigating officer's explanation, they were unwilling to the inflict upon the officer disproportionate disciplinary consequences for committing a relatively trivial offence. Perhaps somewhat surprisingly, it was middle-class complainants who tended to withdraw complaints for these reasons (Russell 1976) suggesting that they were assured that alternative informal action would be taken. Among Maguire and Corbett's sample of investigating officers some admitted to "guiding" complainants towards withdrawing the complaint, which the authors accept might be quite proper in some circumstances, although this is a cause of dissatisfaction among complainants (Maguire & Corbett 1991).

The current British system allows for non-serious complaints to be dealt with through "informal resolution" and this has been one reason for the relatively steep decline in the substantiation rate. Although they commend the introduction of "informal resolution", Maguire and Corbett (1991) suggest that senior officers responsible for this procedure use a variety of "ploys" to persuade complainants to take this course of action. These "ploys" seem to have proven quite successful, since only a few complainants felt that they were "wrongly 'pressured'" in opting for informal resolution.

Once an investigation commences there is the suspicion – reflected in popular opinion, criticisms by commentators, and the views of complainants – that so long as it is in the hands of the police themselves it will be less than vigorous. Apart from the "low" substantiation rate, the evidence in support of this contention is far from overwhelming. The British Police Complaints Board are quoted as saying that they "have sometimes observed that a defensive posture is adopted by both the investigating officers and the deputy chief constable in dealing with complaints. This often finds expression in the assertion that the complainant is anti-police, or that his record makes his evidence unreliable" (Stevens & Willis 1982: 7). This finds support in Maguire and Corbett's research that found that members of its successor body, the Police Complaints Authority, required further inquiries to be made in around a quarter of all investigations. Whether this makes any material difference to the outcome is, however, doubtful: "we were unable ... to identify any clear instance of actions by a [PCA supervisor] having made a difference to the final outcome of a case" (Maguire & Corbett 1991: 154). Investigating officers themselves complain of "overfussiness" on the part of PCA supervisors and this is consistent with Maguire and Corbett's view that while requests for further investigation "may have helped produce more thorough or balanced reports" (p. 154) they did not affect the eventual outcome. Russell insists that before the introduction of a formal complaints procedure "There was absolutely no evidence to suggest that there was selective interviewing of witnesses. The evidence was to the contrary in that investigating officers made considerable efforts to interview all interested parties to the complaint" (Russell 1976: 88). Moreover, Maguire and Corbett volunteer the assessment that "we were generally impressed with the commitment and the abilities of police investigators and of PCA members" (Maguire & Corbett 1991: 193). They also report that complainants regarded the visit from the investigating officers as the most satisfactory part of the whole procedure because their approach was "caring, interested and/or sympathetic" (p. 61). The growing use of confidential "hotlines" and covert surveillance (Marx 1992) to expose misconduct is further indication that the investigation of complaints is vigorously pursued by many police organizations.

The image of the police "closing ranks" in defensive solidarity may accurately describe the behaviour of *peers*, but officers are not investigated by their peers; they are investigated by superiors anxious to "guard" their own "backs" by ensuring no "come-back" from the investigation. As Russell explains:

> . . . for investigating officers to act with partiality, particularly in cases where the allegations are of a criminal nature, exposes them to the possibility of discovery when the report of the investigation goes to the Deputy Chief Constable and/or the Director of Public Prosecutions. Should a complainant persist with his complaint and it was then discovered that the investigating officer had acted improperly he would then become the subject of a complaint himself. (Russell 1976: 89)

Evidence of the vigour with which some investigations are conducted is found in the "ploys" the investigating officers use *against* those whom they are investigating. Some try to delay issuing notification of complaint until shortly before the interrogation to "catch [officers] on the hop" (Maguire & Corbett 1991: 26). Uildriks and Mastrigt remark that the Discipline Branch in the Scottish force they studied was "much feared" and "looked upon as 'the Gestapo'" (1991: 53). A view shared by these officers' counterparts in England:

> Discipline departments . . . were regarded with some distaste and a little fear, and, contrary to the public image of complaints investigations as "whitewash" exercises, [investigating officers] had a reputation of giving junior officers a rough ride in interviews. (Maguire & Corbett 1991: 68)

This view is given substance by an examination of the experiences of British police officers who have shot suspects in the course of their duties. This depicts the officer as abandoned and isolated during a period of intense vulnerability and left to write his official statement of what happened without help or support (Manolias & Hyatt-Williams 1988). As one officer with considerable experience of firearms operations remarked to me, "The sound of senior officers diving for cover is louder than the gunshots". From the perspective of those who are accused, the complaints process amounts to the systematic denial of elementary human rights (Guest 1995); the Police

Complaints Authority is a modern "witch-hunter general" (Peach 1995); and the Crown Prosecution Service applies unduly rigorous standards to police conduct (Howe 1996). Yet, despite the apparent vigour of complaints investigations substantiation rates remain lower than many observers find acceptable.

Independent Review?

Whether or not "low" substantiation rates are the product of the investigations being conducted by the police, if the police are seen as "judges in their own cause" this undermines both the legitimacy of the process and satisfaction of complainants. There would, therefore, seem good grounds for making the process independent of the police in any case. Indeed, the Police Federation of England and Wales (the police union) joined with the Law Society and National Council of Civil Liberties to demand a wholly independent system, claiming that however rigorous police investigations actually were they would never command the confidence of the public (The Law Society & The Police Federation of England and Wales 1983; Gostin 1984; see also *Police*, March 1996). However, Reiner cites chief constables as believing that this was a cynical ploy by the Federation to introduce a less effective alternative to the current system (Reiner 1991b). But what is the experience of different complaints procedures that incorporate more or less independence from the police? As Bayley (1991b) remarks, there are now enough systems of sufficient diversity to enable some preliminary conclusions to be reached.

Wagner and Decker (1993), reviewing North American experience, suggest that there is considerable diversity. The most common option is still to have no civilian involvement, although this has become less common since the 1980s. Otherwise, citizens may be involved in different capacities and at different stages of the process. In some systems civilian involvement is restricted to those who are already within the police bureaucracy. Independent citizen review may be limited to receiving and evaluating the initial complaint, or monitoring the process retrospectively. Alternatively, it can involve overseeing or directly participating in investigations, and being involved in the adjudication of the case. Examples of this range of procedures can be found in Toronto, Detroit, Chicago and Metro Dade County, Miami. In Toronto, the continued role of the police in the investigation of complaints is a cause for criticism; however the complaints commissioner can take over an investigation at any time after 30 days and has a staff of investigators for the purpose. Boards of Inquiry can be established at the discretion of the chief, the commissioners or any officer who appeals, and the decision of the board is final (Lewis 1991). Detroit has a "blue-ribbon" panel serving at the pleasure of the mayor, with its own investigative arm staffed by a mixture of civilians and police officers and extensive powers to receive complaints, monitor or conduct investigations, and affirm or overrule disciplinary action taken by the police. The Chicago system was established on the initiative of police themselves and consists of the Office of Professional Standards appointed by and accountable to the chief. It is staffed by civilian personnel and has its own investigative arm; it receives all complaints from the public and investigates all complaints of assault, shootings (whether or not the subject of complaint), and any case referred to it. Metro Dade County officers are not subject to an exclusively police complaints procedure, but to a system that deals with complaints against *all* county employees. It reviews complaints and can decide to investigate those deemed serious by empanelling three members "Two are selected from the community affected by the incident, while the third is a representative from the bargaining unit of the accused employee" (Terrill 1991: 312). The panel advises the relevant department on questions of guilt, penalty and policy implications of incidents. However, there is little evidence that these differences in institutional arrangements are reflected in their effectiveness or credibility. Loveday (1988, ibid. 1989a) claims that there has been a general tendency for civilians engaged in the review process to become progressively more sympathetic to the police, thus blunting the effectiveness of the procedures.

Britain has passed through three types of complaints process since 1964 when procedural requirements were first laid down by statute. At first, complaints remained wholly a matter for the police; this was followed by the Police Complaints Board, that had review functions; and then by the Police Complaints Authority with supervisory powers over the investigation. However, as Maguire remarks, "the advent of the PCA, like the PCB before it, has made no statistically significant difference to results overall" (Maguire 1991: 187). Under the Scottish system the procurator fiscal is an independent legal agent who is able to supervise complaints of police violence. He sees all complaints alleging any illegality and has at his disposal a legal staff able to conduct some limited investigation, plus the Discipline Branches of the respective police forces and a fiscal's authority to direct officers in the investigation of a case. On the instructions of the Crown Office, fiscals are barred from judging the substance of a complaint solely from police records – the complainant and any eye-witnesses should be independently interviewed. The Crown Office – Lord Advocate and Solicitor General – take the decision whether proceedings should be commenced against a police officer. Yet, Uildriks and Mastrigt conclude: "Despite the existence of an at times applauded 'independent element', the present system contains little to inspire confidence in those who have a perfectly legitimate cause for complaint." (Uildriks & van Mastrigt 1991: 128.) At the other extreme, the Danish police have extensive powers combined with a complaints system overseen by local boards who are accused of supporting the police, probably because investigation is in the hands of the police. Yet Danes remain complacent about their police (Marais & Jenkins 1992).

There are, in short, few grounds for believing that injecting independence into complaints procedures is likely to change very much at all. Indeed, Perez and Muir's analysis reveals that external review results in *fewer* substantiated complaints than internal procedures. In consequence, complainants preferred none of the currently used systems because they usually lose, while police prefer whatever system they already have because it is experienced as less threatening than anything that might replace it (Perez & Muir 1996).

Making the Case

Why, then, do substantiation rates remain so low throughout the liberal democracies? The answer is to be found in the characteristics of policing itself: *low visibility* use of authority to keep *marginal sections of the population* in their place.

Evidentiary problems in most police complaints are formidable, since it is often the complainant's word against that of the officer who, in turn, is likely to be supported by other officers. Had George Holliday not made a video-recording of the beating of Rodney King, it is highly unlikely that any complaint made by King would have been taken seriously (Skolnick & Fyfe 1993). Indeed, when Holliday took his recording to the police the following day, he was curtly dismissed. In the absence of this unequivocal video evidence, the officers could easily have exaggerated the threat that King posed to them so as to justify the force they used. After all, as it was they managed to convince the Simi Valley jury that the 53 baton blows, tasar barbs and sundry kicks did not constitute a criminal assault.

In the absence of independent evidence, the investigation of a complaint easily, and often quickly, degenerates into what Skolnick and Fyfe (1993) call a "swearing contest" in which each party flatly contradicts the other. In these circumstances the relative credibility of the complainant and the police officer play a determining role, which overwhelmingly favours the latter for the police have disproportionate contact with the most marginal sections of the population who tend to lack social skills and suffer discrediting personal characteristics. In Maguire and Corbett's sample of complainants only 60 per cent were employed, and only 30 per cent of those were in non-manual jobs, with 12 per cent in professional/executive positions; half were under 30 years of age; 45 per cent had previous convictions. This is strikingly similar to Russell's profile of complainants, apart from his striking revelation that in 59 per cent of the cases he examined "at some stage the complainant had been treated for mental illness" (Russell 1976: 81). *Who* the complainant is has a marked impact on whether the complaint is substantiated. Home Office research shows that complainants with previous convictions had 3.9 per cent of their complaints substantiated compared to 10 per cent for those without criminal records. The substantiation rate for white complainants was 4.6 per cent compared to 1.5 per cent for blacks and 3.6 per cent for Asians (Stevens & Willis 1982).

Moreover, complaints tend to arise from incidents that discredit the complainant. Maguire and Corbett point out that 27 per cent of complainants were described as drunk at the time of the incident and in at least a third of cases one or more complainant had been drinking (Maguire & Corbett 1991). Freckelton adds that in Victoria, Australia, "All too often the complainants were at the time affected by drugs or alcohol or had already been involved in some form of violent altercation" (Freckelton 1991: 95). Maguire and Corbett also point out that many complainants accepted that they had struggled and resisted arrest sufficient to justify the use of some force by the police, but complained that the officer(s) had used *more* force than was necessary. They conclude that in many complaints of assault, the complainant was "likely to fit the 'stereotype' – that is, to be young and working class, to have previous convictions, and to have been drinking prior to the incident in question" (Maguire & Corbett 1991: 43).

Discrediting characteristics are not simply *possessed* by people: they must be recognized and interpreted as *discreditable* (Goffman 1968). Box and Russell pursue this line of reasoning to the conclusion that investigating officers seek to defuse complaints of misconduct by *actively* discrediting those who make them (Box & Russell 1975). Evidence for this hypothesis is slim, but it does seem inevitable that any investigation in a "swearing contest" will assess the credibility of the complainant by paying attention to their personal characteristics and the circumstances surrounding the complaint. Otherwise, the complaint from a psychiatric patient that an officer was putting "rays" into his head to make him move forward (Graef 1989) would be given as much credibility as a severely injured suspect claiming that they had been assaulted. Russell's contention that this is "contrary to the concept of equality of all citizens before the law" (Russell 1976: 89), is simply bizarre, not least because credibility of witness testimony is one of the most salient considerations in many criminal trials. As the independently-minded Complaints Authority in Victoria, Australia, discovered, "a significant percentage of complaints was made by disturbed, malicious, or vexatious people with an axe to grind" (Freckelton 1991: 94). However, what is undoubtedly true is that assessments of credibility favour "respectable citizens" and adversely affect marginal sections of the population who are thus *doubly* disadvantaged, because they are more vulnerable to policing in the first place.

Box and Russell's (1975) other suggestion is that officers arrest potential complainants as a defensive strategy. It is certainly an accepted informal working rule among police that if officers manhandle a person during a hostile encounter they should arrest that person in order to "guard their backs". As Box and Russell argue, arresting a potential complainant confers a number of advantages: first, it gives the police a bargaining position in which the prosecution is discontinued if the complaint is withdrawn. Secondly, it places the potential complainant in the position of a "criminal suspect" to which attributions of malice can readily be attributed. Thirdly, it provides a ready-made motive for the complaint such as the belief among Scottish officers that the single most common "spurious" allegation is the "standard defence charge" to rebut a criminal prosecution (Uildriks & van Mastrigt 1991: 62–63). However, it would be mistaken to attribute too much deliberation to arrest decisions. As Maguire and Corbett (1991) found, a high proportion of complaints occur in confused and volatile circumstances in which arrests are likely to be made hurriedly and with little reflection. Moreover, the belief among officers that they must "guard their backs" by arresting anyone with whom they have an altercation suggests that the likelihood of being complained against is regarded by them as a serious enough risk to warrant preventive action.

Due Process

Not only do many complainants face evidentiary and credibility obstacles to establishing their case, the legalism of many complaints procedures confers considerable advantages on officers. Most complainants are making a complaint for the first time (Maguire & Corbett 1991) and are thus unfamiliar with procedures, whereas officers are likely to be personally or vicariously familiar with the complaints process. In any event, officers will be more knowledgeable about the law and investigative procedures and they can use rules of evidence as protection. It is, however, difficult to imagine how this could be otherwise. Surprisingly, the constitutional lawyer, Lustgarten, objects to the practice of investigating officers formally reminding officers under investigation of their rights and the punctilious attention shown to proper procedure, which he suggests has the "odour of favouritism" (Lustgarten 1986: 142). He argues that an employee who refuses to answer questions about misconduct in other spheres of employment could be fairly dismissed. What this fails to appreciate is the considerable overlap between disciplinary infractions and criminal offences. Thus a hostile exchange between a police officer and a citizen may give rise to disciplinary allegations of incivility *and/or* criminal charges of assault, and this is unlikely to become clear until the investigation is complete. Investigating officers who failed to attend punctiliously to legal safeguards would find themselves vulnerable to the criticism that they had undermined the prospects of a criminal prosecution because much of the evidence they had collected would prove inadmissible. What is undoubtedly true is that knowledgeable people can use safeguards as a means of protecting themselves from disciplinary or legal action. This is not restricted to police officers; there have been reports that social workers have similarly defended themselves against accusations of failing to protect vulnerable children (Laurance 1986). On the other hand, the fact that a police officer is investigated by a superior under whose command he may work in the future, proves a major *disincentive* to invoking procedural safeguards. Maguire and Corbett found that many officers favoured a wholly independent complaints procedure precisely because they felt they would be freer fully to exercise their rights (Maguire & Corbett 1991).

The rights that police in Britain (and some other jurisdictions [Lewis 1991]) enjoy derive not only from criminal procedures where applicable, but also from the fact that the standard of proof in disciplinary proceedings is that of "beyond a reasonable doubt". Investigating officers told Maguire and Corbett that this standard was so demanding that they had little expectation of substantiating any complaint, and saw informal action as more fruitful (Maguire & Corbett 1991). This has led to a debate in Britain about whether the standard of proof in internal complaints should be lowered. Reforms to the procedure aim to match the standard of proof to the severity of the complaint: for complaints that threaten an officer's career the criminal standard is preserved, but the civil standard of the "balance of probabilities" will be applied in less serious cases (see *Police Review*, 19 July 1996; 21 March 1997). The Home Affairs Select Committee (1998) has suggested further reform to reduce the safeguards for accused officers.

There are three reasons for adopting the civil standard of the "balance of probabilities". The obvious reason is the belief that a change in the standard of proof will lead to the substantiation of more complaints because it is an easier standard to satisfy. Meadus (1990) reports that in Australian states that rely upon the civil standard of proof, substantiation rates are double those in Britain under the criminal standard. However, this relies on an uncritical acceptance of official statistics which have already been shown to be questionable. For the apparent doubling of the substantiation rate might reflect nothing more than relabelling outcomes. Thus, a complaint that under the criminal standard results in the officer receiving "advice" might, under the civil standard, be classed as "substantiated", even though the penalty remained exactly the same. This said, the procedure would probably gain credibility if the full range of actual outcomes was more explicitly acknowledged.

A second reason is one of equity: very few professions impose such a tremendous obstacle to the substantiation of a complaint as do the police. Of course, the police are entitled to point out, as they often do, that few other professions involve routine authoritative intervention in conflict situations. There is a world of difference between the provision of service from which the recipient is intended to benefit and the routine imposition of coercive authority that is likely to be to the detriment of at least some of those whom the police encounter. On the other hand, it might be argued that there is a world of difference between the incompetent provision of a service and being assaulted. However, simply comparing formal standards of proof does not mean that those in other professions are more likely to have a complaint substantiated against them than are the police. Many professions are notorious for failing to discipline their members. Equating one profession with another is more hazardous than might at first appear.

The third reason advanced for adopting the civil standard is that cases brought in the civil courts are more likely to find in favour of the plaintiff than are disciplinary or criminal proceedings. Many onlookers are perplexed when a civil court imposes punitive damages on the police because of the conduct of its officers, but no disciplinary or criminal charges follow. It is sometimes suggested that complainants, despairing of the disciplinary system, are resorting to the civil courts in order to obtain a fair hearing. If the standard of proof in disciplinary proceedings was reduced to the civil standard it is envisaged that officers identified in civil proceedings would also suffer individual disciplinary penalties. Again, this is more complex than it appears initially, because, apart from the standard of proof, civil and disciplinary proceedings differ in terms of who or what is penalized. In a civil case, it might be transparent that a plaintiff has suffered improper treatment for which the police undoubtedly are *corporately* responsible. However, it is quite a different matter to say that an *individual* officer was guilty of wrongdoing.

A further objection to adopting the civil standard of proof is that it might prove *too* punitive. Police officers engage in actions as a matter of duty which are otherwise dubious. They are required to use force and might in some circumstances err in using too much. Fyfe argues that a careful distinction needs to be made between police "brutality", which is "conscious and venal", and the use of unnecessary force, that often arises from incompetence in handling the situation (Skolnick & Fyfe 1993). Likewise, Maguire and Corbett suggest that not all assaults deserve that appellation:

> We interviewed several complainants who had received minor injuries on arrest who willingly admitted that they had struggled, yet continued to feel that the actions of the arresting officer had "gone over the top". Although their complaints were recorded as "assault", a more apt description might have been "excessive use of force". (Maguire & Corbett 1991: 90)

However, even if commonsense dictates that "assault" is not an "apt description", the notion that police use of force can be both "excessive" and not a criminal assault would involve a sea-change in constitutional thought. As things stand, even if the officer successfully convinces the court that he was provoked, this mitigation might alter the sentence, but not the charge. Thus, a gratuitous thump administered after a bruising struggle with a violent suspect becomes a career-threatening offence, the penalty for which is inevitably so draconian as to be regarded as wholly disproportionate to the wrong done. It is difficult to imagine that if the civil standard of proof was adopted, tribunals would abandon such commonsense considerations.

Even if this means that officers who understandably "go over the top" avoid disciplinary charges, the operation of such commonsense considerations has a negative consequence for the police, as well as the public. The result is tacitly to condone "minor" assaults. If it was explicitly acknowledged that police officers are entitled to use force in the course of their duties, they could be granted limited immunity to charges of assault by introducing a lesser disciplinary offence of using "excessive force", the penalty for which was not career-threatening. This would remind officers that "going over the top" was not acceptable, while recognizing that in volatile circumstances anyone might act excessively. However, this would entail a tacit shift away from the ideological myth that police officers are merely "citizens in uniform"; there would indeed then be one law for the police and another for the rest of the population.

Standing Accused

Difficulty in substantiating complaints should not be interpreted as meaning that being the recipient of a complaint has little or no impact on officers, or indeed their colleagues, who commonly find it a most stressful experience. Even if the complaint is not formally substantiated, Russell found that officers believed that it still harmed their career prospects (Russell 1976). Certainly, it does so temporarily: I was accompanying an officer on mobile patrol who arrested a young man on suspicion of driving under the influence of drugs. The suspect's driving had certainly been most erratic, so much so that the driver of another vehicle with which he nearly collided needed to be restrained by the officer. Having been arrested, it was discovered that the suspect was a diabetic and in the judgement of the police physician his erratic behaviour was the result of his condition. Although he was quickly released and not charged with any driving offences, an official complaint was made by his father against the officer (and incidentally against me, for I was assumed to be a plainclothes police officer!). The evidence of the enraged motorist was sufficient to disprove the allegation of fabricating evidence, but even so the officer's career plans were stalled for a year while the complaint was investigated and the decision not to prosecute was taken (for fuller details of this incident, see Waddington 1987b). Even when a complaint is not substantiated officers might receive "advice", which as Maguire and Corbett note is a more serious matter than is often appreciated (Maguire & Corbett 1991).

Occasionally, the public obtains a brief insight into the impact of the police complaints process on individual officers. The most notorious example is that of John Stalker, Deputy Chief Constable of the Manchester force. He was relieved of his command of the investigation into allegations of a "shoot to kill" policy being operated by members of the Royal Ulster Constabulary, after unrelated allegations of corruption were made against him of which he was subsequently cleared (Taylor 1987; Stalker 1988). What is striking about the Stalker case is just how similar his experience was to that of his more humble colleagues. The difference is that because of the circumstances of the case, Stalker received widespread public sympathy for the ordeal through which he was put (Judge 1986; see also the case of the detective Tony Lundy [Short 1992]).

Official Toleration of Malpractice

Police deviancy does not occur in a social, political and legal vacuum, but rather in a context that either facilitates or encourages it. One powerful component of that context is the law and how the courts interpret it. This has two aspects: first, the disinclination of the prosecution authorities to bring cases before the criminal courts and the equal disinclination of juries to convict officers of criminal wrongdoing. In Britain, the Director of Public Prosecutions has explicitly acknowledged that much firmer evidence is required before commencing the prosecution of police officers because of the unwillingness of juries to convict (Lustgarten 1986: 138–40). Glanville Williams has attacked this approach as allowing brutal and corrupt police officers to escape punishment in conditions where their civilian equivalents would not be so fortunate (Williams 1985). However, because so much police deviance is motivated not by personal gain, but by the pursuit of "noble" goals, successful prosecution in almost all jurisdictions seems a rarity.

The most notorious example of this was the acquittal of four police officers charged with the savage beating of Rodney King by a Simi Valley jury. Two of the officers were subsequently convicted of abusing King's civil rights, but the remaining two were acquitted for a second time. Comment and speculation about the trial has drawn attention to its being staged in Simi Valley, a predominantly white middle-class neighbourhood in which any empanelled jury was likely to favour the accused police officers. However, this is to overlook the fact that juries throughout the liberal democracies are singularly disinclined to convict police officers of offences committed in the course of their duty. High-profile examples of this occurred in Britain during a series of police shootings of unarmed people during the 1980s, including a man travelling in a car with the girlfriend of a suspect, the mother of another and the five-year-old son of a third. In each case, the jury accepted the defence that the officer had made a tragic mistake (Waddington 1991). In the only full trial to arise from the series of miscarriages of justice associated with Irish terrorism – the trial of former-detectives involved in the "Guildford Four" case – the jury acquitted the officers on all counts. Likewise, despite severe criticism of the practices of the West Midlands Serious Crime Squad and a succession of successful appeals against conviction (Kaye 1991), in the only case to come to trial the accused officers were acquitted. This acquittal came after a jury retirement of less than half an hour, indicating that they had virtually dismissed the prosecution case out of hand. In Scotland, trials of police before both Sheriffs and juries are unlikely to result in guilty verdicts, a pattern "ascribed to the fact that often people consider the police to have a difficult enough task to rid the streets of criminals without their job needing to be made even more difficult" (Uildriks & van Mastrigt 1991: 65). However, juries are not indiscriminate: when police officers are accused of "ordinary" crimes – drug smuggling, supplying drugs, sexually abusing children, and so forth – there is a much greater willingness to convict (see, for example, *Police Review*, 28 February & 7 March 1997). Disinclination to convict tends to lie in cases where officers are alleged to have committed offences in the course of fulfilling their duties.

One respect in which police wrongdoing is tolerated by the courts is their unwillingness to exclude improperly obtained evidence – one of the most common forms of police deviance. The courts in Britain have become more interventionist in excluding evidence since the passage of legislation in the mid-1980s, but even so many commentators look wistfully across to the United States and demand that Britain follows the American example and incorporates a strict exclusionary rule into criminal procedure (Hewitt 1982; Wallington 1984; Baxter 1985; Lustgarten 1986; Hillyard & Percy-Smith 1988; Uglow 1988; Robertson 1989). They imagine that the courts would then exercise the power to exclude evidence, which would result in acquittals, and this would dissuade officers from breaching rules of criminal procedure. However, American evidence suggests that the exclusionary rule is observed more in the breach than in the observance and the Supreme Court has diluted its effectiveness through a succession of qualifications (Rudovsky 1982; Parenti 1988; Gordon 1990; Uchida & Bynum 1991; Baldwin 1993; Skolnick & Fyfe 1993; Sharpe 1995). Certainly, there is no evidence that American cops behave any better than their British counterparts.

American experience of the exclusionary rule seems to confirm McBarnett's analysis of how "legal rhetoric" is divorced from actual practice (McBarnett 1983). On the one hand, the American courts give the rhetorical pretence of upholding "due process", but in practice, exemptions, qualifications and interpretations of Supreme Court decisions are routinely employed to circumvent procedural safeguards in particular cases. What is striking is not the gulf between legal practice either side of the Atlantic, but the similarities throughout the common law jurisdictions. Dixon has brilliantly analysed the history of judicial interpretation of common law safeguards in England and New South Wales, Australia (Dixon 1997). He convincingly demonstrates how courts in both jurisdictions tolerated police malpractice in relation to detention and interrogation and then subsequently used this history of tolerance as justification for establishing practices as accepted and acceptable. For instance, detaining suspects for the purposes of interrogation was supposedly contrary to criminal procedure, but the courts allowed it to continue until it became customary, whereupon it was enshrined in law. He also shows how the highest courts in both jurisdictions have enunciated principles without providing enforcement mechanisms, thus rendering their own statements of principle vacuous. He exposes how official inquires have recommended changes in the law to legalize explicitly acknowledged routine police illegalities. For example, the Commissioner of the London Metropolitan Police's evidence to the 1980 Royal Commission on Criminal Procedure frankly conceded that officers routinely resorted to breaches of procedural safeguards in order to secure convictions. Far from recommending that these safeguards be strengthened, the Royal Commission accepted the Commissioner's proposal that the law be changed to facilitate such practices!

Nor is such an indulgent legal climate restricted to common law jurisdictions. Bell explains how in France the police actually exercise enormous quasi-judicial powers during investigations, because of the shortage of investigating magistrates; and how the courts are able to make use of evidence improperly obtained at this early stage of the procedure despite apparent safeguards to the contrary (Bell 1993; see also Horton 1995). Likewise, Miyazawa shows repeatedly how the permissive legal culture in Japan facilitates the police "pulling strokes" (Miyazawa 1992).

McBarnett's observation, made in the British context, that the police do not have to "bend" the rules because their practices are actually endorsed by courts (McBarnett 1979), seems to have general applicability. So too does Williams's observation that "in criminal cases, the courts are anxious to facilitate the conviction of villains and they interpret the law whenever possible to secure this" (cited in Dixon 1997: 288). But it is not simply a question of convicting criminals by whatever means are necessary, for courts also tolerate other questionable police practices and behaviour. For example, following a succession of cases in which heavy punitive damages were awarded against the police in the British civil courts, the Metropolitan Police were able to obtain a ruling that the scale of these damages was "excessive" and limitations were then imposed (*Police Review*, 10 May 1996; 28 February 1997). Even death at the hands of the police rarely provokes judicial sanction. British coroners' courts have repeatedly abstained from bringing in verdicts of "unlawful killing", or otherwise criticizing the police, when people have died in police custody in suspicious or controversial circumstances (Scraton 1984; Scraton & Chadwick 1987; Ryan 1996). In Australia, disproportionate deaths of Aboriginal people in police custody have largely escaped judicial censure (Hazlehurst 1991). Deaths of protesters during violent clashes with police have either gone unpunished (Dummett 1980a), or inquiries have exonerated the police from blame (Gilbert 1975; Scarman 1975; Rollo 1980). In Northern Ireland, killings of suspected terrorists by the security forces have rarely been punished (Asmal 1985; Amnesty International 1988); while in South Africa, during the state of emergency, the police were given an explicit immunity from prosecution if they used force "in good faith" and the courts were extremely lenient, even when this permissive standard was breached (Cawthra 1993; Weitzer & Beattie 1994).

In sum, police deviance occurs within a context of tolerance. Thus, the "Dirty Harry problem" (Klockars 1980) is turned on its head: when valiant cops use improper means to defeat the criminal, far from obstructing them, the courts give tacit encouragement.

Political Mobilization

It is not only the courts and legal establishment that indulge questionable and downright illegal police behaviour. Politically too the police have been able to secure *de facto* immunity from scrutiny or sanction.

> The road to independent review of police misconduct is littered with the carcasses of civilian review boards and specialist police ombudsmen, the victims of concerted oppositional alliances of politicians, police administrators, and police unions. (Goldsmith 1991: 32)

Philadelphia is widely acknowledged as initiating civilian review in the 1950s in the teeth of vehement police opposition. Lacking the support of the political establishment and the majority of white voters, it was eventually disbanded after two bruising court cases (Terrill 1991). There were successive attempts in American cities to introduce civilian review throughout the 1970s, but most of these concluded in failure. Elsewhere, the Victoria Police Complaints Authority in Australia suffered a similar fate.

> By the end of the 1980s it was recognized throughout the country that for a political party with an election in the offing to antagonize a police union was tantamount to electoral suicide . . . [it would] run the risk of being portrayed as "soft on crime" and "anti-law-and-order". (Freckelton 1991: 68).

Greater success was forthcoming in Britain, but even so demand for a more independent and active Police Complaints Authority was rejected (predictably enough) by Mrs Thatcher's Conservative government, but also by the all-party parliamentary Home Affairs Select Committee (Cohen 1985). It is not all one-way traffic, however. Toronto police went on strike in an effort to defeat the Complaints Commission but failed to get public backing; but this is clearly the exception rather than the rule (Lewis 1991).

There is a simple explanation for these repeated defeats for independent police complaints procedures – electoral unpopularity.

> Quite simply there are far more votes to be won by "law and order" policies than by support for civil liberties. The latter can thus be comfortably dismissed as the rantings of extremists and intellectuals, despite the fact that such matters vitally concern the lives of everyone, and dictate the type of society in which we live. (Koffman 1985: 15)

This makes itself felt not only on this issue, but also on attempts to increase procedural safeguards for suspects. As Dixon explains, attempts to enact the recommendations of the New South Wales Law Reform Commission that detention for questioning should be regularized, with police being granted powers subject to safeguards for suspects, were dogged by political opposition. The government eventually proposed to give the police virtual *carte blanche*, but this Bill lapsed at the end of that parliament. A revised Bill was presented to the new parliament, but even if passed, will only modestly improved safeguards. In any event:

> Politicians, judges, and police struggle with the idea that suspects have rights which need to be given substance. Their primary concern is the demands and desires of crime control. (Dixon 1997: 226)

Reviewing the history of civilian review in the United States, Brown concludes:

> It is . . . important for public confidence that a civilian element is not introduced purely in response to pressure from particular minority groups or political factions which are opposed to the police. When this happens the resulting identification of complaint procedures with such groups will occasion automatic opposition from those of differing persuasions, and restrict the use of procedures to specific minorities. (Brown 1983: 28)

Bayley puts it succinctly: "If the issue of accountability becomes a matter of high politics, the police will destroy civilian review." (Bayley 1991: vii.) What remains unexplained is why action against police deviancy is so electorally unpopular. The answer is simple: the "policed" section of the population are almost invariably a powerless minority.

What is surprising is that civil libertarian measures *ever* succeed in overcoming popular resistance. They do so via two diametrically opposed strategies: low-key and very high-key. The low-key option is advocated by Bayley who argues that civilian review began to spread during the 1980s and 90s surreptitiously, enlisting the active support of senior officers anxious to improve standards (Bayley 1991). It owed its success to being kept off the political agenda. The very high-key alternative is to capitalize on moral panics. As Bayley notes, concern about police brutality is increasing worldwide.

> In Australia, concern with brutality achieved the status of "moral panic" during the late 1980s. It was given extensive coverage by the media, riveting public attention and forcing governments to respond with a host of special inquiries and commissions: the Royal Commission on Aboriginal Deaths in Custody, the National Inquiry into Racist Violence in Australia by the Human Rights and Equal Opportunity Commission of the Government of Australia, the National Violence Commission, and the coronial inquest into police shootings in Victoria. (Bayley 1996: 284)

Similar flurries of official concern have occurred in Canada and Israel, but were short-lived in the Netherlands and New Zealand. During periods of heightened concern about standards of police conduct, campaign groups can embarrass politicians into enacting legislative safeguards for civil liberties. "Their usual sensitivity to the phenomenon of moral panic does not preclude encouraging one when the folk devils wear blue uniforms" (Reiner 1991b: 212). Judges also might be receptive to campaigning pressure; it is difficult to imagine that the more interventionist stance of the British criminal courts towards procedural safeguards was not the product of public reaction to the series of miscarriages of justice.

It is tempting to regard public opposition to due process reforms as Neanderthal, but even "progressive" movements can be blind to due process when the interests of vulnerable people are at stake. Consider, for example, the due process implications of police policies encouraging the more or less automatic arrest of suspects in cases of domestic violence.

> Simplistically stated, this theory suggests an arrest may be justified, despite no realistic hope of subsequent conviction, if it deters the offender (or any potential offender) from future assaults. Hence, the ability of the police to "shame" the offender by arrest is potentially useful to modify aberrant behaviour. In short, the societal good – control of domestic violence – can be accomplished independently of conviction. It is interesting that academics (staunchly liberal in other contexts) and many feminists have failed to find anything distressing about police powers being used in this manner. While the police as an institution were often deeply mistrusted by these same people, many heartily endorsed statute changes that increased police involvement in intimate disputes and family violence, despite some evidence that police often used such statutes against minority and disadvantaged males rather than against other offenders who were middle class, "respectful" or "respectable" white males. Further, since the lower class was more likely to rely on police for their problems, this inherently reinforced an existing class bias in overall arrest rates. The implications this poses are still apparently either ignored or simply overridden by desperation in effecting change as quickly as possible. (Buzawa & Buzawa 1993)

A example of such "desperation" undermining due process can be found in an experiment conducted in south London. A provision of the law governing police investigation allows for suspects to be bailed by the police to attend a police station at a future time in order for police to make further inquiries and gather additional evidence, if necessary. The experiment makes *creative* use of this provision (Buchan & Edwards 1991; Edwards 1994): suspects are initially bailed under these provisions; their behaviour is monitored in the interim; when they report back to the police station at the designated time, the decision is taken whether to prosecute or not. In other words, the provision is *not* used for its intended purpose – to make inquiries and gather evidence – but as a means of imposing an *ad hoc* form of suspended sentence, probation or bind-over on someone whose guilt has not been established!

Are Police Really "Deviant"?

If the courts tolerate malpractice, juries refuse to convict police officers charged with "noble cause corruption", and public opinion opposes extensions of civil liberties, in what sense are the police acting "deviantly" at all? We have surely all seen George Holliday's video of the beating of Rodney King; it has become an icon of the 1990s. It seems transparent that this was an act of "police brutality": 53 blows, tasar barbs and broken bones tell their own story. Yet, that story was heard in full by the jury in Simi Valley who decided that *no* assault had taken place. Now this evokes, in most commentators, a barely suppressed hollow laugh and accusations that the trial was held in a suburb of Los Angeles specially selected to advantage Sergeant Koon and his co-accused. The tacit assumption is that this was "obviously" an act of "police brutality", but one which the courts refused to punish (Skolnick & Fyfe 1993). Four issues arise from this: first is the epistemological issue of establishing the grounds upon which it is concluded that the beating of Rodney King *was* "police brutality", no matter what the jury concluded. At this point criminologists and hard-bitten detectives swap roles:

criminologists can now be heard intoning the litany "We *know* they're guilty, but the courts won't convict"! The problem is that the competent authority to make judgements of fact in criminal cases is the jury, and insisting that the verdict was perverse is merely to substitute one's own judgement for that of the jury.

Secondly, the legal and sociological fact is (setting aside for the moment the issue of the federal action of denying King his civil rights) that Rodney King was *not* assaulted, however unpalatable that conclusion is. Now, what lessons are cops in Los Angeles to learn from this? The obvious one is that it is acceptable to beat African–Americans with criminal records who lead police on a high-speed car chase and refuse to comply with commands. It is not illegal, it is just doing one's job – a job of which the courts and public approve. It is "dirty work" of which most fellow citizens would rather be kept in ignorance – but such is the hypocrisy of public life. This is reflected even more clearly during the South African state of emergency. When SAP gunned down protesters, hurling rocks and performing other such transparently brutal actions, they were given immunity because they used force "in good faith" (Cawthra 1993). These officers were not "out of control", they were doing their duty (Brogden & Shearing 1993). The courts condoned police actions on those comparatively rare occasions when such actions came before them (Prior 1989; Weitzer & Beattie 1994); politicians praised them; and white public opinion was, at best, indifferent. In sum, if actions are condoned – and much police "deviancy" *is* condoned – then it cannot be "deviant". We might be morally outraged by such actions, but our outrage does not explain the actions of others.

Thirdly, after being acquitted of assaulting Rodney King, the four officers were arraigned on charges of denying King his civil rights. Now, for those who adopt a absolutist view of legality, this presents some difficulties since it amounts to institutionalizing "double jeopardy". Surprisingly, the most detailed analysis of American law on police brutality (Cheh 1996) passes over this problem with an assurance that it is only invoked in cases of "manifest miscarriages of justice". This raises two issues: on the one hand, is the legal–epistemological problem of "manifest" to whom? Justice is procedural, and invoking a procedural aberration when convenient is a denial of justice. On the other, the sociological question arises of whether the federal authorities expediently sacrificed Sergeant Koon and his co-accused in order to placate the "moral panic" that gripped articulate opinion in the wake of the acquittal.

Finally, there is the much wider issue that what is "deviant", or not, is determined retrospectively. Of course, this is something with which we all live: any of us might, in all innocence, commit an act that is later ruled to have been unlawful. However, as noted in the previous chapter, this problem is particularly acute for the police precisely because they are duty bound to act in ways that would otherwise be exceptional, exceptionable or illegal. Beating someone almost senseless is something that police can do with the utmost propriety *if it is appropriate or necessary for a lawful purpose.* This is experienced as precarious by police officers because it rests on an assessment of *fact* made possibly in the dispassionate conditions of a court hearing with the benefit of 20:20 hindsight long after the events themselves. As we have seen, the courts are often generous in their interpretation of the facts, but this does not remove the anxiety of one's fate being held in the balance. In any case, it is a lottery – even in apartheid South Africa a few officers were found guilty: just as many people build dreams on winning the lottery, police officers build nightmares on losing the judicial lottery.

Sometimes, there is no dispute as to the facts, but the law itself is unclear and the courts clarify it *in the course of adjudicating on the guilt or innocence of those accused.* A nice illustration of this was the case of a lawyer whose client deposited at her office a bag that was later found to contain stolen property. The lawyer was invited by the police to make a statement regarding this incident, but declined to do so, claiming legal privilege. She was then arrested and charged with "handling stolen goods", but the case was later dropped by the Crown Prosecution Service. In a civil action against the police she was awarded £45,000 (*Police Review*, 7 March 1997). Did the police exceed their powers in this case? Obviously they did, since the court ruled that they had. But until the court made its ruling, all parties in these very peculiar circumstances might have been equally unclear about the limits of not only police powers, but also legal privilege. However, it could hardly be considered "police deviance", since the circumstances suggest that the police acted in good faith in conditions of legal uncertainty.

Where does this leave us? What is acceptable and unacceptable policing is profoundly uncertain. This arises from the fact that policing entails using methods of intrinsically marginal legality and acceptability – interfering with the person and property of others. That uncertainty is reflected in legal, political and popular opinions on policing generally and specific police actions. This means that policing is intrinsically scandal-prone, as officers tread the shifting terrain between propriety and impropriety.

Alternative Prospects

Given the generally negative assessment of the impact of traditional disciplinary and legal regulation, do alternatives offer better prospects of controlling police practices? In this section four alternatives will be considered: holding the police organization *corporately* responsible for the actions of its members; in some jurisdictions parties to a less serious complaint can opt to resolve it through conciliation; there are moves to improve police practice through professional licensing by peers; and finally empowering officers to perform the tasks they are actually called upon to undertake *within* the law.

Penalizing Police Organizations

According to Lustgarten, the traditional adversarial approach of disciplinary and criminal proceedings:

> . . . is seriously incomplete. That is to say, it reflects the law's traditional emphasis on redress for the victim and punishment of the wrong-doer. This legal outlook is inherently negative, individualistic and oriented towards sanctions. Rewards and incentives and measures devoted to altering misguided group values and solidarities which reinforce objectionable conduct are beyond its capabilities. It does not concern itself directly with the organisational context which stimulates misconduct. Almost certainly the most effective way to reduce racism, brutality, falsification of evidence and what the Discipline Code calls generically "abuse of authority" is for those in charge of the organisation to change its ethos and working atmosphere, career rewards and disincentives, so that its members come to identify their interests, individually and collectively, with the desired behav-

iour. Training and effective management supervision to reinforce its strictures would be a central element in any reform strategy. (Lustgarten 1986: 127)

An example of Lustgarten's point is to be found in the death of Joy Gardner, an illegal immigrant to Britain who died from suffocation after police overpowered her by gagging her mouth with surgical tape and placing her in handcuffs. The individual officers were prosecuted for manslaughter and acquitted, but the trial revealed that the practices used by them were institutionalized and tacitly acceded to by their superiors (*Guardian*, 16 May 1995; see also *Police Review*, 21 July 1995). Kappeler *et al.* argue that tacit consent to deviant practices among senior ranks, provided they are not directly implicated, is not uncommon. Policies forbidding certain conduct are promulgated, not in order to discourage them, but to insulate superiors who can blame subordinates if the practices come to light (Kappeler *et al.* 1994) – an example of the "organizational hypocrisy" to which Ericson (1981) refers.

Civil proceedings enable litigants to expose such corporate responsibilities, inhibiting the police organization from scapegoating individual officers as "rotten apples" and drawing attention instead to the "state of the barrel which contains the apples" (Maguire & Corbett 1991: 12). For example, civil liability claims have had a dramatic impact on police methods in the United States where plaintiffs have been successful (wholly or partially) in more than half the cases brought (Kappeler & Kaune 1993). Thus, in cases concerning the use of force, instead of considering exclusively whether officers who have struck people with batons or shot them acted justifiably in the circumstances in which they found themselves, a much wider range of issues become germane. For example, the police department's policies, and provision of training and supervisory arrangements can become the object of scrutiny. This has led to significant improvements in policies on the use of firearms since the mid-1970s when it was reported that one department's policy was (in its entirety): "Never take me out in anger; never put me back in disgrace!" (Milton *et al.* 1977: 47)

On the other hand, since the civil penalty is the award of damages, it is open to a police department or the municipality that it serves simply to pay up as one of the "costs of doing business". This is allegedly the approach that was taken by the LAPD and City of Los Angeles for many years when it was repeatedly sued for excessive use of force on the part of officers (Chevigny 1995; Skolnick & Fyfe 1993). Such a strategy makes sense when juries remain loath to find against police departments, for: "In 1990 fifty-eight excessive force cases against LAPD officers were tried, with plaintiffs prevailing in only seventeen." (Skolnick & Fyfe 1993: 202.) This may be because defendants settle all but the most hopeless cases out of court, but then once settled, the opportunities for exposure of corporate defects and wrongdoing are removed.

Civil proceedings are not the only means by which organizational deficiencies can be exposed; another is through public inquiries. It is notable how a succession of inquiries into the deaths of vulnerable children whose families were under the supervision of social workers in Britain have directed their most caustic criticisms at *corporate* defects from which individual failings often stemmed (Laurance 1985). In fact, in Britain the police habitually establish internal inquiries following some high-profile incident and these too are often savagely critical of organizational arrangements and senior management, but they rarely reach an external audience and therefore the organization is not held to account for remedying the defects that are identified.

Conciliation Rather than Adversarial Procedures

Another alternative to traditional complaints procedures, in operation in Britain since the mid-1980s, involves abandoning, in less serious complaints, the adversarial style of the legalistic disciplinary process in favour of conciliation. This, together with more recent changes to the standard of proof required in less serious cases, brings the British system into line with that advocated by Bayley: conciliation for "misunderstandings"; expedited hearings at civil standard of proof for "genuine mistakes of judgement"; and full "court-like processes and a high standard of proof" for "very serious abuses of power . . . where career-threatening penalties are appropriate" (Bayley 1991b: ix).

Maguire and Corbett's research (1991) showed that complainants found conciliation to be a more satisfactory procedure than the traditional adversarial proceedings. However, officers were more guarded in their assessment, for they were suspicious about assurances that informal resolution would not be taken as an admission of guilt and adversely affect their subsequent careers. Many complainants gained the impression that officers did not believe they had done anything wrong and informal resolution amounted to "agreeing to differ". (Maguire & Corbett 1991: 84). There appear to be two weaknesses in this conciliation scheme: first, the parties are not brought together but instead the "Appointed Officer" acts as an intermediary. Secondly, it remains under the aegis of the police; this both fails to re-assure officers that if they admit to making a mistake it will not count against them and continues to give the impression to complainants that they are being fobbed off. Nevertheless, it is preferable to more adversarial proceedings; but such a procedure cannot be extended to the most common complaints, since these allege breaches of the criminal law.

Accreditation

An interesting development in the United States has been the growth in accreditation of police agencies to the independent Commission on Accreditation for Law Enforcement Agencies. However, its limitation is that accreditation relies on the adoption of rational–bureaucratic policies and procedures, rather than the standards of conduct delivered by officers on the streets (Skolnick & Fyfe 1993). One positive spin-off has been to create a pool of expert witnesses able to testify whether police procedures in any given incident matched up to professional standards. The aim, then, is to abandon the notion that the police officer is simply a "citizen in uniform", to be judged by the same standards as anyone else. Developing this line of reasoning, Klockars has convincingly argued that when they use force, police officers should be expected to act according to the standards of "a highly skilled officer" (Klockars 1996). In other words, entrusted with the power to use coercion, police officers should shoulder the additional responsibilities that this implies.

This growth of peer evaluation fits the evidence that officers are good judges of the professional competence of their colleagues (Bayley & Garofalo 1989). It is also consistent with demands that the police sub-culture – for so long enjoying only pariah status among academics and senior police ranks – should be enlisted to *improve* standards of conduct. Kelling and Kliesmet argue that the defensiveness of the lower ranks, as expressed through the intransigence of police unions, is a *response* to the punitiveness of traditional management. They suggest that a more consultative style would not only smooth the introduction of organizational change, but tap a rich source of practical knowledge (Kelling & Kliesmet 1996; see also Goldsmith 1990; Bayley 1991b).

Empowering

One means of controlling police that is rarely acknowledged as such is that of empowering officers to perform their role without recourse to deviant practices. Mention was made above in passing that it might be better to recognize that police officers use force by officially giving them that special entitlement coupled with additional responsibilities. Hence, officers might be found guilty of using "excessive force" short of committing a criminal assault. As noted immediately above, this might then enable officers to be required to display higher levels of competence in the use of force. Similarly, policing involves the routine exercise of authority, but short of invoking powers of arrest and so forth, that authority is not officially underwritten. However, if Anglo–Saxon jurisdictions were to follow the continental European tradition and institute a "doctrine of rebellion", police would be freed from the need to resort to "creative" use of "resource charges".

This approach has been adopted to a very limited extent in Britain. The Police and Criminal Evidence Act (PACE), 1985, explicitly empowers officers to search, detain and interrogate suspects. In doing so, as Dixon (1997) makes plain, it effectively legalizes long-established institutionalized police malpractice. Although predictably denounced at the time of its passage as oppressive by civil libertarian campaigners, it has now become a model that is widely admired and sometimes emulated in other jurisdictions. While there are undoubtedly still problems associated with the treatment of suspects, there can be little doubt that it has been a engine for improving police conduct. In order to operate effectively within the constraints of PACE, the police have encouraged "ethical interviewing" and other means of enhancing their own professionalism. The irony is that by *facilitating* the achievement of police goals, policing practice is more effectively *controlled* than it is when restricted.

Conclusion

Policing is intrinsically difficult to control: not only does it occur in relatively invisible circumstances, the recipients of police are also largely powerless and marginal. There is also good reason to doubt the desire on the part of the political and legal establishment, and also popular public opinion, for the police to be subject to much restraint. Yet, the almost universal denial of the police role, as the routine exercise of state authority, is perhaps the most powerful influence conducive to malpractice. Frankly recognizing what the police do and attempting to facilitate it within the law might still be the best hope for effective regulation.

CHAPTER 7

Controlling Police Organizations

Introduction

In the previous chapter we examined attempts to control the behaviour of individual officers and penalize wrongdoing. Apart from the many difficulties in establishing whether officers are guilty of wrongdoing that were identified, disciplinary and legal proceedings can only have a limited impact on police behaviour, not least because action targeted against individuals fails to address the organizational context within which they act. For this reason, reformers have sought to gain influence over, if not direct control of, police policy-making. It is article of faith among many critics of the police in Britain that policing will continue to be unacceptable so long as it remains beyond the control of elected representatives. This debate has largely been conducted in a spirit of intense parochialism. In this chapter I will try to expand empirical horizons to consider the constitutional position of the police in other jurisdictions and assess whether nostrums advanced for improving the police are supported by experience elsewhere.

Independence and Control

The central issue in this debate is that of democratic control of the police as opposed to independence from political influence. The constitutional basis for bringing the police under the direct control and direction of elected representatives is quite clear: "It is a fundamental principle of a democratic system of government that people who are elected, or appointed, to exercise power over others should be accountable for their actions." (Spencer 1985b: 1); and that accountability should be "to the body politic" (Greene 1993: 369). Yet in many jurisdictions the police are not unequivocally accountable to the "body politic". In the eyes of constitutionalists this is a fundamental democratic deficit. Stated more bluntly, one might ask why it is that we entrust the education of our children, the provision of health care, the planning of urban development, the management of the nation's finances, foreign policy, not to mention the waging of war, into the hands of politicians, but are reticent to do the same with policing? Indeed, the case for bringing policing firmly under the control of elected representatives is more compelling than most of the other responsibilities of politicians. The police are custodians of the state's monopoly of legitimate force as it is applied to citizens and, therefore, nothing is more central to the functioning of the state than policing. In a polity that claims to govern by the consent of the governed, it is particularly necessary that citizens should be able to determine how the monopoly of force is used. Again, to put it bluntly, what is the point of politicians providing first-class education to citizens whose civil liberties are routinely abused by a police force beyond democratic control? From this perspective it is not only absurd, it is offensive, that elected representatives are unable to remove chief officers, be they the Director of the FBI, Judge William Sessions, Chief Gates of the LAPD or the Chief Constable of Manchester, Sir James Anderton.

The constitutional case *seems* irrefutable, but it is when the rhetoric is stripped away that problems emerge. In the first place, it is simply untrue to claim that an essential requirement of democracy is that officials who "exercise power over others" are invariably accountable, through the "body politic". There are many bodies exercising power that are independent of political control, including, in Britain, the BBC Board of Governors, the Health and Safety Executive, Parliamentary Boundary Commissioners, the Audit Commission and National Audit Office, Equal Opportunities Commission and, no doubt, many more. These institutions embody the notion that certain functions should be removed from political contention, even though the decisions they must take are occasionally contentious; such as whether the BBC should broadcast an interview with terrorists. Precisely which functions should be removed from the political arena is itself a political decision and varies from one polity to another; but that *some* activities should be removed seems universally accepted in non-totalitarian societies.

It is universally agreed among the liberal democracies that one function that should be removed from political contention is the law. Now, let us be clear, the law *is* quintessentially a function of the state operated by appointed officials (judges, magistrates, and other tribunals) who exercise enormous discretion. Few state functionaries can compete in the "exercis[ing] power over others" stakes with judges who impose fines, imprisonment, or loss of life. Not only are judges unaccountable to politicians, they may dictate what politicians can do. The United States Supreme Court, European Court of Human Rights and similar constitutional courts in other jurisdictions have the power to strike down legislation deemed to be unconstitutional. In Britain, there has been a growth of administrative law over the past 50 years which has limited the scope of political decision-making.

Democracy is rooted in two principles: electoral accountability and the "rule of law" which exist in tension. That tension is embodied in the doctrine of the "separation of powers" that underwrites the American constitution and is often felt to be compromised in Britain by senior law officers also holding ministerial positions in government, notably the Lord Chancellor and Attorney General. As Jefferson and Grimshaw (1984b) argue, the law is distinguished from politics through its "principled discourse", represented most clearly when unpalatable decisions are found to be legally unavoidable because judges' hands are tied by statute and precedent. It is worth noting that when interpreting statutes, judges are not required to interpret the intentions of legislators, but to interpret the law *as it stands*, whether or not that interpretation is to the liking of politicians who created it. This is quite different to the discourse of politics which is rooted in the representation of *interests* that may be particular and transitory.

It is no accident that the law is the principal institution through which the state's monopoly of legitimate coercion is channelled; for the law is the guarantor of the rights of citizens. According to Marshall's classic account (Marshall, T.H. 1950), citizenship evolved in Britain from the eighteenth century extension of *legal* rights to the civil population that limited state power. A good example of this is contained in the 1765 case of *Entick v. Carrington*, quoted by Dixon:

> every official interference with individual liberty and security is unlawful unless justified by some existing and specific statutory or common law rule; any search of private property will similarly be a trespass and illegal unless some recognised lawful authority for it can be produced; in general, coercion should only be brought to bear on individuals and their property at the instance of regular judicial officers acting in accordance with established and known rules of law, and not by executive officers acting at their discretion; and finally it is the law, whether common law or statute, and not a plea of public interest or an allegation of state necessity that will justify acts normally illegal. (cited in Dixon 1997: 55)

Not only are law and politics separate state activities, law is *superior*.

The reason why policing is an acute constitutional issue, lies in the uncertain location of the police between these fundamental principles and the institutions that embody them. For, while policing is a "public good" whose distribution is an unavoidably political issue (Lustgarten 1986), in liberal democracies political issues are resolved in *partisan* terms and it is far from clear whether partisan considerations should apply to issues of policing.

Britain: Political Autonomy Versus Control

Consideration of the constitutional position of the police in Britain (where the debate was intense during the 1980s) usually begins by delving into the medieval origins of the "office of constable". Space precludes a recitation of this history (for details see Critchley 1978), but it is unimportant since there is no doubt that Peel's installation of a professional police changed the rules of the game sufficiently radically to render what went before of antiquarian interest only. What *is* important, is how Peel *used* the historical "office of constable" to placate political opposition to the "New Police" that feared, among other things, that the police would become a oppressive arm of the state. Constables were traditionally servants of justices of the peace and it is instructive that the first Commissioners of Police in London (and many generations of their successors) were *not* police officers, but sworn as justices (a practice repeated under the Birmingham Police Act 1835 [Critchley 1978]) – in other words, those in overall charge of the police were *judicial* officers. It is equally the case that the Metropolitan Police Act 1829 subordinated the Commissioners to the Home Secretary and created thereby a constitutionally ambiguous position for the police that has since been the hallmark of policing in Britain and has given proponents of both sides of the debate plentiful ammunition with which to support their respective arguments. Arrangements for policing urban centres brought the borough police forces firmly under the control and direction of local politicians, through the Watch Committees of local councils. On the other hand, the policing of rural areas was always under pronounced magisterial influence: parliament legislated first to allow and then to compel magistrates sitting in Quarter Sessions to establish a police force for the whole or part of any county. Eventually, this was transformed into a Standing Joint Committee in which magistrates and elected councillors shared equal responsibility. Constitutional reform continued on a piecemeal basis until 1964 when a single constitutional framework was created for all police forces, apart from the London Metropolitan. A "tri-partite" structure was introduced consisting of the Home Secretary, local Police Authority, and the chief constable, and which embodied the ambiguous constitutional position of the police. A uniform structure was imposed on police authorities that would henceforth consist of one-third representation of magistrates and two-thirds councillors. The police authorities' responsibilities were to maintain an "adequate and efficient" force (Lustgarten 1986: 84–94) while the force was to be under the "direction and control" of the chief constable. The meaning and delineation of these responsibilities became a matter of increasingly acrimonious conflict, especially when chief constables asserted their "operational independence" against more assertive left-wing police authorities during the 1980s. Meanwhile, through a series of steps stretching back to the inception of Peel's "New Police", central government had extended its grip on policing throughout the country (Critchley 1978). By 1964 this was explicitly recognized by statutory responsibility imposed on the Home Secretary to "promote" the efficiency of the police, for which the minister is granted wide statutory powers. This placed the Home Secretary in a pivotal position as clashes between local police authorities and their chief constables grew more intense; for whoever gained the support of the Home Office won, and that was almost invariably the chief constable. In 1994 further legislative change reduced the size of police authorities, limited the proportion of locally elected representatives to half and replaced magistrates with central government appointees who were supposed to introduce a measure of business acumen to policing. At the same time, the Home Office strengthened its grip by requiring police authorities to achieve national policing objectives and subordinated chief constables by requiring that they be employed on short-term contracts (Loveday 1994a, ibid. 1995b, ibid. 1996; Butler 1995; McLaughlin & Murji 1995, ibid. 1996; Savage & Charman 1995).

As this brief historical sketch makes clear, the constitutional position of the police in Britain has been shaped by a protracted *struggle* between competing principles and interests: political independence versus electoral accountability; central rather than local power; manufacturing and mercantile interests versus the landed gentry. That struggle has only partly been played out in constitutional legislation; it has also been reflected in debates, controversies and crises surrounding policing. The most persistent theme in these debates, controversies and crises has been the tension between independence and political control. For example, during parliamentary debates on the Local Government Bill 1888, which introduced Standing Joint Committees for county police forces, "Reference was constantly made to questions on which 'political and popular public feeling' might be very strong, and it was suggested that those who controlled the police ought to be persons *free from any sort of popular pressure*" (Critchley 1978: 135 emphasis added). Three-quarters of a century later borough councils fought the government's proposal to incorporate into the 1964 Police Act the practice, previously restricted to standing joint committees, of including magistrates on police authorities. Conflicts between chief constables and their respective local authorities and the activities of such moral entrepeneurs as Mr Raymond Blackburn led the courts to interpret the constitutional status of the police in directions favourable to the principle of independence (Lustgarten 1986). But controversies have extended beyond the narrowly constitutional: a series of conflicts between chief constables and their local Watch Committees repeatedly brought the issue of independence from political control to the forefront even though they ostensibly concerned the policing of drunkenness and prostitution, licensing of pubs and places of entertainment and other such routine aspects of police work (Critchley 1978). The notion that the police officer should be apolitical is manifested in the continuing restrictions on overt political activities by police officers, such as membership of political parties, which before 1919 went so far as to deny police officers the right to vote. It was an insistence upon the independence of the police that persistently fuelled, and still fuels, concerns about the influence of freemasonry (Wall 1994a, ibid. b). It is instructive that a proposal to require police officers to register their membership of such bodies requires the same only of judges and the Crown Prosecution Service (*Police Review*, 28 March 1997) – in other words, criminal justice officials.

How states react to crises can be seen as evidence of expediency or as revealing fundamental values that need to be defended. It seems clear that the notion of "constabulary independence" clearly emerges as a constitutional principle only relatively recently (Marshall 1965). According to Lustgarten (1986) it was an expedient invention designed to emasculate Labour-dominated local councils allied to increasingly militant trade unions during the turmoil that followed the First World War. We saw in Chapter 3 how a strike-breaking machinery, in which the police played a crucial role, was covertly installed between the two World Wars, which would have been greatly facilitated by the assertion of independence from local political control. Whereas Jefferson and Grimshaw (1984b) detect a longer lineage based on traditional "themes". There seems merit in both perspectives, for while the struggle between the principles of electoral representation and independence from political influence undoubtedly stretches back to the inception of professional policing in Britain, it seems to have *crystallized* in the aftermath of World War One. It was not until the Labour movement presented a serious challenge to the hegemony of landed and capitalist interests that the prospect of serious conflict over policing policy became a constitutional issue; when it did, the independence option was selected.

However, it was not *only* when issues explicitly arose that independence was affirmed as a guiding principle. While the Home Secretary had the power to issue directions to the Commissioner(s) of the Metropolitan Police and used it, from the outset the first two Commissioners of the London Metropolitan force strove consciously to establish their independence from such political influence. The most notable example of this was their resistance to sabbatarianism which they feared would drag the police willy-nilly into conflict with the otherwise law-abiding public (Miller 1977b). It is also instructive to examine the national police self-image. This can be gauged from what the British imposed upon or exported to other jurisdictions. The policing of colonial Canada was strongly influenced by the notion that the police should be autonomous (see below, Stenning 1981) and elsewhere in the British Empire the aspiration to adopt a "bobby" style of policing was assumed to entail independence. After the Second World War each of the occupying powers in West Germany imposed their own distinctive style of policing: the British imposed a tri-partite structure like that they would adopt for themselves twenty years later. This illustrates how entrenched was the view that independence and political accountability should be maintained in some kind of balance (Das 1993).

USA: Machine Politics and Progressive Reform

Britain was not alone in this struggle. The United States also grappled with the same issues, albeit approaching them from a different historical direction. When cities like

New York and Boston first adopted professional policing on the London model, they adapted it to the American environment of intense localism and an entrenched democratic ethos. As a result, the police were invariably under the direct control of the local mayor – and in New York "local" sometimes meant the borough rather than the city. In this capacity American police forces were sucked immediately into the political "machine". Not only were the police subordinate to the mayor, police officers were appointed and promoted according to mayoral pleasure and thus wholly dependent upon the occupant of that office for employment. This proved corrupting: as servants of the political machine they not only avoided enforcing laws against their masters but provided often corrupt services such as discouraging votes being cast in opposition to incumbents.

It was this corruption that prompted reform measures designed to remove the police from political influence. This is sometimes divided into "progressive" and "professional" eras, but constitutionally both were intent on treating the police as independent law enforcers. Crucially, the Wickersham Commission of 1931 recommended that police officers be granted "civil service" terms and conditions of employment, designed to free them from political patronage. In "reform" departments police were subject to rational-bureaucratic methods of evaluation, rather than the favours of politicians. The "full enforcement" provisions of some states were intended to negate discretion and thus make the police officer the unequivocal servant, not of politicians, but of the law. This era, lasting from the end of the First World War to the 1970s was notably successful in eradicating police corruption, even in cities otherwise afflicted by corrupt government (Sherman 1978). It is a vision of policing that continues to resonate in American thinking about the police:

> . . . one might view the evolution of the American police as moving away from a concept of "personal authority", rooted in the character of a policeman's relationships with the community being policed, to a concept of "impersonal authority", which is tied closely to the legitimacy of the state and based on a concept of the police as dispassionate servants of society. . . . The police are more than servants, they are professional servants. They stand above the community and assume the responsibility for interpreting and judging what are the serious problems of crime and disorder that a community faces and what should be done about them (Brown, cited in Patterson 1991: 265)

However, probity was bought at the cost of distancing the police from the public they were supposed to serve and encouraging aggressive law-enforcement strategies. These became increasingly untenable and during the 1970s and 80s began to wane in favour of greater community involvement in policing (Patterson 1991; Kappeler *et al.* 1994).

Commonwealth Jurisdictions

As in Britain, policing in the United States represents a struggle between electoral accountability, on the one hand, and independence from political influence, on the other. This was and is also true of Canada where, in Ontario, the Baldwin Act 1849 established boards of commissioners, comprising the mayor, recorder and police magistrate (the latter two both being judicial officers) to oversee municipal policing.

> The scheme of this legislation makes it quite clear that it was intended that the board should have a considerable degree of autonomy and independence from the dictates of the municipal council, no matter what its composition may be. The powers and functions of the board were not powers and function delegated by the council, but statutory powers and functions conferred directly on the board itself. (Stenning 1981: 168)

Elsewhere throughout Canada police boards vary enormously, save that "all have had at least a notionally separate identity from that of their local municipal councils" (Stenning 1981: 176) and seek to adopt the mantle of being "non-political". Like the English courts, the courts in Canada have supported the notion that the police should be independent.

> . . . two things are quite clear. First, the concept [of independence] itself has exerted a considerable influence on the relationship of police boards to the forces that they govern, encouraging a posture of substantial restraint, and a tendency to favour a limited interpretation of their mandate, by the former, and a good measure of hostility toward attempts to impose democratic control on the police, by the latter. Secondly, the precise implications of the notion of police independence for the relationship of a police board to its police force are the subject of substantial disagreement among police chiefs and police board members alike across Canada. (Stenning 1981: 189)

Stenning concludes, however, that the independence of the police from political control is a democratic deficit in contemporary Canada.

Another Commonwealth country, New Zealand, is distinguished by having a Minister of Police, but the relationship of the minister to the national police retains the notion that the latter are operationally independent while the minister is responsible for "administration and control" (Das 1993: 72).

Europe: Political Domination?

In Europe, which is often portrayed as unequivocally committed to the political control of policing, the notion that policing should enjoy some measure of independence is embodied in state institutions. For example, in the Netherlands policing was traditionally under the dual responsibility of burgomasters and local public prosecutors in municipalities, and ultimate political responsibility rested jointly with the Ministry of the Interior and Ministry of Justice (Mawby 1990). This is a division of labour that the recent reorganization of policing in the Netherlands has sought to retain (Wintle 1996). However, it should be noted that the burgomaster was and still is a *centrally* appointed official and that the influence of elected representatives was always indirect and since reorganization has become more so (Jones 1995).

In France too there is division of labour between "administrative" policing such as patrolling the streets for which the civil police are responsible to either local mayors or the Ministry of the Interior, and "judicial" tasks such as criminal investigation that come under the jurisdiction of the Minister of Justice (Horton 1995). Moreover, the involvement of investigating magistrates at an early stage in criminal investigation also reflects an acceptance that at least some "police" functions should belong to legal institutions (Stead 1983). Indeed, the Police Nationale have been subject to considerable public criticism precisely because this division between "administrative" and "judicial" tasks has become blurred.

In Germany, the "principle of legality" is designed to ensure that in their law-enforcement duties police officers pay attention only to legal precept (Linnan 1984).

Reform Agendas

Even radical proposals for reform divide on the crucial issue of the constitutional location of the police between law and politics. On the one hand, proposals advanced independently by Lustgarten (1986) and Spencer (1985b) – the latter on behalf of the National Council for Civil Liberties – both opt for placing the police firmly in the political realm. They recommend that the police should enjoy exactly the same status as any other local authority service. Elected councillors would make police policy in exactly the same way that they decide upon educational policy and would be subject to the usual restraints of administrative law in so doing. Major pre-planned operations, such as raids for drugs and so on, would need the prior approval of the council. Because so much police work is reactive, the police would have to be granted delegated powers to deal with situations as they arise; but that could always be reversed if the issue became contentious, as now happens with other services with a law enforcement role, such as social workers. For instance, if rioting broke out police commanders would of necessity decide upon the initial response to it, but councillors could decide to override commanders if they felt that police actions were inappropriate. Officers would continue to exercise discretion in the application of policy to actual law enforcement, just as planning officers apply guidelines to building applications. On the other hand, equally radical proposals are made by Jefferson and Grimshaw (1984b) who feel that the demands of complying with the law are so great that a separate body would need to be created, which was constitutionally mandated to uphold the law. These elected "commissioners" would be responsible for setting policy on how discretionary aspects of police work should be conducted. In other words, this would place the police more securely under the rubric of the law, albeit with elected representatives.

The diversity of constitutional arrangements, actual and hypothetical, undermines any claim that only one of them is compatible with democracy and the rule of the law (*contra* Lustgarten 1986). Equally, there is ample evidence that the notion of police independence is not something unique to Britain and that the tension between independence, on the one hand, and democratic control, on the other, is one that is widely embodied in police institutions. If democracy dictates that the police be wholly subordinated to elected representatives, then it is doubtful whether democracy is to be found in many parts of the "liberal democratic" world.

Impartiality, Discretion and Law

If the relationship of the police to law requires independence from partisan politics, perhaps that independence should be complete. In other words, the tension between law and politics with which so many jurisdictions struggle, could be eliminated by removing the police from politics entirely and considering the police as a legal institution. This seems to be what some chief constables envisage as their proper constitutional position (Goodson 1984). This is a view that the courts seem to have endorsed, especially in the cases brought by Mr Raymond Blackburn against the London Metropolitan Police (Lustgarten 1986) – in the execution of their duty police officers, whatever their rank, are accountable to no one other than the law itself. This extends to decisions by senior officers to deploy subordinates and other resources in one way rather than another. Several tricky issues arise from this view: first, how far accountability to law can be effective accountability at all; secondly, how far police occupy a quasi-judicial position when exercising discretion; and, finally, whether policy-making is equivalent to law enforcement decisions in particular cases.

Effective Accountability to Law?

The first issue harks back to our previous discussion of police discretion, namely that the police exercise their discretion to *under-enforce* the law. Therefore, their exercise of discretion would only be reviewable by the courts in those comparatively infrequent instances where they opted to invoke the law. The corollary, of course, is that if the police are accountable only to the law for their exercise of discretion, they are effectively *accountable to no one* for the vast majority of the decisions they take, most of which would never come before a court (Grimshaw & Jefferson 1987). As Lustgarten (1986) notes, under-enforcement may become an affront to justice if it is selective, for some sections of the population might routinely escape legal penalty whereas others do not. A good illustration of this has been the common practice among officers in many jurisdictions not to proceed in cases of domestic violence; this has resulted in generations of women being abandoned to the not-so-tender mercies of their abusive husbands. It was not the law that held the police accountable for this, but *political* action by campaigning groups (Jones *et al.* 1994). Nor is it likely that the law could have held the police accountable, for legal institutions were largely ignorant of police *in*action and on those rare occasions where abuse was so serious that prosecution resulted the courts would have found nothing objectionable in the action taken. Hence, advocates of greater political control insist that police must be held accountable for the exercise of discretion to elected representatives who can review the broad spread of police action *and inaction.*

There is, of course, a practical problem that confronts any attempt to make accountable the exercise of police discretion – its low visibility. However, this can be overstated: a political body unencumbered by legal procedures could consider, for example, evidence about the routine practices of police officers that would be inadmissible in court. For instance, there would be nothing to prevent them commissioning surveys and discovering, as did the Policy Studies Institute (Smith 1983), that certain sections of the population were vastly more vulnerable to stop and search than were others. Such a body could also act as a channel through which demands, such as those of feminists for more robust action in cases of domestic violence, could be directed. All this is unexceptionable, but what remains unclear is why such a body need be "political". Now, it depends what is meant by "political" in this context; for if the inclusive meaning is employed, then any distribution of "public goods" become "political". However, as noted already, "political" in liberal democracies is equated with the electoral representation of partisan interests that might be less concerned with pursuing justice than with achieving advantage for those they represent. On the other hand, there seems no reason in principle why such a task could not be performed by a neutral arbiter such as an ombudsman charged with ensuring that police acted impartially.

Quasi-judicial Officers?

This issue becomes entangled with the second – the status of police discretion – for it is sometimes maintained that the police occupy "quasi-judicial" office. The constitutional grounds for this are that, at least in Britain, the powers of a constable are "original": that is, a constable's authority for exercising his or her legal powers is not delegated. No superior can order a constable to invoke legal powers or not in any given case; it is for the constable to make that decision for which he or she will be held directly legally responsible. There are two objections to this view: that it is wrong in principle and untrue in fact. Let us consider the principled objection: this rests on the view that the discretion exercised by the police is no different from that exercised by other state officials (Dixon 1997). Customs officers use their discretion to search some passengers at airports and not others; planning officers object to some building developments and pass others; public health officials close some premises and abstain from doing so in other cases. In each instance, the official exercises his or her discretion by considering the particular facts of the specific cases against general guidelines or instructions. Their powers may be permissive, so Customs Officers may search travellers entering the country, but are not obliged to search particular individuals or a given quota. The grounds for deciding one way or the other *may* be good or bad. Thus, a surgeon who refuses surgery to an habitual cigarette smoker may be acting properly if the decision is based on a assessment of the likelihood that the treatment will prove effective or enhance the patient's quality of life, but could be considered improper if the surgeon merely believed that smokers were a menace and the fewer of them that survived, the better! Thus, a police officer who decides to take no action against a person found committing a minor legal violation because it is judged that in the circumstances little harm is being done, is not engaged in any process of decision-making that is reserved to the police alone.

The problem with this approach to police discretion is that, like our earlier discussion, it remains imprisoned within a legàlistic frame of reference. Lustgarten expresses this with his customary clarity and directness:

> One assumption underpinning the analysis is that the mandate of the police is the executive task of enforcing criminal law. It is true that the police perform many social service functions, but most of these could readily and perhaps more effectively be performed by other agencies. . . . And although sociologically and historically it makes eminent sense to talk about policing primarily in terms of the maintenance of order, in concrete terms this ineluctably political task is carried out by the discretionary invocation of legal powers. (Lustgarten 1986: 161)

On the one hand, this is perfectly justifiable because discussion of constitutional issues is legalistic, but on the other it can prove misleading for it fails to appreciate that legal powers are not merely "invoked" they are "used".

> Those who argue that, for example, offensive language should not be an arrestable offence (as it is in New South Wales) on the ground that a summons will usually be appropriate overlook the ways in which police use such a charge,

> especially in their control of Aboriginal people. Often, this is not (or not simply) to respond to an offence. Rather, an offensive-language charge is a method of control, a justification for removing a person from a public place. (Dixon 1997: 77)

If the power of arrest for the offence of using offensive language was to be removed, the police would simply use another charge to justify "removing a person from a public place". Legal powers are instruments that serve higher purposes; they do not define or prescribe what those purposes are. It is in the purposes they pursue that the police might be regarded as exercising quasi-judicial powers: for example, in the two cases of domestic violence referred to by Chatterton (1983), and discussed above, the decision to take action is based on an assessment of the *culpability* of the parties. The arrest of the "culpable" husband is not on a charge of assault, but for drunkenness; the arrest is *in itself* the imposition of a penalty of sorts. The police perform the *de facto* role of a court of first instance on the streets: they adjudicate in disputes, deciding on culpability; prescribe remedies, and impose penalties. In doing all this they *use* the law, not enforce it.

If it is acknowledged that police perform a "quasi-judicial" role of sorts, this actually strengthens the argument for subjecting them to greater political oversight. As was argued in a previous chapter, the routine exercise of police discretion serves prevailing social values. Radical critics are correct in observing that the police are not impartial when the interests of "respectable" people come into conflict with those of disadvantaged sections of the population (State Research 1981b). To expect that they would be impartial is rather like expecting police to be impartial between the law-abiding and law-breakers! But it does raise a crucial question about how the police identify what values "prevail". There is always the danger that the police begin to impose their own private standards on the rest of the civil population, as has allegedly happened when some chief constables have vigorously pursued certain morals offences, such as pornography. Locally elected representatives can act as a conduit through which shifts in prevailing values make themselves felt.

The second objection to the notion of police as quasi-judicial officers is that they do not, nor can they, exercise unfettered discretion. Police officers are enmeshed within large bureaucracies that subject them to rules, guidelines, and other restraints upon the decisions that they can take, but which are themselves not subject to review. For example, it is common practice in many police forces for complaints of crime to be screened according to set formulæ to determine what resources should be devoted to their investigation. This is a routine administrative task in which discretion plays little part in applying criteria that need not have received any authorization from democratic, or for that matter legal, institutions.

The safest conclusion seems to be that in *some* respects individual officers act in ways that are, at least d*e facto,* quasi-judicial, but that in many others they act as bureaucratic functionaries.

Discretionary Policy-Making

The extent to which policy and administrative rules determine the behaviour of subordinates in the police (or many another) organization can be grossly over-stated, but it is undoubtedly the case that the arguments for the democratic control of the police are on firmest ground when applied to policy-making. In deciding how to allocate resources senior officers are not, and cannot be, accountable to law because they are obliged to prioritize between legally equivalent tasks (Grimshaw & Jefferson 1987). If it is decided, say, that resources should be devoted to traffic offences, or public drunkenness, or mugging, or drug-taking then this is a distribution of a "public good". That is, the decision will be properly taken after some assessment of the harm that these offences create and how much impact the police can realistically expect to have in ameliorating them. It might be decided that the death, injury and damage to property caused by criminal driving, as well as annoyance and delay to other road-users, is sufficiently serious as to warrant a shift in policing priorities. This is not a legal evaluation, but a political (in the broad sense) assessment of what is in the aggregate public interest. However, it is not at all clear that the police have any special competence in deciding upon such matters, for they require no technical expertise, only a moral sense of what the public values.

> Some of these decisions require solely the application of professional experience and expertise. Most, however, are *political* decisions. The word is used, not in the sense of partisanship but to describe the essence of public choice: decisions which entail judgements about moral values, favour certain interests over others, and require weighing competing claims for scarce resources. At this level, policing is politics, just as taxation or education are politics. (Lustgarten 1986: 20)

If left to the police, the public have imposed upon them what the police think the public desire (Reiner 1991a); politicians are neither more nor less capable of making such judgements, but being elected enables the electorate to periodically reject them if they fail adequately to reflect their priorities. Even if the decisions do involve technical issues, this does not establish that they should be taken by technocrats (Spencer 1985b). If, as the aphorism has it, "war is too important to be left to the generals", then so too is policing too important to be left to police officers.

Accommodating Constitutional Tensions

Considering these three issues together, it seems clear that law and politics must exist in tension; therefore, the question arises as to how that tension is to be institutionally accommodated. To what kind of body should the police be responsible? For what range of decision-making should such a body have responsibility? In Britain the attempt was made to differentiate between "operational" matters, that were left to the chief constable, and "administrative or organizational" issues that were the preserve of partially elected committees. This proved unsatisfactory, since it largely excluded elected representatives from deciding on matters of any significance and became a recipe for conflict once local politicians began to explore the full extent of their powers. Thus, on the one hand, it is regarded as a democratic abomination that routine arming of the police can become widespread without the "informed consent" of the public via its elected representatives (McKenzie 1995). On the other hand, police have complained that elected representatives have attempted to impede their operational effectiveness by budgetary manipulation. Thus, disputes arose during the year-long coalminers' strike about the maintenance of police horses, which the police regarded as an attempt by councils supportive of the miners to prevent the use of mounted officers on picket-lines. Similar problems have arisen from attempts to distinguish *policy* from *operational* decisions

(Grimshaw & Jefferson 1987; Spencer 1985b). It seems that policing is destined to remain in an ambiguous constitutional position.

Abuses of Power

The standard objection to granting political control over the police is the potential it offers for abuse and corruption. There can be little doubt that historically and comparatively political control of the police has been associated with corrupt practice. The prime illustration was the Tammany Hall political machines of American cities whose influence the progressive and police professional movements sought to eradicate during the first half of the twentieth century, but which continue to plague some cities (Miller 1995). According to Robinson, politically controlled police in America were used by politicians to suppress the effects of their own failures to prevent urban decay, discrimination and other ills (Robinson 1975). Certainly, it was not the politically controlled police of nineteenth-century American cities that acquired an international reputation for epitomizing civil policing, but the most politically independent and unaccountable police force, the London Metropolitan (Miller 1977a). Elsewhere in Britain, where police forces were controlled by local Watch Committees corruption was much more common, the influence of local brewers and pub owners being legendary (Critchley 1978).

The association between political control and corruption is confined neither to particular historical periods or specific locations. In France the close association between the *Police Nationale* and the Ministry of the Interior and local mayors has been regarded as a corrupting influence from which the Gendarmarie have been saved by their more distant relationship with political figures (Horton 1995). The Fitzgerald Inquiry into policing in Queensland, Australia, identified centralized political control as a principal source of corrupting influence (Finnane 1990). Similar problems arose in Canada where

> . . . by the 1830s cities and towns were authorized to appoint full-time police forces if they wished. Members of the forces were still appointed annually and their selection was based on patronage. The political character of appointees proved nothing short of disastrous when riots and religious rivalry shattered the peace of the community, since the faction in control of the municipal government was not above using the police as a partisan force. (McDougall cited in Stenning 1981: 171; see also Sturgis 1991)

In the Indian state of Kerala under communist rule "the documentation of partiality in the administration of justice was one of the critical factors turning the tide of opinion and impelling the central government to take over the governing of the state" (Bayley 1969: 365). Throughout India there is ample evidence of political interference with the police which results in them being intimidated into inaction and prevarication, and being susceptible to the influence of powerful individuals. In divided societies political control is associated with the oppression of the minority population. In Northern Ireland, prior to the reform of the RUC, the Minister of Home Affairs in the Stormont government and head of the RUC routinely took decisions for reasons of political expediency and partisanship (Ryder 1989; Topping 1991; see also Gamson & Yuchtman 1977 on Israel).

Constitutionalists dismiss fears that if police were brought under exclusively political control they would be used to enforce the law in a partisan manner, by pointing out that no one can instruct a police officer in how to enforce the law (Marshall 1965; Spencer 1985b; Grimshaw & Jefferson 1987).

> ... no superior officer can take away the discretion granted to the individual constable by statute, either by requiring him to arrest, or forbidding him to arrest, a particular individual or anyone who falls into some predefined category.... If the balance of power between chief constables and democratic representatives was to be altered, and police authorities once again exercised executive control of their forces, that change would leave the discretionary power of constables totally unaltered. (Lustgarten 1986: 14)

However, it is not clear that politicians seeking control of the police share this restricted view of their role. Bundred, writing as vice-chairperson of the Greater London Council Police Committee, evidently envisaged instructing the Metropolitan Police in how they should enforce the law (Bundred 1982). This harks back to a long and discreditable tradition in which politicians sought to obstruct the police in British boroughs from interfering with the vested interests they represented. More importantly, Lustgarten merely lays bare the paucity of legalism; for as numerous corruption scandals testify, influence is not necessarily brought to bear so overtly. It is through the power to reward officers who act as their political masters desire and punish those who do not that corrupting influence is often wielded.

The constitutionalist argument is similarly weak when applied to general policy directives, for it is argued that in Britain any policy can be appealed against on the grounds that it is not "reasonable" – the so-called "Wednesbury rules" (Spencer 1985b; Lustgarten 1986). However, it would not test the ingenuity of a police authority to construct a perfectly "reasonable" argument for deploying police resources in their preferred direction. In law "reasonableness" is an enormously elastic category that excludes little. On the other hand, if the constitutionalists are right and it *is* true that the law would restrain elected representatives from interfering with the enforcement of law, one is left wondering what purpose would be served by constitutional change. Police officers would continue to exercise their discretion on the streets untouched by the policy directives of elected representatives, just as they do now.

A Mechanism For Restraint?

Advocates of greater political control of the police do not rest their case entirely on constitutional principle, but add that it will bring tangible benefits – better policing. However, as Reiner points out, "there is no reason for expecting this to be the panacea in terms of improving standards of police work, which critics seem to imply, pretty well without a shred of evidence" (Reiner 1985d: 126). The expectation that policing improves under political direction seems to rest on identifying how police have failed to resolve various problems (Jefferson & Grimshaw 1984b), rather than on how local government has succeeded. Police failures are numerous, but that does not establish that had they been under political control the situation would have been any better. When the police in British cities were under the control of local Watch Committees they were not noted for their enlightened approach. For instance, in the riots that followed the First World War in Cardiff, Liverpool and elsewhere, racism was shown not only by the rioters who attacked ethnic-minority seamen, but also by the police whose coercive interventions were directed not at the rioters but at those in peril (Jenkinson 1993). Indeed, the policies and practices of many politically controlled state agencies are subject to vituperative criticism from many on the left of British politics. Social Security inspectors are accused of hounding the poor (Cook 1989) and the Immigration Service are accused of heavy-handed oppression of ethnic minorities (Gordon 1981, ibid. 1984b, ibid. 1985; Cook 1983; Luthra & Gordon 1984). Enlightenment certainly has not flowed from political control in these cases if radical critics are to be believed.

What little evidence there is of political control of the police in Britain suggests that for the most part political supervision was always supine, even in boroughs with Watch Committees (Brogden 1977, ibid. 1982; Regan 1983a, ibid. b; Reiner 1991a). For a brief historical moment, left-wing Labour-councils succeeded in gaining control of the police authorities of a few conurbations, but in the confrontations that followed they were defeated. It is commonly imagined that defeat was at the hands of the Conservative government that finally abolished these councils. However, McLaughlin's thorough, incisive and sympathetic study of the Manchester police authority tells a rather different tale (McLaughlin 1994). It is one in which those whom the left wing of the Labour-dominated Manchester City Council wished to mobilize through local consultation stubbornly refused to share their agenda of curtailing the activities of the police. Instead, those who attended local meetings demanded *more* "law and order" and victim support groups and neighbourhood watch networks were successfully mobilized by the police and moderate or right-wing politicians to defeat the left. Instead of empowering the most crime-ridden and deprived neighbourhoods, attempts to assert political control condemned these areas to even greater marginality because of their political alignment with the militant factions.

McLaughlin's analysis is of much wider significance than the experience in one English city at a particular time; for it implicitly challenges the fundamental assumption that political control of the police will benefit the poor and marginalized. On the contrary, there are strong grounds for believing that political control of the police would adversely affect precisely this section of the population. What seems not to have occurred to proponents of democratic control is that elected police authorities might insist upon more "law and order" to the disadvantage of marginal groups. In the United States there has been a pronounced shift since the 1970s towards aggressive law enforcement championed by elected representatives under such slogans as the "war on drugs" (Gordon 1990). The growing number of African–American mayors and chiefs of police have obtained political support by tactics that are indistinguishable from those operated by their white predecessors (Skolnick & Bayley 1986; Cashmore & McLaughlin 1991). The reason for this, as McLaughlin discovered in Manchester (McLaughlin 1994), is that the deprived and dispossessed are not as well organized as powerful interests. The repeated experience of public consultation is that forums are captured by the articulate and powerful. This was the conclusion reached by Morgan following his research on Police Liaison Committees in Britain (Morgan & Maggs 1985; Morgan, R. 1987; see also Stratta 1990; Weitzer 1992), confirmed by Dixon and Stanko's evaluation of a community-policing initiative in London (Dixon & Stanko 1993) and Maggs's brief review of New York City precinct community councils (Maggs 1986). My own research on public-order policing in London found that the ability of the police to gain extensive control over mass gatherings was not impeded by the establishment of a public representative body to oversee the Notting Hill Carnival. On the contrary, it facilitated it as organized and articulate opinion was mobilized to resist anything that threatened not only disorder, but wrought further unwelcome depredations on residents (Waddington 1994a, ibid. 1996b). Such democratic representation is easily coopted by the police to legitimate suppression of marginal groups. Thus even in an area of London notable for the opposition of Afro–Caribbeans against the police, the local liaison committee not only authorized, but encouraged police to use riot-squads to support the closure of an unofficial "social club" that had become the centre for oppositional activity (Gordon 1984a).

Apart from their greater political organization, those who seek more vigorous enforcement have other advantages over marginal groups in achieving their goal democratically. The first is the legal precept that no one can instruct a police officer how to enforce the law. This gives a distinct bias towards law enforcement rather than abstinence, for formal penalties could not be imposed on officers who vigorously enforce laws that politicians would rather not have enforced. As Jefferson and Grimshaw (1987) note, most of the English constitutional conflicts between chief constables and their watch committees were resolved in favour of *upholding* the law. Moreover, since access to the courts favours those with the wealth and organizational resources to avail themselves of it, it seems that any attempt to swing police practice towards favouring minorities and the dispossessed at the expense of the powerful would be doomed to failure. Secondly, criminal incidents provide compelling grounds for increased law enforcement through their instigation of "moral panics". Thus, when a deranged gunman killed 16 people in an English country town, this became a "window of opportunity" for the police to introduce armed response vehicles (Waddington 1991; Waddington & Hamilton 1997). Thirdly, the police are in an advantaged position to mobilize public opinion. As Cashmore and McLaughlin concluded in evaluating policing in the aftermath of Britain's inner-city riots:

> . . . the police have commanded authority and their views have sufficient legitimacy to persuade the population that a crisis of colossal proportions is afoot. Far from losing public confidence, the police have strengthened it by demonstrating a hard-edged toughness and resolution in its efforts to maintain order in the face of all manner of threats, the main one of which has been black youth (Cashmore & McLaughlin 1991: 40)

Finally, extending police powers is a means of expressing political will. It is

> . . . one of the clearest way (sic) in which politicians can signify that they take public concerns seriously. When the demand is to "do something about the crime problem", a change in police powers is an attractive option: it is likely to be popular, highly visible, and cheap. (Dixon 1997: 85)

Thus, in Troy, New York, although the roles were reversed the outcome was much the same as in Manchester, England: a progressive and enlightened chief was obstructed and eventually defeated by the mobilization of conservative forces (Guyot 1991).

There is also a directly democratic reason why political control of the police does not produce enlightened policing – there is little public appetite for it. The behaviour of Mayor Daley's cops at the Democratic Party Convention in 1968 appalled liberal opinion and was officially described as a "police riot" (Walker 1968). It did *not* appal Mayor Daley, who publicly applauded the actions of police officers and it seems not to have appalled the voters of Chicago either. An even more dramatic example was Frank Rizzo's reign in Philadelphia that began with a promise, expressed in the most uncompromising language, to pursue tough law and order policies. He was re-elected for a second four-year term and only narrowly defeated in a referendum called to grant him an exceptional third term. Evidently, the decision to suspend the Philadelphia Police Department's erstwhile restrictions on the use of deadly force and the 20 per cent increase in fatal shootings by police that followed, did not dent his electoral popularity. Nor is the public desire for tough law-and-order policies an American curiosity: the PSI survey of Londoners found strong support for tough policing (Smith 1983). During the 1980s the British Labour Party acquired a reputation for being "soft" on crime, which did them enormous political damage and was repudiated by the leader of the party who pledged to support the police in the fight against crime (McLaughlin 1994). Dixon describes how attempts to impose procedural restraints on the police in New South Wales have foundered upon electoral unpopularity (Dixon 1997). Just as telling, has been the political success of opponents of greater external review of complaints against the police mentioned above (Bayley 1991b; Freckelton 1991; Goldsmith 1991). Against this public appetite for "toughness", what is remarkable is not that civil liberties are not more advanced, or in some cases actually eroded, but that they have advanced as far as they have. This has been a victory not for representative politics, but the influence of unelected liberal officials in the civil service (Downes 1993; Downes & Morgan 1994; Rock 1995b) who have been responsive to the influence of civil libertarian campaigners.

On whom does tough policing fall? It is the marginalized, powerless and dispossessed. As Jones and Levi (1987) concluded from their research on popular opinions to law and order issues, the belief that local political control would reduce harassment of minority youth is wishful thinking. Instead, even in radical Manchester:

> [the] truly marginalized, those whose voice was apparently "shrill" and biased . . . those badly treated in police custody, those denied elementary rights, the urban black and female population, the gay and lesbian, the travellers, those with even slight criminal records and even a large section of the unemployed . . . were . . . pushed out of sight and their policing needs dispensed with. (Walker quoted in McLaughlin 1994: 119)

Respectable citizens, whom the exercise of police discretion favours and protects, are much less concerned about the oppressive use of police powers against marginal groups, than they are about the threat of crime and disorder. "For those groups who are subject to the attention of the police the ramifications of the seeming lack of concern about police accountability for their substantive rights of citizenship are staggering." (McLaughlin 1991: 130.) Regrettably it is also wholly predictable. In France, the extension of powers for police to check identity documents was a populist measure against illegal immigrants embodied in a renamed "Central Directorate for the Control of Immigration and Illegal Employment" within the *Police Nationale*.

> In order words, police officers are now officially required, in carrying out identity and residence checks to target those populations not conforming to the majority white French national profile. (Horton 1995: 46)

Moreover, political mobilization of marginal groups is impeded by the fact that they are also the principle victims of crime and disorder, who are just as likely to support tough law-and-order policies as their respectable neighbours (Jones *et al.* 1994). The communities to which police relate are rarely homogeneous, but instead are riven by conflicts between voluntary and involuntary "users" of police services (Dixon *et al.* 1993; see also Jefferson & Shapland 1994). It is voluntary "users" who are more numerous, powerful and in favour of tough "law and order".

Given this popular thirst for "law and order" there seems every justification for Lea and Young's "constant nightmares ... that if there was a completely democratic control of police in areas such as Hackney, the resulting police force would look exactly the same as the present" (Lea & Young 1984: 270). It is precisely to forestall such a likelihood that Jefferson and Grimshaw (1984b) envisage elected "commissioners" committing themselves to a "socialist conception of justice"; but this triumph of ideological hope over historical experience has faded along with socialism itself. No less utopian are suggestions that the police should be held preferentially accountable to those marginal sections of the population who are "policed" – "victims and offenders, the homeless, young, employed, battered wives and certain ethnic groups" (Loveday 1994a: 10–11; see also Bundred 1982; Banton 1983; Pepinsky 1984). What this prescription fails to appreciate is that these groups are the "policed" *because* they are politically impotent (see Crewe 1983). In sum, there seems to be little prospect of an affirmative answer to McLaughlin's "key question":

> whether it would be possible to construct institutional arrangements which would ensure that those sections of the community most disadvantaged and discriminated against by policework – the policed – had their voices heard directly by those in authority and their complaints acknowledged as legitimate. (McLaughlin 1994: 1)

Making a Difference

Ultimately, the objection to demands to increase civilian participation in policing *as a means of injecting liberality, tolerance and empowerment for marginal groups* is that it is sociologically naïve. Does that mean that prospects for change are non-existent? No, but it does mean that the naïve belief in the efficacy of constitutional reform must, at the very least, be substantially qualified. What is required is a sociologically informed appraisal of where police power lies and how it is wielded.

Brogden's analysis of the historical development of police accountability draws attention to how chief constables gradually exploited the tensions between the centre and periphery in the British state, as well as their ambiguous constitutional position, to achieve a position of increased autonomy. One of their principal weapons was the growing professionalism of chief constables, who organized nationally as a coherent group and were able to influence Home Office policy by providing advice and guidance to policy-makers. This was aided and abetted by central government who increasingly detached chief constables from local government through the provision of central training and curbs on the procedures for their appointment (Brogden 1982). A similar process has occurred in the United States as chiefs of police move from one force to another, using smaller forces as an apprenticeship for commanding larger ones. The

FBI, through its training centre at Quantico and the provision of advice and guidance on best-policing practice, has performed a centralizing role in a system still notable for its localism and diversity. Internationally too, police are increasingly talking to and copying from one another (Bayley 1994a; McCarthy *et al.* 1995). As Reiner has argued, these tendencies create a cosmopolitan "power élite" among senior police officers (Reiner 1991a; ibid. 1989b; ibid c; see also Stenning 1981). Thus, the police share characteristics common to many other organizations which seek to insulate themselves from their environment. In business this is achieved by creating cartels and vertical integration of producers and suppliers; but in organizations like the police it is achieved by the creation of ideological shields that present officers as professional experts and public-relations activities that involve outsiders in policing but on the police's own terms (Greene 1993).

In using political power constitutional ambiguity is a useful resource that has undoubtedly been used by chief constables to their advantage. "*They can legitimately free themselves from political accountability at the same time that they enjoy the freedom, if they wish, to enhance their own internal control*" (Brogden 1982: 128, original emphasis). It has also been used by central government who issue government policy on policing via circulars which are notionally only "advisory", but actually enormously influential (Reiner 1989a, ibid. b). When Reiner asked British chief constables whom they would first inform of an outbreak of serious rioting, the general consensus was that it would be the Home Office ahead of the chairperson of their police authority (Reiner 1991a). Despite persuasive arguments to the contrary (such as the dissenting opinion of Dr Goodhart to the 1964 Royal Commission [Willink 1962]) it is highly improbable that a national police force would be established in Britain with the Home Secretary as its political head. This would gain little by way of increased central government influence over police policy (which is already extensive) and sacrifice the currently convenient fiction that allows the Home Secretary to disown responsibility for anything that is politically inconvenient. A similar situation occurred in Canada where police boards were established, not in order to ensure that the police were apolitical, but to free them from local influence and bring them under provincial or central government spheres of influence (Stenning 1981).

Obstacles to external control of policing do not only lie in the political arena, but also in the nature of the task:

> A major problem in constructing adequate institutions of police accountability is that the decisions which ultimately have the greatest effect on ordinary people are low visibility ones, made day-by-day by constables on the streets and in the backstage areas of police stations. (Reiner 1993a: 8)

In making these decisions police are influenced not by external accountability, but by their working practices and their perception of respectability. On the one hand, this encourages scepticism about the possibilities, not only of external control, but managerial control by senior officers. James describes how a robbery squad was established with a remit to gather evidence against "muggers" by systematic surveillance, but because this violated sub-cultural values of action and excitement, the remit was changed in the course of the policy's implementation in ways that continued to court the very dangers of hasty arrests and possible fabrication of evidence that the new strategy was designed to avoid (James 1979). On the other hand, there have been significant recent changes in policing, that indicate that policies can be effective. Perhaps the most glaring example has been the impact of restrictions on police use of deadly force in the United States. The decision whether to draw and/or fire a weapon is quintessentially discretionary and taken in an instant. Yet, throughout America police policies have become more restrictive and the number of killings has markedly declined (Reiss 1980; Fyfe 1982a; Sherman 1983b; Tennenbaum 1994). Strangely, this has occurred *despite* legal confusion about what the restrictions actually are (Alpert & Smith 1994), which indicates that police are not simply complying with the letter of law but are responding to its proverbial "spirit". This same spirit of restraint can be also be seen in the way in which American police changed their public order strategy from "escalated force" to "negotiated management" (McPhail *et al.* 1998).

American police have not been alone in responding to a changed cultural climate in demanding alterations in their working practices. During a 20-year period when the British police became progressively less accountable, they also became sensitive to demands voiced by democratic interests. This has recently been documented by Jones *et al.* (1994) who point, for example, to how police have responded to feminist demands for more sensitive treatment of women victims of sexual crimes and domestic violence. One of the strongest influences prompting this change was a television documentary that displayed the callous and offensive way in which detectives treated a woman who alleged that she had been raped by several men. The public outrage that followed its screening represented a "cultural shift" (Jones *et al.* 1994: 301–3). But it was also an expression of a wider, indeed international, cultural change towards women as victims of sexual crimes and domestic violence, which was the achievement of the feminist social movement.

All this is consistent with Bayley's contention that political culture is far more important in determining whether policing is "congruent with the values of the community" than is either the mode of accountability procedures and forums, or the structure of the police organization (such as its degree of centralization). Constitutional reform is, he maintains, for symbolic rather than instrumental purposes (Bayley 1982b). Culture is so influential precisely because it insinuates itself into low-visibility policing. For when police officers exercise their discretion by upholding respectability, prevailing values are not only applied to those to whom they direct their actions – victims, bystanders and suspects – but also reflexively to themselves. While the police as an institution may robustly resist constitutional restraints, policing as an activity is far more precarious. The "generalized other" to which the police orient their actions are "ordinary decent people" on whose behalf they see themselves acting. Police recognize that they themselves can be "out of order" in using the exceptional powers at their command. The televized interview with the woman complaining that she had been raped was the source of intense embarrassment to many officers who saw on the screen the embodiment of practices that brought them into disrepute in the eyes of those with whom they identified – hence the "cultural shift".

Brogden describes how police throughout this century have striven to appeal directly to public opinion over the heads of elected representatives (Brogden 1982). This is portrayed as a strategy for gaining autonomy from local political control, and so it undoubtedly is, but it also makes the police sensitive to criticism. The "in the job trouble" that police seek to avoid is not restricted to formal criticism, but extends also and powerfully to their public image as represented in the media. For this reason, they strive to control the media as much as possible (Chibnall 1977; Schlesinger & Tumber 1993, ibid. 1994); however their success is limited. In Britain policing has been transformed from the "sacred" to the "profane" through "desubordination" of marginal sections of the population (Reiner 1995) aided by those who campaign for universal rights of citizenship – the contemporary inheritors of the "Whiggish tradition". (Dixon 1997: 299). This has been witnessed in the growth of "police monitoring" by unofficial radically inclined groups during the 1980s (Field 1985; Jefferson *et al.* 1984); a succession of inquiries into the policing of major public order operations by local councils (Hytner 1981; Silverman 1986); and campaigning civil liberties groups (Dummett 1980a, ibid. b; Gifford 1986; McCabe *et al.* 1988), all of which sullied the police occupational image. All these pale into insignificance, however, compared to the impact that the Scarman report on the 1981 inner-city riots had on police attitudes (Scarman 1981). Indeed, Scarman became overnight the singular authority to which senior police officers, at least, rhetorically deferred. The fact that Scarman was a senior judicial figure was not irrelevant, for while what he concluded was intrinsically "political", his was not a partisan voice that could be dismissed as partial and selective; he represented instead the authoritative expression of respectable opinion. In response, the police have striven hard to re-legitimate their broad political authority through embracing (and, of course, co-opting) public consultation (Morgan 1989). The danger, however, is that when a police force is universally distrusted as brutal, malign and corrupt, it can begin to live *down* to its reputation. This was the situation in India in the 1960s described by Bayley (1969), where lack of popular respect for the police was translated into wholesale non-co-operation which only exacerbated an already bad situation. Any system of control needs to balance the "stick" of public opprobrium with the "carrot" of popular esteem.

There is also a dark side of cultural influence, for where respectable opinion cares little for how the police suppress marginal groups, then constitutional protections will count for hardly anything. This is most apparent in some South American states where prevailing attitudes based upon fear of crime and traditions rooted in militarism have licensed the routine slaughter of "suspects" (Chevigny 1995). However, it is not limited to states whose democratic credentials would, by any criterion, be considered questionable. It is, for instance, noteworthy that not only does the LAPD have a long history of aggressive policing, but this is shared with the Los Angeles County Sheriff's Department, the chief of which is directly elected (Chevigny 1995: 89). This suggests that explanations of the use of excessive force that have focused on the organizational culture and structure of the LAPD alone (Skolnick & Fyfe 1993) are too limited – its source would appear to lie in the local political culture.

Constructing Constitutionalism

Constitutional arguments are limited not only by their omission of any understanding of how power and influence are actually exerted, but also by an unreflexive stance towards constitutional principles. Concepts like "democracy", "law", "due process", "rights" are treated as wholly unproblematic: they are taken to exist *sui generis* as non-relativistic benchmarks. This stands in stark contrast to the scepticism rightly shown towards such concepts as the "independence" or "impartiality" of the police. Thus, when McBarnett demonstrates a disparity between the rhetoric and practice of law, it is against the rhetoric that practice is measured (McBarnett 1983; Dixon 1997). But why accord privileged status to what is, even according to this analysis, mere rhetoric?

Surely, the law is how it is created and maintained *in practice.* Lustgarten might well be justified in his remarks on Lord Denning's judgement in the Blackburn case that "seldom have so many errors of law and logic been compressed into one paragraph"; but this does not negate the fact that it "has become the Bible of those supporting the independence doctrine, and is quoted in virtually all legal writing on police" (Lustgarten 1986: 64). In other words, Denning's view *became* law and the law is in a constant process of *becoming* as cases are decided. Constitutionalists might wish that the law would become something other than it is and use legal discourse to argue accordingly. However, that does not establish that the law is mistaken, for to do so would reify the law itself. The doctrine of "constabulary independence" might be of only recent origin in British law, but to imply that it is an aberration is to deny the fluidity of legal reasoning in which many other principles are of equally recent origin.

This is worthy of greater sociological attention than it has hitherto received. "Democracy", "law" and "rights" are continually being negotiated in changing social, economic and political conditions. They are a cultural arena in which citizenship itself is being repeatedly re-constructed as competing visions of the individual's relationship to state institutions is contested. It is, at least, arguably the case that how these concepts are contested and with what outcome, is by far the most potent means of exerting control over the police institution.

CHAPTER 8

Reform and change

Introduction

The struggle to accommodate policing within a liberal democratic polity is reflected in the frequency with which it is subject to reform. Throughout the nineteenth century reform took the guise mainly of expansion as the authority of the state expanded, but throughout the twentieth century attempts have been made in many jurisdictions to limit the authority that the police wield over citizens. In Britain there have been a succession of inquiries and royal commissions and major legislative changes introduced in the 1980s and changes to the constitutional position of the police made in the 1990s; in the United States there was the multifarious activity associated with the progressive, reform and professionalizing movements to which judicial activism in the Supreme Court in the 1960s and since have added; Canada witnessed a major inquiry into the intelligence-gathering function of the Royal Canadian Mounted Police and the adoption of a Charter of Rights; Australian police forces have been subjected to many inquiries into alleged abuses; the Dutch have amalgamated the hundreds of small municipal police forces into a few regional forces; in Belgium steps have been taken to de-militarize the gendarmerie and following the child abuse scandal of the mid-1990s radical reforms of the civil police have been promised; Italy has introduced a shift from the inquisitorial to a more adversarial system of justice; and in France the *Police Nationale* has been the object of reformist policies.

In this chapter, I will examine three reform movements that seem to have international significance: community policing; police managerialism; and the growth of private involvement in policing. Not only do we need to consider whether they achieve their aims, but also what they tell us about policing and police work.

Community Policing

Community policing appeared in the mid-1970s as a topic of discussion among police administrators and academics, since when it has spread worldwide as the credo of enlightened police thinking. The enormous influence of this approach to policing raises the question: what is it and why has it been so successful?

Community Policing in Theory

One of the foremost advocates of community policing in Britain has been the former chief constable, John Alderson, who in 1979 published the classic statement of the community-policing creed (Alderson 1979). This represented an attempt to reverse what he saw as the headlong and foolhardy reliance on technology and return to a style of policing more in tune with the priorities of local residents. The aim was to enhance social cohesion and integration and thus prevent crime through these positive social influences. As chief constable of Devon and Cornwall, he encouraged experimentation to implement these general principles (Moore & Brown 1981). This involved police officers engaging in activities removed from overt law enforcement, such as co-operating with local government agencies, like those responsible for housing, and consulting the public to discover what they thought about problems of law and order. Meanwhile, in America, Herman Goldstein, was advocating "problem-oriented policing" (POP) (Goldstein 1977, ibid. 1979, ibid. 1987, ibid. 1990). He argued that instead of police restricting themselves to the symptoms of social malaise, in the form of crime and disorder, they should address the underlying causes of those symptoms. This could be as simple as appreciating that rowdy youngsters are a problem to local residents because there is inadequate transport from a place of entertainment. Convincing those responsible to provide transport addresses the problem and avoids police coming into needless confrontation with the young people who seek only to have a good time. Although there are differences of terminology and emphasis between "community" and "problem-oriented policing" they share many affinities and can legitimately be considered together. "Problems" to be addressed are identified by the "community" and community-based resources are mobilized in their resolution (Goldstein 1987). Although each approach can be distinguished from the other, they have sufficient "family resemblance" to be considered together as a general approach to policing.

This is an approach that succeeds in pulling together several otherwise disparate strands in the diverse role that the police fulfil. Just as importantly, perhaps, it does so *in opposition* to the law-enforcement model that predominated during the 1960s in many jurisdictions, when police – buoyed by the promise of technology – came to define their role increasingly narrowly.

> Compared to the enforcement model, the community policing approach takes a different inspiration from the police mandate. Civil order, peace and security are given priority over crime control, which is seen as a means of enhancing peace and security. This approach accords with the idea that the first and pre-eminent duty of the police is to secure public tranquillity. (Fielding 1996: 51)

Under this mandate the order-maintenance function that the police actually perform is explicitly recognized and given priority as some early researchers on policing had explicitly advocated: Banton argued that the police should see their role as "peacekeepers", rather than law enforcers, keeping closely in touch with those whom they policed and committed to crime prevention through what would later be called proactive, multi-agency methods (Banton 1974). Likewise, Wilson had concluded that, while it presented all manner of dilemmas, the order-maintenance role must be recognized as the prime function of the police (Wilson 1968). This emphasis on order-maintenance is justified by its effectiveness in *preventing* or minimizing crime through knowledge of the community. For instance, woven around a vignette of how an officer skilfully defuses a potentially violent situation, Muir shows how order is better maintained through negotiation based on understanding of the people involved, than by an aggressive enforcement approach (Muir 1980). "Community policing" also recognized what subsequent research would confirm: that disorder and "incivility" were at least as serious as crime in their impact on people's lives (Lewis & Maxfield 1980; Maxfield 1984, ibid. 1987; Hope & Hough 1988). The fear of crime that "incivility" created encourages a spiral of decline in which people avoided public places that become even more forbidding when abandoned to the depredations of minor delinquents and vandals; thereby undermining local businesses that collapse to be replaced by more "seedy" alternatives, and so on, until the area becomes a haven for criminals and a nightmare for those unable to escape (Wilson & Kelling 1982; Skogan 1990). This notion also honestly acknowledges the limited impact that law enforcement can have on crime compared to informal social controls (Bayley 1994a). As Skogan indicates, it is neighbourhoods rich in informal social resources that are best able to withstand urban deterioration, since decline is best arrested before it becomes an avalanche. Thus, low-level controls, such as mere watching, are most effective but need to be far more ubiquitous than the police could ever be (Shapland & Vagg 1988). The police role is to encourage and support these informal methods of social control as happened in north London when Jewish organizations co-operated with police in maintaining control over Jewish youth gathering in the high street of a suburb (Factor & Stenson 1989). However, problem-solving does not rely on informal intervention alone; "community policing" seeks to enlist the assistance of other agencies, public and private, in addressing local issues under the banner of "inter-agency" co-operation. Finally, the "community policing" vision recognizes and values the service role that the police have long performed, regarding it as one of the means of bringing them closer to the community through non-conflictual contact (Cumming *et al.* 1965; Punch & Naylor 1973; Punch 1979b). Instead of emphasising the controlling function of the police, "community policing" pays attention to how the police also *care* for those whom they police (Stephens 1988; Stephens & Becker 1994a, ibid. b). Bayley has summed up "community policing" as consisting of four elements: *consultation* with local people; *adaptation* of policing methods to local conditions; *mobilization* of local people and agencies against crime and disorder; and *problem-solving* – captured by the acronym "CAMP." (Bayley 1994a).

"Community policing" is a vision that has captured wide adherence, not only internationally (see, for example, Steenhuis 1980), but also ideologically. Even some of its critics accept that good intentions lie behind the concept. McConville and Shepherd acknowledge "community policing is intended to transform policing *of* the community into policing *for* the community" (McConville & Shepherd 1992: 11, original emphasis). Young and his various collaborators have argued that it is an attempt to reverse "fire brigade" and militarized styles of policing that seek to impose control upon alienated – usually ethnic-minority – youth (Lea & Young 1984; Kinsey, Lea & Young 1986).

Implementation

The adherence shown to "community policing" has been matched by a research effort to evaluate its impact on police and people in the community. This effort has largely been concentrated in the United States, where the localization of policing is conducive to comparative research – especially when backed by federal funding. The omnibus nature of the "community policing" approach is reflected in the variety of programmes that have been implemented under this banner. However, despite this diversity, there has been little to encourage proponents.

The most favourable conclusions come from Skogan's systematic evaluation of community-policing programmes in six cities which reveals that there appears to be no *adverse* effects. Strangely this conclusion receives little comment despite its practical significance; for if community policing has few costs then any benefits that accrue must make reform profitable overall. Residents' views of the police show the most consistently positive effect, however crime reduction was largely absent (Skogan 1994). Comparative evaluation of community-policing strategies in Houston and Newark found that "softer" community-policing strategies designed to bring patrolling officers into contact with the community were more successful than more aggressive alternatives – especially where they relied on autonomous action by officers themselves (Pate *et al.* 1986). A review of community-policing evaluation studies in twelve locations also portrayed "community policing" in a favourable light with both police and local residents expressing more positive attitudes after programmes had been implemented. However, the authors entertain serious reservations regarding the methodology of the individual studies that they reviewed (Lurigio & Rosenbaum 1994). More equivocal were the conclusions of an examination of community-policing programmes in eight cities which found modest success at best and sometimes those successes were paradoxical, as when fear of crime was reduced even though *perceived* crime levels remained unaffected (Sadd & Grinc 1994). A comparison of three case studies showed that perfectly legitimate POP initiatives had only a modest impact in one case and no discernible impact in the other two (Copowich & Roehl 1994). A special programme for reducing drug-dealing through community-policing initiatives in eight cities found "that community residents generally have no interest in becoming involved in community policing efforts" (Grinc 1994: 446). This is due to fear of reprisals; distrust of the police born of long experience of animosity in poor neighbourhoods; apathy and community disorganization. What residents wanted was for the police to act as "crime-fighters" but to be permanently assigned to their beats.

Individual evaluation studies have also arrived at mixed conclusions. A project in Hartford, Connecticut, was intended to "weed" out drug dealers from four selected areas of the city by vigorous enforcement activity and then to "seed" the newly reclaimed area with businesses providing alternative employment. Police achieved some success in "weeding" out drug dealers, but attempts at "seeding" failed because of local government chaos (Tien & Rich 1994). Another project aimed at rehabilitating an area plagued by drug dealing received saturation policing followed by additional foot patrols. Evaluation found that the saturation policing and foot patrols *did* have the desired effect, but were less influential than changes in housing policy. Moreover, while foot patrols seemed to maintain gains in order maintenance, they had no pretensions to "community policing" (Cordner 1994).

Elsewhere the aim has been to reduce fear of crime. This was the aim of an experimental initiative in London and Birmingham in which officers were deployed to make contact with residents. The evaluation found that the primary aim of reducing fear of crime was not achieved, but both programmes did succeed in improving some aspects of the quality of life and enhancing police–public relations (Bennett 1991). In Canada, it has been found that even when crime rates do not fall, "fear-reducing projects are successful in strengthening already favourable attitudes towards the police and in decreasing fear of crime" (Friedmann 1992: 102). On the other hand, such initiatives can have paradoxical effects. For example, an experimental study of a programme designed to enhance police service to victims found that it had either no positive effect on any group of victims and may even have had a negative effect on Hispanic and Asian fears about their neighbourhood (but this was possibly an artefact of the research) (Skogan & Wycoff 1987).

"Community-policing" initiatives have also sought improvements in police–public relations. A three-year evaluation of an Experimental Police Division in Madison found that there was significant improvement in officers' attitudes towards internal management, but *not* in relation to the wider community. The attitude of residents showed modest, but favourable changes (Wycoff & Skogan 1994a). The authors suggest that internal change is a necessary precondition to wider changes. However, an attempt to implement appropriate internal change in the Philadelphia police – a department with a notorious reputation for "tough law enforcement" – found that despite the valiant efforts of the new reform-minded chief, there was little shift in police attitudes. For their part, the public remained divided in their attitudes towards the police: this "tough" force received the positive endorsement of the white working class, but African–Americans and Latinos remained deeply distrustful. Much the same fate befell a reforming chief of Troy, New York, who was opposed by conservatives both within and beyond his department (Guyot 1991). Moreover, as Copowich & Roehl found, the gulf between a public that defines its problems in terms of disorder and quality of life and the police who are narrowly crime-oriented, is not easily bridged (Copowich & Roehl 1994).

In Britain, central Home Office influence has meant a more uniform endorsement of the "community policing" ethos than in the USA and, as Bennett reports, police forces have become almost hyper-active in initiating schemes of many different kinds (Bennett 1994c). The weakness had lain in the evaluation of these schemes, much of which is done "in-house" where there is considerable pressure to report favourably – schemes are thereby "doomed to succeed" (Weatheritt 1983, ibid. 1986, ibid. 1987). One exception to this was the introduction of sector-policing in London, the initial trial of which took place at Notting Hill and was independently evaluated by the Police Foundation (Irving *et al.* 1989). The evaluation documents with embarrassing clarity how this vague notion – intended to bring officers into closer contact with people – was implemented half-cocked. Despite a deluge of training and propaganda, lower ranks remained largely ignorant of its purposes, becoming increasingly disenchanted with the scheme and eventually positively disaffected from it as it collided ever more directly with their perceptions and values. Precious few improvements in police–community relations could be identified by evaluators, although there was widespread endorsement of "community policing" among residents in the area. However, public attitudes turned out to be rather more complex than either policy-makers or evaluators had imagined.

> Underlying the belief that it was feasible to establish and maintain community contact between local officers and community groups was the assumption that the population would be acquiescent to the idea of, and already supportive, of the work of the police in the area. This was fundamentally wrong, particularly with respect to sections of the black community. Even with those groups who were generally supportive of the police, it was clear that they reacted to their local

> policing in a complex and changing way depending on national and local factors, personal and organisation demands, and political and ethnic differences. At any one time, what satisfied one set of people annoyed and irritated another. The most common divide was between those who believed that the police should take a harder line with muggers and drug pushers, and those – particularly members of the black community – who wanted the police to stop what they saw as racial harassment and discrimination, particularly in stop-and-search operations. . . .
>
> Fifteen per cent of the community group representatives (mostly residents' associations) were concerned that neighbourhood policing would be too soft on those elements of the community who were causing trouble, and mistrusted the gentle methods of community liaison. . . . Another 20 per cent thought neighbourhood policing would give officers too much discretion in their actions, and so increase harassment against black youngsters. (Irving *et al.* 1989: 153–4)

Even among the most supportive groups there was a tendency to value highly dedicated Community Liaison Officers, but *not* to generalize this positive sentiment to the rest of the police. The behaviour of younger patrol officers continued to be regarded as something of "a problem" (p. 153).

Relations with other agencies in the area were also fraught with unanticipated difficulties:

> An analysis of the different agencies' reactions to interagency cooperation indicated an uneven spread across the scale from unquestioning support of the police to outright hostility, with each agency's position determined by their view of their own best interests. (Irving *et al.* 1989: 157)

Housing and public health departments were eager to co-operate with police, believing that they shared common purposes. Whereas social workers felt torn between, on the one hand, the relationships of trust they had painstakingly built with black clients and, on the other, addressing issues of mutual concern with the police. The staff of youth centres were seen by police as unequivocally committed to protecting petty criminals, while the local law centre and Mangrove community association (a centre for Black activism) were seen as being even more hostile. Yet the irony was that in order for the experiment to succeed, it was precisely those sections of the population and organizations most hostile to the police whose co-operation was essential.

> In summary this work exposed the inherent problems of creating cooperative practices between the police and local professional and voluntary groups, and the extreme disaffection of some sectors of the local community with the police. This in turn highlighted the practical difficulties of moving towards a contract between the police and this heterogeneous and often transient community. (Irving *et al.* 1989: 150)

This savagely critical evaluation did not temper the enthusiasm of senior officers for sector policing, which was subsequently introduced throughout the Metropolitan Police. Its implementation in another area of London was evaluated by Stanko and Dixon and what emerges is a remarkably similar tale of vague and purposeless management, resistance from the lower ranks, marginalization of "community constables" and a public largely ignorant of the policy but who are, in any case, mainly satisfied when the police respond to any emergency or problem that they experience (Dixon & Stanko 1993, ibid. 1995; Dixon *et al.* 1993; see also Gray 1994).

Perhaps the problems of implementation have arisen from the "grand design" of wholesale reform. The alternative has been to introduce piecemeal schemes that address specific aspects of service delivery or particular issues. A very common one has been to dedicate certain patrol officers to a "community policing" role freed from the demands of reactive policing. Bayley characterizes such officers (whom he calls Neighbourhood Police Officers) as the general practitioners of policing (Bayley 1994a). As Fielding has described, these officers can develop a very different orientation towards their work from that of their patrol colleagues. Theirs is a more long-term perspective and allows positive policing outcomes other than arrest, whereas patrol officers are oriented to short-term avoidance of negative sanctions (Fielding *et al.* 1989). Yet despite the potentially valuable function these officers can perform they seem universally prone to marginalization within and subversion by the remainder of the police organization. In the London Metropolitan Police, Fielding found that despite organisational claims to the contrary, these "community constables" were marginalized and despised by patrol officers; frequently subjected to ineffective and capricious management; and suffered conflicting and confusing role expectations (Fielding 1994b; see also McConville & Shepherd 1992). Throughout Britain Bennett and Lupton's national survey reveals a less uniformly bleak picture with some "community" officers expressing general satisfaction; but the position is highly variable with most forces devoting only a modest proportion of their personnel to these duties, which are insufficiently distinctive when compared to ordinary patrol, in which women officers are under-represented and where there is a familiar litany of complaint that officers are re-deployed at short notice and on an ad hoc basis to fill gaps in the organization (Bennett & Lupton 1990, ibid. 1992). Fielding found that the effectiveness of these "community" officers was crucially affected by the commitment of their superiors which was frequently lacking (Fielding 1994b). Where the role of "community constable" was given status, seen as a route to detective work, and protected from ad hoc re-deployment, there was greater satisfaction with the role (Fielding *et al.* 1989). On the other hand, as Horton confirms (Horton 1989), vague or non-existent definition of the "community" officer's role, and lacking clear policy direction, is the fate that many of these officers suffer. However, this is not simply due to mismanagement, since the officers themselves resist attempts to constrain their autonomy by defining too closely their role. Indeed, contradictory expectations extend to the public who both desire increased foot patrolling, but also demand rapid response to emergency calls (McConville & Shepherd 1992). Similarly, "Community Liaison Officers", who have special responsibilities for fostering police–public relations, suffer much the same malaise: lack of role definition, despised by colleagues as not "real police officers", and because they lack credibility, are unable to act as the voice of the community *within* the police (Phillips & Cochrane 1988) – an echo of the same authors' conclusions regarding Schools Liaison Officers (Phillips & Cochrane 1986).

"Community policing" is not restricted to changing deployments of police officers, but also attempts to *mobilize the community* to counter crime and disorder. One of the most conspicuous means of doing that has been through "Neighbourhood Watch", "Block Watch" and other programmes originally pioneered in the United States. Such ventures have proven very popular with membership steadily increasing, especially among the elderly (Dowds & Mayhew 1994). Unfortunately, this popularity is concentrated among the white middle class where problems of crime are least apparent. In crime-infested ghettos it is much more difficult to initiate and sustain such programmes in the face of intimidation and reprisals (Skolnick & Bayley 1986; Skogan 1990). The sad conclusion is that neighbourhood watch works best where it is needed least, and vice versa. In Britain too, evaluations of the impact of neighbourhood watch on crime have not been encouraging (Bennett 1990); nor is there any evidence that it acts as a stimulus for residents to become involved in other local groups and thus foster a sense of "community" (Bennett 1989). A study of neighbourhood watch in three British cities found that it was of only marginal significance even to those who were members; for it rests on the flawed assumption that crime is a major concern among the public and that they are in a position to do anything effectively about it. The increasingly domestic style of life in many neighbourhoods means that few people see what is happening on the streets and in public places (McConville & Shepherd 1992). On the other hand, the British Crime Survey did find that residents in such schemes were more likely to report suspicious activity, perhaps because they were sensitized to it and felt obliged to take action (Dowds & Mayhew 1994).

McConville and Shepherd suggest that the police themselves are highly sceptical, if not cynical, about neighbourhood watch. Attention is paid to establishing new schemes that can be favourably portrayed as positive endorsements of police–public relations; but existing schemes very often atrophy without being officially "written off", thus giving a false impression. Moreover, police encourage the skewing of participation in favour of middle-class neighbourhoods because they act on the expectation that poor neighbourhoods with a high proportion of ethnic-minority residents will prove difficult to mobilize. Because officers saw "no point" in trying to recruit in high-crime estates, "whole sections of the black community of London and Bristol were written off by local officers as unfit for neighbourhood watch or other community-based policing initiatives" (McConville & Shepherd 1992: 140). Moreover, what contact the police have with local people tends to be highly concentrated on those with particular vested interests, such as proprietors of small businesses. Thus, neighbourhood watch, argue McConville and Shepherd (1992), may succeed in actually *exacerbating* divisions within communities, rather than fostering integrity and cohesion.

Reviewing these evaluations, it is difficult to avoid the conclusion that "nothing works". "Community policing" – be it the wholesale attempt to reconstruct the police organization, or highly targeted initiatives to reduce public drunkenness (Brown & Knox 1994), or crime supposedly caused by children truanting from school (Ekblom 1979) – fairs no better than previous investments in rapid response, preventative patrol, or "team policing" (Kelling 1978).

Why "Community Policing" Fails

Why, then, does "community policing" fail to "work'? There is general agreement that it suffers from serious flaws both practical and conceptual. These flaws tend to become entwined in the process of policy creation and implementation, but analytically they can be separated.

Implementation Failures

Evaluators have identified recurring reasons for failures of "community policing" schemes. Skogan (1994) identifies three reasons for programme failure: first, the level of emergency demands which swamp departments and commandeer organizational resources. Secondly, the opposition of middle management who face additional burdens and responsibilities. Thirdly, an organizational culture that is often antagonistic to a "community-policing" orientation. Sadd & Grinc (1994) attribute failure slightly differently: they found patrol officers ignorant and unenthusiastic about what they regarded as "top-down", "flavour of the month" initiatives. Also, the need for more effective inter-agency collaboration is not always forthcoming. The "community" is often stratified with activists aware and favourably disposed towards programmes, but ordinary people ignorant of them. Finally, a major impediment to improved police–public relations is the history of fear and suspicion by residents. Whichever appraisal one takes, the question remains why is implementation so universally inept? Why, if "community policing" is such a good idea, do police officers and at least some sections of the population resist it? Could it be that the idea itself is defective?

Resistance of Lower Ranks

Implementation of "community policing" faces a number of problems, not least resistance from police officers who are emotionally wedded to the law-enforcement definition of their role. It involves reversing their traditional isolation from the communities they police (Clark 1965), exposing them to consultation and receiving feedback on how well the police are addressing community problems. Instead of seeing policing in terms of a succession of discrete incidents, officers need to identify underlying causes and substitute indirect means of dealing with them rather than authoritative intervention (Shapland & Vagg 1987a). Traditional "macho" police sub-cultural values are directly assaulted by the implicit, but strong, emphasis on "care" rather than "control" (Stephens 1988; Stephens & Becker 1994a, ibid. b).

It is no surprise, therefore, that resistance from the lower ranks is a recurring theme in evaluations of "community-policing" initiatives (Bennett 1994a; Lurigio & Rosenbaum 1994) This can be expressed as a generalized "culture of resistance" on the part of the lower ranks who are hostile to the assault on the "shibboleths" of policing (Dixon & Stanko 1993; ibid 1995). Such antipathy is not distributed evenly throughout the police organization, with officers from ethnic-minority backgrounds, or those who are older than average, or in senior positions tending to be most favourably disposed (Lurigio & Skogan 1994). At the other extreme, resistance can arise from much more prosaic considerations: a team-policing experiment in one quarter of a Dutch town was halted after six months because in summer months it impeded opportunities for days off and holidays (Broer & van der Vijver 1983)! Sometimes resistance manifests itself in conflict within the police between officers committed to "community-policing" duties and those involved in routine patrolling. Attention has already been drawn to how "community" officers are marginalized and despised by their colleagues who do not share their long-term perspective and their tolerance of minor delinquencies in pursuit of solutions to much more general problems (Fielding 1995). Where "community-policing" programmes are given clear organizational support, splits might arise from the envy and resentment of officers who are *not* selected for specialist roles, but whose co-operation is necessary nevertheless for the success of the venture (Pate & Shtull 1994).

The quality of police management seems to be important, but not determinate. Skogan (1994) insists that the "battle", fought by senior officers, to overcome the resistance of the lower ranks "can be won". Fielding (1995) suggests that a way of achieving that is to make participation in "community policing" the route through which ambitious and able officers are able to progress within the police organization. However commitment is not enough, for the chief of Joliet, Illinois, was clearly committed to "community–policing" but it had little impact on officers in this force when compared to another that claimed few "community-policing" pretensions (Rosenbaum *et al.* 1994). Wycoff & Skogan (1994b) found that the participative and decentralized management of the Madison police was successful in improving officers' attitudes. This conclusion receives support from a comparison of "community policing" in two cities, which found that the more rigid, top-down bureaucratic style of one of the police departments was ill-suited to overcoming resistance (Wilkinson & Rosenbaum 1994). However, resistance itself is not universal: Weisel & Eck (1994) found wide differences in programmes and implementation strategies in the six cities they examined. Despite this, support for community policing was remarkably and consistently high. This support was also unconnected to a series of demographic or structural variables, the only exception being age: rookies were particularly keen.

In short, there is little doubt that "community policing" presents a challenge to the police, both institutionally and culturally, but it is not at all clear how that challenge can most effectively be met.

Conceptual Confusion

When a "good idea" fails it is tempting to blame those whose task it is to implement it rather than recognize that the idea itself is flawed. It is just possible that junior ranks within disparate police organizations realize that this notion and the schemes that it spawns are deeply defective. Indeed, perhaps they know what we know: "community policing" is a vague notion that fails to identify any particular goals or means of achieving them. As Manning explains:

> The concept of community police has a least four meanings. On one level, it is an *ideological system* of beliefs which asserts that communities in previous times were more unitary, that police were a more legitimate and accepted part of communities, that crime and disorder were once better controlled through co-operative effort, and that social control on the whole was tighter, more coherent, and pervasive.
>
> A second meaning of community policing is programmatic. . . . [It] entails *programs* with broad political aims intended to restore police "closeness" to the community, . . . to assuage community fear, and to assure community members by police presence and accessibility.
>
> A third meaning of community policing is *pragmatic.* It contrasts with current police practice. . . . Programs are responses to perceived citizen discontent with police organizations that are bureaucratic, impersonal, focused on specific incidents, "professional," crime-focused and centralized.
>
> A fourth meaning of community police is a set of programmatic elements and organizational structures. . . . Note that the emphasis is on working in a given area

> as a team, participating and communicating with community groups, and attempting to provide organizational and managerial support for the teams, especially by combining patrol and investigative functions. (Manning 1993: 422–23)

Eck and Rosenbaum (1994) attempt to inject some clarity into the concept by suggesting that it aims to achieve three goals: effectiveness, especially in reducing crime; equity, particularly in relation to ethnic minorities; and efficiency by matching resources to problems identified through consultation and inter-agency collaboration. However, as they admit, the achievement of any of these goals has been meagre indeed.

Despite these attempts to lend some semblance of clarity to the concept, it remains steeped in a romantic sentimentality that harbours many dubious assumptions. Manning identifies many of them:

> 1. People desire to see police officers in their local areas of residence and business on a regular and casual basis.
> 2. The more police they see, the more they will be satisfied with police practices.
> 3. The more police they see (to some unknown limit), the more secure they will feel.
> 4. People yearn for personal contact of a nonadversarial character with police.
> 5. The public is more concerned about crime than disorder.
> 6. There is a single public, a single public mood, and a "common good" that is known and coherently represented.
> 7. People are dissatisfied with current police practices.
> 8. Previous policing schemes have been shown to have failed.
> 9. Public satisfaction as measured in polls is a valid index of "public opinion".
> 10. The police are responsible for defending, defining, expanding, and shaping the common good of the community by active means.
>
> Community policing best meets the above needs. (Manning 1993: 425)

Key to these assumptions is the belief that crime and disorder, or indeed more broadly defined "problems", can be resolved by *police* action. While it is recognized that *direct* police action can only have a limited impact on crime, disorder and other problems, the doctrine of "community policing" continues to maintain that the police are best equipped to orchestrate collective action on behalf of the community – an assumption that is, at best, *untested*. While the police may have the appearance of a formidably powerful institution, their command of the levers that affect crime levels is much more doubtful. Of course, there are the big issues of the effect on crime of unemployment, education, family life and so forth, which the police could only influence by mainstream partisan political action. However, even more managable problems embroil the police in political action. For instance, tackling the crime of "burglary artifice" (in which thieves fraudulently gain access to premises posing as legitimate officials, such as utility meter readers), relies on the co-operation of powerful commercial organizations. As Don (1990) has cogently argued, utilities that make frequent ad hoc and unplanned visits to homes create the conditions that "bogus officials" exploit. Thus, he argues utilities must change their practices in order to facilitate crime prevention by only visiting the homes of vulnerable people by appointment; but the costs that this imposes on the utilities is a serious disincentive to co-operation. Even where crime and disorder are locally generated, the assumption implicit in "community policing" is that the community has the resources to prevent it. As Buerger (1994) points out, informal social controls have been eroded by fundamental socio-economic trends that "community policing" is in no position to reverse. The emphasis on restoring informal community controls is, he argues, a version of "blaming the victim", instead of recognizing how crime is just one manifestation of a deeper malaise. One might go further and argue that the restoration of local social control (even if possible) might act as a palliative that makes living in decaying ghettos, inner-cities and "dump" housing estates merely bearable.

Weatheritt asked of community policing, "does it work and how do we know?" (Weatheritt 1983). She concluded that it is simply too vague to allow rational evaluation and the assumptions on which it rests are, at best, untested and often *prima facie* doubtful (Weatheritt 1983, ibid. 1987). It is difficult to disagree with this assessment.

Why "Community Policing" Succeeds

What, then, is the attraction of "community policing"? For despite its inherent conceptual and practical weaknesses enthusiasm for "community policing" remains undiminished and this itself is a phenomenon worthy of serious attention. "Community policing" has been an unparalleled *political* success because it satisfies important *interests.*

Vagueness

The first is that it *is* vague, imprecise and ill-thought out. As a broad "philosophy" of policing that covers a multitude of sins "community policing" serves the interests of police administrators (Reiner 1991a; Seagrave 1996). It enables senior police officers to assert that their policies – whatever they happen to be – are those of "community policing" without fear of contradiction. The imprecision that defeats rational evaluation acts as a safeguard against the policy being shown to have failed, for however much evidence of failure is stacked up there will always be other aspects of the policy that can plausibly be claimed as successes. Moreover, the positive associations of individual programmes, particular policies and the general principles become diffused into an ideological framework that is difficult to criticize or reject (Manning 1993). By moving the debate onto the wide and imprecise terrain of "community policing", police administrators have succeeded in blunting criticism derived from increasing crime and decreasing detection rates.

Virtuous Policing

What this does not explain is why anyone should be taken in by such a stratagem. To explain this we need to appreciate the ideological appeal of "community policing". As Bayley remarks, it has proven such a popular doctrine worldwide because it is associated with *virtue* (Bayley 1994b). Those virtues are the antithesis of most of the characteristics associated with the exercise of coercive authority. "Community policing" is associated with "caring" rather than "controlling" and thus mines a deep seam in liberal sentimentality (Stephens 1988; Stephens & Becker 1994a, ibid. b). It rhetorically emphasizes "*partnership*" with *local* people and organizations to address issues of *common* concern by police organized on the *small scale* (Bennett 1994b). In its Dutch variant it is presented as a democratic influence encouraging harmony through social integration (Nordholt & Straver 1983). The concept of "community" elides definitions based on geographical residence to notions such as "community of interest" and feelings of belonging (Smith, D. 1987).

"Golden Age"

However, its strongest ideological appeal lies in its promise of recovering a "golden age" of policing where officers were respected, if not universally loved; and when the society that was policed was harmonious and relatively crime-free. Manning argues that it represents the "*Nostalgia Theme*" of contemporary policing that offers not only a return to the past, but a rejection of the present; "a *metaphor* based on yearning and the wish for personalization of service which contrasts with bureaucratic/professional policing" (Manning 1993: 421–22). For the British, it affirms the virtuous myth of "policing by consent" (Newman 1984; Oxford 1984) epitomized in the fictional television character "Dixon of Dock Green". However much of this is an uncritical and "vain pursuit of an ideal type" (Howes 1975: 5) founded upon "fractured" history (Walker 1993): its evocation of a past characterized by harmony is appealing. It reconstructs policing in a way that is essentially non-coercive. Police officers are kindly gentle people who seek to help and assist; not purveyors of violence willing to confront.

Responding to Crisis

There have been programmes and initiatives that would now qualify as "community policing" before that designation became popular (see, for example, Schaffer 1980); however the ideological banner of "community policing" came to prominence in the 1970s and this timing is not mere happenstance. It came in the wake of 1960s turmoil and the growing demand for civil rights from various, previously excluded sections of the population. This had thrown the legitimacy of the police into question: they were depicted as racist oppressive thugs who had prompted, rather than prevented, disorder. It is no surprise that the notion emerges in the United States, where the 1960s onslaught on police legitimacy had been most acutely felt. In Britain, "community policing" received its greatest boost in the aftermath of the inner-city riots of 1981, and especially Lord Scarman's endorsement of the view that the maintenance of "public tranquility" should take precedence over the enforcement of law (Scarman 1981). In France, "community policing" was only of marginal interest until serious public disorder erupted in the *banlieues* (large public housing estates on the fringes of many large cities) in the "hot summer" of 1981 (Horton 1995). Police in New South Wales introduced "community policing" initiatives as part of a general strategy of police reform adopted in the wake of a succession of scandals (Chan 1997). Elsewhere, "community policing" was introduced not in an atmosphere of crisis, but against a background of chronically poor police–public relations. This was the situation in Israel where concern at the gulf between police and public was addressed by the deployment of Neighbourhood Police Officers (Friedmann 1992). The Canadians have embraced the "community policing" ethos without prompting by a crisis, but in the face of tremendous changes in the structure of Canadian society. The influx of non-European immigrants transformed Canada into a more heterogeneous society that posed a challenge for policing to which "community policing" was seen as an appropriate response (Friedmann 1992; Leighton 1994). Perhaps Singapore is the only country in which "community policing", in the form of a Japanese Koban style of policing, has been introduced without external prompting (Quah & Quah 1987). Where the crisis has passed so commitment to "community policing" has waned: Friedmann complains that in America many schemes "have shrunk to nothing more than a public relations officer in a department". (Friedmann 1992: 160).

Legitimation

Whether "community-policing" initiatives achieve their professed goals is much less important than that they effectively legitimate the police as an institution. This is a lesson that is often lost on evaluators who accept at face value the expressed aims of some initiative or other. For instance, Norris is damning in his appraisal of a police–community relations programme that conspicuously failed to achieve its hopelessly idealistic avowed aims. He fails to recognize its transparent success in achieving its latent, but primary, purpose of winning public support (Norris 1973). The search for legitimation tends to provoke accusations of bad faith from academic commentators who accuse initiatives of "cosmetic, superficial, public relations" (Friedmann 1992: 160). However, analytically it indicates just how strong is the imperative in liberal democracies for the police to create and sustain widespread legitimacy. Programmes and initiatives can be almost entirely spurious and yet fulfil admirably the purpose of legitimation. This is made brutally apparent in the evaluation report on the Notting Hill sector policing experiment. For this initiative was founded upon a pair of undergraduate dissertations completed by junior officers who had been seconded to university courses. As the evaluators somewhat incredulously remark, "Undergraduate theses are not often taken up and turned into major projects by organisations the size of the Metropolitan Police" (Irving *et al.* 1989: 11). The reason why this occurred was, to put it in a nutshell, that these dissertations were the answer to a police commissioner's prayer: in the wake of the 1981 riots and Scarman report, the Metropolitan Police had to be seen to "do something" and the idea of sector policing had the *appearance* of taking radical action. The "management-speak" in which the project was wrapped merely enhanced its appeal as a new and dynamic innovation. Hence, even the damning evaluation report on the implementation of sector policing on one division did not prevent its extension force-wide. It was, like so many other "community policing" initiatives, "doomed to succeed" (Weatheritt 1986) because success is legitimating.

On the other hand, we must not succumb to total cynicism, for "community policing" can have *valuable* legitimating functions. It provides a rationale for releasing police officers from the constraints of being regarded solely, or mainly, as law enforcers. It justifies a much wider conception of the police role and the use of discretion. As Fielding notes, the irony of the "golden age" view of "community policing" is that officers are now enjoined to engage in the kinds of activities, such as having a cup of tea with a local resident, that would have earned their predecessors in the 1950s a disciplinary penalty (Fielding 1986). Policing involves officers in routinely making difficult discretionary decisions in difficult situations and the dilemmas arising from so doing can be openly recognized. The central dilemma that such policing encounters is that in order to establish satisfactory reciprocal relationships with marginal sections of the population, the police officer must tolerate minor delinquencies (Fielding 1995) – precisely the kind of exercise of discretion that legal purists previously condemned. The overt acceptance that this is a line that officers must tread militates against the potentially corrupting influences that secrecy encourages.

"Community Leaders"

The police do not and probably cannot legitimate themselves in the eyes of everyone, but universal legitimation is less important than acquiring legitimacy from those in positions of power. "Community policing" has been a mechanism through which locally powerful figures among otherwise marginal populations can be co-opted into policing. Like sentimental conservatives who regard "the community" as homogeneous, those who occupy locally prominent positions often present the same image of "their community", steadfastly refusing to recognise the divisions and conflicts that exist within it. Yet, theirs are the voices that matter, for they can mobilize opinion, not only within the local area, but also beyond it, through articulating grievances in the media. If they can be drawn into partnership with the police, opposition is blunted, if not eradicated. Thus, while Fielding is correct in saying that, "Policing has been liable to the 'take me to your community leader' ideology which has dogged the race relations industry.... Self-appointed leaders often represented only their own interests" (Fielding 1995: 14), he fails to appreciate the political importance of such a strategy.

In sum, what "community policing" does is to redefine citizenship within a policing context. It is both an ideology and set of practices that *accords respect* to sections of the population hitherto considered disreputable. Thereby it attempts to transform the relationship of the police to this section of the public.

The Dangers of "Community Policing"

Viewed from the perspective of radical scepticism "community policing" contains many dangers, some of them being the very same features that make this ethos so appealing to police administrators and other more conservative commentators. Common to these perceived dangers is the fear that "community policing" entails an expansive vision of the police role that surreptitiously injects continental-style traditions – equating it with the maintenance of good order and administration – instead of resurrecting traditional Anglo-Saxon values of policing as locally determined, as it pretends to do.

Elevating Police Concerns

Goldstein envisages the police role as that of social diagnostician identifying and remedying a wide range of social problems (Goldstein 1977, ibid. 1990); by any standards an extravagant aspiration that contains the danger that the police will impose *their* agenda upon local communities. There are two objections voiced to this vision: first, that articulated most powerfully by McConville and Shepherd: it distorts the concerns of residents and other interested parties, for whom "crime, if it figures at all, is a background consideration of their lives and not the organizing matrix of their normal activities" (1992: 59). Even in inner-city areas crime is just one problem among others, "a latent rather than manifest issue" (ibid, 60). People recognize that much crime is petty and largely property offences rather than personal violence to people, and did not figure prominently in their lives. From this perspective, "fear of crime" is artificially generated by, among other things, official statistics and pronouncements that are then used to justify giving priority to crime-related policies. However, this view of McConville and Shepherd flies in the face of successive victim surveys, both national and local, that seem to show considerable levels of genuine, albeit often misplaced, concern about crime (Garofalo 1979; Hough & Mayhew 1983, ibid. 1985; Maxfield 1984, ibid. 1987; Gottfredson 1986; Jones *et al.* 1986; Mayhew *et al.* 1989, ibid. 1993; Anderson *et al.* 1990; Crawford *et al.* 1990; van Dijk *et al.* 1990; Mayhew & Maung 1992; Mirrlees-Black *et al.* 1996). Given the methodological limitations and weaknesses of McConville and Shepherd's own survey, this would seem a slender basis upon which to jettison such an extensive body of research (Waddington 1993d). There is also a semantic problem concerning the definition of "crime" that McConville and Shepherd employ.

> For most people, crime is not at the forefront of their social concerns, which tend instead to be dominated by what the police would term "grief". Noisy neighbours, kids kicking a ball against the side of their house, unemployment, environmental mess, transport, poor local facilities – these are the stuff of everyday life. (McConville & Shepherd 1992: 61)

Indeed so, but these, or at least many of them, are also the stuff of "community policing", the aim of which is to elevate *these* concerns of ordinary people to a position of prominence within the policing agenda. These may not constitute "crime", according to some definitions, but they *do* constitute the kind of minor incivilities that cause misery for many people and are associated with "fear of crime" (Maxfield 1984, ibid. 1987; Hough 1995).

A second, and more substantial, objection to the notion of "police officer as social diagnostician" is that even if crime is a serious problem in the eyes of many people this is not to say that the police have any specialist knowledge about its causation and no particular expertise in its prevention (de Lint 1997). This dubious diagnostic pretension unjustifiably entrusts yet more authority to the police to interfere in community life. The danger is that public consultation is used, not to hear from the community what problems it suffers, but to convince the public of the police diagnosis of problems, their causes and remedies – what one senior police officer has called "issue advertising" (Davies 1986). Apart from imposing one particular professional perspective, this has additional – possibly adverse – consequences such as feeding popular racism through the spurious legitimation of "officially generated statistics" purporting to show disproportionate involvement in crime by young Afro-Caribbeans. This is, "simply one graphic illustration of the way in which the 'crime problem' is socially constructed by the police and other state officials in ways which advanced the argument of those who seek increased police powers and a 'stronger' state" (McConville &

Shepherd 1992: 76–77). "Community policing" also legitimates direct political intervention by the police (Rawlings 1985), a fear that gains some credibility from the demand by one divisional commander for the local council to cease financial support for local groups whom he considered "politically extremist organizations" (*Independent* 19 June 1989, p. 6). Less seriously, giving priority to the police as social diagnosticians means that they will dictate the agenda of other official bodies, leading to disputes about "turf" (Eck 1987).

Undermining Accountability

In seeking to give pre-eminence to police concerns, "community policing" subtly undermines the accountability of the police to the local community. Despite appearances to the contrary, "community policing" envisages the community serving the interests of the police, rather than vice versa (Rawlings 1985). Certainly, "community policing" advocates rarely suggest and occasionally explicitly reject the notion that it entails the community having an influence over police decision-making (Kettle & Hodges 1982). "The 'velvet glove' of police–community relations programmes at once provided a way for the police to gain broad-based public support, while at the same time masking the autonomy of action and decision making they exercise" (Greene 1993: 374). Thus, local opposition to the police is subverted and locally influential individuals and groups are co-opted into legitimating police activity. This was illustrated in the south London district of Brixton, the scene of serious inner-city riots in 1981 and 1985, and the location for the first experiment in local police–community liaison. As already noted, the result of which was the deployment of riot-police to *support* a local council initiative to close premises that had long been the focus for opposition to the police (Gordon 1984a).

Whose Community?

It has already been noted that "community policing" suffers from a romantic view of community as a homogeneous and integrated whole maintaining stability through informal sanctions, but there is also a dark side to the sentimentality of this "Golden Ageist" view: the refusal to acknowledge the divisions and conflicts that exist in communities can perversely be used as means of exploiting those very divisions and conflicts. The natural state of communal life is represented as homogeneous, harmonious and integrated, a state of affairs that is undermined in contemporary society by an "alien presence" who have destroyed traditional values and against whom the community should unite, a view that contains transparently racist overtones (Rawlings 1985). What might seem an unduly pessimistic interpretation receives credibility from the views of some senior officers who hark back to a romantic vision of the past and then relate its decline into contemporary disarray with the arrival of "immigrants" who do not share the same culture as the host society (Marshall 1975). Thus, "community policing", while on the surface a philosophy of inclusion, can become an ideological justification for excluding the already marginal, especially young lower-class members of ethnic-minority populations.

> The reason why the adoption of community policing as a policy does not immediately solve problems between ethnic youth and the police is quite simple: the "community" being served by the police in community-policing strategies does not include young people, especially those who are judged to be "not from good homes". If the aim of policing is to maintain order in the community, then it usually means the removal of nuisances and troublesome elements such as "youth gangs". (Chan 1994: 185)

In Britain this has justified and won approval for the imposition of curfews on youngsters causing problems in south London (Gibbons 1997b); local residents collecting intelligence on youngsters in a Gloucester housing estate who create nuisance (Morgan 1997); police and local housing authorities collaborating to remove "problem families" from their homes (Potter 1995); and combined action by police and local authorities to rid tourist areas in the cathedral city of Winchester of unsightly alcoholics (Green 1996).

In a literal sense, "community policing" is an oxymoron, for if the police could serve the *whole* community there would be little point in having a police at all. As Chan correctly observes "... there is not going to be a consensus about the kind of policing the community wants. There is not one, but many publics and policing is about dealing with conflicts, often between some of these publics" (Chan 1994: 187). Policing is the imposition of authority on *someone;* from this perspective, "community policing" is a strategy for identifying more selectively who that "someone" is. As Fielding points out, "differentiating the community is something the police have always done but to keep one's categories up to date one has to be close to the people" (Fielding 1995: 15). Employing such refinement avoids antagonizing those whose support (or, at least, passive acquiescence) the police need to cultivate, but it also involves a process of renegotiating standards of respectability that will guide discretion. On the other hand, the more successful police officers are in identifying those who are friendless, the more assuredly are those individuals and groups marginalized or excluded. In other words, as the boundaries of inclusion and exclusion have become more fluid police have devised methods of patrolling that boundary that are more responsive and sensitive but, perhaps, no less oppressive.

Licensing Aggressive Policing

A number of commentators have noted, with more or less approval, that "community policing" complements, rather than replaces, "harder" styles of policing (Kettle & Hodges 1982; Reiner 1992).

> It is not a question of the police having to make a choice between two different styles. Community policing has an important part to play in the legitimation of coercive policing, it is a mobilisation of the support of the "silent" majority around increases in the powers and autonomy of the police. (Rawlings 1985: 86)

This is most obviously the case at the level of police organization, where a commitment to "community policing" co-exists with the maintenance of militaristic units. Indeed, in London local community officers have been deployed alongside riot-squads to guide them around riot-afflicted areas and identify rioters.

Apart from "community policing" acting as a "velvet glove" that covers the "iron fist", it poses, in the view of some radical critics, even more insidious threats to civil liberties. Penetration of the community becomes a means of acquiring intelligence that can then be used to suppress dissent and resistance to the state, thus a potent mechanism for establishing a local "police state" (Gilroy 1982; Scraton 1987). Of course, this conclusion relies on a normative perspective that celebrates criminal and disorderly actions as "resistance". An alternative, but still radical, perspective points to how such criminality and disorder adversely affects, not the rich and powerful, but other local residents for whom high-crime rates are an added deprivation (Lea & Young 1984, ibid. 1993; Kinsey *et al.* 1986; Campbell 1993). Moreover, as McConville and Shepherd observe, programmes such as "neighbourhood watch" do not seem to be as effective in generating criminal intelligence as the authorities had hoped and critics feared (McConville & Shepherd 1992).

On the other hand, there is clearly a conflict between "community policing" which aims to close the gap between police and local people, and the safeguarding of civil liberties that relies on the state (and its representatives) being kept at arm's length. This fundamental contradiction can lead to serious policy entanglement. For instance, the Danes established an uncontentious programme in which the police liaised with diverse social agencies. Independently, parliament passed civil libertarian legislation restricting *inter alia* the ability of public bodies to release information to third parties about individuals without the individual's permission. Since exchange of information was crucial to the liaison programme this effectively prevented it from functioning. The government then encouraged agencies involved in the programme to ignore the Act, but the Ombudsman demanded that this advice be rescinded. Parliament has since reconsidered the issue, but with what effect is not yet known. Meanwhile, the programme continues to operate by being economical with the truth (Thomas 1990).

While some radical critics have been busily looking under the proverbial "bed" for subversive policing, a more serious threat has been developing quite openly. Local and national public support has been mobilized in favour of more aggressive styles of policing, most notably the doctrine of "zero tolerance" pioneered in New York City by Commissioner Bratton, and which is being enthusiastically emulated elsewhere throughout the liberal democratic world. This doctrine is derived from Wilson and Kelling's notion of "broken windows" (Wilson & Kelling 1982) which drew attention to the value of foot patrol in reducing fear of crime by suppressing minor incivilities such as vandalism, public drunkenness and low-level disorder. While their theory did suggest that the toleration of these minor depredations should be reversed, it was a more subtle argument than the doctrine of "zero tolerance" has become. Drunks were not simply hounded, but regulated by the local patrol officer who might allow them to continue drinking provided they did so discreetly. Police were envisaged as working in collaboration with local agencies to remove signs that "nobody cares" – such as vandalism and abandoned car wrecks – and thus improve the physical environment of localities. However, the danger is that the narrow doctrine of "zero tolerance" successfully mobilizes public hostility to marginal sections of the population to produce "community policing with the gloves off" (Waddington 1997). There is some anecdotal evidence that at least some sections of the public in New York City have begun to tire of this more aggressive style of policing, despite its apparent success in reducing crime levels (Read 1997).

Is Integration a Good Thing?

Essential to "community policing" is the integration of the police and local people.

> In community policing there is a concern for developing personalized forms of control, an extension of an informal, differentiated moral system in which the officer acts as if he or she were a member of the community and not as an officer of an external police system, an absolutist legal system, and an authoritative state. (Manning 1993: 429)

Such integration is uncritically accepted by "community-policing" activists as desirable, but this fails to consider what the community values are into which the police are integrated. There is evidence that some of the *least* desirable aspects of policing owe their origins to precisely this local integration. For instance, rural police throughout the United States are far more integrated into their local communities than are their more urban counterparts and this is reflected in higher approval ratings and the provision of a wide range of services. However, it is also reflected in a greater potential for corruption and the mobilization of communal support for tough police action against youthful delinquents (Weisheit *et al.* 1994). Websdale and Johnson compared rural with urban and state police in Kentucky and found that rural officers were much *less* effective in protecting women from abusive husbands than were their urban or state counterparts. They attribute this relative ineffectiveness to rural officers being so closely integrated into their local communities, which tend to tolerate such abuse (Websdale & Johnson 1997). Moreover, integration is likely to be variable, with police being more integrated into some communities, or groups within communities, than they are with others. This can then result in discriminatory treatment that favours those with whom the police are integrated. For example, Ferdinand & Luchterhand (1970) attributed the more lenient treatment of white youths to the fact that white police officers could make more informed judgements of how to proceed based on their intimate knowledge of white culture and values, whereas their estrangement from African–Americans left them reliant on superficial information when dealing with black youths. A similar conclusion was arrived at in a comparative analysis of the treatment of African–American, Latino and white juveniles in two contrasting communities (Dannefer & Schutt 1982). In ethnically divided communities there is the danger than the dominant group effectively hi-jacks the programme to the disadvantage of the minority (Skogan 1994).

A related problem arises when the police and community become so integrated that the division of labour is blurred to the point that it permits or even encourages vigilantism. This, of course, is most apparent when "community policing" is extended to include some element of local community participation in patrolling (Marx & Archer 1971). In Israel, the "Civil Guard" intended to "provide a neighbourhood-based armed security patrol" was responsible for a number of "excesses" and needed reform (Friedmann 1992). Similarly, the creation of "people's courts" and "self-defence units" in the South African townships during the 1970s licensed residents to take brutal action against marginalized youths (Scharf 1989) and a similar situation arose on the West Bank when, during the Intifada, armed gangs alarmed the Palestinian leadership by their oppressive and violent methods (Milton-Edwards 1997). (On the other hand, areas from which the police are excluded can still suffer such vigilantism, as areas of Belfast testify [McCorry & Morrisey 1997].)

Conclusion

What, then, is "community policing" and, to quote Weatheritt (1983), "does it work and how do we know?". "Community policing" seems only to make sense as an ideological re-definition and re-legitimation of the policing mandate in the context of an increasingly plural and culturally heterogeneous society. Police authority is justified, not as the enforcement of universal standards, be it "the law" or a single dominant notion of "respectability", but as the discretionary implementation of possibly divergent "communal" values. While this appeals to sentimental myth of homogeneous communities, the police can be guided in their exercise of discretionary authority by locally dominant values when dealing with *intra*-communal conflict. The result is that "police property" comes to be defined more narrowly, minimizing the risk that locally "respectable" people will be subjected to the needless exercise of coercive authority. However, "communities" in highly plural societies overlap and intertwine leading to the possibility of *inter*-communal conflict. It is this that gives the police crucial room for manœuvre and hence autonomy, for ultimately they become arbiters of "community" boundaries.

Police Management

The fate of "community-policing" initiatives illustrates an endemic failure of police management worldwide. Repeatedly, well-intentioned programmes are implemented inadequately with the result that they fail or have perverse effects (Skogan & Wycoff 1987). Programmes are introduced without clear aims or any definite plan for implementation. In the Notting Hill sector policing trial evaluators came to the conclusion that senior management was beguiled by the vacuous "management speak" that surrounded the scheme – a triumph of appearance over substance (Irving *et al.* 1989). At least this programme was properly evaluated – albeit that little attention seems to have been paid to its conclusions – but many "bright ideas" are implemented without any systematic evaluation at all, or if evaluated they are "doomed to succeed" because senior officers cannot be seen to have erred. When faced with the results of systematic evaluation police managers frequently respond with hostility (Smith 1989), presumably because they believe that facts undermine beliefs. This even extends to positive evaluation: when I conducted an evaluation of the organizational effects on a police division of supplying a large proportion of its officers to aid other police forces during the 1984–85 dispute in the coalfields (Waddington 1985a, ibid. 1985b), senior officers rejected the conclusion that their organization had continued to operate reasonable well. This favourable news was unwelcome because they had been publicly announcing throughout the dispute that the demands it made on manpower was having a deleterious effect and my data contradicted those claims. They also feared that my evidence would be used against them; for if the division could operate so well with a much depleted workforce then it might be argued that the division was over-staffed and the force over-resourced.

Despite the appearance of the police organization as a archetypal legal–rational bureaucracy in the Weberian mould, policy is formulated and implemented with a characteristic lack of attention to the precepts of rationality (Weatheritt 1985, ibid. 1986, ibid. 1989; Brown & Waters 1993). Research evidence is rarely considered with the result that police organizations repeatedly find themselves committed to achieving the impossible, the classic illustration of which is, of course, to reduce crime levels. Senior officers have little information about or control over their principal resource – subordinate ranks. There is an absence of strategic planning and little attempt to identify and disseminate good practice (Smith 1989). Most attention is paid to the avoidance of negative consequences. In conditions of managerial drift police forces operate differently for reasons that are difficult to fathom. For instance, Bennett and Lupton's (1992a) national activity survey found considerable, but inexplicable, differences in the proportion of time that officers spent in the station as opposed to on patrol. Frequently, what passes for policy are mere platitudes, hence the absence of any clear policy for recruiting and retaining officers from the ethnic minority despite the oft-repeated desire to increase their numbers (Holdaway 1991). In Britain there is no dearth of managerial ranks, but policy formulation and implementation is not discernibly better than elsewhere (Clarke & Greene 1987).

This is not just some recent affliction, but one that has a long historical pedigree in many jurisdictions (Bordua & Reiss 1966). Since the inception of professional policing senior officers have struggled to control the organization for which they are responsible. In a earlier era patrolling officers in Britain were compelled to patrol "fixed beats" so that their every movement was known to their superiors and later were compelled to be at appointed places at designated times so that contact could be made (Chatterton 1979). Supervision was traditionally oppressive, with sergeants and inspectors touring the area trying to catch subordinates unawares (Brogden 1991; Weinberger 1995). Yet, subordinate ranks continued to enjoy enormous autonomy with which their superiors colluded (Cain 1973). It is also not an affliction that debilitates *all* aspects of police decision-making, for Grimshaw and Jefferson found that when making decisions about, say, the replacement of patrol vehicles senior officers acted in a passably rational-bureaucratic manner. Perversely, it was when decisions had to be taken about the deployment of officers that rationality deserted the process and subordinates were left to decide more or less for themselves (Grimshaw & Jefferson 1987). Thus, where it matters most police management is least effective.

The consequences of such management-by-default are not only that police organizations seem chronically unable to implement policy or are inefficient, they may actually be *dangerous*. The FBI (1993) analysis of officers killed in the line of duty found that while many of those who died had committed procedural errors, many others had scrupulously abided by procedures and still been exposed to unacceptable danger. Many departments simply did not have procedures to cover the circumstances in which officers found themselves; in other circumstances procedures conflicted leaving officers to make fateful decisions for themselves. In many cases procedures either allowed or actually *prescribed* actions that were dangerous. Poor training in "street survival" skills was endemic: 41 per cent of those killed approached a vehicle improperly and 65 per cent did not have control of the person or situation. It is not only officers who can pay the price of such an abdication of management, but also members of the public. Skolnick and Fyfe (1993) point to how the LAPD allowed officers to apply choke holds to suspects who were resisting arrest, with the result that a number died and the suspicion grew that officers were using choke holds as a method of "street punishment".

As public funding has come under increasingly close scrutiny, so the inability of the police to "deliver" has been regarded as unacceptable. In Britain central government has sought to inject greater managerial discipline into the police service. After a brief "honeymoon", the Thatcher government of the 1980s became increasingly disillusioned with the police service and commenced a programme of budgetary controls and organizational reform intended to establish control over burgeoning police costs (Loveday 1994b). Like the rest of the public sector, the police were subjected to the doctrines of "new public management", especially the insistence on providing "value for money" (Leishman *et al.* 1995; Savage & Charman 1995). A series of circulars from the Home Office made it clear that the police would not receive additional resources without demonstrating that they were making the best use of the resources already at their disposal (Collins 1985). Her Majesty's Inspectorate of Constabulary was transformed from its erstwhile role as a retirement home for chief constables to the driving force for the introduction of a "performance culture" among senior ranks, through the application of performance indicators and other similar managerial devices (Davidoff 1993). The Audit Commission commenced a series of reports that reviewed performance in a number of areas with predictably damning conclusions and recommendations for more or less radical change (see, for example, Audit Commission 1990a, ibid. b, ibid. 1993, ibid. 1996). All forces in Britain are now subjected to an annual performance assessment and the results are published in the form of league tables to the embarrassment of those not at, or near, the top of the list. Devolving budgetary control to chief constables (rather than local authorities) and, within many forces, to local divisional commanders has meant that police managers at all levels are increasingly obliged to make hard choices (Chatterton *et al.* 1996). Yet, in Britain, as elsewhere, policing remains stubbornly resistant to rational management.

The Military Model

Responsibility for this state of affairs is often placed at the door of the military model of police organization that is virtually ubiquitous, but regarded by critics and commentators as nonetheless wholly unsuitable for policing. The military model was appropriate to continental European gendarmeries who enjoyed a close, albeit subordinate, relationship with the army. What is odd is that despite Robert Peel's explicit rejection of the gendarmerie model, his "New Police" has, since its inception in 1829, adopted precisely the same form of organization. Moreover, despite the aggressive commitment to *civilian* policing in the United States – manifested, for example, in the refusal to attire the early New York police officers in uniforms beyond a badge of office (Miller 1977a) – police organizations throughout America evolved along military lines also. If the military model is so inappropriate, why have so many police organizations adopted it?

Is Policing Really a Quasi-military Organization?

It is more often assumed, than proved, that the police is a quasi-military organization. Yes, police officers typically wear uniforms, hold rank within a military-style structure, salute and indulge in other militaristic displays, but does this surface appearance penetrate far into the organization? Well, there are reasons to doubt it, at least in some police systems. First, police in the Anglo–Saxon tradition typically have no officer caste separately recruited. Secondly, police officers often make their career largely within a single force, whereas military officers typically spend only limited tours of duty on any task so as to prevent them becoming too closely attached to people and places. Thirdly, police officers are typically not subject to superior orders for which those who issue them are responsible (Brownlee 1989).

Moreover, it is far from clear that these departures from militarism are regarded favourably, even by critics of militarism. For instance, despite their opposition to the military organization of the police, Skolnick and Fyfe seem to approve of a military-style officer caste who have not worked their way up the ranks They also believe that complaints should be treated as a management tool through which superiors control their subordinates in a top-down manner typical of military hierarchies (Skolnick & Fyfe 1993). They commend the New York Police Department's policy of instituting immediate investigation of all shootings by *superior* officers who report to the Commissioner. I have argued that a more militaristic approach to public-order policing can result in greater discipline and restraint (Waddington 1987a, ibid. 1991, ibid. 1994a, ibid. 1995), and although this has been hotly disputed as a generalization (Jefferson 1987, ibid. 1990, ibid. 1993; Waddington, D. 1992, ibid. 1996), there is far more agreement that the absence of command and control has impeded the effective response to incidents of public disorder (see, for example, Webster & Williams 1992). Reiss has gone so far as to suggest that the non-militaristic insistence that officers cannot be commanded to shoot or not, means that in serious violent confrontations the police act with *organized indiscipline* (Reiss 1980). In France, it is the explicitly militaristic Gendarmerie that has won public respect and approval, rather than their less militaristic colleagues in the *Police Nationale* (Horton 1995).

Management by Default

The problem with police organizations is not that they are subjected to too much military-style command, but too little command of any kind. It is not only that officers police the streets largely beyond the control of the organization they supposedly serve, but that that organization has positively harmful effects.

Devaluing the Lower Ranks

It is the near-universal credo of senior officers that the most important person in the organization is the officer who deals with the public on the street. This is the kind of claptrap that frequently drops from the lips of highly paid people in senior positions in a wide range of bureaucracies; that is why those at the bottom of so many hierarchies suffer the worst pay and conditions! But in the case of policing it has particular force, since those at the base of hierarchy have tremendous power. As Wilson observed, the curiosity of policing is that discretion *increases* as one *descends* the rank structure (Wilson 1969). Street-level officers routinely make decisions – such as to arrest – that are not only fateful for the citizen, but also for the organization. Arrests made on insufficient or fabricated evidence can plunge an entire police service into scandal and public disrepute, as the succession of "miscarriages of justice" did to the British police at the end of the 1980s. Yet, it is the experience of those officers that they are despised by their senior officers whom they in turn often ridicule as inhabitants of "the dream factory".

That the lower ranks should feel this way is no mere accident; despite appearances, incompetence is not a entrance qualification to senior police management worldwide. In perhaps one of the most perceptive analysis of policing, a British senior police officer convincingly argues that the routine practices of police organizations systematically devalue the lower ranks and belie the rhetoric that they are of prime importance (Jones 1980). He identifies two mutually reinforcing processes within the organization that work to "push" and "pull" officers off the streets. The "push" lies in the boredom and uncongenial nature of patrol work: it consists of untold hours of wandering around with little to occupy one's mind and yet having little control over one's work because one must be able to react to public demands as and when they arise. The tasks that patrol officers perform have little value in the eyes of the organization or themselves: rarely do patrol officers become involved in law enforcement – most of their activities being the policing equivalent of rescuing cats from trees. On rare occasions when officers become involved in serious law enforcement they are likely to find that specialist or senior personnel assume almost immediate responsibility – exciting, it ain't. These activities are undertaken throughout day and night and in all weather conditions – fun, it ain't. Explaining why officers dislike patrol work and seek to escape it as soon as possible is not difficult.

In escaping from the streets, able and ambitious officers find that they are "pushing at an open door", for the organization actively seeks to draw them away from the activity that it rhetorically most values. The engine that drives this "pulling" mechanism is the requirement to fill vacancies in higher ranks and specialist departments. Thus, vacancies arising in higher echelons and specialisms, such as detective work, must be filled, whereas vacancies in the patrol complement need not. Moreover, those who fill these vacancies are the best qualified – they have the training, experience, maturity and acumen for such responsibility. Those who remain in patrol work are, by implication, those unable to fill more valuable positions. Just in case the patrol force fails to read the signals that senior officers routinely send them through personnel selection, those senior or specialist officers who fail to satisfy organizational goals tend to be returned to the patrol force as *demotion*. Thus, whatever its rhetoric, the organization sends a strong message to those engaged in patrol work that they and what they do is of little value; they are, at best, a pool from which the best escape.

Indirect support for Jones's analysis is to be found in my own study of the effects of staff depletion during the 1984–85 miners' dispute (Waddington 1985b) which demonstrated *inter alia* how the processes to which he draws attention can be reversed when it is in the interests of the organization to do so. First, because it was essential for officers to be available for duty in the coalfields the normal process of drawing officers out of the pool ceased. Abstractions for purposes of training, recruitment to specialisms, and temporarily "acting up" in higher ranks also ceased. Second, this had no apparently adverse consequence upon the organization, despite the fact that it was acting under tremendous stress.

It is tempting to fulminate against such idiocies, but we should pause before doing so and ask why police forces worldwide find self-inflicted damage so attractive. Cynicism might dictate that we look for self-aggrandizement in devising an organization that removes those with ability from the boredom and uncongeniality of the streets. There are grounds for this view, not least because most organizations work on the principle that the least able are left to do the most important work: the best teachers move into administration; the most skilled and experienced nurses administer tender loving care to a desk; the most formidable warriors do battle over military budgets. However, in the police this general organizational tendency is reinforced by others, the most potent of which is the fact that patrol work is an unskilled activity conducted mainly in relation to a low-status clientele. As this book has been at pains to emphasise, police exercise authority predominantly over the marginal and excluded sections of the population who tend to be powerless. Even if the exercise of that authority is incompetent or illegal, the consequences for the organization are unlikely to be serious. The "punishment-centred bureaucracy" operates to ensure that any responsibility for wrongdoing remains with the lower echelons and rarely implicates their superiors. However, because discretion is more severely circumscribed by the visibility of one's actions as one moves up the hierarchy, it becomes progressively more important to ensure that those who take visible decisions that might jeopardize the organization are carefully selected. Detectives are valued more than patrol officers not because they catch criminals – which they do not – but because they "legalize" police decisions (Dixon 1997). Transforming the messy reality of the streets into the clinical world of "evidence" that will be *publicly examined* in court is an enterprise fraught with danger for the police organization if done incompetently. Likewise, senior police officers do not often deal with the marginalized and dispossessed, but with those who have power, such as politicians and the mass media. Thus, the reason why patrol officers are treated so badly is that, save for the most exceptional circumstances, what they do is of little consequence for the organization, however important it might be for others.

Inter-rank Conflict

Given what has been written above it is hardly surprising that police organizations are riven with conflict between "street". and "management" cops (Punch 1983; Reuss-Ianni & Ianni 1983). Patrol officers dislike the arduous and unsociable conditions under which they work and envy those with a "cushy number'; they resent the under-valuation of their work; but most of all they resist the punitive nature of police discipline. From their perspective, senior ranks are divorced from reality, living a comfortable and trouble-free existence on the upper floors of police headquarters. Attempts by senior officers to evaluate performance are regarded as, at best, ill-conceived distractions from genuine priorities that rarely receive the attention they deserve (Chatterton 1987). Senior officers view their subordinates across the same divide with as much wariness. They know that their ability to "command" those for whom they are notionally responsible is tenuous. Hence, the existence on the upper floors of police headquarters tends to be experienced as living on a volcano that might erupt at any time with career-jeopardizing consequences. When the "volcano" erupts, senior officers are politically compelled to "do something" to ensure that it does not recur and this becomes a symbolic act of tightening rules and procedures that only exacerbates the counter-productive approach of the "punishment-centred bureaucracy". In the United States the result of this mutual antagonism has been the growth of the police union movement that has channelled resistance to managerial imposition and had a negative impact on reform (Kelling & Kliesmet 1996). Britain too has seen the *de facto* power of the Police Federation grow, reaching its climax with its successful opposition to the government-appointed Sheehy Committee's proposals to change terms and conditions of employment by such management innovations as performance-related pay (Sheehy 1993).

Specialists

The organizational response to the growth in demand for police services has been to create a plethora of specialist departments, squads and units. On the one hand, this allows the police to avoid the implication of their all-embracing generalist role, by apportioning responsibilities to those with specific skills and knowledge (Wiles 1993). It also gives senior officers a limited measure of control over the allocation of police resources, since any department can only do as much as its resources allow. It also allows the police to be seen to "do something" in response to a particular issue. Thus, the growing concern about domestic violence and child abuse, has been matched by the growth of organizational structures dedicated to this area of police work. Nevertheless, the increased specialization in policing has evident organizational drawbacks.

The first drawback is that it serves to exacerbate the problems that Jones identifies since it creates enhanced opportunities for escape from the drudgery of patrol (Jones 1980). Worse still, as specialist units are created, they effectively deskill patrol work, leaving patrol officers to deal with the rump of tasks that no one else in the police organization has responsibility for. This makes patrol work even less attractive and lends further encouragement to officers to escape. It is, perhaps, ironic that "community policing", by creating yet another specialism – that of the community officer – tends to exacerbate rather than mitigate these organizational problems. In particular, by allowing patrol officers to refer more complex problems requiring long-term solutions to their "community" colleagues, it encourages still further their "short-termism" and thirst for excitement.

Secondly, the creation of a plethora of specialist units can perversely *reduce* skill levels among those who staff them. This arises from the way in which ambitious officers use specialist positions to develop their careers. For instance, upwardly mobile officers must gain sufficient experience of different types of police work to demonstrate their grasp of the full range of policing (Wiles 1993). The result is that they move frequently from one department to the next earning themselves the unkind sobriquet of "butterflies" in the process. More seriously, it incidentally means that as upwardly mobile officers take successive command of a variety of specialist units, those units are commanded by those with little or no specialist knowledge. Since knowledge is power in many circumstances, this is a recipe for the emasculation of command and its *de facto* delegation to subordinates who *do* possess the specialist knowledge needed. Moreover, frequent changes in command personnel tends to create the "three-year rule". This "rule" maintains that new commanders feel compelled to introduce sweeping policy changes in order to establish their managerial credentials, by the time those changes have been implemented it is time for the commanders to move to their next positions, whereupon they are succeeded by other commanders who, under the same compulsion, dismantle the policies of their predecessors and introduce sweeping policy changes. The result is "continuous revolution" at the policy level, but little change at the operational level where subordinates continue their working practices safe in the knowledge that any change is only temporary and can safely be ignored.

Such perverse effects are not restricted to upwardly mobile officers, but extend throughout all ranks. The more highly prized a specialist unit is, the more aspiring members of it must create a *curriculum vitae* enhancing their eligibility. These officers tend to seek short-term appointment to less highly prized specialist units on the margins of their preferred specialism so as to acquire as much relevant experience as possible. This is most evident in relation to detective work, where aspiring sleuths join a succession of subdetective investigative units in an effort to enhance their *CVs*. Of course, not all of them are successful by any means, but whether they are or are not, the effect on the specialist units through which they pass can be deleterious. The most obvious negative impact is that these specialist units are rarely staffed by personnel with specialist abilities; instead staff tend to be at various stages of *acquiring* relevant skills and knowledge which, once acquired, are lost to the unit as the person moves elsewhere in pursuit of their career ambitions (Waddington 1993a).

Thirdly, to the extent that officers stay in particular specialisms there is the danger that they acquire a narrow and distorted perspective on policing, coming to equate their specialist priorities with those of the organization *per se*. In Britain, where most officers do not routinely carry firearms, dedicated firearms units have a reputation among their colleagues of viewing armed operations solely in terms of the armed threat and disregarding all other considerations, such as the impact on community relations. To ensure that officers do not lose sight of the wider context of their specialist actions it has become common practice in Britain to limit the time that anyone can spend in a specialist unit. Of course, this has the effect of denuding units of precisely the specialist knowledge and skills that experienced staff have acquired and is the *raison d'être* of the unit itself. It can also amount to a costly exercise in continuously training new personnel to replace already trained staff.

Fourthly, one supposed advantage of specialist units is that they can be dissolved when conditions and priorities change. Again, this is easily subverted by those who staff such specialist units and who acquire a vested interest in the continued existence of the specialism. This can take various forms: members of a unit can try to generate evidence of its productivity by such practices as aggressive enforcement. Thus, it is often suggested that the scale of a drug problem in an area reflects the size of the drug squad that needs to demonstrate a continuing need for its existence. Units can also lobby, both internally and externally, to raise awareness and increase the priority given to its task, alliances can be formed with interested groups to maintain pressure for the police to continue to "do something" about a particular problem. This may, of course, reflect genuine concerns and may not be at all malign, as illustrated by the growth of specialist units concerned with domestic violence which have expanded to embrace sexual offences and child abuse. On the other hand, lobbying can militate against the most rational allocation of resources when viewed from the perspective of the organization as a whole.

Reforming Management

What, then, can be done to improve the effectiveness of police organizations? Two largely contradictory strategies have been proposed: professionalizing and managing.

Professionalizing

The professional model seeks to abandon the hierarchical structure of command and control in favour of treating all officers as quasi-professional practitioners exercising their discretion within a framework that acknowledges their skills and emphasizes self-regulation through a code of ethics. In doing so, it recognizes that the bureaucratic model is ill-suited to a discretionary activity that is largely conducted in isolation and beyond the gaze of the organization. This is consistent with the view of those academic commentators who emphasize the skill and "craftsmanship" that good policing entails (Muir 1977; Bittner 1983; Bayley & Bittner 1984). While this argument has undoubted force, it fails to convince because policing is a low-status activity. The skills and knowledge that the police deploy are difficult to formulate as theoretical principles that can be taught through professional education – it is a *craft*. Unlike other crafts – such as antique restoration – its product is not of intrinsically high value; on the contrary much of it is "dirty work". Police patrol the boundaries of respectability, keeping the disreputable in their place, which becomes visible only when things go wrong and rarely lends dignity to any of those involved.

It is because policing treads a path so perilously close to oppression and illegality that strong central control has been enhanced in the wake of successive scandals (Bordua & Reiss 1966). However, this not only hinders the claims of many early police reformers, especially in America, that the police should be considered a profession, but also some argue that it impedes the adoption of more effective methods of control. Whereas imposition of external rules has singularly failed to prevent police wrongdoing, the self-imposition of a code of ethics could prove more effective (Richards 1985, ibid. 1992; Kleinig 1996).

> The need for high levels of individual accountability is not unique to the police. Many other occupations attempt to guarantee such accountability by a system of professional ethics supported by contractual obligations, rather than by a disciplined command structure. It is not at all obvious that high levels of individual accountability are best achieved by a structure which combines command and hierarchical discipline. It is debatable whether the public believes that the individual accountability of police officers is greater than that of employees in other public service organisations. (Wiles 1993: 56)

De-centralization is, of course, consistent with the ethos of "community policing" and some evaluation reports have concluded that rigid, "top-down" organizations have greater difficulty in implementing this type of police reform than do departments with more participative styles of management (Wilkinson & Rosenbaum 1994; Wycoff & Skogan 1994b). However, *if* participation by the lower ranks in decision-making results in "community policing" reforms being abandoned, should senior officers abdicate their responsibility to impose reforms that they and perhaps the public believe are desirable? Just how much respect should the views of lower ranks be accorded?

Policing by Policy

A very different answer to the question of organizational reform has been to attempt to make "command" a reality, albeit disguised as quasi-commercial management rather than emulating military structures. It seeks to make policing *policy-driven*. This is an approach that is attractive to a new generation of senior police officers that Reiner has characterized as "bureaucrats" rather than "bobbies" or "bosses" (Reiner 1991a). It is also chimes with government policies in Britain which have shifted markedly in the direction of seeking to ensure that the police achieve objectives established nationally and deliver "value for money" (Leishman *et al.* 1995; Loveday 1995a; Savage & Charman 1995). Officers at all levels of management find themselves increasingly under pressure to account for their achievements and the setting of objectives is regarded as a necessary discipline (Ackroyd & Helliwell 1991). Budgets have been devolved throughout the police organization requiring officers at all levels of seniority to appraise more self-consciously than in the past how best to deploy their limited resources.

Unlike traditional quasi-military models of organization, "policing by objectives" (as it is commonly known) does not rely simply on the issuing of orders by superiors, it is much more sophisticated than that. Central to this approach is the "policy-cycle", in which views are solicited from interested parties as to what the objectives of the police should be; these objectives are then implemented through carefully formulated "action plans" and their success evaluated, with those evaluations providing valuable information in the formulation of future objectives and their associated "action plans" (for a more detailed exposition see Butler 1984). The issue is whether this model, adopted from business management, can be validly applied to the police and a protracted debate with Butler (Waddington 1986b, ibid. c; Johnston 1997; Butler 1985, ibid. 1986) fails to convince me that it can. The reason is fundamental: policing is *of necessity* reactive. Because they are custodians of state authority on the streets, when members of the public find themselves in circumstances that breach the boundaries of acceptability and with which they are unable to cope, they habitually call the police. Policing is "crisis management"; that is managing other people's crises. This has profound consequences for police management, for the activity that must be managed is indefinite. Crises can occur at any time and must be reacted to there and then; not when it is organizationally convenient. Moreover, crises can take *any* form. Britain is not often struck by hurricane force winds, but on one night in October 1987 it was, and the police were at the forefront of the emergency response; wild animals do not often escape from zoos, but if they do it is the police who spearhead attempts to re-capture them; at the other end of the spectrum, confused elderly people do not often call the police in the early hours of the morning complaining that they cannot change the channel on their television, but in February 1986 that is exactly what happened at the divisional control room that I was observing. It is because *unforeseen* situations tend to become crises that it is difficult to plan for them beyond making available a generic response capability – the police. This is fatal for attempts to introduce policy-driven policing. There will always be crises – large or small – that will prevent the achievement of objectives (Waddington 1993a).

Because it is unachievable, does not prevent the police trying to achieve it. So what have been the consequences of this pursuit of rational management through objectives? Well, it has certainly been influential: police authorities in Britain are required to published their objectives and are evaluated in their achievements by central government who publish annual league tables of performance (Ackroyd & Helliwell 1991). Divisional commanders are normally required to state their objectives and some impose the same discipline on subordinates with specialist responsibilities. However, early attempts at "policing by objectives" foundered on the vague, unachievable and immeasurable nature of the objectives that were being set (Southgate 1985). Subordinates quickly learnt to "work the system" by setting objectives retrospectively, giving the appearance that actual achievements had been purposively produced (Chatterton 1991). Chatterton found that in only one division that he studied was the exercise taken seriously, but that engendered serious opposition from the lower ranks. Chatterton *et al.* went on to compare two police forces, one with a strong commitment to "policing by objectives", and the other not. He and his colleagues found that few differences emerged between the two forces, and that what was common to both was that officers were ignorant of force aims and objectives (Chatterton *et al.* 1993)

The Limits of Management

The experience of "policing by objectives" serves to highlight the severe limitations that there are on any attempt to *manage* policing.

Discretion and Control

The discretion of individual officers exercising authority in conditions of low visibility undermines the command of their superiors just as assuredly as it negates other attempts to control police behaviour. Indeed, Manning has consistently argued that policing is relatively immune to legal–rational bureaucracy, because of its wide discretionary element (Manning 1977, ibid. 1979). Despite its appearance as an organization that processes information in the rational pursuit of declared aims, he maintains that police activity is always so context-specific, conditional and interpretable that it cannot be standardized. He illustrates this in his in-depth analysis of control rooms in both an English and American police force (Manning 1983, ibid. 1988). The choice of control rooms in which to examine this thesis is deliberate, since this purports to be the heart of the rational information-processing machine: inputs are received in the form of messages from the public and elsewhere, and they are converted into outputs in the form of the deployment of police resources. Delving deeply into this process what Manning reveals is the continuous need for control-room operatives to read between the lines of incoming calls to reconstruct the situation that has prompted the call and arrive at an appropriate response. I too found that decision-making in a divisional control room was highly context-specific and relatively immune to policy direction (Waddington 1993a). However closely they are supervised and however tightly rules are drawn operatives retain such enormous discretion as to defeat naïve attempts to constrain their actions in the name of increased efficiency (Audit Commission 1990a; see also Shearing 1981a, ibid. 1984; Scott & Percy 1983).

It is the inability of policy-makers to ensure that their policies are fulfilled that makes the police, in Shearing's view, a deviant organization (Shearing 1981b). Holdaway maintains that the power of the lower ranks to subvert policy is so great in the police that improvement will only come from greater external influence over the police (Holdaway 1978), but it remains unexplained why external influences should be any more immune to subversion than those emanating from superior ranks. Research on the policing of domestic violence in Phoenix illustrates the scope that exists for the subversion of policies with which subordinates disagree (Buzawa & Buzawa 1993). In response to a policy requiring the arrest of violent spouses, officers adopted their own *de facto* policy of arresting *both* partners, which undermined the credibility of the abused woman and reduced the likelihood that their abuser would be convicted. This had the predictable consequence of dissuading abused women from calling the police again. However, it would be misleading to suggest that policy is subverted only by the lower ranks; for often senior officers and their subordinates enter into an unholy alliance in which illicit activities are tolerated so long as they prove effective (Kappeler *et al.* 1994). Moreover, senior officers themselves manipulate evidence of performance so as to give a favourable public impression of the organization to powerful audiences (Diez 1995).

Symbolism of Policing

The problems posed by police discretion for management are widely recognized and often remarked upon, but perhaps an even more serious challenge to the management ethos lies in the symbolism of policing. This contradicts the central assumption of "policing by objectives" (or, indeed, any other rational management approach), which maintains that policing is an *instrumental* activity. If, as was argued in Chapter 1, patrolling is a symbolic exercise of police (and through them, state) authority, then its aims are achieved in the course of its enactment. Evaluating whether patrolling reduces crime or enhances public attitudes to the police is irrelevant, since they are at most merely incidental benefits of an activity that is essentially symbolic. Law and order in the Bogside of Londonderry was probably as secure under the *de facto* authority of the Provisional IRA when it was "Free Derry" in the early 1970s than before or since; but the British Army still mobilized a huge force to re-capture the Bogside in "Operation Motorman" because this "no-go" area *symbolized* the impotence of the authority of the British State. "Free Derry" was an issue of symbolism rather than instrumentality, and that same symbolism is enacted when cops the world over patrol the areas for which they are responsible.

The limits of the rationalist case are neatly identified by one of its most persuasive exponents. Sherman has been at the forefront of policies to arrest those who perpetrate domestic violence. It is important to appreciate the grounds upon which Sherman has advocated such policies, for they are quite different to those of feminist writers who have largely been concerned with *justice* for women. Sherman's argument is that careful evaluation has shown that the policy *works*; that is, that violent spouses tend to curb their violence once the threat of arrest becomes a realistic possibility. Sherman is too rigorous an analyst to have allowed his empirical claims to rest on one experimental evaluation; but as the original experiment in Milwaukee has been repeated so the picture has become more complex. It turns out that the arrest policy has greatest impact on those spouses with the most to lose – that is the middle classes. Working-class abusers are less influenced in their behaviour and arresting them might even prove counter-productive (Sherman & Berk 1984; Martin & Sherman 1986; Sherman 1986, ibid. 1990, ibid. 1992a, ibid. b; Sherman *et al.* 1992). What, then, should the police do? Sherman has advocated that they should exercise discretion selectively guided by the results of empirical research (Sherman 1984). Hence, middle-class men would be arrested, while their working-class counterparts would not. The objection to this, which Sherman openly acknowledges, lies in what he calls the "justice model': not only might abusive middle-class husbands feel they have been unjustly treated when they are arrested in conditions where working-class counterparts are not; abused working-class women are equally likely to conclude that the plight of their middle-class counterparts is taken more seriously by the police than is their own. Sherman is correct: justice *is* principally symbolic. If positive consequences happen to flow from just actions that is bonus, but one cannot act unjustly in order to achieve positive consequences – justice is something that is good in itself and needs no instrumental justification.

This symbolism permeates policing, especially in liberal democratic societies, because of the need to legitimate and re-legitimate police authority. Sykes argues that the reason why police organizations have the trappings of militarism is in order to reassure the civil population that police officers are under command and control even though, in fact, they are not (Sykes 1993). Decisions are taken in police hierarchies not because those who take them are the most knowledgeable, able, or in any other regard rationally appropriate, but because they are of the appropriate rank. In Britain, officers may be equipped with firearms only with the authority of a superior of chief officer rank. Those who give authorization are rarely specialists in the use of firearms and are often wholly reliant on the advice they receive from their subordinates, who are not infrequently the very individuals who are seeking the authority to deploy firearms. This ritual – for that is what it often is – is enacted in order symbolically to demonstrate that in an unarmed police like that in Britain the arming of officers is exceptional and not undertaken lightly. The same applies to the legal requirement that officers of certain rank must authorize the detention of suspects beyond certain time limits, or authorize stop-and-search operations in high crime areas, and so forth. These are symbolic assertions of the seriousness with which such decisions are taken.

Management (Mis)information

Information is crucial for the management of any organization and one commodity of which police organizations tend not to be short is information – virtually everything is recorded – the problem is that such information is rarely used for management purposes. It is stored for the eventuality that it may be needed as evidence in a prosecution or complaint against an officer. The notion that these records might be treated as data, the analysis of which could provide valuable information about the patterns of public demand on the police, the occurrence of crime, the deployment of officers, and so forth, has only recently received even the most cursory acknowledgement within the police institution.

> . . . it was apparent that police managers did not routinely ask themselves the kinds of questions which the information could have helped them to answer. . . . For the most part, local managers were not pursuing defined policies in a systematic way, so they found information about public demand and policing activity much less useful. (Horton 1989: 35)

Information is often fragmentary, ad hoc and not used to guide police actions, which is illustrated by how repeat calls to complaints of domestic violence at the same address are each treated in isolation, instead of being recognized as part of a recurring pattern (Horton & Smith 1988). Chatterton and Rogers found that supervising officers made little attempt to orchestrate the use of patrol time to focus on continuing problems. Instead of using what management information was available, "blind faith" was placed in the amount of local knowledge possessed by patrolling officers (Chatterton & Rogers 1989). Moreover, police organizations collect inappropriate information, especially about crime, and gather insufficient useful data, such as that relating to public expectations and experiences of the police (Tremblay & Rochon 1991).

This inability or refusal to use information to guide and direct police practice reflects how information is regarded and used within police organizations. Information is something to be guarded closely and released with care. This is for two reasons: first, information may be used to enhance one's own interests, for example by making a "good arrest" that brings esteem and career advancement – it enables one to "win" (Irving *et al.* 1989). Secondly, denying information to others enables officers to retain autonomy and avoid censure (Chatterton 1987). Thus, unless an incident is dealt with formally, officers disclose as little as possible about their actions, which thereby denies superiors the information with which to assess effectiveness and make appropriate changes (Kemp *et al.* 1992b). When information *is* disclosed, it is couched so as to give the actions of the officers organizational legitimacy – knowing how to account for the same incident differently to different audiences being an essential component of police competence (Fielding 1984). All of this militates against policy formulation and evaluation, as well as evaluating the performance of officers. It encourages instead "management by consequences"; that is in the absence of complaints senior officers leave well alone (Chatterton 1991). It also undermines an integrated corporate strategy that relies on sharing information. This can range from defeating sector policing in which local officers are encouraged to share their knowledge of the local area so as to find general solutions (Irving *et al.* 1989), to hindering collaboration on a national scale to defeat organized crime (Hilliard 1995).

External Constraints on Resource Management

It is not only internal processes that subvert the command that superiors can exercise, there are external constraints too. The most significant constraint is the pattern and content of calls for police assistance from members of the public. This quite directly shapes, albeit does not determine, police activity. As such it acts as a "democratic" restraint on policing, for the police usually intrude only when members of the public believe that situations are beyond their capacity to cope with. However, this "democracy" is very imperfect, since those with the most economic, organizational and social power exert disproportionate influence. A good example of this is the way that commercial companies are able effectively to commandeer police resources through fitting automatic intruder alarms linked to security companies. When the alarm is activated, the security company contacts the police (often through a specially dedicated telephone line) to advise them of a possible burglary. What, on the face of it, should be a valuable contribution to crime prevention has other, less valuable, consequences. Firstly, the commercial imperative dictates that in so far as the alarm will be triggered in error, that should occur preferentially in conditions when no intruder is present. An alarm that failed to activate when intruders were on the premises would have little commercial attraction, whereas "false positives" incur little cost to either the installer or customer. It does however incur considerable cost for the police, and hence the public purse, as officers are dispatched to reported alarms, the vast majority of which turn out to be false (Waddington 1993a). Secondly, the ability of commercial companies to obtain an urgent response from the police to an activated alarm that all parties believe is probably false, is assisted by organizational procedures that expose individual officers to potential "comeback". For instance, in the control room that I observed, calls from security companies were accompanied by a well-rehearsed routine in which the company operative gave their individual identity code and officers replied with their divisional number. Thus, officers felt individually accountable for any action taken and this encouraged an urgent response in order to "cover their backs". The result is that large numbers of officers are routinely deployed to seal off commercial premises in response to alarms that overwhelmingly turn out to be false. A similar situation arises with suspected shoplifters arrested by store detectives. Store detectives have no powers of arrest beyond those of any other citizen, so police feel considerable compulsion to attend and "regularize" the arrest. This is a task often allocated to junior officers who have recently completed training. Those officers find that when they attend the store they are confronted by an experienced and knowledgeable store detective who presents them with an already completed witness statement in conditions that leaves little *de facto* opportunity in which to exercise discretion. Officers are effectively compelled to arrest the suspect, even if the goods allegedly stolen are quite meagre in value, and to complete "paperwork" that almost invariably results in an official caution being administered. The consequence is to remove officers from the street to attend to the priorities of the stores, irrespective of the priorities of the police organization (Waddington 1993a).

Evaluation by Numbers

Another external pressure comes from the increased demand for police organizations to give the appearance that they are achieving objectives. There is the tendency of bureaucracies generally to substitute means for ends, which in terms of evaluation becomes assessing what can be assessed, preferably in measurable form. Hence, police forces are evaluated in terms of crude measures of effectiveness in reducing crime. When government pressure first began to be felt by the police in Britain, effectiveness and efficiency were treated as coterminous, but as Jones and Silverman pointed out at the time, considerations of efficiency tend to predominate because cost per unit of outcome is relatively easy to quantify. So, the result is that police forces might have become more efficient – in that what they do they do at minimum cost – but not necessarily any more effective from the public's point of view (Jones & Silverman 1984).

A further problem with "number crunching" has been identified by Waters (1995) who points to the clash between the demands for efficiency and the desire to improve "quality of service". This is neatly illustrated by police response to household burglaries. Most victims express satisfaction at how the police response to their burglary: the police usually attend directly; display care and concern for the welfare of the victim; and make an awful mess as they "dust" for fingerprints (Maguire 1982). None of these activities have any connection with capturing the burglar; for example, less than half of one per cent of all detections are attributable to fingerprint evidence (although this evidence can provide corroboration of suspicions aroused in other ways). In terms of rational instrumentality what police do in response to household burglaries is virtually a waste of time, but it does help reassure victims – those in authority are taking their plight seriously. Hard-nosed management, guided by the objective of reducing burglaries would be obliged to abandon such a response, advise victims to clear up the mess and claim on their insurance, then wait for a burglar to fall into the police lap and pump him to confess to all the burglaries that he has committed, for that is how the vast majority of burglaries are actually detected (Burrows 1986).

There is also the danger that beneath the veil of apparent rationality there lurks the irrational desire for the "quick fix" married to arrogance bred by ignorance. This seems to have been behind a series of Audit Commission reports in Britain during the early 1990s. The *modus operandi* is clear: a brief and superficial investigation, paying little heed to existing criminological research, results in a report that castigates current practice and dictates how deficiencies can be rectified. A good example of this was the enthusiasm shown for "intelligence-led" policing as the cost-effective alternative to traditional reactive methods. Police should target suspected offenders, collect evidence and then swoop and make the arrest (Audit Commission 1993). This amounted to little more than telling the police what they wanted to hear, since it authoritatively endorsed an approach pioneered in London against burglars under the title "Operation Bumblebee". But is this advice as rational as it appears? Dunnighan and Norris (1995a) have carefully costed informer handling by the police and concluded that the Audit Commission's figures are hopelessly optimistic and Morgan and Newburn (1997) conclude that, on the Audit Commission's own estimates, there are at least 300,000 repeat offenders who need targeting, a figure clearly beyond the resources of the police.

Managing Organizational Change

The wonder is that senior officers are able to exert *any* control or influence over their subordinates; but they can and they do. Where it matters, police forces have succeeded in transforming practice. Perhaps the most startling example of this has been the substantial reduction in police shootings in the United States which is almost entirely attributable to changes in departmental policy brought about through external pressure (Fyfe 1978, ibid. 1982a; Reiss 1980; Chapman 1982; Sherman 1983b). However, this not an isolated case: in Britain the rigorous enforcement of disciplinary rules concerning "drink driving" has had an enormous impact on alcohol consumption among officers, even when off-duty. There have also been substantial improvements in the way in which victims of domestic violence and sexual crimes are treated (Buchan & Edwards 1991; Edwards 1994).

Why precisely these changes have proven so effective while others have not is difficult to fathom. It is tempting to see change as a response to scandal (Sherman 1978). In Britain few could doubt the magnitude of the scandal that overwhelmed the police at the end of the 1980s as a wave of "miscarriages of justice" and police wrongdoing in the investigation of serious crime burst into the public arena. Yet, legislators and police management have avoided taking relatively modest action that would, at least, reduce the likelihood of a recurrence of these scandals (Maguire & Norris 1994). Frankly, research has yet to even glimpse why reform occurs where and when it does, or takes the form it does.

Managing From the Bottom Up

If the search for rational police management is the pursuit of chimera, does this mean that policing is unmanageable, indeed uncontrollable? The answer is yes, if management and control is taken to mean the issuing of directives, guidance or any other means of influencing police behaviour *in advance* of the situations they deal with. Policing is largely reactive and attention should be given to how those reactive interventions can be improved. This entails concentrating, not on the amorphous generality of "the public", but on those who actually *use* the service.

> By trying to gratify the whimsical demands of the abstract public, police have a tendency to ignore the demands of the actual users of their services, with the end result that the predicament of a given victim of crime becomes a secondary issue relative to the interests of the police to apprehend the often unapprehendable offenders; demands by individuals for police to resolve conflict or to provide noncriminal emergency services become low-priority items on the police agenda; and police devote excessive amounts of resources on unproductive proactive tactics to prevent crime at the expense of the more productive tactic of reactive policing. (Vanagunas 1982: 43)

However, a straightforward consumerist approach is equally fraught with difficulty, for, as Dixon *et al.* (1993) make clear, the police often intercede *between* different users of their services. Authoritative intervention in conflict often results in one of the parties "winning" at the expense of others. Any evaluation of police action might, therefore, reflect whether the evaluator was on the "winning" or "losing" side.

POP Goes the Management Structure

What these arguments have not questioned is a commitment to solving problems. The crucial difference between rational management and community policing, especially problem-oriented policing, is that the latter reflects the reality that policing is driven, not by policy, but by problems brought to the attention of the lowest echelons in the organization. Police typically cease their involvement in a situation when their authority is exercised and acceptable order is restored. As Goldstein argues, this is to address symptoms rather than their causes (Goldstein 1979, ibid. 1990) and he advocates the adoption of a problem-oriented approach towards those underlying causes. However, while some problems might be resolvable by concerted action of the lower ranks, the organizational reality is that patrol officers cannot devote sustained attention to almost any problem because of the demands of unscheduled calls for service from the public, but more so the requirements of shift work. What this suggests is that senior ranks should see their role as *supporting* their subordinates by identifying problems that are manifested in particular incidents and co-ordinating a response to them that might entail mobilizing resources well beyond the confines of the police service. In other words, the structure of the police organization should reflect the task it is call upon to discharge and also be bottom-up (Waddington 1993a).

Conclusion

The omnibus and indeterminate responsibilities that the police acquire as custodians of state authority defeat attempts to impose rational management. Instead of emulating the flawed models of commercial management, policing needs to develop organizational forms appropriate to its distinctive task.

Privatization

While reformers have been seeking to improve policing through policy and managerial innovation, other developments have been occurring that threaten to have a far more profound impact on policing in future. These developments reflect wider socio-economic changes and once more direct our attention to the fact that policing is largely determined by the society that is policed.

So, what are these socio-economic changes that threaten to transform policing? They are often referred to under the umbrella term "globalization". There is now an extensive literature on this phenomenon that has many ramifications only some of which I will outline in the barest terms here. Basically, it refers to the growth of international trade that homogenizes goods and services worldwide. This has many consequences – economically, culturally and politically – one of which is to liberate financial capital for firms that no longer operate within a national territory, but manufacture wherever it is economically most advantageous to do so. Countries compete to attract investment capital to their respective territories and this applies downward pressure on costs. This has two direct impacts on policing: first, the downward pressure on costs is felt most directly on public services funded by taxation. Taxes raised by direct levies on firms obviously drive up costs and discourage investment, but the taxation of workers also applies upward pressure on wage rates that has an adverse effect on competitiveness. Since the 1970s countries throughout the western world have been retreating from the "welfare state" paid for by taxation, albeit with more or less enthusiasm. Policing has been less adversely affected by this development than many other public services, such as health, education and social work; but even in Britain – where they were shielded from the full effects of Thatcherism by the prime minister's addiction to authoritarian solutions to social problems – they did not escape the impact of financial stringency. Since 1983 the government has sought to impose on police the rigours of its "new financial management" (Leishman *et al.* 1995; Savage & Charman 1995) in which "value for money" is the watchword (Home Office 1983). Police resources have been increasingly stretched in pursuit of "effectiveness" and "efficiency" (Jones & Silverman 1984). This has been coupled with a growth in managerialism which, though it found an enthusiastic ally in "policing by objectives", goes much further. Basically, the aim has been to make senior police officers far more *financially accountable* (Reiner 1993b). Police forces are now obliged to recognize that they allocate economic resources and must make hard choices between equally attractive options. This has been coupled with the introduction of a "performance culture" in which senior officers are appointed for a limited period and their contract renewed or discontinued at its conclusion. Attempts to impose performance-related pay (Sheehy 1993) were effectively resisted by the lower ranks, but vestigial structures continue to operate. Adherence to current managerial wisdom (if that is not a contradiction in terms) dictates that the police hierarchy is "delayered" and two ranks have been removed, albeit that there are distinct signs of surreptitious, and effective, resistance. However, there can be little doubt that the police, in common with other public services, find themselves increasingly subject to financial stringency.

Secondly, the impact of globalization is felt in the increasing demands being made upon the police. In part this arises from financial stringency and its associated insistence on managerial accountability. More importantly, the society that is policed is more demanding. Downward pressure on labour costs throughout the economy results in higher rates of unemployment as labour markets become more "flexible". However, because of the retreat from the welfare state, those who suffer unemployment receive less financial support and are subject to pressures to return to whatever employment can be found. This encourages the growth of a section of the labour force that is perpetually trapped by low wages and insecure employment. Concentrated in rotting public housing in urban areas and facing the progressive withdrawal of public welfare, this increasingly racialized section of the population is exposed to the cocktail of social deprivation and environmental decay that has long been associated with lawlessness and criminality (for an admirable summary of the British data see Morgan & Newburn 1997). From the perspective of the political right this is seen as the creation of a new feckless "underclass" (Murray 1990, ibid. 1994); from a liberal-left perspective it amounts to the virtual abandonment of possibly a third of the population (Hutton 1995); either way it entails the removal of the "disciplines" that were apparently responsible for the decline in crime during the second half of the nineteenth century (Lane 1992). It is not just that the perpetrators and victims of crime are concentrated among this increasing section of the population, but that whole areas are becoming more difficult to police as workless young men assert themselves by rejecting the authority of the police (Power & Tunstall 1997). Apart from the direct demands on police services that these developments encourage, they also fuel fear of crime among the general population and demands for more "law and order".

So policing in the last quarter of the twentieth century finds itself caught increasingly between the "hard place" of financial stringency and the "rock" of increasing demand. Police forces throughout the western world have struggled to come to terms with these developments and in doing so may be setting the stage for a fundamental transformation of policing in the twenty-first century. That transformation amounts to the growth of "grey policing" (Hoogenboom 1991), lying neither clearly within the ambit of the state nor private institutions, but occupying a vague status between the two.

The Case of the Shrinking Police

One response to socio-economic change has been to improve the cost-effectiveness of police organizations, so that adequate levels of policing are maintained but at lower unit costs. The major difficulty that confronts the pursuit of police efficiency is that policing is manpower intensive and officers are expensive. This expense lies in the need to offer salaries that attract recruits of an acceptable calibre and to train, and frequently retrain, them in the essentials of criminal law and procedure, forensic techniques, self-defence and weapons handling, and much more besides. Yet, this contains a paradox: for the tasks that officers are mainly engaged in, and which the public tends to value most (such as patrolling), rarely require the skills and personal qualities of a fully fledged police officer. As Wiles has argued (1993), refusal to specialize in policing increases costs and decreases efficiency as all police personnel need to be reasonably competent across a broad range of duties. The police have come to appreciate this and under cost pressure police have abandoned the assumption of "omnicompetence" and hived off various tasks to unsworn personnel. Thus, routine office work tends increasingly to be undertaken by civilian clerical staff, and in some jurisdictions civilian staff take such relatively front-line roles as Scenes of Crimes Officers (collecting physical evidence, taking photographs, and so forth), control-room operators, receptionists in police stations, parking-meter attendants and even bomb-disposal personnel. Cost-savings have encouraged this tendency, since civilian staff rarely enjoy such advantageous terms and conditions of employment as do sworn officers (Loveday 1989b). In some jurisdictions the number of civilians employed by the police is beginning almost to match the number of sworn personnel.

This principle has begun to be extended into the patrol function – until recently the last bastion of the sworn officer. Some Dutch cities have introduced two new policing roles: the "stadswacht" (or city warden) and the "politiesurveillant" (or police patroller), the latter having greater powers than the former, but both acting as less costly patrolling auxiliaries of the public police (Wiles 1993; Hofstra & Shapland 1997). In Britain increasing emphasis has been given to recruiting unpaid police auxiliaries known as "Special Constables" (Leon 1989; Gill & Mawby 1990) and some forces have begun using the special skills and knowledge possessed by such auxiliaries in organizational and law-enforcement roles. Thus, Special Constables with computing expertise are being used as unpaid consultants (Howe & Graham 1995). However, the use of unpaid or less well-paid auxiliaries provides only limited scope for reducing the costs of policing, especially since schemes, such as those in Holland, are usually predicated on *expanding* the patrol function.

Policing Tiers

Another means of reducing costs has been to specialize police forces themselves. In France there has been a recent and significant increase in the number of municipalities installing their own police force (Loveday 1994c; Horton 1995). In Britain the Independent Committee of Inquiry into the Role and Responsibilities of the Police (Cassells 1994; see also ibid. 1996) considered the creation of local municipal police as a possible response to public demands for more "bobbies on the beat" (see also Morgan & Newburn 1997). The United States and Canada both have long-established traditions of local policing within state or provincial, and federal or national structures. However, it is widely recognized that dangers lurk in the localization of policing: first, problems of co-ordination arise from the overlapping jurisdictions of several police and law-enforcement agencies, and increasing tiers of policing entails greater overlap and more problems. Secondly, local policing tends to be highly variable with some highly professional police forces in better-resourced municipalities but correspondingly less professional departments elsewhere. Thirdly, the municipalities that are most able to afford their own police forces tend not to be those who need them most. It is in deprived areas where taxation income is least that the problems of law and order tend to be most acute. Hence, municipalization might result in further disadvantaging the already disadvantaged.

Growth of the Private Sector

A parallel development, especially in Anglo–Saxon jurisdictions where the populus has long been suspicious of state intervention (Loveday 1994d), has been the growth of private security – or, as some commentators prefer to call it, "private policing". Of course, there is nothing new about private security; long before the state established a police force private individuals paid retainers to protect them and their property, and "thief-takers" to apprehend criminals and recover property (South 1987, ibid. 1988). Many of these practices were retained after the installation of public policing and were progressively commercialized. Thus, night watchmen have been replaced by uniformed security guards and the paraphernalia of alarm systems. What is noticeable is the explosion in the scale of private security provision during the last quarter of the twentieth century across so many jurisdictions (Hamilton *et al.* 1972; Kakalik & Wildhorn 1977; House of Commons Expenditure Committee 1977; Shearing & Stenning 1981, ibid. 1982, ibid. 1987a; Johnston 1992). In Britain, even some police and military premises are guarded by private security firms. More importantly, perhaps, private security companies have begun to penetrate mainstream criminal justice activities such as transporting remand prisoners to and from court, as well as staffing privately run prisons (Bottomley *et al.* 1996). The Conservative government instigated an inquiry into which policing tasks could better be performed by the private sector. Although the recommendations were more modest than many feared (*Police*, July 1994, June 1995), it was proposed that private security companies should take over a range of responsibilities such as escorting "abnormal loads" (trucks that are longer, wider or heavier than would normally be allowed on the roads). The case for such a transfer seems compelling: it would relieve the police of a tedious task that currently detracts from enforcing traffic laws and would provide a better, if more costly, service to hauliers.

What opponents of privatization fear is the threat to civil liberties. When these fears are expressed by the police, it is tempting to see in their protests the expression of vested interests by a monopoly producer (Blair 1994; Gibbons 1994; Broughton 1995; Alexandrou 1996; see also *Police*, November 1994). On the other hand, when private security guards are employed to prevent environmental protesters from obstructing the building of new roads similar concern is echoed from other quarters who fear the threat to civil liberties (Wilderman 1991; Gallagher 1995; Crandon 1996; Vidal 1996). Like the "slugging detectives" in pre-1940s American labour relations (Weiss 1987), the security guard is not an agent of the state constrained by constitutional safeguards, but the servant of a private master whose particular interests are served. But there are many ways in which liberty is threatened just as assuredly but far more insidiously. First, private security has insinuated itself into many aspects of daily life without any form of public debate or consent. For example, there is now extensive video surveillance operated by private security companies. One might accept that entering private premises might imply being subjected to such surveillance. We will return to the question of private space shortly; however, the investigation of city-centre terrorist bombings in Britain has incidentally revealed just how extensive is the video surveillance of *public* space in the vicinity of commercial premises. Much of this is passive, but operatives of surveillance cameras retain the option of focusing on particular individuals and keeping them under close scrutiny without the person knowing; still less agreeing.

Secondly, the relationship that police have with private security firms might blur the distinction between the two and the rights of citizens. South (1989) has identified how the relationship between the police and private security risks civil liberties as private security carves out for itself an area of responsibility previously exercised by the state. Private security defines who are the "target population" and this reflects clients' interests; for instance it is employees that are subject to surveillance, not management. It is private security that exercises the option of invoking the police when it is in *its* interests to do so. Private security firms retain the option of dealing with matters informally; say, by dismissal, or through the civil or criminal courts. Marx goes further and points to how policing and private security have become entwined in ways that threaten civil liberties because the police can leave it to private security firms to take action that would otherwise breach constitutional safeguards (Marx 1987). For example, private security may have far wider powers of search and seizure over employees than the police and may be used by police to obtain evidence that could not otherwise be lawfully obtained. When private security interests dictate that suspects are reported to the police, commercial "muscle" tends to ensure that police respond compliantly to such demands; as was noted above with regard to shoplifters. One implication of this is that private security (and the interests they serve) come to define "peace and order" and this is an incipient challenge to state authority (Shearing & Stenning 1987b).

The third threat posed by privatization is the assumption of full law-enforcement powers by private security companies. In authoritarian societies facing insurrectionary threats private security can readily be mobilized in defence of the state. This is what happened in the dying days of apartheid when various private interests were required to perform security roles. For instance, nominated "key points" such as strategic industries (arms manufacture, energy production and so forth) were required to protect themselves from terrorist attack and formed paramilitary (in the strict sense of the term) units for such a purpose. Nor were these units used only for static defence, but often patrolled nearby townships in an active policing role. Elsewhere, tribal authorities (such as traditional chiefs) were encouraged to exert none-too-subtle control over young people, and in the townships a "blind eye" was turned to the activities of vigilante groups so long as they suppressed militant youth (Grant 1989; Scharf 1989; Brogden & Shearing 1993; Cawthra 1993). All this might seem very alien to western democracies; but in Britain one of the very few routinely armed police forces is that employed to guard privately owned nuclear-powered electricity generating plant (Potter 1996). Less dramatically, it has been seriously mooted that store detectives should be sworn as Special Constables to reduce the duplication of effort by police who effectively arrest a suspect who has already been arrested *de facto* by the store detective. What apartheid South Africa represents is the terminal point in a process where the distinction between public and private is progressively blurred.

Perversely, attempts to regulate and improve the efficiency of private security can actually encourage further encroachment into public policing roles. Police representative associations, like the Police Federation, have consistently demanded the registration and licensing of private security companies (*Police*, November 1994, June 1995), but during the 1980s government resisted these demands and then only proposed modest legislation (*Police Review*, 14 June 1996, 10 January 1997). Meanwhile police have become involved in schemes to improve the training of private security personnel (*Police Review*, 9 February 1996, 14 April 1996). The irony of this is that licensing and enhanced training will improve the credibility of private security and facilitate its encroachment into public policing.

Fourthly, the blurring of public and private does not only arise from incursions of private security into public policing, but also from the growth of private activity by the police ranging from providing dedicated patrols to receiving corporate sponsorship. One cash-strapped British police force began charging for services such as registering the "keyholders" of business premises and escorting abnormal loads during busy periods and have also marketed their own security devices. One senior officer in the force supported a proposal at the Superintendents' Association conference for police forces to compete openly with private security firms in order to generate income (Jenkins 1997). There has been a growth in recent years in public bodies, such as hospitals and housing authorities, paying for dedicated police patrols (*Police Review*, 3 March 1995, 26 July 1996). Loveday perceives in these developments the opportunity for local authorities and other public bodies to reduce the autonomy of the police and enhance their democratic accountability (Loveday 1995b). Elsewhere, he has suggested that this contractual arrangement could be extended to municipalities purchasing police services from competing providers (Loveday 1993). Whether one shares his enthusiasm for such arrangements or not, he correctly recognizes that by entering into such private arrangements the police lose their independence. Instead of being of agents of the state, they become servants of particular sectional interests while appearing to retain their constitutional position. This is not uncommon in the United States where bodies like hospitals, universities, transport authorities, art galleries and museums, and a host of others, maintain fully sworn police services. In Britain this is not nearly so fully developed, but the now-privatized railways are policed by their own sworn officers and so too are the Royal Parks in London. The kind of problems that this can pose are illustrated by the latter. Prior to the Royal Parks Police assuming full responsibility for Hyde Park (a traditional site for protest gatherings), the London Metropolitan Police frequently declined to enforce park regulations forbidding the display of banners and placards. They did so because it would invite confrontation with protesters at the entrance to the park and the threat of disorder erupting in its vicinity. However, this caused intense irritation to the park authorities who consistently pressed for the regulations to be enforced. The Royal Parks Police are much more vulnerable to this pressure than the Metropolitan Police, because of their employer–employee relationship and the lack of wider responsibility for the streets of the capital generally. While both police forces enjoy the same constitutional status, the realities of power are quite different and may have serious consequences.

Private Space

A major boost to the growth of private security has been the development of office plazas, shopping malls, and entertainment and sports complexes that blur the distinction between private and public space. In entering a shopping mall one also enters a private contract with its owners that implicitly subjects one to security surveillance and general scrutiny. The owners are not obliged to enter into such a contract and their agents (private security guards located at entrances) can refuse entry to whomsoever they wish, provided they do not discriminate against certain types of person too overtly. Moreover, the contract can be terminated at will, thus allowing those who offend the owners to be removed. In other words, visitors to a mall or similar premises leave many of their constitutional safeguards at the entrance; for they enter into a relationship, not with the state, but with the proprietor – citizenship is exchanged for becoming a customer. The irony is that this is one of the features of such premises that make them so popular, for they offer the appearance of security to customers (Reiss 1987; Graham 1995). As Shearing and Stenning (1982) point out, the growth of private security has been based upon the *preventative* surveillance of private space; a surveillance that is virtually unfettered by constitutional safeguards. It is this that gives such premises the feeling of safety that customers find attractive. But for the young, lower-class and ethnic-minority population such premises are less attractive; for while malls are public places in which to hang out and meet peers, they are subject to the oppressive and possibly capricious control of private security guards (White 1994). Malls and similar premises effectively privatize what was once the epitome of the public space – the shopping street.

The nightmare scenario to which this development gives rise is that public space will increasingly be privatized with housing and, indeed, entire villages, being privately guarded, as is allegedly already happening in southern California (Davis 1990). Already, some local authorities in Britain have contracted private security firms to provide regular patrols. Thus, for those who can afford it, the prospect looms of leaving one's home in a privately guarded compound; travelling (possibly along private toll roads privately policed) to work in privately guarded and secure offices; shopping and being entertained in the security of private malls; and when holidays arrive one relaxes in a fenced compound in a Third World Country, away from the starving population. What role beckons for the public police? It would be to control that section of the population that cannot afford private security – the deprived and dispossessed from whom the affluent pay to be protected. There would be little incentive for those who are affluent enough to purchase private security to ensure more than minimum resourcing of such policing. The function of such a police would inevitably be to suppress the rebelliousness of the excluded population and the limited means at their disposal would invite heavy-handedness. In other words, it would be the application of colonial style policing to the domestic population.

This is an unpalatable future; but like all prophecies it could easily be falsified by changes in events. It is possible that instead of global competition tearing economies apart, national governments will respond to the pressures that it brings by the formation of huge trading blocks that reinforce, rather than undermine, state authority. But that is – as they say – another story!

Conclusion

Police reform can be assessed according to how effectively it achieves desirable goals; but it can also indicate how this state institution struggles to adapt to changing social conditions. From this latter perspective we can detect two contrary influences on policing. For much of the second half of the twentieth century, policing has been coming to terms with the worldwide demand for civil rights for previously excluded or marginalized sections of the population – ethnic minorities, women, gays and lesbians. "Community policing" was an ethos that encapsulated the need to be responsive to *all* sections of the population. However, the realities of material power are not easily swept aside and changes in the economic structure have reversed the processes of inclusion and re-asserted patterns of exclusion. Whether it is through fighting the "war on drugs" or pursuing "zero tolerance" of minor incivilities in the name of "quality of life", policing is less problematic than it was. Excluded sections of the population are increasingly seen as a threat that must be contained and there is less concern about how that containment is achieved. If pressure for inclusion was founded on demands that the rights of individuals should be respected, another aspect of individualism has fuelled exclusion. Security is a commodity that can be purchased and those who can afford do so are providing for their own security. This transforms the relationship of individuals to authority, for the citizen's relationship to the state is replaced by the consumer's contract with the supplier. Security is maintained against external threat and that threat is embodied in excluded sections of the population.

Bibliography

Abbott, P. & R. Sapsford 1990. Health Visiting: Policing the Family? In *The Sociology of the Caring Professions*, P. Abbott & C. Wallace (eds), 120–52. London: Falmer.

Ackroyd, C., J. Rosenhead, T. Shallice 1977. *The Technology of Political Control.* Harmondsworth, Middlesex: Penguin.

Ackroyd, S. & C. Helliwell 1991. What Happened to Objectives? *Policing* **7** (2, Summer), 132–43.

Adams, K. 1996. Measuring the Prevalence of Police Abuse of Force. In *Police Violence: Understanding and Controlling Police Abuse of Force*, W.A. Geller & H. Toch (eds), 52–93. New Haven, Conn.: Yale University Press.

Adorno, T.W., E. Frenkel-Brunswick, D.J. Levinson, R.N. Sanford 1950. *The Authoritarian Personality.* York: Harper and Row.

Ahire, P.T. 1991. *Imperial Policing: The Emergence and Role of the Police in Colonial Nigeria 1860–1960. New Directions in Criminology.* Milton Keynes: Open University Press.

Albertson Fineman, M. & R. Mykitiuk 1994. *The Public Nature of Private Violence: The Discovery of Domestic Abuse.* New York: Routledge.

Alder, C. 1994. The Policing of Young Women. In *The Police and Young People in Australia*, R. White & C. Alder (eds), 159–74. Cambridge: Cambridge University Press.

Alderson, J.C. 1979. *Policing Freedom.* Plymouth: MacDonald and Evans.

Alexander, D.A. & A. Wells 1991. Reactions of Police Officers to Body-Handling After a Major Disaster: A Before-and-After Comparison. *British Journal of Psychiatry* **159**, 547–55.

Alexandrou, A. 1996. Will Private Finance Put the Police Service in Hock? *Police* (October), 26–28.

Allatt, P. 1984. Residential Security: Containment and Displacement of Burglary. *Howard Journal* **23**, 99–116.

Allen, R.F. & C.H. Adair 1969. *Violence and Riots in Urban America.* Worthington, Ohio: Charles A. Jones.

Alpert, G.P. & W.C. Smith 1994. How Reasonable is the Reasonable Man?: Police and Excessive Force. *Journal Criminal Law and Criminology* **85** (2, Fall), 481–501.

Ames, W. 1981. *Police and Community in Japan.* Berkeley: University of California Press.

Amnesty International 1988. *United Kingdom: Northern Ireland: Killings by Security Forces and "Supergrass" Trials.* London.

BIBLIOGRAPHY

Anderson, D.M. & D. Killingray (eds) 1991. *Policing the Empire: Government, Authority and Control, 1830–1940.* Manchester: Manchester University Press.

Anderson, D.M. & D. Killingray (eds) 1992. *Policing and Decolonisation: Politics, Nationalism and the Police, 1917–65.* Manchester: Manchester University Press.

Anderson, S., C. Grove-Smith, R. Kinsey, J. Wood 1990. *The Edinburgh Crime Survey: First Report. Central Research Unit Paper.* Edinburgh: Scottish Office.

Anderson, S., R. Kinsey, I. Loader, C. Smith 1994. *Cautionary Tales: Young People, Crime and Policing in Edinburgh.* Aldershot: Avebury.

Anderton, J. 1981. Statement of James Anderton, Chief Constable of Greater Manchester Police, to the Greater Manchester Police Committee. Unpublished paper, Manchester.

Antunes, G. & E.J. Scott 1981. Calling the Cops: Police Telephone Operators and Citizen Calls for Service. *Journal of Criminal Justice* **9**, 165–79.

Armstrong, F. & M. Wilson 1973. City Politics and Deviance Amplification. In *Politics and Deviance*, I. Taylor & L. Taylor (eds), 61–89. London: Penguin.

Ashworth, A.J. 1975. Self-Defence and the Right to Life. *Cambridge Law Journal* **34** (2, November), 282–307.

Asmal, K. 1985. *Shoot to Kill? International Lawyers' Inquiry into the Lethal Use of Firearms by the Security Forces in Northern Ireland.* Dublin: Mercier Press.

Audit Commission 1990a. *Calling All Forces: Improving Police Communications Rooms. Police Papers: Number 5.* London: HMSO.

Audit Commission 1990b. *Effective Policing – Performance Review in Police Forces. Police Papers: Number 8.* London: HMSO.

Audit Commission 1993. *Helping with Enquiries. Police Paper: No. 12.* London: HMSO.

Audit Commission 1996. *Streetwise: Effective Police Patrol.* London: HMSO.

Bachrach, P. & M.S. Baratz 1970. *Power and Poverty: Theory and Practice.* Oxford: Oxford University Press.

Baldwin, F.N., Jnr. 1993. The Impact of the Exclusionary Rule on Police Deviance and Accountability. In *Policing the Conflict in South Africa*, M.L. Mathews, P.B. Heymann, A.S. Mathews (eds), 92–105. Gainesville: University Press of Florida.

Baldwin, J. & M. McConville 1980. *Confessions in the Crown Courts Trials. Royal Commission on Criminal Procedure: Research Study No. 5.* London: HMSO.

Ball-Rokeach, S.J. 1972. The Legitimation of Violence. In *Collective Violence*, J.F. Short Jnr & M.E. Wolfgang (eds), 100–11. New York: Aldine Atherton.

Banfield, E. 1974. Rioting Mainly for Fun and Profit. In *The Unheavenly City Revisited*, E. Banfield (ed.), 212–33. Boston: Little Brown.

Banton, M. 1964. *The Policeman in the Community.* London: Tavistock.

Banton, M. 1974. The James Smart Lecture: Policing a Divided Society. *Police Journal* (October–December), 1–18.

Banton, M. 1983. Policies for Police-Minority Relations. In *Minorities: Community and Identity*, C. Fried (ed.), 299–313. Berlin: Dahlem Konferenzen.

Baxter, J. 1985. Policing and the Rule of Law. In *Police: The Constitution and the Community*, J. Baxter & L. Koffman (eds), 38–61. Abingdon, Oxon: Professional Books.

Bayley, D.H. 1969. *The Police and Political Development in India.* Princeton: Princeton University Press.

Bayley, D.H. 1976. *Forces of Order: Police Behaviour in Japan and the United States.* Berkeley: University of California Press.

Bayley, D.H. 1982a. A World Perspective on the Role of the Police in Social Control. In *Maintenance of Order in Society*, R. Donelan (ed.), 1–7. Ottowa: Canadian Police College.

Bayley, D.H. 1982b. Accountability and Control of Police: Lessons for Britain. In *The Future of Policing. Cropwood Conference Series.* No. 15, T. Bennett (ed.), 146–62. Cambridge: Institute of Criminology, University of Cambridge.

Bayley, D.H. 1985. *Patterns of Policing: A Comparative International Analysis.* New Brunswick, NJ: Rutgers University Press.

Bayley, D.H. 1991a. *Forces of Order: Police Behaviour in Japan and the United States*, 2nd edn. Berkeley: University of California Press.

Bayley, D.H. 1991b. Preface. In *Complaints Against the Police*, A.J. Goldsmith (ed.), v-xi. Oxford: Clarendon.

Bayley, D.H. 1992. Comparative Organization of the Police in English-Speaking Countries. In *Modern Policing. Crime and Justice. A Review of Research*, vol. 15, M. Tonry & N. Morris (eds), 509–47. Chicago: University of Chicago Press.

Bayley, D.H. 1994a. *Police for the Future. Studies in Crime and Public Policy.* New York: Oxford University Press.

Bayley, D.H. 1994b. International Differences in Community Policing. In *The Challenge of Community Policing: Testing the Promises*, D.P. Rosenbaum (ed.), 278–81. Thousand Oaks: Sage.

Bayley, D.H. 1996. Police Brutality Abroad. In *Police Violence: Understanding and Controlling Police Abuse of Force*, W.A. Geller & H. Toch (eds), 273–91. New Haven, Conn.: Yale University Press.

Bayley, D.H. & E. Bittner 1984. Learning the Skills of Policing. *Journal of Law and Contemporary Social Problems* **47** (4), 35–59.

Bayley, D.H. & E. Bittner 1985. The Tactical Choices of Police Patrol Officers. *Journal of Criminal Justice* **14**, 329–48.

Bayley, D.H. & J. Garofalo 1989. The Management of Violence by Police Patrol Officers. *Criminology* **27** (1), 1–23.

Bayley, D.H. & H. Mendelsohn 1969. *Minorities and the Police.* New York: Free Press.

Beck, G.N. 1972. SWAT – the Los Angeles Police Special Weapons and Tactics Teams. *FBI Law Enforcement Bulletin* (April), 8–30.

Bell, J. 1992. Justice and the Law. In *Justice: Interdisciplinary Perspectives*, K.R. Scherer (ed.), 114–42. Cambridge: Cambridge University Press.

Bell, J. 1993. The French Pre-Trial System. In *Justice in Error*, C. Walker & K. Starmer (eds), 226–45. London: Blackstone.

Belson, W.A. 1975. *The Public and the Police.* London: Harper and Row.

Bem, S.L. 1974. The Measurement of Psychological Androgyny. *Journal of Consulting and Clinical Psychology* **42** (2), 155–62.

Benn, M. 1985. Policing Women. In *Police: The Constitution and the Community*, J. Baxter & L. Koffman (eds), 124–39. Abingdon, Oxon: Professional Books.

Bennett, T. 1979. The Social Distribution of Criminal Labels. *British Journal of Criminology* **19** (2, April), 134–45.

Bennett, T. 1989. Factors Related to Participation in Neighbourhood Watch Schemes. *British Journal of Criminology* **29** (3), 207–18.

Bennett, T. 1990. *Evaluating Neighbourhood Watch.* Aldershot: Gower.

Bennett, T. 1991. The Effectiveness of a Police-Initiated Fear Reducing Strategy. *British Journal of Criminology* **31** (1, Winter), 1–14.

Bennett, T. 1994. Recent Developments in Community Policing. In *Police Force, Police Service*, M. Stephens & S. Becker (eds), 107–30. Basingstoke: Macmillan.

Bennett, T. 1994a. Community Policing on the Ground: Developments in Britain. In *The Challenge of Community Policing: Testing the Promises*, D.P. Rosenbaum (ed.), 224–46. Thousand Oaks: Sage.

Bennett, T. 1994b. Police Strategies and Tactics for Controlling Crime and Disorder in England and Wales. *Studies on Crime and Crime Prevention* **3**, 146–67.

Bennett, T. & R. Lupton 1990. A National Review of the Community Constable Scheme. Report to the Home Office Research and Planning Unit. Institute of Criminology.

Bennett, T. & R. Lupton 1992a. A National Activity Survey of Police Work. *Howard Journal of Criminal Justice* **31** (3, August), 200–23.

Bennett, T.H. & R. Lupton 1992b. A Survey of the Allocation and Use of Community Constables in England and Wales. *British Journal of Criminology* **32** (2), 167–82.

Benyon, J. 1984a. The Riots: Perceptions and Distortions. In *Scarman and After*, J. Benyon (ed.), 37–45. London: Pergamon.

Benyon, J. (ed.) 1984b. *Scarman and After: Essays Reflecting on Lord Scarman's Report, The Riots and Their Aftermath.* Oxford: Pergamon.

Benyon, J. 1987a. Interpretations of Civil Disorder. In *The Roots of Urban Unrest*, J. Benyon & J. Solomos (eds), 23–41. Oxford: Pergamon.

Benyon, J. 1987b. Unrest and the Political Agenda. In *The Roots of Urban Unrest*, J. Benyon & J. Solomos (eds), 165–80. Oxford: Pergamon.

Benyon, J. & J. Solomos 1987a. British Urban Unrest in the 1980s. In *The Roots of Urban Unrest*, J. Benyon & J. Solomos (eds), 3–22. Oxford: Pergamon.

Benyon, J. & J. Solomos 1987b. The Roots of Urban Unrest. In *The Roots of Urban Unrest*, J. Benyon & J. Solomos (eds), 181–95. Oxford: Pergamon.

Bergesen, A. 1980. Official Violence during the Watts, Newark and Detroit Race Riots of the 1960s. In *A Political Analysis of Deviance*, P. Lauderdale (ed.), 138–74. Minneapolis: University of Minnesota Press.

Berk, R.A. 1972. The Controversy Surrounding Analyses of Collective Violence: Some Methodological Notes. In *Collective Violence*, J.F. Short & M.E. Wolfgang (eds), 112–18. Chicago: Aldine-Atherton.

Bieck, W. 1977. *Response Time Analysis.* Kansas City: Kansas City Police Department.

Binder, A. & P. Scharf 1980. The Violent Police–Citizen Encounter. *Annals of the American Academy of Political and Social Science* **452** (November), 111–21.

Birkbeck, C. & L.G. Gabaldon 1996. Avoiding Complaints: Venezuelan Police Officers' Situational Criteria for the Use of Force Against Citizens. *Policing and Society* **6** (2), 113–29.

Bittner, E. 1967a. Police Discretion in Emergency Apprehension of Mentally Ill Persons. *Social Problems* **14**, 279–92.

Bittner, E. 1967b. The Police on Skid-Row: A Study of Peace Keeping. *American Sociological Review* **32** (5), 699–715.

Bittner, E. 1970. *The Functions of the Police in a Modern Society.* Washington, DC.: US Government Printing Office.

Bittner, E. 1974. Florence Nightingale in Pursuit of Willie Sutton: A Theory of the Police. In *Potential for Reform of Criminal Justice*, H. Jacob (ed.), 17–44. Beverly Hills: Sage.

Bittner, E. 1976. Policing Juveniles: The Social Context of Common Practice. In *Pursuing Justice for the Child*, Margaret K. Rosenheim (ed.), 69–93. Chicago: Chicago University Press.

Bittner, E. 1983. Legality and Workmanship: Introduction to Control in the Police Organization. In *Control in the Police Organization*, M. Punch (ed.), 1–12. Cambridge, Mass.: MIT.

Black, D.J. 1970. The Production of Crime Rates. *American Sociological Review* **35**, 733–48.

Black, D.J. 1971. The Social Organization of Arrest. *Stanford Law Review* **23**, 1087–111.

Black, D.J. & A.J. Reiss 1970. Police Control of Juveniles. *American Sociological Review* **35**, 63–77.

Blair, I. 1994. Public Property. *Police Review* (14, October), 18–22.

Bloch, P.B. & D. Anderson 1974. *Policewomen on Patrol: Final Report.* Washington, DC: Police Foundation.

Blom-Cooper, L. & R. Drabble 1982. Police Perceptions of Crime: Brixton and the Operational Response. *British Journal of Criminology* **22** (2, April), 184–7.

Blumberg, A.S. 1967. The Practice of Law as a Confidence Game: Organizational Co-optation of a Profession. *Law and Society*.

Bordua, D.J. & A.J. Reiss 1966. Command, Control, and Charisma: Reflections of Police Bureaucracy. *American Journal of Sociology* **72** (July), 68–76.

Bottomley, A.K. 1973. *Decisions in the Penal Process*. London: Martin Robertson.

Bottomley, K. & K. Pease 1993. *Crime and Punishment: Interpreting the Data*. Milton Keynes: Open University.

Bottomley, K., A. James, E. Clare, A. Liebling 1996. *Wolds Remand Prison – An Evaluation. Home Office Research and Statistics Department, Research Findings No. 32*. April.

Bourlet, A. 1990. *Police Intervention in Marital Violence*. Milton Keynes: Open University Press.

Bowden, T. 1975. Policing Palestine 1920–36: Some Problems of Public Security Under the Mandate. In *Police Forces in History. Readings in 20th Century History*, vol. 2, G.L. Mosse (ed.), 115–30. Beverly Hills: Sage.

Bowden, T. 1978. *Beyond the Limits of the Law*. Harmondsworth: Penguin.

Bowes, S. 1966. *The Police and Civil Liberties*. London: Lawrence and Wishart.

Bowling, B. 1993. Racial Harassment and the Process of Victimisation. *British Journal of Criminology* **33** (2), 231–50.

Box, S. & K. Russell 1975. The Politics of Discreditability: Disarming Complaints Against the Police. *Sociological Review* **23** (2), 315–46.

Braithwaite, J. & B. Fisse 1987. Self-Regulation and the Control of Corporate Crime. In *Private Policing. Sage Criminal Justice System Annuals*, vol. 23, C.D. Shearing & P.C. Stenning (eds), 221–46. Newbury Park, California: Sage.

Brewer, J.D. 1990a. *Inside the RUC*. Oxford: Clarendon.

Brewer, J.D. 1990b. Talking About Danger: The RUC and the Paramilitary Threat. *Sociology* **24** (4, November), 657–74.

Brewer, J.D. 1991a. Policing in Divided Societies: Theorising a Type of Policing. *Policing and Society* **1**, 179–91.

Brewer, J.D. 1991b. Hercules, Hippolyte and the Amazons – Or Policewomen in the RUC. *British Journal of Sociology* **42** (2, June), 231–47.

Brewer, J.D. 1993. The History and Development of Policing in Northern Ireland. In *Policing the Conflict in South Africa*, M.L. Mathews, P.B. Heymann, A.S. Mathews (eds), 184–93. Gainesville: University Press of Florida.

Brewer, J.D. 1994. *Black and Blue: Policing in South Africa*. Oxford: Clarendon.

Brim, O. 1960. Personality Development as Role Learning. In *Personality Development in Children*, I. Iscoc & H. Stevenson (eds), 127–59. Austin: Texas University Press.

British Society for Social Responsibility in Science 1983. *Technocop*. London: Free Association.

Brodeur, J.-P. 1981. Legitimizing Police Deviance. In *Organisational Police Deviance*, C. Shearing (ed.), 127–60. Toronto: Butterworths.

Broer, W. & K. van der Vijver 1983. Research and Organizational Control. In *Control in the Police Organization*, M. Punch (ed.), 60–74. Cambridge, Mass: MIT Press.

Brogden, M. 1977. A Police Authority – The Denial of Conflict. *Sociological Review* **25** (2), 325–49.

Brogden, M. 1982. *The Police: Autonomy and Consent*. London: Academic.

Brogden, M. 1983. The Myth of Policing by Consent. *Police Review* (22, April), 760–761.

Brogden, M. 1985. Stopping the People – Crime Control Versus Social Control. In *Police: The Constitution and the Community*, J. Baxter & L. Koffman (eds), 91–110. Abingdon, Oxon: Professional Books.

Brogden, M.E. 1989. The Origins of the South African Police – Institutional Versus Structural Approaches. In *Acta Juridica*, W. Scharf (ed.), 1–19. Cape Town: Faculty of Law, University of Cape Town.

Brogden, M. 1991. *On the Mersey Beat.* Oxford: Oxford University Press.

Brogden, M. & C. Shearing 1993. *Policing For a New South Africa.* London: Routledge.

Brooks, L.W. 1993. Police Discretionary Behaviour: A Study of Style. In *Critical Issues in Policing: Contemporary Readings*, 2nd edn., R.G. Dunham & G.P. Alpert (eds), 140–64. Prospect Heights, Illinois Waveland.

Broughton, F. 1995. Drive the Cowboys Out of Business. *Police* (June), 13–14.

Brown, B. 1994. *Assaults on Police Officers: An Examination of the Circumstances in which Such Incidents Occur. Police Research Series: Paper 10.* London: Home Office Police Department.

Brown, D. 1988. The Police Complaints Procedure. A "Consumer" View. *Howard Journal* **27** (3, August), 161–71.

Brown, D. 1994. The Incidence of Right to Silence in Police Interviews: The Research Evidence Reviewed. *Home Office Research Bulletin* **35** (Winter), 57–75.

Brown, D.C. 1983. *Civilian Review of Complaints Against the Police: A Survey of the United States Literature. Research and Planning Unit: Paper 19.* London: Home Office.

Brown, D. & T. Ellis 1994. *Policing Low-level Disorder: Police Use of Section 5 of the Public Order Act. Home Office Research Studies: 135.* London: HMSO.

Brown, J. & I. Waters 1993. Professional Police Research. *Policing* **9** (Winter), 323–34.

Brown, J., E.A. Campbell, C. Fife-Schaw 1995. Adverse Impacts Experienced By Police Officers Following Exposure to Sex Discrimination and Sexual Harassment. *Stress Medicine* **11**, 221–28.

Brown, L. & A. Willis 1985. Authoritarianism in British Police Recruits: Importation, Socialization or Myth? *Journal of Occupational Psychology* **58**, 97–108.

Brown, W. & C. Knox 1994. A Law Without Teeth, *Police Review* (22, July), 24–25.

Brownlee, I.D. 1989. Superior Orders: Time for a New Realism? *Criminal Law Review*, 396–411.

Bryant, L., D. Dunkerley, G. Kelland 1985. One of the Boys. *Policing* **1** (4, Autumn), 236–44.

Bryett, K. & A. Harrison 1993. *An Introduction to Policing: Policing In the Community* vol. 4. Sydney: Butterworth.

Buchan, I. & S. Edwards 1991. *Adult Cautioning for Domestic Violence. Police Requirement Support Unit, Science and Technology Group.* London: Home Office.

Bucke, T. 1994. Equal Opportunities and the Fire Service. *Home Office Research and Statistics Department, Research Findings No. 13.* September.

Buerger, M.E. 1994. A Tale of Two Targets: Limitations of Community Anticrime Actions. *Crime and Delinquency* **40** (3, July), 411–36.

Bundred, S. 1982. Accountability and the Metropolitan Police: A Suitable Case for Treatment. In *Policing the Riots*, D. Cowell, T. Jones, J. Young (eds), 58–81. London: Junction.

Burrows, J. 1986. *Burglary: Police Actions and Victims' Views. Research and Planning Unit: Paper 37.* London: Home Office.

Bush, T. & J. Hood-Williams 1995. Domestic Violence on a London Housing Estate. In *Research Bulletin*, Home Office Research and Statistics Department (ed.), 11–18. London: Home Office Research and Planning Unit.

Butler, A.J.P. 1984. *Police Management.* Gower: Aldershot.

Butler, A.J.P. 1995. Managing the Future: A Chief Constable's View. In *Core Issues in Policing*, F. Leishman, B. Loveday, S.P. Savage (eds), 218–30. London: Longman.

Butler, A.J.P. & R. Cochrane 1977. An Examination of Some Elements of the Personality of Police Officers and Their Implications. *Journal Police Science and Administration* **5**, 441–50.

Butler, T. 1985. Objectives and Accountability. *Policing* **1** (4, Autumn), 174–86.

Butler, T. 1986. Purposes and Process. *Policing* **2** (2, Summer), 160–6.

Button, J.W. 1978. *Black Violence: Political Impact of the 1960s Riots.* Princeton, NJ: Princeton University Press.

Buzawa, E.S. & C.G. Buzawa 1993. Opening the Door – The Changing Police Response to Domestic Violence. In *Critical Issues in Policing: Contemporary Readings*, 2nd edn., R.G. Dunham & G.P. Alpert (eds), 551–67. Prospect Heights, Illinois Waveland.

Buzawa, E., T.L. Autin, C.G. Buzawa 1995. Responding to Crimes of Violence Against Women: Gender Differences Versus Organizational Imperatives. *Crime and Delinquency* **41** (4, October), 443–66.

Cain, M. 1973. *Society and the Policeman's Role.* London: Routledge & Kegan Paul.

Cameron, Lord *et al.* 1969. *Report of the Commission on Disturbances in Northern Ireland.* Belfast: Government of Northern Ireland.

Campbell, B. 1993. *Goliath: Britain's Dangerous Places.* London: Methuen.

Carr-Hill, R.A. & N.H. Stern 1979. *Crime, The Police and Criminal Statistics: An Analysis of Official Statistics for England and Wales Using Econometric Methods.* London: Academic.

Carson, W.G. 1970. White-Collar Crime and the Enforcement of Factory Legislation. *British Journal of Criminology* **10** (4, October), 383–398.

Carter, T. & D. Clelland 1979. A Neo-Marxian Critique, Formulation and Test of Juvenile Dispositions As a Function of Social Class. *Social Problems* **27** (1, October), 96–108.

Cascio, W.F. 1977. Formal Education and Police Officer Performance. *Journal Police Science and Administration* **5**, 89–96.

Cashmore, E. 1991. Black Cops Inc. In *Out of Order*? E. Cashmore & E. McLaughlin (eds) 87–108. London: Routledge.

Cashmore, E. & E. McLaughlin 1991. Out of Order? In *Out of Order*, E. Cashmore & E. McLaughlin (eds), 10–41. London: Routledge.

Cashmore, E. & B. Troyna 1982. Growing up in Babylon. In *Black Youth in Crisis*, E. Cashmore & B. Troyna (eds), 72–86. London: Allen & Unwin.

Cassels, Sir John 1994. *Independent Committee of Inquiry into the Role and Responsibilities of the Police: Discussion Document.* London: Police Foundation and Policy Studies Institute.

Cassels, Sir John 1996. *Independent Committee of Inquiry into the Role and Responsibilities of the Police.* London: Police Foundation/Policy Studies Institute.

Cawthra, G. 1993. *Policing South Africa.* London: Zed Books.

Center for Research on Criminal Justice 1977. *The Iron Fist and the Velvet Glove: An Analysis of the US Police*, 2nd edn. Berkeley, CA.

Chambers, G. & A. Millar 1983. *Investigating Sexual Assault. Scottish Office Social Research Study.* Edinburgh: HMSO.

Chambliss, W.J. 1975. Towards a Political Economy of Crime. *Theory and Society* **2** (Summer), 149–70.

Chambliss, W.J. 1982. Toward a Radical Criminology. In *The Politics of Law*, D. Kairy (ed.), 230–41. New York: Pantheon.

Chan, J. 1994. Policing Youth in "Ethnic" Communities: Is Community Policing the Answer? In *The Police and Young People in Australia*, R. White & C. Alder (eds), 175–98. Cambridge: Cambridge University Press.

Chan, J. 1996. Changing Police Culture. *British Journal of Criminology* **36** (1), 109–34.

Chan, J.B.L. 1997. *Changing Police Culture: Policing in a Multicultural Society.* Cambridge: Cambridge University Press.

Chapman, S.G. 1982. Police Policy on the Use of Firearms. In *Readings on the Police Use of Deadly Force*, J.J. Fyfe (ed.), 224–57. Washington, DC: Police Foundation.

Chatterton, M.R. 1976a. Police in Social Control. In *Control Without Custody. Cropwood Papers.* No. 7, J. King (ed.), 104–25. Cambridge: Institute of Criminology.

Chatterton, M.R. 1976b. Police Arrest Powers as Resources in Peace-keeping. *Social Work Today* **7**, 234–7.

Chatterton, M.R. 1979. The Supervision of Patrol Work Under the Fixed Points System. In *The British Police*, S. Holdaway (ed.), 83–101. London: Edward Arnold.

Chatterton, M.R. 1983. Police Work and Assault Charges. In *Control in the Police Organization*, M. Punch (ed.), 194–221. Cambridge, Mass.: MIT Press.

Chatterton, M.R. 1987. Assessing Police Effectiveness: Future Prospects. *British Journal of Criminology* **27** (1), 80–86.

Chatterton, M.R. 1991. Organisational Constraints on the Uses of Information and Information Technology in Problem-Focused Area Policing. Paper presented at British Criminology Conference, June.

Chatterton, M. & M. Rogers 1989. Focused Policing. In *Coming to Terms with Policing*, R. Morgan & D.J. Smith (eds), 64–81. London: Routledge.

Chatterton, M.R., C. Humphrey, A.J. Watson 1996. *On the Budgetary Beat: An Investigation of the Development of Management Accounting Systems in the Police Service in England and Wales*. London: Chartered Institute of Management Accountants.

Chatterton, M.R., M. Weatheritt, A. Wright 1993. Rational Management in Police Organisations: A Comparative Study in Two Forces. Joint project by: Hentry Fielding Centre for Police Studies, University of Manchester, and the Police Foundation. July.

Cheh, M.M. 1996. Are Lawsuits An Answer to Police Brutality? In *Police Violence: Understanding and Controlling Police Abuse of Force*, W.A. Geller & H. Toch (eds), 247–72. New Haven, Conn.: Yale University Press.

Chevigny, P. 1969. *Police Power: Police Abuses in New York City*. New York: Vintage.

Chevigny, P. 1995. *Edge of the Knife: Police Violence in the Americas*. New York: New Press.

Chibnall, S. 1977. *Law and Order News*. London: Tavistock.

Choongh, S. 1997. *Policing As Social Discipline*. Oxford: Clarendon.

Christian, L. 1985. Restriction Without Conviction. The Role of the Courts in Legitimising Police Control in Nottinghamshire. In *Policing the Miners' Strike*, B. Fine & R. Millar (eds), 120–36. London: Lawrence & Wishart.

Christopher, W. 1991. Report of the Independent Commission on the Los Angeles Police Department. Los Angeles.

Cicourel, A.V. 1968. *The Social Organisation of Juvenile Justice*. New York: Wiley.

Clark, J.P. 1965. Isolation of the Police: A Comparison of the British and American Situations. *Journal of Criminal Law, Criminology and Police Science* **56** (3), 307–19.

Clarke, R.V. & J.R. Greene 1987. Cutting Down on Supervision. *Policing* **3** (2), 88–105.

Clisby, D. 1990. Assistant Division Officer Dick Clisby. In *The Ruffian on the Stair: Reflections on Death*, R. Dinnage (ed.), 146–65. London: Viking.

Clutterbuck, R. 1973. *Protest and the Urban Guerrilla*. London: Cassell.

Clutterbuck, R. 1980. *Britain in Agony*. Revised edition, Harmondsworth, Middx.: Penguin.

Coates, R.B. & A.D. Miller 1974. Patrolmen and Addicts: A Study of Police Perception and Police–Citizen Interaction. *Journal Police Science and Administration* **2** (3), 308–21.

Cohen, B. 1985. Police Complaints Procedure: Why and For Whom? In *Police: The Constitution and the Community*, J. Baxter & L. Koffman (eds), 246–67. Abingdon, Oxon: Professional Books.

Cohen, L.E. & J.R. Kluegel 1979. The Detention Decision: A Study of the Impact of Social Characteristics and Legal Factors in Two Metropolitan Juvenile Courts. *Social Forces* **58** (1, September), 146–61.

Cohen, P. 1979. Policing the Working Class City. In *Capitalism and the Rule of Law*, B. Fine, R. Kinsey, J. Lea, S. Picciotto, J. Young (eds), 118–36. London: Hutchinson.

Cohen, P. 1980. The "Effective Force" of the Fatal Blow. *New Statesman* **99** (6, June), 838.

Cohen, S. 1972. *Folk Devils and Moral Panics*. Oxford: Martin Robertson.

Coleman, C.A. & A.K. Bottomley 1976. Police Conceptions of Crime and "no crime". *Criminal Law Review* (June), 344–60.

Collin, R.O. 1985. The Blunt Instruments: Italy and the Police. In *Police and Public Order in Europe*, J. Roach & J. Thomaneck (eds), 185–214. London: Croom Helm.

Collins, K. 1985. Efficiency Revisited. *Policing* **1** (2), 70–76.

Colman, A.M. & L.P. Gorman 1982. Conservatism, Dogmatism, and Authoritarianism in British Police Officers. *Sociology* **16** (1), 1–11.

Comrie, M.D. & E. Kings 1975. Urban Workloads. *Police Research Services Bulletin* **23**, 32–8.

Conway, H. 1996. Dangerous Liaisons. *Police Review* (14, February), 24–25.

Cook, D. 1989. *Rich Law, Poor Law: Different Responses to Tax and Supplementary Benefit Fraud.* Milton Keynes: Open University Press.

Cook, S. 1983. The Bitter Reality of Our Race Laws. *New Society* (3, November), 187–9.

Copowich, G.E. & J.A. Roehl 1994. Problem-Oriented Policing: Actions and Effectiveness in San Diego. In *The Challenge of Community Policing: Testing the Promises*, D.P. Rosenbaum (ed.), 127–46. Thousand Oaks: Sage.

Cordner, G.W. 1994. Foot Patrol Without Community Policing: Law and Order in Public Housing. In *The Challenge of Community Policing: Testing the Promises*, D.P. Rosenbaum (ed.), 182–91. Thousand Oaks: Sage.

Cordner, G.W., J.R. Greene, T.S. Bynum 1983. The Sooner the Better: Some Effects of Police Response Time. In *Police at Work. Perspectives in Criminal Justice*, No. 5. R.R. Bennett (ed.), 145–64. Beverly Hills: Sage.

Coulter, J., S. Miller, M. Walker 1984. *State of Siege: Miners' Strike 1984.* London: Canary Press.

Cowell, D., T. Jones, J. Young (eds) 1982. *Policing the Riots.* London: Junction Books.

Cox, B., J. Shirley, M. Short 1973. *The Fall of Scotland Yard.* London: Penguin.

Crandon, L. 1996. Tug-of-War. *Police Review* (3, May), 22–24.

Crawford, A., T. Jones, T. Woodhouse, J. Young 1990. *The Second Islington Crime Survey. Centre for Criminology.* Middlesex: Middlesex Polytechnic.

Crewe, I. 1983. Representation and the Ethnic Minorities in Britain. In *Ethnic Pluralism and Public Policy*, N. Glazer & K. Young (eds), 258–84. Lexington, Mass.: D.C. Heath.

Criminal Law Revision Committee 1972. *Eleventh Report: Evidence (General).* London: HMSO.

Critcher, C. 1996. On the Waterfront: Applying the Flashpoints Model to Protest Against Live Animal Exports. In *Policing Public Order: Theoretical and Practical Issues*, C. Critcher & D. Waddington (eds), 53–70. Aldershot: Avebury.

Critchley, T. 1970. *The Conquest of Violence.* London: Constable.

Critchley, T.A. 1978. *A History of Police in England and Wales.* London: Constable.

Cruse, D. & J. Rubin 1973. Police Behaviour: Part 1. *Journal of Psychiatry and Law* **1**, 18–19.

Cumming, E., I. Cumming, L. Edel 1965. Policeman as Philosopher, Guide and Friend. *Social Problems* **17**, 276–86.

Cunningham, H. 1977. The Metropolitan Fairs: A Case Study in the Social Control of Leisure. In *Social Control in Nineteenth Century Britain*, A.P. Donajgrodzki (ed.), 163–84. London: Croom Helm.

Currie, E. & J.H. Skolnick 1972. A Critical Note on Conceptions of Collective Behaviour. In *Collective Violence*, J.F. Short & M.E. Wolfgang (eds), 61–71. Chicago: Aldine-Atherton.

Curtis, L. 1986. Policing the Streets. In *The Police: Powers, Procedures and Proprieties*, J. Benyon (ed.), 95–102. Oxford: Pergamon.

Dahrendorf, R. 1985. *Law and Order, The Hamlyn Lectures 37th series.* London: Stevens.

Dalley, A.F. 1975. University and Non-University Graduated Policeman: A Study of Police Attitudes. *Journal Police Science and Administration* **3**, 458–68.

Damer, S. 1974. Wine Alley: The Sociology of a Dreadful Enclosure. *Sociological Review* **22** (2, May), 221–48.

Dannefer, D. & R.K. Schutt 1982. Race and Juvenile Justice Processing in Court and Police Agencies. *American Journal of Sociology* **87** (5), 1113–32.

Darley, J.M. & C.D. Batson 1984. 'From Jerusalem to Jericho': A Study of Situational and Dispositional Variables in Helping Behaviour. In *Readings About the Social Animal*, E. Aronson (ed.), 37–51. New York: W.H. Freeman.

Das, D.K. 1993. *Policing in Six Countries Around the World.* Chicago: OICJ.

Davidoff, L. 1993. Performance Indicators for the Police Service. Paper Presented at British Criminology Conference; University College, Cardiff, 28–31 July.

Davies, M. 1986. Community Consultation. *Policing* **2** (2), 141–50.

Davis, K.C. 1975. *Police Discretion.* St Paul: West.

Davis, M. 1990. *City of Quartz: Excavating the Future in Los Angeles.* London: Vintage.

de Friend, R. & S. Uglow 1985. Policing Industrial Disputes. In *Police: The Constitution and the Community*, J. Baxter & L. Koffman (eds), 62–71. Abingdon, Oxon: Professional Books.

de la Haye Davies, H. 1997. Custody Battle. *Police Review* (31, October), 16–17.

de Lint, W. 1997. The Constable Generalist As Exemplary Citizen, Networker, and Problem-Solver: Some Implications. *Policing and Society* **6** (4), 247–64.

Deane-Drummond, A. 1975. *Riot Control.* London: Royal United Services Institute for Defence Studies.

Dear, G.J. 1986. *Report of the Chief Constable West Midlands Police, Handsworth/Lozells – September 1985.* West Midlands: West Midlands Police.

Decker, S.H. & A.E. Wagner 1982. Race and Citizen Complaints Against the Police. In *Managing Police Work: Issues and Analysis. Perspectives in Criminal Justice*, No. 4. J.R. Greene (ed.), 107–22. Beverly Hills: Sage.

della Porta, D. 1994a. The Political Discourse on Protest Policing: Italy and Germany From the 1960s to the 1980s. Paper Presented at International Sociological Association, XIII World Congress of Sociology, Bielefeld, Germany, 18–23 July.

della Porta, D. 1994b. Social Movements and the State: Thoughts on the Policing of Protest. In *The Dynamics of Social Movements*, D. McAdam, J. McCarthy, M. Zald (eds), 62–92. Cambridge: Cambridge University Press.

della Porta, D. 1997a. *Police Knowledge and Protest Policing: Some Reflections on the Italian Case.* See della Porta & Reiter (1998), 228–52.

della Porta, D. 1997b. *The Policing of Protest in Contemporary Democracies. EUI Working Papers: RSC 97/1.* Badia Fiesolana, San Domenico, Italy: European University Institute, Robert Schuman Centre.

della Porta, D. & H. Reiter (eds) 1998. *Policing Protest: The Control and Mass Demonstrations in Western Democracies. Social Movements, Protest, and Contention*, vol. 6. Minneapolis: University of Minnesota Press.

Department of Employment 1969. *In Place of Strife.* Cmnd 3888 ed. London: HMSO.

Diez, L. 1995. *The Use of Call Grading: How Calls to the Police are Graded and Resourced. Police Research Series: Paper 13.* London: Police Research Group, Home Office.

Ditchfield, J.A. 1976. *Police Cautioning in England and Wales. Home Office Research Study: No. 37.* London: HMSO.

Ditton, J. 1977. *Part-Time Crime: An Ethnography of Fiddling and Pilferage.* London: Macmillan.

Dixon, B. & E. Stanko 1993. *Serving the People: Sector Policing and Public Accountability.* Uxbridge, Middlesex: Centre for Criminal Justice Researcy, Brunel University.

Dixon, B. & E. Stanko 1995. Sector Policing and Public Accountability. *Policing and Society* **5** (4), 171–84.

Dixon, B., J. Kimber, B. Stanko 1993. Sector Policing, Public Accountability, and Use of Police Services. Paper Presented at British Criminology Conference; University College, Cardiff, 28–31 July.

Dixon, D. 1989. Consent and the Legal Regulation of Policing. Paper Presented at Australian Law and Society Conference, La Trobe University.

Dixon, D. 1997. *Law in Policing: Legal Regulation and Police Practices. Clarendon Studies in Criminology.* Oxford: Clarendon.

Dixon, D., C.A. Coleman, A.K. Bottomley 1990. Consent and the Legal Regulation of Policing. *Journal of Law and Society* **17**, 345–62.

Don, D. 1990. The Man From the Gas Board. *Policing* **6** (3, Autumn), 559–72.

Donovan, Lord 1968. *Royal Commission on Trade Unions and Employers Associations.* London: HMSO.

Dowds, L. & P. Mayhew 1994. Participation in Neighbourhood Watch: *Findings from the 1992 British Crime Survey. Home Office Research and Statistics Department, Research Findings, No. 11.* July.

Downes, D. 1993. Review of "Public Order and Private Lives: The Politics of Law and Order" by Michael Brake and Chris Hale. *British Journal of Criminology* **33** (1, Winter), 108–10.

Downes, D. & R. Morgan 1994. "Hostages to Fortune"? The Politics of Law and Order in Post-War Britain. In *The Oxford Handbook of Criminology*, M. Maguire, R. Morgan, R. Reiner (eds), 183–232. Oxford: Clarendon.

Drechon, P. & S.K. Mitra 1992. The National Front in France – The Emergence of an Extreme Right Protest Movement. *Comparative Politics* **25**, 63–82.

Dummett, M. 1980a. *The Death of Blair Peach.* London: National Council for Civil Liberties.

Dummett, M. 1980b. *Southall 23 April 1979.* London: National Council for Civil Liberties.

Dunnighan, C. & C. Norris 1995a. The Detective, the Snout, and the Audit Commission: Or What Are the Real Costs Involved in Using Informers? Paper Presented at British Criminology Conference, University of Loughborough, 18–21 July.

Dunnighan, C. & C. Norris 1995b. Practice, Problems and Policy: Management Issues in the Police Use of Informers. Report Compiled from the Findings of an Economic and Social Research Council Funded Project: "The Role of the Informer in the Criminal Justice System". Department of Social Policy and Professional Studies, University of Hull, May.

Dunnighan, C. & C. Norris 1996. Subterranean Blues: Conflict As an Unintended Consequences of the Police Use of Informers. Department of Social Policy and Professional Studies, University of Hull, Hull HU6 7RX.

Dunning, E., P. Murphy, T. Newburn, I. Waddington 1987. Violent Disorders in Twentieth Century Britain. In *The Crowd in Contemporary Britain*, G. Gaskell & R. Benewick (eds), 19–75. London: Sage.

East, R. & P. Thomas 1985. Road Blocks: The Experience in Wales. In *Policing the Miners' Strike*, B. Fine & R. Millar (eds), 137–44. London: Lawrence & Wishart.

East, R., H. Power, P. Thomas 1985. The Death of Mass Picketing. *Journal of Law and Society* **12** (3, Winter), 305–19.

Easton, S.M. 1991. *The Right to Silence.* Aldershot: Avebury.

Eck, J.E. 1987. Who Ya Gonna Call? The Police as Problem-Busters. *Crime and Delinquency* **33** (1, January), 31–52.

Eck, J.E. & D.P. Rosenbaum 1994. The New Police Order: Effectiveness, Equity, and Efficiency in Community Policing. In *The Challenge of Community Policing: Testing the Promises*, D.P. Rosenbaum (ed.), 3–23. Thousand Oaks: Sage.

Edgar, D. 1988. Festivals of the Oppressed. *Race and Class* **XXIX** (4), 61–76.

Edwards, J., R. Oakley, S. Carey 1987. Street Life, Ethnicity and Social Policy. In *The Crowd in Contemporary Britain*, G. Gaskell & R. Benewick (eds), 76–122. London: Sage.

Edwards, S. 1989a. *Policing "Domestic" Violence.* London: Sage.

Edwards, S.M. 1989b. "Provoking Her Own Demise": From Common Assault to Homicide. In *Women, Policing and Male Violence*, J. Hanmer, J. Radford, E.A. Stanko (eds), 152–68. London: Routledge.

Edwards, S.M. 1990. Women and Crime. *Policing* **6** (2, Summer), 448–61.

Edwards, S.S.M. 1994. Domestic Violence and Sexual Assault. In *Police Force, Police Service*, M. Stephens & S. Becker (eds), 131–50. Basingstoke: Macmillan.

Ekblom, P. 1979. Police truancy patrols. In *Crime Prevention and the Police. Home Office Research Study, No. 55*, J. Burrows, P. Ekblom, K. Heal (eds), 17–33. London: HMSO.

Ekblom, P. & K. Heal 1982. *The Police Response to Calls from the Public. Research and Planning Unit Paper, No. 9.* London: Home Office.

Emsley, C. 1983. *Policing and Its Context.* London: Macmillan.

Emsley, C. 1996. *The English Police: A Political and Social History* (2nd edn). Hemel Hempstead: Harvester Wheatsheaf.

Ericson, R.V. 1982. *Reproducing Order.* Toronto: University of Toronto Press.

Ericson, R.V. 1981. Rules for Police Deviance. In *Organisational Police Deviance*, C. Shearing (ed.), 83–110. Toronto: Butterworths.

Evans, R. 1993. *The Conduct of Police Interviews with Juveniles. Royal Commission on Criminal Justice Research Studies, No. 8.* London: HMSO.

Evans, R. 1994. Police interrogation and the Royal Commission on Criminal Justice. *Policing and Society* **4** (1).

Evans, R. & S. Rawstorne 1995. PACE and the protection of vulnerable suspects. Paper presented at British Criminology Conference, University of Loughborough 18–21 July.

Ewing, K.D. & C.A. Gearty 1990. *Freedom Under Thatcher.* Clarendon: Oxford.

Factor, F. & K. Stenson 1989. Community Control and the Policing of Jewish Youth. Paper presented at British Criminology Conference, Bristol Polytechnic, July.

Farrell, G. & A. Buckley 1993. Repeat Victimisation As a Police Performance Indicator: A Case Study of a Domestic Violence Unit in Merseyside. Paper presented at British Criminology Conference; University College, Cardiff, 28–31 July.

Farrington, D.P. & E.A. Dowds 1985. Disentangling Criminal Behaviour and Police Reaction. In *Reactions to Crime: The Public, the Police, Courts and Prisons*, D.J. Farrington & J. Gunn (eds), 41–72. Chichester: Wiley.

FBI, Uniform Crime Reports Section, United States Department of Justice. 1993. *Killed in the Line of Duty: A Study of Selected Felonious Killings of Law Enforcement Officers.* Washington, DC: United States Department of Justice.

Ferdinand, T.N. & E.G. Luchterhand 1970. Inner-City Youth, the Police, the Juvenile Court, and Justice. *Social Problems* **17**, 510–27.

Field, J. 1985. Police Monitoring: The Sheffield Experience. In *Policing the Miners' Strike*, B. Fine & R. Millar (eds), 204–16. London: Lawrence and Wishart.

Field, S. 1984. *The Attitudes of Ethnic Minorities. Home Office Research Study: No. 80.* London: HMSO.

Field, S. 1990. *Trends in Crime and Their Interpretation: A Study of Recorded Crime in Post-War England and Wales. Home Office Research Study: No. 119.* London: HMSO.

Fielding, N. 1981a. *The National Front.* London: Routledge.

Fielding, N. 1981b. The Credibility of Accountability. *Polytechnic Law Review* **6** (2, Spring), 89–93.

Fielding, N. 1984. Police Socialization and Police Competence. *British Journal of Sociology* **XXXV** (4), 568–90.

Fielding, N. 1986. Social Control and the Community. *Howard Journal* **25** (3, Aug), 172–89.

Fielding, N. 1994a. Cop Canteen Culture. In *Just Boys Doing Business: Men, Masculinity and Crime*, T. Newburn & E. Stanko (eds), 46–63. London: Routledge.

Fielding, N. 1994b. The Organizational and Occupational Troubles of Community Police. *Policing and Society* **4**, 305–22.

Fielding, N. 1996. Enforcement, Service and Community Models of Policing. In *Themes in Contemporary Policing*, W. Saulsbury, J. Mott, T. Newburn (eds), 42–59. London: Independent Committee of Inquiry into the Role and Responsibilities of the Police.

Fielding, N. & J. Fielding 1991. Police Attitudes to Crime and Punishment: Certainties and Dilemmas. *British Journal of Criminology* **31** (1, Winter), 39–53.

Fielding, N. & J. Fielding 1992. A Comparative Minority: Female Recruits to a British Constabulary Force. *Policing and Society* **2**, 205–18.

Fielding, N., C. Kemp, C. Norris 1989. Constraints on the Practice of Community Policing. In *Coming to Terms with Policing*, R. Morgan & D.J. Smith (eds), 49–63. London: Routledge.

Fielding, N.G. 1988. *Joining Forces: Police Training, Socialization, and Occupational Competence*. London: Routledge.

Fielding, N.G. 1995. *Community Policing. Clarendon Studies in Criminology*. Oxford: Clarendon.

Fillieule, O. & F. Jobard 1998. *The Policing of Protest in France: Towards a Model of Protest Policing*. See della Porta & Reiter (1998), 70–90.

Fine, B. & R. Millar (eds) 1985. *Policing the Miners' Strike*. London: Lawrence and Wishart.

Finnane, M. (ed.) 1987. *Policing in Australia: Historical Perspectives*. Kensington, NSW: New South Wales University Press.

Finnane, M. 1990. Police Corruption and Police Reform: The Fitzgerald Inquiry in Queensland, Australia. *Policing and Society* **1** (2), 159–71.

Finnane, M. 1994. Larrikins, Delinquents and Cops: Police and Young People in Australian History. In *The Police and Young People in Australia*, R. White & C. Alder (eds), 7–26. Cambridge: Cambridge University Press.

Finnegan, R. 1978. Do the Police Make Decisions? In *Criminal Justice: Selected Readings*, J. Baldwin & A.K. Bottomley (eds), 64–70. London: Martin Robertson.

Fisher, C. & R. Mawby 1982. Juvenile Delinquency and Police Discretion in an Inner-City. *British Journal of Criminology* **22** (1), 141–63.

Fisher, G. & H. Joshua 1982. Social Policy and Black Youth. In *Black Youth in Crisis*, E. Cashmore & B. Troyna (eds), 129–42. London: Allen and Unwin.

Flanagan, T.J. & M.S. Vaughn 1996. Public Opinion About Police Abuse of Force. In *Police Violence: Understanding and Controlling Police Abuse of Force*, W.A. Geller & H. Toch (eds), 113–28. New Haven, Conn.: Yale University Press.

Flanders, D. 1991. Poll Tax Demonstration, 20th October 1990. A Review of Policing Arrangements. Unpublished. London: Metropolitan Police.

Fletcher, G.P. 1984. Some Unwise Reflections About Discretion. *Law and Contemporary Problems* **47** (4, Autumn), 269–86.

Fogelson, R.M. 1970. Violence and Grievances: Reflections of the 1960s Riots. *Journal of Social Issues* **26**, 141–63.

Fogelson, R.M. 1971. *Violence as Protest*. Garden City, NY: Doubleday.

Fountain, J. 1993. Dealing with Data. In *Interpreting the Field*, D. Hobbs & T. May (eds), 145–73. Oxford: Clarendon.

Fox, C. 1997. Taking a Firm Line on Officer Discipline. *Police Review* (7, November), 14.

Freckelton, I. 1991. Shooting the Messenger: The Trial and Execution of the Victorian Police Complaints Procedures. In *Complaints Against the Police*, A.J. Goldsmith (ed.), 63–114. Oxford: Clarendon.

Friedmann 1992. *Community Policing: Comparative Perspectives and Prospects*. Hemel Hampstead: Harvester Wheatsheaf.

Friedrich, R.J. 1980. Police Use of Force: Individuals, Situations and Organizations. *Annals of the American Academy of Political and Social Science* **452** (November), 82–97.

Funk, A. 1995. The German Police System in a European Context. In *Comparisons in Policing: An International Perspective*, J.-P. Brodeur (ed.), 69–85. Aldershot: Avebury.

Furneaux, R. 1963. *Massacre at Amritsar.* London: George Allen and Unwin.

Furstenberg, F. & C. Wellford 1973. Calling the Police: The Evaluation of Police Service. *Law and Sociological Review* **7** (Spring), 393–406.

Fyfe, J.J. 1978. Administrative Interventions on Police Shooting Discretion. *Journal of Criminal Justice* **7**, 309–23.

Fyfe, J.J. 1981. Who Shoots? A Look At Officer Race and Police Shootings. *Journal of Police Science and Administration* **9** (4), 367–82.

Fyfe, J.J. 1982a. Administrative Intervention on Police Shooting Discretion: An Empirical Examination. In *Readings on Police Use of Deadly Force*, J.J. Fyfe (ed.), 258–81. Washington, DC: Police Foundation.

Fyfe, J.J. 1982b. Race and Extreme Police-Citizen Violence. In *Readings on Police Use of Deadly Force*, J.J. Fyfe (ed.), 173–94. Washington: Police Foundation.

Fyfe, J.J. 1982c. Blind Justice: Police Shootings in Memphis. *Journal Criminal Law and Criminology* **73**, 707–20.

Gallagher, J. 1995. Anti-Social Security. *New Statesman and Society* (31, March), 22–24.

Galliher, J.F. 1971. Explanations of Police Behaviour: A Critical Review and Analysis. *Sociological Quarterly* **12** (Summer), 308–18.

Gamson, W.A. 1975. *The Strategy of Social Protest.* Homewood, Illinois: Dorsey.

Gamson, W.A. & E. Yuchtman 1977. Police and Society in Israel. In *Police and Society*, D.H. Bayley (ed.), 195–218. Beverly Hills: Sage.

Gardiner, J. 1969. *Traffic and the Police: Variations in Law Enforcement.* Cambridge, Mass.: Harvard University Press.

Garofalo, J. 1979. Victimisation and Fear of Crime. *Journal of Research in Crime and Delinquency* **16**, 80–97.

Geary, R. 1985. *Policing Industrial Disputes: 1893 to 1985.* Cambridge: Cambridge University Press.

Gemmill, R. & R.F. Morgan-Giles 1980. *Arrest, Charge and Summons. Royal Commission on Criminal Procedure: Research Study No. 9.* London: HMSO.

Genz, J.L. & D. Lester 1976. Authoritarianism in Policemen as a Function of Experience. *Journal Police Science and Administration* **4** (1), 9–13.

Gibbons, S. 1994. Private Insecurity. *Police Review* (9, December), 16–17.

Gibbons, S. 1995. Resign Call After Condon Talks of "Noble Corruption". *Police Review* (17, March), 6.

Gibbons, S. 1997a. Searching Questions. *Police Review* (21, February), 14–16.

Gibbons, S. 1997b. Exclusion Orders. *Police Review* (17, January), 18–19.

Gifford, Lord 1986. *Report of the Independent Inquiry into Disturbances of October 1985 at the Broadwater Farm Estate, Tottenham.* London: The Broadwater Farm Inquiry.

Gilbert, T. 1975. *Only One Died: An Account of the Scarman Inquiry into the Events of 15 June 1974 in Red Lion Square when Kevin Gately Died Opposing Racism and Fascism.* London: Kay Beauchamp.

Gill, M.L. & R.I. Mawby 1990. *A Special Constable: A Study of the Police Reserve.* Aldershot: Avebury.

Gilroy, P. 1982. Police and Thieves. In *The Empire Fights Back: Race and Racism in 70s Britain*, Centre for Contemporary Cultural Studies (ed.), 143–82. London: Hutchinson.

Gilroy, P. 1983. Perspectives on Southall. In *Growing Up With Racism*, P. Cohen & H. Singh (eds). London: Macmillan.

Gilroy, P. 1987. The Myth of Black Criminality. In *Law, Order and the Authoritarian State*, P. Scraton (ed.), 107–20. Milton Keynes: Open University.

Glauser, M.J. & W.L. Tullar 1985. Citizen Satisfaction with Police Officer/Citizen Interaction: Implications for the Changing Role of Police Organisations. *Journal Applied Psychology* **70** (3), 514–27.

Goffman, E. 1968. *Stigma: Notes on the Management of Spoiled Identity.* Harmondsworth, Middlesex: Pelican.

Goldkamp, J.S. 1982. Minorities as Victims of Police Shootings: Interpretations of Racial Disproportionality and Police Use of Deadly Force. In *Readings on Police Use of Deadly Force*, J.J. Fyfe (ed.), 128–51. Washington, DC: Police Foundation.

Goldsmith, A. 1990. Taking Police Culture Seriously: Police Discretion and the Limits of the Law. *Policing and Society* **1** (2), 91–114.

Goldsmith, A.J. 1991. External Review and Self-Regulation: Police Accountability and the Dialetic of Complaints Procedures. In *Complaints Against the Police*, A.J. Goldsmith (ed.), 13–62. Oxford: Clarendon.

Goldstein, H. 1964. Police Discretion: The Ideal vs the Real. *Public Administration* **23** (Sep), 140–8.

Goldstein, H. 1977. *Policing a Free Society.* Cambridge, Mass: Ballinger.

Goldstein, H. 1979. Improving Policing: A POP Approach. *Crime and Delinquency* (April).

Goldstein, H. 1987. Towards Community Oriented Policing. *Crime and Delinquency* **33** (No. 1), 6–30.

Goldstein, H. 1990. *Problem-Oriented Policing.* New York: McGraw-Hill.

Goldstein, J. 1960. Police Discretion Not to Invoke the Criminal Process. Low Visibility Decisions in the Administration of Justice. *Yale Law Journal* **69** (4, March), 543–94.

Goldstone, His Honour R.J. 1990. *Report of the Commission of Enquiry into the Incidents at Sebokeng, Boipatong, Lekoa, Sharpeville and Evaton on 26 March 1990.* Johannesburg: South African Government.

Gomez-Preston, C. & J. Trescott 1995. Over the Edge: One Police Woman's Story of Emotional and Sexual Harassment. In *The Criminal Justice System and Women: Offenders, Victims, and Workers*, 2nd edn, B.R. Price & N.J. Sokoloff (eds), 398–403. New York: McGraw-Hill.

Goode, E. & N. Ben-Yehuda 1994. *Moral Panics: The Social Construction of Deviance.* Oxford: Blackwell.

Goodson, A. 1984. Police and the Public. In *Scarman and After*, J. Benyon (ed.), 143–51. London: Pergamon.

Gordon, D.R. 1990. *The Justice Juggernaut: Fighting Street Crime, Controlling Citizens.* New Brunswick: Rutgers University Press.

Gordon, P. 1981. *Passport Raids and Checks.* London: Runnymede Trust.

Gordon, P. 1983. *White Law.* London: Pluto Press.

Gordon, P. 1984a. Community Policing: Towards the Local Police State. *Critical Social Policy* **10** (Summer), 39–58.

Gordon, P. 1984b. Outlawing Immigration, 1: Anwar Ditta and Britain's Immigration Laws. In *Causes for Concern: Questions of Law and Justice*, P. Scraton & P. Gordon (eds), 114–34. Harmondsworth, Middlesex: Penguin.

Gordon, P. 1985. *Policing Immigration: Britain's Internal Controls.* London: Pluto.

Gostin, L. 1984. A Common Cause for Complaints. *The Times* (12, March).

Gottfredson, M.R. 1986. The Substantive Contribution of Victimization Surveys. In *Crime and Justice: an Annual Review of Research*, vol. 7, M. Tonry & N. Morris (eds), 251–88. Chicago: University of Chicago.

Gould, L. 1969. Who Defines Delinquency: A Comparison of Self-Reported and Officially-Reported Indices of Delinquency for Three Racial Groups. *Social Problems* **16** (Winter), 325–35.

Graef, R. 1989. *Talking Blues.* London: Collins Harvill.

Graham, V. 1995. Talking Shops. *Police Review* (17, November), 26–28.

Grant, E. 1989. Private Policing. In *Acta Juridica*, W. Scharf (ed.), 92–117. Cape Town: Faculty of Law, University of Cape Town.

Grant, J.D. & J. Grant 1996. Officer Selection and the Prevention of Abuse of Force. In *Police Violence: Understanding and Controlling Police Abuse of Force*, W.A. Geller & H. Toch (eds), 150–64. New Haven, Conn.: Yale University Press.

Gray, B.J. 1994. Sector Policing: Just an Illusion. *Police Review* (15, July), 22–24.

Green, E. 1970. Race, Social Status and Criminal Arrest. *American Sociological Review* **35**, 476–90.

Green, P. 1990. *The Enemy Without.* Milton Keynes: Open University Press.

Green, R. 1996. Off limits. *Police Review* (6, September), 18–19.

Greene, J.R. 1993. Civic Accountability and the Police. In *Critical Issues in Policing: Contemporary Readings*, 2nd edn, R.G. Dunham & G.P. Alpert (eds), 369–94. Prospect Heights, Illinois: Waveland.

Greenwood, C. 1975. The Evil Choice. *Criminal Law Review* (January), 4–11.

Greenwood, P.W. 1980. The Rand Study of Criminal Investigation: The Findings and Its Impact to Date. In *The Effectiveness of Policing*, R.V.G. Clarke & J.M. Hough (eds), 35–43. Aldershot: Gower.

Greer, S. 1990. The Right to Silence: A Review of the Current Debate. *Modern Law Review* **53** (6, November), 709–730.

Greer, S. & R. Morgan (eds) 1990. *The Right to Silence Debate.* Bristol: Bristol and Bath Centre for Criminal Justice.

Grennan, S.A. 1987. Findings on the Role of Officer Gender in Violent Encounters with Citizens. *Journal Police Science and Administration* **15**, 78–85.

Grieve, C.J. 1993. Thinking the Unthinkable. In *Taking Drugs. Criminal Justice Matters*, R. Matthews & J. Braggins (eds), No. 12, Summer, p. 8. London: Institute for the Study and Treatment of Delinquency.

Grimshaw, R. & T. Jefferson 1987. *Interpreting Policework: Policy and Practice in Forms of Beat Policing.* London: Allen and Unwin.

Grinc, R.M. 1994. Angels in Marble – Problems in Stimulating Community Involvement in Community Policing. *Crime and Delinquency* **40** (3, July), 437–68.

Gudjonsson, G.H. 1994. Psychological Vulnerability. In *Suspicion and Silence: The Right to Silence in Criminal Investigation*, D. Morgan & G. Stephenson (eds), 91–106. London: Blackstone.

Gudjonsson, G., I. Clare, S. Rutter, J. Pearse 1993. *Persons at Risk During Interviews in Police Custody: The Identification of Vulnerabilities. Royal Commission on Criminal Justice Research Studies: No. 12.* London: HMSO.

Guest, J. 1995. Officers are Denied Common Law Rights. *Police Review* (21, July), 12–13.

Gutzmore, C. 1978. Carnival, the State and the Black Masses in the United Kingdom. *Black Liberator* **1**, 8–27.

Guyot, D. 1991. *Policing As Though People Matter.* Philadelphia: Temple University Press.

Hagan, J. & C.P. Morden 1981. The Police Decision to Detain: A Study of Legal Labelling and Police Deviance. In *Organisational Police Deviance*, C. Shearing (ed.), 9–28. Toronto: Butterworths.

Hahn, H. 1971. A Profile of Urban Police. *Law and Contemporary Problems* **36** (Autumn), 449–66.

Hahn, H. & J.R. Feagin 1973. Perspectives on Collective Violence: A Critical Review. In *Violence as Politics*, H. Hirsch & D.C. Perry (eds), 125–55. New York: Harper & Row.

Hall, S. 1979. *Drifting Into a Law and Order Society.* London: Cobden Trust.

Hall, S. 1982. The Lessons of Lord Scarman. *Critical Social Policy* **2**, 66–72.

Hall, S., C. Chricher, T. Jefferson, J. Clarke, B. Roberts 1978. *Policing the Crisis.* London: Macmillan.

Hamilton, P., P. Wiles, F. McClintock (eds) 1972. *The Security Industry in the United Kingdom.* Cambridge: Institute of Criminology.

Haney, C., C. Banks, P. Zimbardo 1973. A Study of Prisoners and Guards in a Simulated Prison. *Naval Research Reviews* (September). Reprinted in *Readings About the Social Animal* (4th edn), Aronson, E. (ed.), 52–67. Freeman, New York, 1984.

Hanmer, J. & Maynard (eds) 1987. *Women, Violence and Social Control.* London: Macmillan.

Hanmer, J. & S. Saunders 1988. Domestic Doesn't Mean It's Not a Crime. *Community Care* **736**, 19.

Hanmer, J., J. Radford, E.A. Stanko (eds) 1989. *Women, Policing, and Male Violence.* London: Routledge.

Harding, R.W. 1970. The Legality of Killings by Australian Police. *Journal of Research in Crime and Delinquency* **7** (2), 177–87.

Harring, S. 1983. *Policing a Class Society: The Experience of American Cities 1865–1915.* New Brunswick, NJ: Rutgers University Press.

Hartjen, C.A. 1972. Police–Citizen Encounters. *Criminology* **10** (May), 61–84.

Hawkins, H. & R. Thomas 1991. White Policing of Black Populations: A History of Race and Social Control in America. In *Out of Order?*, E. Cashmore & E. McLaughlin (eds), 65–86. London: Routledge.

Haysom, N. 1989. Policing the Police: A Comparative Survey of Police Control Mechanisms in the United States, South Africa and the United Kingdom. In *Acta Juridica*, W. Scharf (ed.), 139–64. Cape Town: Faculty of Law, University of Cape Town.

Hazlehurst, K.M. 1991. Passion and Policy: Aboriginal Deaths in Custody in Australia 1980–1989. In *Crimes by the Capitalist State*, G. Barak (ed.), 21–48. Albany: State University of New York.

Heal, K. & P. Morris 1985. The Effectiveness of Patrol. In *Policing Today*, K. Heal (ed.), 107–114. London: HMSO.

Hedderman, C. & M. Hough 1994. Does the Crime Justice System Treat Men and Women Differently? *Home Office Research and Statistics Department, Research Findings, No. 10.* May.

Heidensohn, F. 1992. *Women in Control: The Role of Women in Law Enforcement.* Oxford: Oxford University Press.

Heirich, M. 1976. The Spiral of Conflict: Berkeley 1964. In *Readings in Collective Behaviour*, R. Evans (ed.), 241–75. Chicago: Rand McNally.

Hepburn, J.R. 1978. Race and the Decision to Arrest. *Journal of Research in Crime and Delinquency* **15** (January), 54–73.

Hewitt, P. 1982. *The Abuse of Power: Civil Liberties in the UK.* Oxford: Martin Robertson.

Hill, R. 1986. *History of the New Zealand Police – The Theory and Practice of Coercive Social and Racial Control in New Zealand, 1767–1867,* vol. One. Wellington, New Zealand: Historical Publications Branch, Department of Internal Affairs.

Hill, R.S. 1991. The Policing of Colonial New Zealand: From Informal to Formal Control, 1840–1907. In *Policing the Empire: Government, Authority and Control, 1830–1940*, D.M. Anderson & D. Killingray (eds), 52–70. Manchester: Manchester University Press.

Hilliard, B. 1995. Suspicious Minds. *Police Review* (22, September), 18–19.

Hills, A. 1995. Militant Tendencies. *British Journal of Criminology* **35** (3, Summer), 450–58.

Hills, A. 1997a. Care and Control: The Role of the UK Police in Extreme Circumstances. *Policing and Society* **7** (3), 177–90.

Hills, A. 1997b. Policing, Enforcement and Low Intensity Conflict. *Policing and Society* **7** (4), 291–308.

Hillyard, P. & J. Percy-Smith 1988. *The Coercive State.* London: Fontana.

Hindelang, M.J. 1969. Equality Under the Law. *Journal of Criminal Law, Criminology and Police Science* **60** (3), 306–13.

Hindelang, M.J. 1978. Race and Involvement in Common Law Personal Crimes. *American Sociological Review* **43** (February), 93–109.

Hindelang, M.J. & M.R. Gottfredson 1976. The Victim's Decision Not to Invoke the Criminal Process. In *The Victim and the Criminal Justice System*, W. McDonald (ed.), 57–78. Beverley Hills: Sage.

Hobbs, D. 1988. *Doing the Business: Entrepeneurship, the Working Class, and Detectives in the East End of London.* Oxford: Clarendon.

Hodgson, J. & M. McConville 1993. Silence and the Suspect. *New Law Journal* **143** (7, May), 659.

Hofstra, B. & J. Shapland 1997. Who is in Control? *Policing and Society* **6** (4), 265–82.

Hohenstein, W.H. 1969. Factors Influencing the Police Disposition of Juvenile Offenders. In *Delinquency*, T. Sellin & M.E. Wolfgang (eds), 138–49. New York: Wiley.

Holdaway, S. 1978. The Reality of Police-Race Relations: Towards An Effective Community Relations Policy. *New Community* **6** (part 3), 258–67.

Holdaway, S. 1983. *Inside the British Police.* Oxford: Blackwell.

Holdaway, S. 1986. The Holloway Road Incident. *Policing* **2** (2), 101–13.

Holdaway, S. 1991. Race Relations and Police Recruitment. *British Journal of Criminology* **31** (4, Autumn), 365–82.

Holdaway, S. 1995. Culture, Race and Policy: Some Themes of the Sociology of the Police. *Policing and Society* **5** (2), 109–20.

Holdaway, S. 1996. *The Racialisation of British Policing.* Basingstoke: Macmillan.

Holdaway, S. 1997. Constructing and Sustaining "Race" Within the Police Workforce. *British Journal of Sociology* **48** (1, March), 18–34.

Home Affairs Select Committee 1980. *Race Relations and the "Sus" Law.* London: HMSO.

Home Affairs Select Committee 1986. *Racial Attacks and Harassment.* London: HMSO.

Home Affairs Select Committee 1998. *Police Disciplinary and Complaints Procedure.* London: HMSO.

Home Office 1983. Circular 114/1983: Manpower, Effectiveness and Efficiency in the Police Service.

Home Office 1993. *Police Reform: A Police Service for the Twenty-First Century.* London: HMSO.

Hoogenboom, B. 1991. Grey Policing: A Theoretical Framework. *Policing and Society* **2** (1), 17–30.

Hope, T. & M. Hough 1988. Area, Crime and Incivilities: Findings from the British Crime Survey. In *Communities and Crime Reductions*, T. Hope & M. Shaw (eds), 30–47. London: HMSO.

Horowitz, D.L. 1983. Racial Violence in the United States. In *Ethnic Pluralism and Public Policy*, N. Glazer & K. Young (eds), 187–211. Lexington, Mass.: D.C. Heath.

Horton, C. 1989. Good Practice and Evaluating Policing. In *Coming to Terms with Policing*, R. Morgan & D.J. Smith (eds), 31–48. London: Routledge.

Horton, C. 1995. *Policing Policy in France.* London: Policy Studies Institute.

Horton, C. & D.J. Smith 1988. *Evaluating Police Work: An Action Research Project.* London: Police Studies Institute.

Hough, J.M. & R.V.G. Clarke 1980. Introduction. In *The Effectiveness of Policing*, R.V.G. Clarke & J.M. Hough (eds), 1–16. Aldershot: Gower.

Hough, M. 1995. Anxiety About Crime: Findings from the 1994 British Crime Survey. *Home Office Research and Statistics Department, Research Findings, No. 25.* December.

Hough, M. 1996. The Police Patrol Function: What Research Can Tell Us. In *Themes in Contemporary Policing*, W. Saulsbury, J. Mott, T. Newburn (eds), 60–71. London: Independent Committee of Inquiry into the Role and Responsibilities of the Police.

Hough, M. & P. Mayhew 1983. *The British Crime Survey: First Report. Home Office Research Study: No. 76.* London: HMSO.

Hough, M. & P. Mayhew 1985. *Taking Account of Crime: Key Findings from the Second British Crime Survey. Home Office Research Study: No. 85.* London: HMSO.

House of Commons Expenditure Committee 1977. *Ninth Report from the Expenditure Committee, Session 1976–77: The Employment of Civilians for Police Purposes.* London: House of Commons.

Howe, S. 1996. CPS Pledge Sought After "Unfair" Police Officer Prosecutions Raised. *Police Review* (24, May), 5.

Howe, S. & V. Graham 1995. Special Duties. *Police Review* (22, September), 22–24.

Howes, G. 1975. Introduction. In *The Police and the Community*, J. Brown & G. Howes (eds), 1–6. Farnborough: Saxon House.

Hudson, J.R. 1970. Police–Citizen Encounters That Lead to Citizen Complaints. *Social Problems* **18**, 179–93.

Huggins, M.K. 1997. From bureaucratic consolidation to structural devolution: police death squads in Brazil. *Policing & Society* **7** (4), 207–34.

Huggins, M.K. & M.P. Mesquita 1995. Scapegoating Outsiders: The Murders of Street Youth in Modern Brazil. *Policing and Society* **5** (4), 265–80.

Hughes, E.C. 1962. Good People and Dirty Work. *Social Problems* **10** (1, Summer), 3–11.

Humphry, D. 1972. *Police Power and Black People.* London: Panther.

Hurd, D. 1987. Police Foundation Annual Lecture. Given at the Guildhall, London, 30 July.

Hutter, B.M. 1989. *The Reasonable Arm of the Law.* Oxford: Clarendon.

Hutton, W. 1995. *The State We're In.* London: Jonathan Cape.

Hyder, K. 1995. Research Shows Five to One Odds on Blacks Being Stopped. *Police Review* (26, January), 10.

Hytner, B.A. 1981. *Report of the Moss Side Enquiry Panel to the Leader of the Greater Manchester Council.* Manchester: Greater Manchester Council.

Independent Inquiry Panel 1985. *Inquiry into Leon Brittan's visit to Manchester University Students' Union, 1 March 1985.* Manchester: Manchester City Council.

Information on Ireland 1987. *They Shoot Children.* London: Information on Ireland.

Institute of Race Relations. 1981. *Police Against Black People. Race and Class, No. 6.* London.

Institute of Race Relations 1987. *Policing Against Black People.* London: Institute of Race Relations.

Irving, B. 1986. The Interrogation Process. In *The Police: Powers, Procedures and Proprieties*, J. Benyon (ed.), 136–49. Oxford: Pergamon.

Irving, B. & C. Dunnighan 1993. *Human Factors in the Quality Control of CID Investigations. Royal Commission on Criminal Justice Research Studies, No. 21.* London: HMSO.

Irving, B. & L. Hilgendorf 1980. *Police Interrogation: the Psychological Approach. Royal Commission on Criminal Procedure, Research Study No. 1.* London: HMSO.

Irving, B. with the assistance of Linden Hilgendorf 1980. *Police Interrogation: A Case Study of Current Practice. Royal Commission on Criminal Procedure, Research Study No. 2.* London: HMSO.

Irving, B., C. Bird, M. Hibberd, J. Willmore 1989. *Neighbourhood Policing: The Natural History of a Policing Experiment.* London: Police Foundation.

Jackson, B. with T. Wardle 1986. *The Battle for Orgreave.* Brighton: Vanson Wardle.

Jackson, P. 1989. Street Life: The Politics of Carnival. *Environment and Planning* **6**, 248–61.

Jacob, H. & M. Rich 1980. The Effects of the Police on Crime: A Second Look. *Law and Society* **15** (1), 109–22.

Jacob, H. & M. Rich 1981. The Effects of the Police on Crime: A Rejoinder. *Law and Society* **16** (1), 171–72.

Jaime-Jimenez, O. & F. Reinares 1998. *The Policing of Mass Demonstrations in Spain: From Dictatorship to Democracy*. See della Porta & Reiter (1998), 166–87.

Jakubs, D.L. 1977. Police Violence in Times of Political Tension: The Case of Brazil, 1968–71. In *Police and Society*, D.H. Bayley (ed.), 85–106. Beverly Hills: Sage.

James, D. 1979. Police–Black Relations: The Professional Solution. In *The British Police*, S. Holdaway (ed.), 66–82. London: Edward Arnold.

James, S.P. 1994. Contemporary Programs with Youth People: Beyond Traditional Law Enforcement? In *The Police and Young People in Australia*, R. White & C. Alder (eds), 199–231. Cambridge: Cambridge University Press.

Janowitz, M. 1970. *Political Conflict: Essays in Political Sociology*. Chicago: Quadrangle Books.

Jarman, N. & D. Bryan 1996. *Parade and Protest: A Discussion of Parading Disputes in Northern Ireland*. Coleraine: Centre for the Study of Conflict, University of Ulster.

Jefferson, T. 1987. Beyond Paramilitarism. *British Journal of Criminology* **27** (1, Winter), 47–53.

Jefferson, T. 1990. *The Case Against Paramilitary Policing*. Milton Keynes: Open University.

Jefferson, T. 1991. Discrimination, Disadvantages and Police-Work. In *Out of Order?*, E. Cashmore & E. McLaughlin (eds), 166–88. London: Routledge.

Jefferson, T. 1993. Pondering Paramilitarism. *British Journal of Criminology* **33** (3), 374–81.

Jefferson, T. & R. Grimshaw 1984a. The Problem of Law Enforcement Policy in England and Wales: The Case of Community Policing and Racial Attacks. *International Journal of Sociology* (12, May), 117–135.

Jefferson, T. & R. Grimshaw 1984b. *Controlling the Constable*. London: Frederick Muller/ Cobden Trust.

Jefferson, T. & J. Shapland 1994. Criminal-Justice and the Production of Order and Control – Criminological Research in the UK in the 1980s. *British Journal of Criminology* **34** (3), 265–90.

Jefferson, T. & M.A. Walker 1993. Attitudes to the Police of Ethnic-Minorities in a Provincial City. *British Journal of Criminology* **33** (2), 251–66.

Jefferson, T., E. McLaughlin, L. Robertson 1984. Police Watching: Results of a Pilot Study in London. Paper presented at Third European Conference of Critical Legal Studies, University of Kent, April 13–15.

Jeffery, K. & P. Hennessy 1983. *States of Emergency*. London: Routledge and Kegan Paul.

Jenkins, C. 1997. Market Forces. *Police Review* (3, October), 20–21.

Jenkinson, J. 1993. The 1919 Riots. In *Racial Violence in Britain, 1840–1950*, P. Panayi (ed.), 92–111. Leicester: Leicester University Press.

Johnston, L. 1992. *The Rebirth of Private Policing*. London: Routledge.

Joint Consultative Committee 1990. *Operational Policing Review*. Surbiton: The Joint Consultative Committee.

Jones, M.J. 1980. *Organisational Aspects of Police Behaviour*. Farnborough: Gower.

Jones, S. 1986. *Policewomen and Equality: Formal Police v Informal Practice?* London: Macmillan.

Jones, S. & M. Levi 1987. Law and Order and the Causes of Crime: Some Police and Public Perspective. *Howard Journal* **26** (1, Feb), 1–14.

Jones, S. & E. Silverman 1984. Manpower and Efficiency. *Policing* **1** (1), 31–48.

Jones, T. 1995. *Policing and Democracy in the Netherlands*. London: Policy Studies Institute.

Jones, T., B. MacLean, J. Young 1986. *The Islington Crime Survey*. Aldershot: Gower.

Jones, T., T. Newburn, D.J. Smith 1994. *Democracy and Policing*. London: Policy Studies Institute.

Joshua, H., T. Wallace, H. with the assistance of Booth 1983. *To Ride the Storm.* London: Heinemann.

Judge, T. 1986. A Necessary Ordeal? *Police* (1, Sep), 20–22.

Judge, T. 1994. "When I Was a Lad . . .". *Police* (July), 20–23.

JUSTICE 1994. *The Right to Silence Debate: The Northern Ireland Experience.* London: JUSTICE.

Kakalik, J.S. & S. Wildhorn 1977. *The Private Police: Security and Danger.* New York: Crane Russak and Co.

Kannenmeyer, D.D.V. 1985. Report of the Commission Appointed to Inquire into the Incident which Occurred on 21 March 1985 at Uitenhage. Pretoria, South Africa.

Kappeler, V.E. & M. Kaune 1993. Legal Standards and Civil Liability of Excessive Force. In *Critical Issues in Policing: Contemporary Readings*, 2nd edn, R.G. Dunham & G.P. Alpert (eds), 526–36. Prospect Heights, Illinois: Waveland.

Kappeler, V.E., R.D. Sluder, G.P. Alpert 1994. *Forces of Deviance: Understanding the Dark Side of Policing.* Prospect Heights, Illinois: Waveland.

Kaye, T. 1991. *Unsafe and Unsatisfactory? Report of the Independent Inquiry into the Working Practices of the West Midlands Serious Crime Squad.* London: Civil Liberties Trust.

Keith, M. 1991. Policing a Perplexed Society? No-Go Areas and the Mystification of Police–Black Conflict. In *Out of Order?*, E. Cashmore & E. McLaughlin (eds), 189–214. London: Routledge.

Kelling, G.L. 1978. Police Field Services and Crime – The Presumed Effects of a Capacity. *Crime and Delinquency* **24** (April), 173–84.

Kelling, G.L. & R.B. Kliesmet 1996. Police Unions, Police Culture, and Police Use of Force. In *Police Violence: Understanding and Controlling Police Abuse of Force*, W.A. Geller & H. Toch (eds), 191–213. New Haven, Conn.: Yale University Press.

Kelling, G.L., T. Pate, D. Dieckman, C.E. Brown 1974. *The Kansas City Preventive Patrol Experiment: A Technical Report.* Washington, DC: Police Foundation.

Kemp, C. & R. Morgan 1989. David and Goliath – Using Private Citizens to Monitor a Public Service: Lay Visitors to Police Stations. Paper presented at British Criminology Conference, Bristol Polytechnic, July.

Kemp, C. & R. Morgan 1990. *Lay Visitors to Police Stations: Report to the Home Office.* Bath: Bristol and Bath Centre for Criminal Justice.

Kemp, C., C. Norris, N.G. Fielding 1992a. *Negotiating Nothing: Police Decision-Making in Disputes.* Aldershot: Avebury.

Kemp, C., C. Norris, N. Fielding 1992b. Legal Manoeuvres in Police Handling of Disputes. In *Criminal Justice*, A. Bottomley, A. Fowles, R. Reiner (eds), 55–74. London: British Society for Criminology.

Kendrick, D. 1995. *De-brief Report into the Disorder in Hyde Park and Park Lane on Sunday 9th October 1994.* London: Metropolitan Police.

Kerner, O. 1968. *The Report of the National Advisory Commission on Civil Disorders.* Washington, DC: US Government Printing Office.

Kerstetter, W.A. 1996. Toward Justice for All: Procedural Justice and the Review of Citizen Complaints. In *Police Violence: Understanding and Controlling Police Abuse of Force*, W.A. Geller & H. Toch (eds), 234–47. New Haven, Conn.: Yale University Press.

Kettle, M. 1985. The National Reporting Centre and the 1984 Miners' Strike. In *Policing the Miners' Strike*, B. Fine & R. Millar (eds), 23–33. London: Lawrence and Wishart.

Kettle, M. & L. Hodges 1982. *Uprising.* London: Pan.

Killian, L.M. 1984. Organization, Rationality and Spontaneity in the Civil Rights Movement. *American Sociological Review* **49**, 770–83.

Kinsey, R., J. Lea, J. Young 1986. *Losing the Fight Against Crime.* Oxford: Blackwell.

Kirkham, G.L. 1974. From Professor to Patrolman. *Journal of Police Science and Administration* **2** (June), 127–37.

Kleinig, J. 1996. *The Ethics of Policing. Cambridge Studies in Philosophy and Public Policy.* Cambridge: Cambridge University Press.

Klockars, C.B. 1980. The Dirty Harry Problem. *Annals of the American Academy of Political and Social Science* **452** (November), 33–47.

Klockars, C.B. 1985. *The Idea of Police. Law and Criminal Justice: Volume 3.* Beverly Hills: Sage.

Klockars, C.B. 1996. A Theory of Excessive Force and its Control. In *Police Violence: Understanding and Controlling Police Abuse of Force*, W.A. Geller & H. Toch (eds), 1–22. New Haven, Conn.: Yale University Press.

Knapp, W. 1972. *The Knapp Report on Police Corruption.* New York: Braziller.

Kock, E. & B. Rix 1997. *A Review of Police Trials of the CS Aerosol Incapacitant. Police Research Series: Paper 21.* London: Police Research Group, Home Office.

Kock, E., T. Kemp, B. Rix 1993. *Assessing the Expandable Side-Handled Baton. Police Research Series: Paper 11.* London: Police Research Group, Home Office.

Koffman, L. 1985. Safeguarding the Rights of the Citizen. In *Police: The Constitution and the Community*, J. Baxter & L. Koffman (eds), 11–37. Abingdon, Oxon: Professional Books.

Kraska, P.B. & L.J. Cubellis 1997. Militarizing Mayberry and Beyond: Making Sense of American Paramilitary Policing. *Justice Quarterly* **14** (4, December), 607–29.

Kraska, P.B. & V.E. Kappeler 1997. Militarizing American Police: The Rise and Normalization of Paramilitary Units. *Social Problems* **44** (1, February), 1–18.

Kraska, P.B. & D.J. Paulsen 1997. Grounded Research into US Paramilitary Policing: Forging the Iron Fist Inside the Velvet Glove. *Policing and Society* **7** (4), 253–70.

LaFave, W.R. 1962a. The Police and Non-Enforcement of the Law (Part 1). *Wisconsin Law Review* (January), 104–37.

LaFave, W.R. 1962b. The Police and Non-Enforcement of the Law (Part 2). *Wisconsin Law Review* (March), 179–239.

LaFave, W. 1965. *Arrest: The Decision to Take a Suspect into Custody.* Boston: Little Brown.

Lambert, J.R. 1970. *Crime, Police and Race Relations: A Study in Birmingham.* London: Oup.

Landau, S.F. 1981. Juveniles and the Police: Who is Charged Immediately Who is Referred to the Juvenile Bureau? *British Journal of Criminology* **21** (1, January), 27–46.

Lane, R. 1992. Urban Police and Crime in Nineteenth-Century America. In *Modern Policing. Crime and Justice. A Review of Research*, vol. 15, M. Tonry & N. Morris (eds), 1–50. Chicago: University of Chicago Press.

LaPiere, R.T. 1934. Attitudes vs Actions. *Social Forces* **13**, 230–37.

Larson, R. 1976. What Happened to Patrol Operations in Kansas City? A Review of the Kansas City Preventive Patrol Experiment. *Journal of Criminal Justice*, **3** (4), 267–97.

Laurance, J. 1985. Learning the Lessons. *New Society* (6, December).

Laurance, J. 1986. Is the Tyra Henry Inquiry Doomed? *New Society* (4, April), 16–17.

Law Society & The Police Federation of England and Wales 1983. The Police Complaints and Discipline Scheme. Proposed by The Law Society and the Police Federation of England and Wales.

Laycock, G. & R. Tarling 1985. Police Force Cautioning: Policy and Practice. In *Managing Criminal Justice*, D. Moxon (ed.). London: HMSO.

Layzell, A. 1985. Enforcement Discretion. *Policing* **1** (4, Autumn), 245–53.

Lea, J. & J. Young 1982. The Riots in Britain 1981: Urban Violence and Political Marginalisation. In *Policing the Riots*, D. Cowell, T. Jones, J. Young (eds), 5–20. London: Junction Books.

Lea, J. & J. Young 1984. *What Is To Be Done About Law and Order?* Harmondsworth, Middx: Penguin.

Lea, J. & J. Young 1993. *What Is To Be Done About Law and Order? Crisis in the Nineties.* London: Pluto.

Lee, J.A. 1981. Some Structural Aspects of Police Deviance in Relations with Minority Groups. In *Organisational Police Deviance*, C. Shearing (ed.), 49–82. Toronto: Butterworth.

Lefkowitz, J. 1973. Attitudes of Police Towards Their Job. In *The Urban Policeman in Transition*, J.R. Snibbe & H.M. Snibbe (eds), 203–32. Springfield, Illinois: Charles Thomas.

Leighton, B.N. 1994. Community Policing in Canada: An Overview of Experience and Evaluations. In *The Challenge of Community Policing: Testing the Promises*, D.P. Rosenbaum (ed.), 209–23. Thousand Oaks: Sage.

Leishman, F., S. Cope, P. Starie 1995. Reinventing and Restructuring: Towards a "New Police Order". In *Core Issues in Policing*, F. Leishman, B. Loveday, S.P. Savage (eds), 9–25. London: Longman.

Leng, R. 1993. *The Right to Silence in Police Interrogation: A Study of Some of the Issues Underlying the Debate. Royal Commission on Criminal Justice Research Studies, No. 10.* London: HMSO.

Leng, R. 1994. The Right to Silence Debate. In *Suspicion and Silence: The Right to Silence in Criminal Investigation*, D. Morgan & G. Stephenson (eds), 18–38. London: Blackstone.

Leon, C. 1989. The Special Constabulary. *Policing* **5** (4, Winter), 265–86.

Lester, D. 1996. Officer Attitudes Toward Police Use of Force. In *Police Violence: Understanding and Controlling Police Abuse of Force*, W.A. Geller & H. Toch (eds), 180–90. New Haven, Conn.: Yale University Press.

Lewis, C.E. 1991. Police Complaints in Metropolitan Toronto: Perspectives of the Public Complaints Commissioner. In *Complaints Against the Police*, A.J. Goldsmith (ed.), 153–76. Oxford: Clarendon.

Lewis, D.A. & M.G. Maxfield 1980. Fear in Neighbourhoods: An Investigation of the Impact of Crime. *Journal of Research in Crime and Delinquency* **17**, 140–59.

Lidstone, K. 1985. Magistrates and the Pre-Trial Process. In *Managing Criminal Justice*, D. Moxon (ed.), 45–53. London: HMSO.

Lidstone, K.W., R. Hogg, Sutcliffe 1980. *Prosecutions by Private Individuals and Non-police Agencies. Royal Commission on Criminal Procedure, Research Study*, vol. 10. London: HMSO.

Linnan, D.K. 1984. Police Discretion in a Continental European Administrative State: The Police of Baden-Wurttemberg in the Federal Republic of Germany. *Journal of Law and Contemporary Social Problems* **47** (4), 185–223.

Lipset, S.M. 1969. The Politics of the Police. *New Society* **13** (336), 355–58.

Lipset, S.M. 1971. Why Cops Hate Liberals – And Vice Versa. In *The Police Rebellion: A Quest for Blue Power*, W.J. Bopp (ed.), 23–39. Springfield, Illinois: Thomas.

Liska, A.E. & M. Tausig 1979. Theoretical Interpretations of Social Class and Race Differentials in Legal Decision-Making for Juveniles. *Sociological Quarterly* **20** (Spring), 197–207.

Liska, A.E. & J. Yu 1992. Specifying and Testing the Threat Hypothesis: Police Use of Deadly Force. In *Social Threat and Social Control*, A.J. Liska (ed.), 53–68. Albany: State University of New York.

Loader, I. 1996. *Youth, Policing and Democracy.* Basingstoke: Macmillan.

Locke, H.G. 1996. The Color of Law and the Issue of Color: Race and the Abuse of Police Power. In *Police Violence: Understanding and Controlling Police Abuse of Force*, W.A. Geller & H. Toch (eds), 129–49. New Haven, Conn.: Yale University Press.

Loveday, B. 1986. Central Coordination, Police Authorities and the Miners' Strike. *Political Quarterly* **57** (Jan–Mar), 60–73.

Loveday, B. 1988. Police Complaints in the USA. *Policing* **4** (3, Autumn), 173–94.

Loveday, B. 1989a. Recent Developments in Police Complaints Procedure: Britain and North America. *Local Government Studies* (May/June), 25–57.

Loveday, B. 1989b. Poor Prospects for Police Civilians. *Policing* **5** (2, Summer), 86–96.

Loveday, B. 1993. The Local Accountability of Police in England and Wales. In *Accountable Policing: Effectiveness, Empowerment and Equity*, R. Reiner & S. Spencer (eds), 55–80. London: Institute for Public Policy Research.

Loveday, B. 1994a. Police Reform: Problems of Accountability and the Measurement of Police Effectiveness. *Strategic Government* **2** (1, Spring), 7–23.

Loveday, B. 1994b. Ducking and Diving – Formulating a Policy for Police and Criminal Justice in the 1990s. *Public Money and Management* (July/September), 25–30.

Loveday, B. 1994c. Government Strategies for Community Crime Prevention Programmes in England and Wales: A Study in Failure? *International Journal of Sociology* **22**, 181–202.

Loveday, B. 1994d. The Competing Role of Central and Local Agencies in Crime Prevention Strategies. *Local Government Studies* **20** (3, Autumn), 361–73.

Loveday, B. 1995a. Crime at the Core. In *Core Issues in Policing*, F. Leishman, B. Loveday, S.P. Savage (eds), 73–100. London: Longman.

Loveday, B. 1995b. Contemporary Challenges to Police Management in England and Wales: Developing for Effective Service Delivery. *Policing and Society* **5** (4), 281–302.

Loveday, B. 1996. Business As Usual? The New Police Authorities and the Police and Magistrates' Courts Act. *Local Government Studies* **22** (2, Summer), 22–39.

Lundman, R.J. 1979. Organisational Norms and Police Discretion: An Observational Study of Police Work with Traffic Law Violators. *Criminology* **17**, 159–71.

Lundman, R.J., R.E. Sykes, J.P. Clark 1978. Police Control of Juveniles: A Replication. *Journal of Research in Crime and Delinquency* **15** (January), 74–91.

Lurigio, A.J. & D.P. Rosenbaum 1994. The Impact of Community Policing on Police Personnel: A Review of the Literature. In *The Challenge of Community Policing: Testing the Promises*, D.P. Rosenbaum (ed.), 147–63. Thousand Oaks: Sage.

Lurigio, A.J. & W.G. Skogan 1994. Winning the Hearts and Minds of Police Officers – An Assessment of Staff Perceptions of Community Policing in Chicago. *Crime and Delinquency* **40** (3, July), 315–30.

Lustgarten, L. 1986. *The Governance of Police.* London: Sweet and Maxwell.

Luthra, P. & P. Gordon 1984. Outlawing Immigration, 2: The Bestways Passport Raid and Britain's Internal Immigration Controls. In *Causes for Concern: Questions of Law and Justice*, P. Scraton & P. Gordon (eds), 135–53. Harmondsworth, Middlesex: Penguin.

MacDonald, I.R. 1985. The Police System of Spain. In *Police and Public Order in Europe*, J. Roach & J. Thomaneck (eds), 215–54. London: Croom Helm.

MacDonald, L. 1969. *Social Class and Delinquency.* London: Faber and Faber.

Maggs, C. 1986. Community Liaison in New York. *Policing* **2** (1, Spring), 4–16.

Maguire, M. 1982. *Burglary in a Dwelling.* London: Heinemann.

Maguire, M. 1991. Complaints Against the Police: The British Experience. In *Complaints Against the Police*, A.J. Goldsmith (ed.), 177–210. Oxford: Clarendon.

Maguire, M. & C. Corbett 1991. *A Study of the Police Complaints System.* London: HMSO.

Maguire, M. & C. Norris 1992. *The Conduct and Supervision of Criminal Investigations. Royal Commission on Criminal Justice Research Studies, No. 5.* London: HMSO.

Maguire, M. & C. Norris 1994. Police Investigations – Practice and Malpractice. *Journal of Law and Society* **21** (1), 72–84.

Malyon, T. 1995. Nowhere to Stay, Nowhere to Go. In *Taking Liberties: Civil Liberties and the Criminal Justice Act*, New Statesman and Society, 22–3.

Manksch, H. 1963. Becoming a Nurse: A Selective View. *Annals of the American Academy of Political and Social Science* **346**, 88–98.

Mann, M. 1996. Ruling Class Strategies and Citizenship. In *Citizenship Today: The Contemporary Relevance of T.H. Marshall*, M. Bulmer & A.M. Rees (eds), 125–44. London: UCL.

Manning, P.K. 1974. Police Lying. *Urban Life* **3**, 283–306. Revised and reprinted in Peter K. Manning and John van Maanen (eds), *Policing: A View from the Street*. New York: Random House, 1978.

Manning, P.K. 1977. *Police Work*. Cambridge, Mass.: MIT Press.

Manning, P.K. 1979. The Social Control of Police Work. In *The British Police*, S. Holdaway (ed.), 41–65. London: Edward Arnold.

Manning, P.K. 1980a. Organisation and Environment: Influences on Police Work. In *The Effectiveness of Policing*, R.V.G. Clarke & J.M. Hough (eds), 98–123. Aldershot: Gower.

Manning, P.K. 1980b. Violence and the Police Role. *Annals of the American Academy of Political and Social Science* **452** (November), 135–44.

Manning, P.K. 1983. Organizational Constraints and Semiotics. In *Control in the Police Organization*, M. Punch (ed.), 169–93. Cambridge, Mass.: MIT. Press.

Manning, P.K. 1988. *Symbolic Communication: Signifying Calls and the Police Response*. Cambridge, Mass.: MIT Press.

Manning, P.K. 1993. Community-Based Policing. In *Critical Issues in Policing: Contemporary Readings* 2nd edn, R.G. Dunham & G.P. Alpert (eds), 421–31. Prospect Heights, Illinois Waveland.

Manning, P.K. & J. Redlinger 1977. Invitational Edges of Corruption. In *Policing: A View From the Street*, P.K. Manning & J. van Maanen (eds), 147–66. New York: Random House.

Manning, P.K. & J. van Maanen 1977. Rules, Colleagues and Situationally Justified Actions. In *Policing: A View From the Street*, P.K. Manning (ed.), 71–89. New York: Random House.

Manolias, M. & A. Hyatt-Williams 1988. *Post-Shooting Experiences in Firearms Officers*. London: Joint Working Party on Organisational Health and Welfare.

Mansfield, M. 1995. The Bounds of Silence. In *Taking Liberties: Civil Liberties and the Criminal Justice Act*, New Statesman and Society, 16 & 21.

Manwaring-White, S. 1983. *The Policing Revolution*. Brighton: Harvester.

Mapstone, R. 1992. The Attitudes of Police in a Divided Society – The Case of Northern-Ireland. *British Journal of Criminology* **32** (2), 183–92.

Marais, E. & I. Jenkins 1992. Policing in Denmark: Report on the IDASA Study Tour to Denmark, 9–20 November 1992.

Marenin, O. 1982. Parking Tickets and Class Repression: The Concept of Policing in Critical Theories of Criminal Justice. *Contemporary Crises* **6**, 241–66.

Market & Opinion Research International Limited 1984. Public Attitudes Towards Police Complaints Procedures: Research Study Conducted for the Police Federation. London.

Marshall, G. 1965. *Police and Government: The Status and Accountability of the English Constable*. London: Methuen.

Marshall, P. 1975. Urban Stress and Policing. In *The Police and the Community*, J. Brown & G. Howes (eds), 17–30. Farnborough: Saxon House.

Marshall, T.H. 1950. *Citizenship and Social Class and Other Essays*. Cambridge: Cambridge University Press.

Martin, S.E. 1979. POLICEwomen and policeWOMEN: Occupational Role Dilemmas and Choices of Female Officers. *Journal Police Science and Administration* **2/3**, 314–23.

Martin, S.E. 1995. The Interactive Effects of Race and Sex on Women Police Officers. In *The Criminal Justice System and Women: Offenders, Victims, and Workers*, 2nd edn, B.R. Price & N.J. Sokoloff (eds), 383–97. New York: McGraw–Hill.

Martin, S.E. & L.W. Sherman 1986. Selective Apprehension: A Police Strategy for Repeat Offenders. *Criminology* **24** (1), 155–72.

Marx, G.T. 1972. Issueless Riots. In *Collective Violence*, J.F. Short (ed.), 47–59. Chicago: Aldine-Atherton.

Marx, G.T. 1987. The Interweaving of Public and Private Police in Undercover Work. In *Private Policing. Sage Criminal Justice System Annuals*, vol. 23. C.D. Shearing & P.C. Stenning (eds), 172–93. Newbury Park, California: Sage.

Marx, G.T. 1988. *Undercover: Police Surveillance in America.* Berkeley: University of California.

Marx, G.T. 1992. When the Guards Guard Themselves: Undercover Tactics Turned Inward. *Policing and Society* **2** (3), 151–72.

Marx, G. & D. Archer 1971. Citizen Involvement in the Law Enforcement Process: The Case of Community Police Patrols. *American Behavioral Scientist* **15** (1), 52–71.

Masterman, L. 1985. The Battle of Orgreave. In *Television Mythologies*, L. Masterman (ed.), 99–109. London: Comedia.

Matza, D. 1969. *Becoming Deviant.* Englewood Cliffs, NJ: Prentice Hall.

Maung, N. & C. Mirrlees-Black 1994. *Racially Motivated Crime: a British Crime Survey Analysis. Research and Planning Unit: Paper 82.* London: Home Office.

Mawby, R. 1979. *Policing the City.* Farnborough: Saxon House.

Mawby, R.I. 1990. *Comparative Policing Issues.* London: Unwin Hyman.

Maxfield, M. 1984. *Fear of Crime in England and Wales. Home Office Research Study, No. 78.* London: HMSO.

Maxfield, M. 1987. *Explaining Fear of Crime: Evidence from the 1984. British Crime Survey. Research and Planning Unit Papers: No 43.* London: Home Office.

Mayhew, P. & N.A. Maung 1992. Surveying Crime: Findings from the 1992 British Crime Survey. *Home Office Research and Statistics Department, Research Findings, No 2.* October.

Mayhew, P., D. Elliot, L. Dowds 1989. *The 1988 British Crime Survey. Home Office Research Studies, No. 111.* London: HMSO.

Mayhew, P., N.A. Muang, C. Mirrlees-Black 1993. *The 1992 British Crime Survey. Home Office Research Study, No. 132.* London: HMSO.

Mayhew, P., N. A. Maung, C. Mirrlees-Black 1994. Trends in Crime: Findings from the 1994 British Crime Survey. *Home Office Research and Statistics Directorate, Research Findings, No. 14.* September.

McAdam, D. 1982. *Political Process and the Development of Black Insurgency.* Chicago: University of Chicago Press.

McAdam, D. 1983. Tactical Innovation and the Pace of Insurgency. *American Sociological Review* **48** (December), 735–54.

McAdam, D. 1988. *Freedom Summer.* New York: Oxford University Press.

McBarnett, D.J. 1979. Arrest: The Legal Context of Policing. In *The British Police*, S. Holdaway (ed.), 24–40. London: Edward Arnold.

McBarnett, D. 1983. *Conviction.* 2nd edn. London: Macmillan.

McCabe, S. & F. Sutcliffe 1978. Defining Crime. Oxford University Centre for Criminological Research. Oxford Occasional Paper No. 9. Oxford: Blackwell.

McCabe, S., P. Wallington, J. with Alderson, L. Gostin, C. Mason 1988. *The Police, Public Order and Civil Liberties: Legacies of the Miners' Strike.* London: Routledge.

McCarthy, J.D., C. McPhail, J. Crist 1995. The Emergence and Diffusion of Public Order Management Systems: Protest Cycles and Police Responses. A Paper Presented at international workshop on "The Policing of Mass Demonstrations in Contemporary

Democracies", Robert Schuman Centre, European University Institute, San Domenico di Fiesole, Florence, 13–14 October.
McClure, J. 1980. *Spike Island.* London: Pan.
McCone, J.A. 1965. *Violence In The City – An End Or A Beginning? A Report By The Governor's Commission On The Los Angeles Riots.* Los Angeles, California.
McConville, M. & C. Mirsky 1992. The Skeleton of Plea Bargaining. *New Law Journal* (9 October), 1373–81.
McConville, M. & D. Shepherd 1992. *Watching Police, Watching Communities.* London: Routledge.
McConville, M., A. Sanders, R. Leng 1991. *The Case for the Prosecution.* London: Routledge. McConville, M. & D. Shepherd 1992. *Watching Police, Watching Communities.* London: Routledge.
McConville, M., J. Hodgson, L. Bridges, A. Pavlovic 1994. *Standing Accused: The Organisation and Practices of Criminal Defence Lawyers in Britain.* Oxford: Clarendon.
McCormack, R.J. 1996. Police Perceptions and the Norming of Institutional Corruption. *Policing and Society* **6** (3), 239–46.
McCorry, J. & M. Morrisey 1997. Community Crime and Punishment in West Belfast. *Howard Journal of Criminal Justice* **28** (4), 282–90.
McEachern, A.W. & R. Bauzer 1967. Factors Related to Disposition in Police-Juvenile Contacts. In *Juvenile Gangs in Context*, M.B. Klein & B.G. Meyerhoff (eds), 148–60. Englewood Cliffs, NJ: Prentice Hall.
McElree, F. & K. Starmer 1993. The Right to Silence. In *Justice in Error*, C. Walker & K. Starmer (eds), 58–72. London: Blackstone.
McKenzie, I. 1995. Violent Encounters: Force and Deadly Force in British Policing. In *Core Issues in Policing*, F. Leishman, B. Loveday, S.P. Savage (eds), 131–46. London: Longman.
McKenzie, I., R. Morgan, R. Reiner 1990. Helping the Police with Their Inquiries: The Necessity Principle and Voluntary Attendance at the Police Station. *Criminal Law Review*, 22–33.
McLaughlin, E. 1991. Police Accountability and Black People: Into the 1990s. In *Out of Order?*, E. Cashmore & E. McLaughlin (eds), 109–33. London: Routledge.
McLaughlin, E. 1994. *Community, Policing and Accountability.* Aldershot: Avebury.
McLaughlin, E. & K. Murji 1995. The End of Public Policing? Police Reform and 'the New Managerialism'. In *Issues in Contemporary Criminology*, L. Noaks, M. Levi, M. Maguire (eds), 110–27. Cardiff: University of Wales Press.
McLaughlin, E. & K. Murji 1996. Times Change: New Formations and Representations of Police Accountability. In *Policing Public Order: Theoretical and Practical Issues*, C. Critcher & D. Waddington (eds), 207–18. Aldershot: Avebury.
McMullen, J. 1985. Legal Strategy and the Unions. In *Policing the Miners' Strike*, B. Fine & R. Millar (eds), 217–26. London: Lawrence and Wishart.
McNab, A. 1993. *Bravo Two Zero.* London: Corgi.
McNamara, J.H. 1967. Uncertainties in Police Work: The Relevance of Police Recruits' Background and Training. In *The Police: Six Sociological Essays*, D. Bordua (ed.), 163–252. New York: Wiley.
McPhail, C., J. McCarthy, D. Schweingruber 1998. *Policing Protest in the United States: 1960–1995.* See della Porta and Reiter (1998), 46–69.
Meadus, D. 1990. Complaints in Australia. *Policing* **6** (3, Autumn), 550–58.
Medalia, N.Z. & O.N. Larsen 1958. Diffusion and Belief in a Collective Delusion: The Seattle Windshield Pitting Epidemic. *American Sociological Review* **23** (2, April), 180–86.
Menzies, I. 1960. A Case Study in the Functioning of Social Systems as a Defense Against Anxiety. *Human Relations* **13**, 95–121.

Merton, R.K. 1957. *Social Theory and Social Structure.* New York: Free Press.

Metcalfe, J. 1991. Public Order Debriefing: Trafalgar Square Riot. London: unpublished paper Metropolitan Police.

Metropolitan Police 1981. The Scarman Inquiry into the Brixton Disorders of April 1981, written submission by the Commissioner of Police of the Metropolis. Unpublished paper.

Metropolitan Police 1985. Report on the Brixton Disorders, 28/29 September 1985. Unpublished paper.

Meyer, M.W. 1982. Police Shootings at Minorities: The Case of Los Angeles. In *Readings on Police Use of Deadly Force*, J.J. Fyfe (ed.), 152–72. Washington, DC: Police Foundation.

Mhlanga, B. 1993. The Colour of English Justice: A Multivariate Analysis. Paper Presented at British Criminology Conference, University of Wales, Cardiff, 28–31 July.

Milgram, S. 1974. *Obedience to Authority.* London: Tavistock.

Miller, J. & L. Fry 1976. Reexamining Assumptions About Education and Professionalism in Law Enforcement. *Journal of Police Science and Administration* **4**, 187–98.

Miller, R. 1995. The Big Sleazy. *Sunday Times Magazine* (8 October), 20–27.

Miller, W.R. 1977a. *Cops and Bobbies: Police Authority in New York and London, 1830–1870.* Chicago: University of Chicago Press.

Miller, W.R. 1977b. Never on Sunday: Moralistic Reformers and the Police in London and New York City, 1830–1870. In *Police and Society*, D.H. Bayley (ed.), 127–48. Beverly Hills: Sage.

Mills, B. 1996a. Law and Order. *Police Review* (11 October), 25–27.

Mills, B., QC 1996b. It's Not Them and Us Any More. *Police* (October), 12–14.

Milne, S. 1994. MI5's Secret War. *New Statesman and Society* (25 November), 18–21.

Milton, C.H., J.W. Halleck, J. Lardner, G.L. Abrecht 1977. *Police Use of Deadly Force.* Washington, DC: Police Foundation.

Milton-Edwards, B. 1997. Policing Palestinian Society. *Policing and Society* **7** (1), 19–44.

Mirrlees-Black, C. 1995. Estimating the Extent of Domestic Violence: Findings from the 1992 BCS. In *Research Bulletin*, Home Office Research and Statistics Department (ed.), 1–9. London: Home Office Research and Planning Unit.

Mirrlees-Black, C., P. Mayhew, A. Percy 1996. *The 1996 British Crime Survey: England and Wales. Home Office Statistical Bulletin: 19/96.* London: Government Statistical Service.

Mischel, W. 1973. Toward a Cognitive Social Learning Reconceptualization of Personality. *Psychological Review* **80**, 252–83.

Mitchell, M. 1996. Police Coping With Death: Assumptions and Rhetoric. In *Contemporary Issues in the Sociology of Death, Dying and Disposal*, G. Howarth & P.C. Jupp (eds), 137–48. London: Macmillan.

Miyazawa, S. 1992. *Policing in Japan: A Study on Making Crime.* Translated by Frank G. Bennett, Jr with John O. Haley. Albany: State University of New York Press.

Mollen Commission 1994. *Report of the Commission to Investigate Allegations of Police Corruption and the Anti-Corruption Procedures of the Police Department.* New York: New York City.

Monjardet, D. 1995. The French Model of Policing. In *Comparisons in Policing: An International Perspective*, J.-P. Brodeur (ed.), 49–68. Aldershot: Avebury.

Moody, S. & J. Tombs 1982. *Prosecution in the Public Interest.* Edinburgh: Scottish Academic Press.

Moore, C. & J. Brown 1981. *Community Versus Crime.* London: Bedford Square Press.

Moore, M.H. 1980. The Police and Weapon Offences. *Annals of the American Academy of Political and Social Science* **452** (November), 22–32.

Morgan, D. 1997. Parents in Law. *Police Review* (7 February), 30–1.

Morgan, D. & G. Stephenson (eds) 1994. *Suspicion and Silence.* London: Blackstone.

Morgan, J. 1987. *Conflict and Order: The Police and Labour Disputes in England and Wales 1900–1939.* Oxford: Clarendon.

Morgan, R. 1987. The Local Determinants of Policing Policy. In *Policing and the Community*, P. Willmott (ed.), 29–53. London: Policy Studies Institute.

Morgan, R. 1989. "Policing By Consent": Legitimating the Doctrine. In *Coming to Terms with Policing*, R. Morgan & D.J. Smith (eds), 217–34. London: Routledge.

Morgan, R. & C. Maggs 1985. *Setting the PACE: Police Community Consultation Arrangements in England and Wales. Bath Social Policy Papers: No. 4.* Bath: Centre for the Analysis of Social Policy, School of Humanities and Social Sciences, University of Bath.

Morgan, R. & T. Newburn 1997. *The Future of Policing.* Oxford: Clarendon.

Morris, P. & K. Heal 1981. *Crime Control and the Police: A Review of Research. Home Office Research Study, No. 67.* London: Home Office.

Morrison, W.R. 1975. The North-West Mounted Police and the Klondike Gold Rush. In *Police Forces in History. Readers in 20th Century History*, vol. 2. G.L. Mosse (ed.), 263–75. Beverly Hills: Sage.

Morrison, W.R. 1991. Imposing the British Way: The Canadian Mounted Police and the Klondike Gold Rush. In *Policing the Empire: Government, Authority and Control, 1830–1940*, D.M. Anderson & D. Killingray (eds), 92–104. Manchester: Manchester University Press.

Moston, S. & T. Williamson 1990. The Extent of Silence in Police Stations. In *The Right to Silence Debate: Proceedings of a Conference at the University of Bristol in March 1990*, S. Greer & R. Morgan (eds), 36–43. Bristol: University of Bristol.

Moxon, D. & P. Jones 1984. Public Reactions to Police Behaviour: Some Findings from the British Crime Survey. *Policing* **1** (1), 49–56.

Muir, W.K. 1977. *Police: Streetcorner Politicians.* Chicago: Chicago University Press.

Muir, W.K., Jnr. 1980. Power Attracts Violence. *Annals of the American Academy of Political and Social Science* **452** (November), 48–52.

Murdock, G. 1984. Reporting the Riots: Images and Impact. In *Scarman and After*, J. Benyon (ed.), 73–95. London: Pergamon.

Murray, C. 1990. *The Emerging British Underclass.* London: Institute for Economic Affairs.

Murray, C. 1994. *Underclass: The Crisis Deepens.* London: Institute for Economic Affairs.

Nathan, L. 1989. Troops in the Townships 1984–1987. In *War and Society*, J. Cock & L. Nathan (eds), 67–78. Cape Town: David Philip.

National Council for Civil Liberties 1984. *Civil Liberties and the Miners' Dispute: First Report of the Independent Inquiry.* London: National Council for Civil Liberties.

National Council for Civil Liberties 1986. *Stonehenge: A Report into the Civil Liberties Implications of the Events Relation to the Convoys of Summere 1985 and 1986.* London: National Council of Civil Liberties.

National Council for Civil Liberties 1987. *No Way in Wapping.* London: National Council for Civil Liberties.

Nelken, D. 1994. White-Collar Crime. In *The Oxford Handbook of Criminology*, M. Maguire, R. Morgan, R. Reiner (eds), 355–92. Oxford: Clarendon.

Neville, M. & J. Brown 1996. Fair Cops. *Police Review* (31 May), 20–21.

New Law Journal 1992. Is It a Bargain? (19 June), 849.

New Law Journal 1993. The Debate Continues (4 June), 801.

Newman, D.J. 1956. Pleading Guilty for Considerations: A Study in Bargain Justice. *Journal of Criminal Law, Criminology and Police Science* **46**, 780–90.

Newman, Sir K. 1984. *Policing By Consent (James Smart Lecture).* Glasgow: Strathclyde Police.

Niederhoffer, A. 1967. *Behind the Shield: The Police in Urban Society.* Garden City: Doubleday.

Noaks, L. & S. Christopher 1990. Why Police are Assaulted. *Policing* **6** (4, Winter), 625–38.

Nordholt, E. & R. Straver 1983. The Changing Police. In *Control in the Police Organization*, M. Punch (ed.), 36–46. Cambridge, Mass.: MIT. Press.

Norris, C. 1989. Avoiding Trouble: The Patrol Officer's Perception of Encounters with the Public. In *Police Research: Some Future Prospects*, M. Weatheritt (ed.), 89–106. Aldershot: Avebury.

Norris, C. 1993. Some Ethical Considerations on Field-work with the Police. In *Interpreting the Field*, D. Hobbs & T. May (eds), 122–44. Oxford: Clarendon.

Norris, C., N. Fielding, C. Kemp, J. Fielding 1992. Black and Blue: An Analysis of the Influence of Race on Being Stopped By the Police. *British Journal of Sociology* **43** (2, June), 207–24.

Norris, D.F. 1973. *Police–Community Relations: A Program that Failed.* Lexington, Mass.: D.C. Heath.

North, D.P. 1997. *Report of the Independent Review of Parades and Marches.* Belfast: The Stationery Office.

Northam, G. 1985. A Fair Degree of Force. *The Listener* **114** (2933, 31 Oct), 3.

Northam, G. 1988. *Shooting in the Dark.* London: Faber and Faber.

O'Connor, I. 1994. Young People and Their Rights. In *The Police and Young People in Australia*, R. White & C. Alder (eds), 76–101. Cambridge: Cambridge University Press.

Ogletree, C.J., M. Prosser, A. Smith, W. Talley Jr. 1995. *Beyond the Rodney King Story: An Investigation of Police Conduct in Minority Communities.* For the National Association for the Advancement of Colored People. Boston: Northeaster University Press.

Okojie, P. 1985. Chief Constables and Police Interference: The Case of Anderton and Greater Manchester. In *Policing the Miners' Strike*, B. Fine & R. Millar (eds), 54–64. London: Lawrence and Wishart.

Oxford, K. 1984. Policing By Consent. In *Scarman and After*, J. Benyon (ed.), 114–24. London: Pergamon.

Oxford, K.G. 1981. *Public Disorder on Merseyside, July–August 1981: Report of the Chief Constable to the Merseyside Police Committee.* Liverpool: Merseyside Police.

Packer, H. 1968. *The Limits of the Criminal Sanction.* Stanford: Stanford University Press.

Palmer, S.H. 1988. *Police and Protest in England and Ireland, 1780–1850.* Cambridge: Cambridge University Press.

Panayi, P. 1993a. Anti-Immigrant Riots in Nineteenth- and Twentieth-century Britain. In *Racial Violence in Britain, 1840–1950*, P. Panayi (ed.), 1–25. Leicester: Leicester University Press.

Panayi, P. (ed.) 1993b. *Racial Violence in Britain, 1840–1950.* Leicester: Leicester University Press.

Parenti, M. 1988. *Democracy for the Few*, 5th edn. New York: St Martin's.

Parnas, R.I. 1967. The Police Response to Domestic Disturbances. *Wisconsin Law Review* (Fall), 914–60.

Parnas, R.I. 1970. Judicial Response to Intra-Family Violence. *Minnesota Law Review* **54** (January), 585–644.

Parry, G., G. Moyser, M. Wagstaffe 1987. The Crowd and the Community: Context, Content and Aftermath. In *The Crowd in Contemporary Britain*, G. Gaskell & R. Benewick (eds), 212–55. London: Sage.

Pate, A.M. & P. Shtull 1994. Community Policing Grows in Brooklyn – An Inside View of the New York City Police Departments Model Precinct. *Crime and Delinquency* **40** (3, July), 384–410.

Pate, A.M., M.A. Wycoff, W.G. Skogan, L.W. Sherman 1986. *Reducing Fear of Crime in Houston and Newark: A Summary Report.* Washington, DC: Police Foundation.

Pate, T., R.A. Bowers, R. Parks 1976. *Three Approaches to Criminal Apprehension in Kansas City: An Evaluation.* Washington, DC: Police Foundation.

Pater, M.E. 1996. Expert Opinion? *Police Review* (31 May), 26–27.

Patterson, W.E. 1991. Police Accountability and Civilian Oversight of Policing: An American Perspective. In *Complaints Against the Police*, A.J. Goldsmith (ed.), 259–90. Oxford: Clarendon.

Peach, S.L. 1995. We're Far from Being Witch-Hunter Generals. *Police Review* (11 August), 12.

Pearson, G. 1975. *The Deviant Imagination.* London: Macmillan.

Pearson, G. 1983. *Hooligan: A History of Respectable Fears.* London: Macmillan.

Pepinsky, D.M. 1971. Informal Norms and Police Practice: The Traffic Ticket Quota System. *Sociology and Social Research* **55** (April), 354–62.

Pepinsky, H.E. 1984. Better Living Through Police Discretion. *Law and Contemporary Problems* **47** (4, Autumn), 249–67.

Perez, D.W. & W.K. Muir 1996. Administrative Review of Alleged Police Brutality. In *Police Violence: Understanding and Controlling Police Abuse of Force*, W.A. Geller & H. Toch (eds), 213–33. New Haven, Conn.: Yale University Press.

Petersilia, J., A. Abrahamse, J.Q. Wilson 1990. The Relationship Between Police Practice, Community Characteristics, and Case Attrition. *Policing and Society* **1** (1), 23–38.

Phillips, S. & R. Cochrane 1986. The Police Schools Liaison Programme. *Policing* **2** (1, Spring), 68–82.

Phillips, S.V. & R. Cochrane 1988. *The Role and Function of Police Community Liaison Officers. Research and Planning Unit Papers: No. 51.* London: Home Office.

Piliavin, I. & S. Briar 1964. Police Encounters with Juveniles. *American Journal of Sociology* **70**, 206–14.

Pistone, J.D. & R. Woodley 1988. *Donnie Brasco: My Undercover Life in the Mafia.* London: Pan.

Police Monitoring and Research Group 1987a. *Police Response to Domestic Violence. Briefing Paper: No. 1.* London: London Strategic Policy Unit.

Police Monitoring and Research Group 1987b. *Policing Wapping: An Account of the Dispute 1986/7. Briefing Paper: No. 3.* London: London Strategic Policy Unit.

Pope, C.E. 1978. Post-arrest Release Decisions: An Empirical Examination of Social and Legal Criteria. *Journal of Research in Crime and Delinquency* **15** (January), 35–53.

Porter, S. 1996. Contra-Foucault: Soldiers, Nurses and Power. *Sociology* **30** (1, February), 59–78.

Potter, K. 1995. Law and Order Restored. *Police Review* (17 March), 20–21.

Potter, K. 1996. Meltdown at the AEAC. *Police Review* (24 May), 22–24.

Power, A. & R. Tunstall 1997. *Dangerous Disorder: Riots and Violent Disturbances in Thirteen Areas of Britain, 1991–92.* York: Joseph Rowntree Foundation.

Pratt, M. 1980. *Mugging As a Social Problem.* London: Routledge.

President's Commission on Law Enforcement and Administration of Justice 1967. *Task Force Report: "The Police".* Washington DC: US Government Printing Office.

Prior, A. 1989. The South African Police and the Counter-Revolution of 1985–1987. In *Acta Juridica.* W. Scharf (ed.), 189–205. Cape Town: Faculty of Law, University of Cape Town.

Pulle, S. 1973. *Police–Immigrant Relations in Ealing: Report of an Investigation Conducted on Behalf of the Ealing CRC.* London: Runnymede Trust.

Punch, M. 1979a. *Policing the Inner City.* London: Macmillan.

Punch, M. 1979b. The Secret Social Service. In *The British Police*, S. Holdaway (ed.), 102–17. London: Edward Arnold.

Punch, M. 1983. Officers and Men: Occupational Culture, Inter-rank Antagonism, and the Investigation of Corruption. In *Control in the Police Organization*, M. Punch (ed.), 227–50. Cambridge, Mass.: MIT Press.

Punch, M. 1985. *Conduct Unbecoming: The Social Construction of Police Deviance and Control.* London: Tavistock.

Punch, M. & T. Naylor 1973. The Police: A Social Service. *New Society* **24** (554), 358–61.

Quah, S.R. & J.S. Quah 1987. *Friends in Blue: The Police and the Public in Singapore.* Oxford: Oxford University Press.

Radford, J. 1978. Policing Male Violence – Policing Women. In *Women, Male Violence and Social Control*, J. Hanmer & M. Maynard (eds), 30–45. London: Macmillan.

Radford, L. 1978. Legalising Women Abuse. In *Women, Male Violence and Social Control*, J. Hanmer & M. Maynard (eds), 135–51. London: Macmillan.

Rafky, D.M. 1973. Police Race Attitudes and Labelling. *Journal of Police Science and Administration* **1** (1), 65–86.

Rainwater, L. 1967. Open Letter on White Justice and the Riots. *Transaction* (September).

Rawlings, P. 1985. "Bobbies", "Aliens" and Subversives: The Relationship Between Community Policing and Coercive Policing. In *Police: The Constitution and the Community*, J. Baxter & L. Koffman (eds), 72–90. Abingdon, Oxon: Professional Books.

Read, S. 1997. Below Zero. *Police Review* (17 January), 16–17.

Reed, D. & O. Adamson 1985. *Miners Strike 1984–1985: People Versus State.* London: Larkin Publications.

Regan, D. 1983a. *Are the Police Under Control? Research Reports: 1.* London: Social Affairs Unit.

Regan, D. 1983b. Enhancing the Role of Police Committees. *Public Administration* 61 (1).

Reicher, S.D. 1984. The St Paul's Riot: An Explanation of the Limits of Crowd Action in Terms of a Social Identity Model. *European Journal of Social Psychology* **14**, 1–21.

Reiner, R. 1978a. *The Blue-Coated Worker.* London: Cambridge University Press.

Reiner, R. 1978b. Scarborough Fair Cop. *Police Journal* **78** (1).

Reiner, R. 1980. Fuzzy Thoughts: The Police and Law-and-Order Politics. *Sociological Review* **28**, 377–413.

Reiner, R. 1985a. *Politics of the Police.* London: Wheatsheaf.

Reiner, R. 1985b. Police and Race Relations. In *Police: The Constitution and the Community*, J. Baxter & L. Koffman (eds), 149–87. Abingdon, Oxon: Professional Books.

Reiner, R. 1985c. Retrospect on the Riots. *New Society* (25 October).

Reiner, R. 1985d. Sauce for the Cops. *New Society* (26 Jul), 126.

Reiner, R. 1989a. The Politics of Police Research in Britain. In *Police Research: Some Future Prospects*, M. Weatheritt (ed.), 3–20. Aldershot: Avebury.

Reiner, R. 1989b. Thinking at the Top. *Policing* **5** (2, Summer), 181–99.

Reiner, R. 1989c. Where the Buck Stops: Chief Constable's Views on Police Accountability. In *Coming to Terms with Policing*, R. Morgan & D.J. Smith (eds), 195–216. London: Routledge.

Reiner, R. 1991a. *Chief Constables.* Oxford: Oxford University Press.

Reiner, R. 1991b. Multiple Realities, Divided Worlds: Chief Constables' Perspectives on the Police Complaints System. In *Complaints Against the Police*, A.J. Goldsmith (ed.), 211–32. Oxford: Clarendon.

Reiner, R. 1992. *Politics of the Police*, 2nd edn. London: Wheatsheaf.

Reiner, R. 1993a. Police Accountability: Principles, Patterns and Practices. In *Accountable Policing: Effectiveness, Empowerment and Equity*, R. Reiner & S. Spencer (eds), 1–24. London: Institute for Public Policy Research.

Reiner, R. 1993b. Accountability and Effectiveness. In *Reforming British Policing Missions and Structures*, R. Dingwall & J. Shapland (eds), 33–50. Sheffield: Faculty of Law, University of Sheffield.

Reiner, R. 1995. From Sacred to Profane: The Thirty Years' War of the British Police. *Policing and Society* **5** (2), 121–28.

Reiss, A.J. 1968. Police Brutality – Answers to Key Questions. *Transaction* **5**, 10–19.

Reiss, A.J. 1971. *The Police and the Public.* New Haven, Conn.: Yale University Press.

Reiss, A.J. 1980. Controlling Police Use of Deadly Force. *Annals of the American Academy of Political and Social Science* **452** (November), 122–34.

Reiss, A.J. 1983. The Policing of Organizational Life. In *Control in the Police Organization*, M. Punch (ed.), 78–97. Cambridge, Mass.: MIT Press.

Reiss, A.J. 1984. Consequences of Compliance and Deterrence Models of Law Enforcement for the Exercise of Police Discretion. *Journal of Law and Contemporary Social Problems* **47** (4), 83–122.

Reiss, A.J., Jr. 1987. The Legitimacy of Intrusion into Private Space. In *Private Policing. Sage Criminal Justice System Annuals*, vol. 23, C.D. Shearing & P.C. Stenning (eds), 19–44. Newbury Park, California: Sage.

Reiss, A.J. & D.J. Bordua 1967. Environment and Organisation: A Perspective on the Police. In *The Police: Six Sociological Essays*, D.J. Bordua (ed.), 25–55. New York: Wiley.

Report of the Working Group on the Right to Silence 1989. London: Home Office.

Reuss-Ianni, E. 1983. *Two Cultures of Policing: Street Cops and Management Cops.* London: Transaction Books.

Reuss-Ianni, E. & F.A. Ianni 1983. Street Cops and Management Cops: The Two Cultures of Policing. In *Control in the Police Organization*, M. Punch (ed.), 251–74. Cambridge, Mass.: MIT Press.

Rex, J. 1982. West Indian and Asian Youth. In *Black Youth in Crisis*, E. Cashmore & B. Troyna (eds), 53–71. London: Allen and Unwin.

Reynolds, G.W. & A. Judge 1969. *The Night the Police Went on Strike.* London: Weidenfeld.

Richards, M.D. 1986. *Public Disorder in Tottenham, 6th October 1985.* London: Metropolitan Police.

Richards, N. 1985. A Plea for Applied Ethics. In *Contemporary Policing*, J.R. Thackrah (ed.), 13–32. London: Sphere Reference.

Richards, N. 1992. A Question of Loyalty. *Criminal Justice Ethics*, 48–56.

Roach, J. 1985. The French Police. In *Police and Public Order in Europe*, J. Roach & J. Thomaneck (eds), 107–42. London: Croom Helm.

Roach, J. & J. Thomaneck (eds) 1985. *Police and Public Order in Europe.* London: Croom Helm.

Roberg, R.R. 1978. An Analysis of the Relationships Among Higher Education, Belief Systems, and Job Performance of Patrol Officers. *Journal Police Science and Administration* **6**, 336–44.

Robertson, G. 1989. *Freedom, The Individual and the Law.* London: Penguin.

Robinson, C.D. 1975. The Mayor and the Police – The Political Role of the Police in Society. In *Police Forces in History. Reading in 20th Century History*, vol. 2, G.L. Mosse (ed.), 277–315. Beverly Hills: Sage.

Rock, P. 1995a. Sociology and the Stereotype of the Police. *Journal of Law and Society* **22** (1, March), 17–25.

Rock, P. 1995b. The Opening Stages of Criminal Justice Policy Making. *British Journal of Criminology* **35** (1, Winter), 1–16.

Rogaly, J. 1977. *Grunwick.* Harmondsworth, Middx.: Penguin.

Rokeach, M. 1960. *The Open and Closed Mind.* New York: Basic Books.

Rollo, J. 1980. The Special Patrol Group. In *Policing the Police*, vol. 2, P. Hain (ed.), 153–208. London: Calder.

Rose, D. 1992. *A Climate of Fear: The Murder of PC Blakelock and the Case of the Tottenham Three.* London: Bloomsbury.

Rosenbaum, D.P. (ed.) 1994. *The Challenge of Community Policing: Testing the Promise.* Thousand Oaks: Sage.

Rosenbaum, D.P., S. Yeh, D.L. Wilkinson 1994. Impact of Community Policing on Police Personnel – A Quasi-Experimental Test. *Crime and Delinquency* **40** (3, July), 331–53.

Roseneil, S. 1995. *Disarming Patriarchy: Feminism and Political Action at Greenham.* Milton Keynes: Open University.

Rosenhead, J. 1981. The Technology of Riot Control. *New Scientist* **91**, 210.

Rosenhead, J. 1985. Plastic Bullets – A Reasonable Force? *New Scientist* (17 Oct), 26–7.

Rubenstein, J. 1973. *City Police.* New York: Farrar, Strauss and Giroux.

Rudovsky, D. 1982. The Criminal Justice System and the Role of the Police. In *The Politics of Law*, D. Kairy (ed.), 242–52. New York: Pantheon.

Russell, K. 1976. *Complaints Against the Police: A Sociological View.* Leicester: Milltak.

Russell, K. 1986. *Complaints Against the Police Which Are Withdrawn.* Leicester: Leicester Polytechnic.

Ryan, M. 1996. *Lobbying from Below: Inquest in Defence of Civil Liberties.* London: UCL.

Ryder, C. 1989. *The RUC: A Force Under Fire.* London: Methuen.

Sadd, S. & R. Grinc 1994. Innovative Neighborhood Oriented Policing: An Evaluation of Community Policing Programs in Eight Cities. In *The Challenge of Community Policing: Testing the Promises*, D.P. Rosenbaum (ed.), 27–52. Thousand Oaks: Sage.

Sanders, A. 1988. Personal Violence and Public Order: The Prosecution of "Domestic" Violence in England and Wales. *International Journal of the Sociology of Law* **16**, 359–82.

Sanders, A. & L. Bridges 1993. The Right to Legal Advice. In *Justice in Error*, C. Walker & K. Starmer (eds), 37–54. London: Blackstone.

Sanders, A., L. Bridges, A. Mulvaney, G. Crozier 1989. *Advice and Assistance at Police Stations and the 24 Hour Duty Solicitor Scheme.* London: Lord Chancellor's Department.

Saunders, K. & H. Taylor 1987. The Impact of Total War Upon Policing: The Queensland Experience. In *Policing in Australia: Historical Perspectives*, M. Finnane (ed.), 143–69. Kensington, NSW: New South Wales University Press.

Savage, S.P. & S. Charman 1995. Managing Change. In *Core Issues in Policing*, F. Leishman, B. Loveday, S.P. Savage (eds), 39–53. London: Longman.

Scarman, J. *et al.* 1972. *Report of the Tribunal of Inquiry on the Violence and Civil Disturbances in Northern Ireland in 1969.* Government of Northern Ireland.

Scarman, The Rt Hon. The Lord 1975. *The Red Lion Square Disorders of 15 June 1974.* London: HMSO.

Scarman, The Rt Hon. The Lord 1981. *The Brixton Disorders 10–12 April 1981: Report of An Inquiry by the Rt Hon. The Lord Scarman, OBE* Cmnd 8427 ed. London: HMSO.

Schaffer, E. 1980. *Community Policing.* London: Croom Helm.

Scharf, W. 1989. Community Policing in South Africa. In *Acta Juridica*. W. Scharf (ed.), 206–33. Cape Town: Juta.

Schlesinger, P. & H. Tumber 1993. Fighting the War Against Crime – Television, Police, and Audience. *British Journal of Criminology* **33** (1), 19–32.

Schlesinger, P. & H. Tumber 1994. *Reporting Crime: The Media Politics of Criminal Justice.* Oxford: Clarendon.

Scott, E.J. & S.L. Percy 1983. Gatekeeping Police Services: Police Operators and Dispatchers. In *Police at Work. Perspectives in Criminal Justice*, No. 5, R.R. Bennett (ed.), 127–44. Beverly Hills: Sage.

Scraton, P. 1982. Policing and Institutionalised Racism on Merseyside. In *Policing the Riots*, D. Cowell, T. Jones, J. Young (eds), 21–38. London: Junction Books.

Scraton, P. 1984. The Coroner's Tale: The Death of Jimmy Kelly. In *Causes for Concern: Questions of Law and Justice*, P. Scraton & P. Gordon (eds), 43–66. Harmondsworth, Middlesex: Penguin.

Scraton, P. 1985. *The State of the Police*. London: Pluto Press.

Scraton, P. 1987a. Unreasonable Force: Policing, Punishment and Marginalization. In *Law, Order and the Authoritarian State*, P. Scraton (ed.), 145–89. Milton Keynes: Open University.

Scraton, P. (ed.) 1987b. *Law, Order and the Authoritarian State*. Milton Keynes: Open University.

Scraton, P. & K. Chadwick 1987. "Speaking Ill of the Dead": Institutionalized Responses to Deaths in Custody. In *Law, Order and the Authoritarian State*, P. Scraton (ed.), 212–37. Milton Keynes: Open University.

Scripture, A.E. 1997. The Source of Police Culture: Demographic or Environmental Variables. *Policing and Society* **7** (3), 163–76.

Seagrave, J. 1996. Community Policing: The Views of Police Executives in British Columbia. *Policing and Society* **6** (2), 163–80.

Seegers, A. 1991. One State, Three Faces: Policing in South Africa (1910–1990). *Social Dynamics* **17** (1), 36–48.

Shannon, L.W. 1963. Types and Patterns of Delinquency Referral in a Middle-Sized City. *British Journal of Criminology* **3**, 24–36.

Shapland, J. & D. Hobbs 1989. Policing Priorities on the Ground. In *Coming to Terms with Policing*, R. Morgan & D.J. Smith (eds), 11–30. London: Routledge.

Shapland, J. & J. Vagg 1987a. Policing by the Public and Policing by the Police. In *Policing and the Community*, P. Willmott (ed.), 21–28. London: Policy Studies Institute.

Shapland, J. & J. Vagg 1987b. Using the Police. *British Journal of Criminology* **27** (1, Winter), 54–63.

Shapland, J. & J. Vagg 1988. *Policing by the Public*. London: Routledge.

Sharpe, A.N. 1995. Police Performance Crime as Structurally Coerced Action. *Policing and Society* **5** (4), 201–20.

Shaw, M. & W. Williamson 1972. Public Attitudes to the Police. *The Criminologist* **7** (26, Autumn), 18–33.

Shearing, C. 1974. Dial-a-Cop: A Study of Police Mobilizations. In *Crime Prevention and Social Control*, R. Aker & E. Sagarin (eds). New York: Praeger.

Shearing, C. 1981a. Deviance and Conformity in the Reproduction of Order. In *Organisational Police Deviance*, C. Shearing (ed.), 29–48. Toronto: Butterworths.

Shearing, C. (ed.) 1981b. *Organisational Police Deviance*. Toronto: Butterworths.

Shearing, C.D. 1984. *Dial a Cop*. University of Toronto: Centre of Criminology.

Shearing, C.D. & R.V. Ericson 1991. Culture as Figurative Action. *British Journal of Sociology* **42** (4), 481–506.

Shearing, C.D. & P.C. Stenning 1981. Modern Private Security: Its Growth and Implications. In *Crime and Justice: An Annual Review of Research*, vol. 3, M. Tonry & N. Morris (eds), 193–245. Chicago: University of Chicago.

Shearing, C.D. & P.C. Stenning 1982. "Snowflakes" or Good Pinches? – Private Security's Contribution to Modern Policing. In *Maintenance of Order in Society*, R. Donelan (ed.), 96–105. Ottowa: Canadian Police College.

Shearing, C.D. & P.C. Stenning (eds) 1987a. *Private Policing. Sage Criminal Justice System Annuals: Vol. 23*. Newbury Park, California: Sage.

Shearing, C.D. & P.C. Stenning 1987b. Reframing Policing. In *Private Policing. Sage Criminal Justice System Annuals*. Vol. 23, C.D. Shearing & P.C. Stenning (eds), 9–18. Newbury Park, California: Sage.

Shelley, L.I. 1990. The Soviet Militsiia: Agents of Political and Social Control. *Policing and Society* **1** (1), 23–58.

Shelley, L.I. 1996. Policing Soviet Society. The Evolution of State Control. New York: Routledge.

Sheehy, Sir Patrick 1993. *Inquiry into Police Responsibilities and Rewards. Vol. 1*. London: HMSO.

Sheptycki, J.W.E. 1993. *Innovtions in Policing Domestic Violence*. Aldershot, Hants.: Avebury.

Sherman, L.W. 1975. An Evaluation of Policewomen on Patrol in a Suburban Police Department. *Journal of Police Science & Administration* **3**, 434–8.

Sherman, L.W. 1978. *Scandal and Reform: Controlling Police Corruption*. Berkeley, Cal.: Univ. of California Press.

Sherman, L.W. 1980a. Causes of Police Behaviour: The Current State of Quantitative Research. *Journal of Research in Crime and Delinquency* **17** (January), 69–99.

Sherman, L.W. 1980b. Perspectives on Police and Violence. *Annals of the American Academy of Political and Social Science* **452** (November), 1–12.

Sherman, L.W. 1983a. After the Riots: Police and Minorities in the United States, 1970–1980. In *Ethnic Pluralism and Public Policy*, N. Glazer & K. Young (eds), 212–35. Lexington, Mass.: D.C. Heath.

Sherman, L.W. 1983b. Reducing Police Gun Use: Critical Events, Administrative Policy, and Organizational Change. In *Control in the Police Organization*, M. Punch (ed.), 98–125. Cambridge, Mass.: MIT Press.

Sherman, L.W. 1984. Experiments in Police Discretion: Scientific Boon or Dangerous Knowledge. *Journal of Law and Contemporary Social Problems* **47** (4), 61–81.

Sherman, L. 1986. Policing Communities: What Works? In *Crime and Justice: a Review of Research*, Communities and Crime, vol. 8, A. Reiss & M. Tonry (eds), 343–86. Chicago: Chicago University Press.

Sherman, L. 1990. Police Crackdowns: Initial and Residual Deterrence. In *Crime and Justice: A Biannual Review of Research*, vol. 12, M. Tonry & N. Morris (eds), 1–48. Chicago: Chicago University Press.

Sherman, L. 1992a. Attacking Crime: Policing and Crime Control. In *Modern Policing. Crime and Justice. A Review of Research*, vol. 15, M. Tonry & N. Morris (eds), 159–230. Chicago: University of Chicago Press.

Sherman, L. 1992b. *Policing Domestic Violence: Experiments and Dilemmas*. New York: Free Press.

Sherman, L.W. 1993. Police in the Laboratory of Criminal Justice. In *Critical Issues in Policing: Contemporary Readings*, 2nd edn, R.G. Dunham & G.P. Alpert (eds), 72–94. Prospect Heights, Illinois: Waveland.

Sherman, L. & R. Berk 1984. The Specific Deterrent Effects of Arrest for Domestic Assault. *American Sociological Review* **49** (April).

Sherman, L.W., J.D. Schmidt, D.P. Rogan, D.A. Smith, P.R. Gartin, E.G. Cohn, D.J. Collins, A.R. Bacich 1992. The Variable Effects of Arrest on Criminal Careers – the Milwaukee Domestic Violence Experiment. *Journal Criminal Law and Criminology* **83** (1), 137–69.

Sherr, A. 1989. *Freedom of Protest, Public Order and the Law*. Oxford: Blackwell.

Sherr, A. 1993. The Policing of Mass Demonstrations and Riot Control: The View from Great Britain. In *Policing the Conflict in South Africa*, M.L. Mathews, P.B. Heymann, A.S. Mathews (eds), 161–83. Gainesville: University Press of Florida.

Short, B. 1991. Earth First! and the Rhetoric of Moral Confrontation. *Communication Studies* **42** (2, Summer), 172–88.

Short, M. 1992. *Lundy*. London: Grafton.

Silver, A. 1967. The Demand for Order in Civil Society: A Review of Some Themes in the History of Urban Crime, Police and Riot. In *The Police: Six Sociological Essays*, D. Bordua (ed.). New York: Wiley.

Silverman, J. 1986. *Independent Inquiry into the Handsworth Disturbances, September 1985*. Birmingham: City of Birmingham District Council.

Simpson, I.H. 1967. Patterns of Socialization into Professions: The Case of the Student Nurse. *Sociological Inquiry* **37**, 47–54.

Skogan, W.G. 1984. Reporting Crimes to the Police: The Status of World Research. *Journal of Research in Crime and Delinquency* **21** (2, May), 113–38.

Skogan, W.G. 1990. *Disorder and Decline*. New York: Free Press.

Skogan, W.G. 1994a. *Contacts Between Police and Public: Findings from the 1992 British Crime Survey. Home Office Research Study: No. 134*. London: HMSO.

Skogan, W.G. 1994b. The Impact of Community Policing on Neighborhood Residents: A Cross-site Analysis. In *The Challenge of Community Policing: Testing the Promises*, D.P. Rosenbaum (ed.), 167–81. Thousand Oaks: Sage.

Skogan, W.G. & M.A. Wycoff 1987. Some Unexpected Effects of a Police Service for Victims. *Crime and Delinquency* **33** (4, Oct), 490–501.

Skogan, W., S.F. Bennett, S. Nartnett, P.J. Lavrakas, J. DuBois, A. Lurigio, J. Lovig, R. Block, L. Higgins, D. Rosenbaum, G. Dantzker 1994. Community Policing in Chicago, Year One: An Interim Report. Prepared by The Chicago Community Policing Evaluation Consortium, Illinois Criminal Justic Information Authority.

Skolnick, J.H. 1966. *Justice Without Trial*. New York: Wiley.

Skolnick, J.H. 1969. *The Politics of Protest: A Task Force Report to the National Commission on the Causes and Prevention of Violence*. New York: Simon and Schuster.

Skolnick, J.H. & D.H. Bayley 1986. *The New Blue Line: Police Innovation in Six American Cities*. New York: Free Press.

Skolnick, J.H. & J.J. Fyfe 1993. *Above the Law: Police and the Excessive Use of Force*. New York: Free Press.

Small, S. 1983. *A Group of Young Black People. Police and People in London: vol. 2*. London: Policy Studies Institute.

Smelser, N.J. 1962. *Theory of Collective Behaviour*. London: Routledge and Kegan Paul.

Smith, A.T.H. 1982. Breaching the Peace and Disturbing the Public Quiet. *Public Law* (Summer).

Smith, A.T.H. 1987. *Offences Against Public Order*. London: Sweet and Maxwell.

Smith, D. 1987. The Police and the Idea of Community. In *Policing and the Community*, P. Willmott (ed.), 54–67. London: Policy Studies Institute.

Smith, D.J. 1983a. *A Survey of Londoners. Police and People in London: vol. 1*. London: Policy Studies Institute.

Smith, D.J. 1983b. *A Survey of Police Officers. Police and People in London: vol. 3*. London: Policy Studies Institute.

Smith, D.J. 1986. The Framework of Law and Policing Practice. In *The Police: Powers, Procedures and Proprieties*, J. Benyon (ed.), 85–94. Oxford: Pergamon.

Smith, D.J. 1989. Evaluating Police Work. *Policing* **5** (4, Winter), 254–64.

Smith, D.J. 1994. Race, Crime, and Criminal Justice. In *The Oxford Handbook of Criminology*, M. Maguire, R. Morgan, R. Reiner (eds), 1041–119. Oxford: Clarendon.

Smith, D.J. 1997. Case Construction and the Goals of Criminal Process. *British Journal of Criminology* **37** (3, Summer), 319–46.

Smith, D.J. & J. Gray 1983. *The Police in Action. Police and People in London: vol. 4*. London: Policy Studies Institute.

Smith, D., C.A. Visher, L.A. Davidson 1984. Equity and Discretionary Justice: The Influence of Race on Police Arrest Decisions. *Journal Criminal Law and Criminology* **75** (1, Spring), 234–49.

Smith, L.J.F. 1989. *Domestic Violence: an Overview of the Literature. Home Office Research Study: No. 107.* London: HMSO.

Solomos, J. (ed.) 1993. *Race and Racism in Britain*, 2nd edn. London: Macmillan.

Solomos, J. & T. Rackett 1991. Policing and Urban Unrest: Problem Constitution and Policy Response. In *Out of Order?*, E. Cashmore & E. McLaughlin (eds), 42–64. London: Routledge.

South, N. 1987. Law, Profit, and "Private Persons": Private and Public Policing in English History. In *Private Policing. Sage Criminal Justice System Annuals*, vol. 23, C.D. Shearing & P.C. Stenning (eds), 72–109. Newbury Park, California: Sage.

South, N. 1988. *Policing for Profit: The Private Security Sector.* London: Sage.

South, N. 1989. Reconstructing Policing: Differentiation and Contradiction in Post-War Private and Public Policing. In *Privatizing Criminal Justice*, R. Matthews (ed.), 76–104. London: Sage.

Southgate, P. 1985. Police Output Measures: Past Work and Future Possibilities. In *Policing Today*, K. Heal, R. Tarling, J. Burrows (eds), 30–41. London: HMSO.

Southgate, P. & D. Crisp 1993. *Public Satisfaction with Police Services. Research and Planning Unit Papers: No. 72.* London: HMSO.

Southgate, P. & P. Ekblom 1984. *Contacts Between Police and Public: Findings From the British Crime Survey. Home Office Research Study, No. 77.* London: HMSO.

Southgate, P. & P. Ekblom 1986. *Police–Public Encounters. Home Office Research Study, No. 90.* London: HMSO.

Spencer, S. 1985a. The Eclipse of the Police Authority. In *Policing the Miners' Strike*, B. Fine & R. Millar (eds), 34–53. London: Lawrence and Wishart.

Spencer, S. 1985b. *Called to Account: The Case for Police Accountability in England and Wales.* London: National Council for Civil Liberties.

Stalker, J. 1988. *Stalker.* London: Penguin.

Stark, R. 1972. *Police Riots: Collective Violence and Law Enforcement.* Belmont: Wadsworth Press.

State Research 1981a. *Policing the Eighties – the Iron Fist. State Research Pamphlet: No. 2.* London: Independent Research Publications.

State Research 1981b. Controlling the Police: Police Accountability in the UK. (*Bulletin* **23**, April/May), 97–123.

Stead, J.S. 1977. The New Police. In *Police and Society*, D.H. Bayley (ed.), 73–84. Beverly Hills: Sage.

Stead, P.J. 1983. *The Police of France.* New York: Macmillan.

Stead, P.J. 1985. *The Police of Britain.* New York: Macmillan.

Steenhuis, D.W. 1980. Experiments on Police Effectiveness: The Dutch Experience. In *The Effectiveness of Policing*, R.V.G. Clarke & J.M. Hough (eds), 124–38. Aldershot: Gower.

Steer, D. 1970. *Police Cautions – A Study of the Exercise of Police Discretion.* Oxford: Blackwell.

Steer, D. 1980. *Uncovering Crime: The Police Role. Royal Commission on Criminal Proceedure Research Study, No. 7.* London: HMSO.

Stenning, P.C. 1981. The Role of Police Boards and Commissions as Institutions of Municipal Police Governance. In *Organisational Police Deviance*, C. Shearing (ed.), 161–208. Toronto: Butterworths.

Stephens, M. 1988. *Policing: The Critical Issues.* Hemel Hampstead: Harvester Wheatsheaf.

Stephens, M. & S. Becker (eds) 1994a. *Police Force, Police Service: Care and Control in Britain.* Basingstoke, Hampshire: Macmillan.

Stephens, M. & S. Becker 1994b. The Matrix of Care and Control. In *Police Force, Police Service*, M. Stephens & S. Becker (eds), 213–30. Basingstoke: Macmillan.

Stevens, A., R. Ostini, P. Dance, M. Burns, D.A. Crawford, G. Bammer 1995. Police Opinions of a Proposal for Controlled Availability of Heroin in Australia. *Policing and Society* **5** (4), 303–12.

Stevens, P. & C.F. Willis 1979. *Race, Crime and Arrests. Home Office Research Study, No. 58.* London: HMSO.

Stevens, P. & C. Willis 1982. *Ethnic Minorities and Complaints Against the Police.* Research and Planning Unit Papers No. 5. London: Home Office.

Stinchcombe, A.L. 1963. Institutions of Privacy in the Determination of Police Administrative Practice. *American Journal of Sociology* **69**, 150–60.

Stoddard, E.R. 1968. The Informal "Code" of Police Deviancy: A Group Approach to "Blue-Coat Crime'. *Journal of Criminal Law, Criminology and Police Science* **58** (2), 201–13.

Storch, R. 1976. The Policeman as Domestic Missionary: Urban Discipline and Popular Culture in Northern England, 1850–1880. *Journal of Social History* **IX** (4, Summer), 481–509.

Stratta, E. 1990. A Lack of Consultation. *Policing* **6** (3, Autumn), 523–49.

Sturgis, J.L. 1991. "Whisky Detectives" in Town: The Enforcement of the Liquor Laws in Hamilton, Ontario, *c.* 1870–1900. In *Policing the Empire: Government, Authority and Control, 1830–1940*, D.M. Anderson & D. Killingray (eds), 202–18. Manchester: Manchester University Press.

Sunday Times Insight Team 1985. *Strike.* London: Coronet.

Sykes, G.M. & D. Matza 1957. Techniques of Neutralization. *American Sociological Review* **22**, 664–70.

Sykes, G.W. 1993. The Functional Nature of Police Reform: The "Myth" of Controlling the Police. In *Critical Issues in Policing: Contemporary Readings*, 2nd edn, R.G. Dunham & G.P. Alpert (eds), 292–303. Prospect Heights, Illinois: Waveland.

Sykes, R. & J. Clark 1975. A Theory of Deference Exchange in Police – Civilian Encounters. *American Journal of Sociology* **81** (3), 584–600.

Sykes, R.E. & E.E. Brent 1983. *Policing: A Social Behaviourist Perspective.* New Brunswick, N.J.: Rutgers University Press.

Taft, P. & P. Ross 1979. American Labor Violence: Its Causes, Character, and Outcome. In *Violence in America*, rvd. edn, H.D. Graham & T.R. Gurr (eds), 187–241. Beverly Hills: Sage.

Tait, D. 1994. Cautions and Appearances: Statistics About Youth and Police. In *The Police and Young People in Australia*, R. White & C. Alder (eds), 60–75. Cambridge: Cambridge University Press.

Takagi, P. 1982. A Garrison State in a "Democratic" Society. In *Readings on Police Use of Deadly Force*, J.J. Fyfe (ed.), 195–213. Washington: Police Foundation.

Tarling, R. & J. Burrows 1984. The Work of Detectives. *Policing* **1** (1), 57–62.

Taylor, I. 1981. Crime Waves in Post-War Britain. *Contemporary Crises* **5**, 43–62.

Taylor, Lord Justice 1989. *The Hillsborough Stadium Disaster, 15 April 1989. Interim Report: Cm. 765.* London: HMSO.

Taylor, P. 1987. *Stalker: The Search for the Truth.* London: Faber & Faber.

Taylor, S. 1984. The Scarman Report and Explanations of Riots. In *Scarman and After*, J. Benyon (ed.), 20–35. London: Pergamon.

Tennenbaum, A. 1994. The Influence of the Garner Decision on Police Use of Deadly Force. *Journal Criminal Law and Criminology* **85** (1, Summer), 241–60.

Terrill, R.J. 1991. Civilian Oversight of the Police Complaints Process in the United States: Concerns, Developments, and More Concerns. In *Complaints Against The Police*, A.J. Goldsmith (ed.), 291–322. Oxford: Clarendon.

Terry, R.M. 1967. The Screening of Juvenile Offenders. *Journal of Criminal Law, Criminology and Police Science* **58** (2), 173–81.

Thomas, J.E. 1972. *The English Prison Officer Since 1850*. London: Routledge.

Thomas, T. 1990. Multi-agency Policing. *Policing* **6** (3, Autumn), 582–5.

Thornberry, T.P. 1973. Race, Socio-Economic Status and Sentencing in the Juvenile Justice System. *Journal Criminal Law and Criminology* **64** (1), 90–99.

Thornberry, T.P. 1979. Sentencing Disparities in the Juvenile Justice System. *Journal Criminal Law and Criminology* **70**, 164–71.

Thorpe, D. 1994. Police and Juvenile Offending. In *Police Force, Police Service*, M. Stephens & S. Becker (eds), 169–90. Basingstoke: Macmillan.

Thurlow, R. 1987. *Fascism in Britain: A History, 1918–1985*. Oxford: Blackwell.

Tien, J.M. & T.F. Rich 1994. The Hartford COMPASS Program: Experiences with a Weed and Seed-Related Program. In *The Challenge of Community Policing: Testing the Promises*, D.P. Rosenbaum (ed.), 192–206. Thousand Oaks: Sage.

Toch, H. 1969. *Violent Men*. Harmondsworth, Middlesex: Penguin.

Toch, H. 1996. The Violence-Prone Officer. In *Police Violence: Understanding and Controlling Police Abuse of Force*, W.A. Geller & H. Toch (eds), 94–112. New Haven, Conn.: Yale University Press.

Topping, I. 1991. The Police Complaints System in Northern Ireland. In *Complaints Against the Police*, A.J. Goldsmith (ed.), 233–58. Oxford: Clarendon.

Townshend, C. 1992. Policing Insurgency in Ireland, 1914–23. In *Policing and Decolonisation: Politics, Nationalism and the Police, 1917–65*, D.M. Anderson & D. Killingray (eds), 22–41. Manchester: Manchester University Press.

Tremblay, P. & C. Rochon 1991. Police Organizations and Their Use of Knowledge: A Grounded Research Agenda. *Policing and Society* **1** (4), 269–83.

Trojanowicz, R.C. 1971. The Policeman's Occupational Personality. *Journal of Criminal Law, Criminology and Police Science* **52** (4), 551–59.

Tuck, M. 1989. *Drinking and Disorder: A Study of Non-Metropolitan Violence. Home Office Research Study, No. 108*. London: HMSO.

Tuck, M. & P. Southgate 1981. *Ethnic Minorities, Crime and Policing: A Survey of the Experiences of West Indian and Whites. Home Office Research Study, No. 70*. London: Home Office.

Turner, B.S. 1990. Outline of a Theory of Citizenship. *Sociology* **24** (2), 189–217.

Turner, B.S. 1993a. *Citizenship*, vol. 1. London: Routledge.

Turner, B.S. 1993b. *Citizenship and Social Theory*, vol. 2. London: Routledge.

Turner, R.H. 1969. The Public Perception of Protest. *American Sociological Review* **32**, 815–31.

Uchida, C.D. & T.S. Bynum 1991. Search Warrants, Motions to Suppress and "lost cases": The Effects of the Exclusionary Rule in Seven Jurisdictions. *Journal of Criminal Law and Criminology* **81** (4), 1034–66.

Uglow, S. 1988. *Policing Liberal Society*. Oxford: Oxford University Press.

Uildriks, N. & H. van Mastrigt 1991. *Policing Police Violence*. Aberdeen: Aberdeen University Press.

Urban, M. 1992. *Big Boys' Rules*. London: Faber and Faber.

US Department of Justice 1976–1998. *Criminal Victimization in the United States National Crime Survey report 1976–1998*. Washington, DC: Government Printing Office.

van Dijk, J.J.M., P. Mayhew, M. Killias 1990. *Experiences of Crime Across the World*. Deventer, Netherlands: Kluwer.

van Maanen, J. 1973. Observations on the Making of Policemen. *Human Organization* **32** (4, Winter), 407–18.

van Maanen, J. 1974. Working the Street: A Developmental View of Police Behaviour. In *The Potential for Reform of Criminal Justice*, H. Jacob (ed.), 83–130. Beverly Hills, Ca: Sage.

van Maanen, J. 1975. Police Socialization: A Longitudinal Examination of Job Attitudes in an Urban Police Department. *Administrative Science Quarterly* **20**, 207–22.

van Maanen, J. 1978. On Watching the Watchers. In *Policing: A View From the Street*, P.K. Manning & J. van Maanen (eds), 309–50. New York: Random House.

van Maanen, J. 1980. Beyond Account: The Personal Impact of Police Shootings. *Annals of the American Academy of Political and Social Science* **452** (November), 145–56.

van Outrive, L. & C. Fijnaut 1983. Police and the Organization of Prevention. In *Control in the Police Organization*, M. Punch (ed.), 47–59. Cambridge, Mass.: MIT Press.

Vanagunas, S. 1982. Planning for the Delivery of Urban Police Services. In *Managing Police Work: Issues and Analysis. Perspectives in Criminal Justice*, No. 4, J.R. Greene (ed.) 37–52. Beverly Hills, Ca: Sage.

Venner, M. 1981. The Disturbances in Moss Side, Manchester. *New Community* **9**, 374–7.

Vidal, J. 1996. In the Forest, in the Dark. *Guardian* (25 January), 2–3.

Viorst, M. 1979. *Fire in the Streets: America in the 1960s.* New York: Simon and Schuster.

Vogler, R. 1991. *Reading the Riot Act: The Magistracy, the Police and the Army in Civil Disorder. New Directions in Criminology.* Milton Keynes: Open University.

Waddington, D. 1992. *Contemporary Issues in Public Disorder.* London: Routledge.

Waddington, D. 1996. Key Issues and Controversies. In *Policing Public Order: Theoretical and Practical Issues*, C. Critcher & D. Waddington (eds), 1–35. Aldershot: Avebury.

Waddington, D., K. Jones, C. Critcher 1989. *Flashpoints: Studies in Public Disorder.* London: Routledge.

Waddington, P.A.J. 1985a. *The Effects of Police Manpower Depletion During the NUM Strike, 1984–85.* London: Police Foundation.

Waddington, P.A.J. 1985b. Manpower Depletion. *Policing* **1** (3), 149–60.

Waddington, P.A.J. 1986a. Mugging As a Moral Panic: A Question of Proportion. *British Journal of Sociology* **2**, 245–59.

Waddington, P.A.J. 1986b. Defining Objectives. *Policing* **2** (1, Spring), 17–26.

Waddington, P.A.J. 1986c. The "Objective" Debate. *Policing* **2** (3, Autumn), 225–35.

Waddington, P.A.J. 1987a. Towards Paramilitarism? Dilemmas in Policing Civil Disorder. *British Journal of Criminology* **27** (1, Winter), 37–46.

Waddington, P.A.J. 1987b. Paying Back the "Old Bill". *Spectator* (28, February), 20.

Waddington, P.A.J. 1990. "Overkill" or "Minimum Force"? *Criminal Law Review* (Oct)", 695–707.

Waddington, P.A.J. 1991. *The Strong Arm of the Law.* Oxford: Clarendon.

Waddington, P.A.J. 1992. An Inquiry into the Police Response to, and Investigation of, Events in Boipatong on 17 June 1992. Submitted to the Commission of Inquiry Regarding the Prevention of Public Violence and Intimidation, His Honour Mr Justice Goldstone, Chairman, Pretoria, South Africa.

Waddington, P.A.J. 1993a. *Calling the Police.* Aldershot, Hants.: Avebury.

Waddington, P.A.J. 1993b. "The Case Against Paramilitary Policing" considered. *British Journal of Criminology* **33** (3, Oct), 14–16.

Waddington, P.A.J. 1993c. Dying in a Ditch: The Use of Police Powers in Public Order. *International Journal of Sociology* **21** (4), 335–53.

Waddington, P.A.J. 1993d. Review of Watching Police, Watching Communities by McConville, M., Shepherd, D. *British Journal of Criminology* **33** (3), 453–57.

Waddington, P.A.J. 1994a. *Liberty and Order: Public Order Policing in a Capital City.* London: UCL Press.

Waddington, P.A.J. 1994b. Coercion and Accommodation: Policing Public Order After the Public Order Act. *British Journal of Sociology* **45** (3, September), 367–85.

Waddington, P.A.J. 1994c. Policing South-Africa – the South-African Police and the Transition from Apartheid – Cawthra,G. *British Journal of Criminology* **34** (4), 507–8.

Waddington, P.A.J. 1995. Public Order Policing: Citizenship and Moral Ambiguity. In *Core Issues in Policing*, F. Leishman, B. Loveday, S.P. Savage (eds), 114–30. London: Longman.

Waddington, P.A.J. 1996a. The Other Side of the Barricades: Policing Protest. In *To Make Another World: Studies in Protest and Collective Action*, C. Barker & P. Kennedy (eds), 219–36. Aldershot: Avebury.

Waddington, P.A.J. 1996b. The Politics of Public Order Policing: A "Typographical Analysis"! In *Policing Public Order: Theoretical and Practical Issues*, C. Critcher & D. Waddington (eds), 129–44. Aldershot: Avebury.

Waddington, P.A.J. 1997. Community Policing With the Gloves Off. *Police Review* (25, April), 26–27.

Waddington, P.A.J. & Q. Braddock 1991. "Guardians" or "Bullies"?: Perceptions of the Police Amongst Adolescent Black, White and Asian Boys. *Policing and Society* **2**, 31–45.

Waddington, P.A.J. & M. Hamilton 1997. The Impotence of the Powerful: Recent British Police Weapons Policy. *Sociology* **31** (1, February), 91–109.

Wagner, A.E. & S.H. Decker 1993. Evaluating Citizen Complaints Against the Police. In *Critical Issues in Policing: Contemporary Readings*, 2nd edn, R.G. Dunham & G.P. Alpert (eds), 275–91. Prospect Heights, Illinois: Waveland.

Walker, D. 1968. *Rights in Conflict: The Violent Confrontation of Demonstrators and Police, During the Week of the Democratic National Convention.* New York: Banton.

Walker, N. 1996. Defining Core Police Tasks: The Neglect of the Symbolic Dimension. *Policing and Society* **6** (1), 53–71.

Walker, S. 1993. "Broken Windows" and Fractured History: The Use and Misuse of History in Recent Police Patrol Analysis. In *Critical Issues in Policing: Contemporary Readings*, 2nd edn, R.G. Dunham & G.P. Alpert (eds), 408–20. Prospect Heights, Illinois: Waveland.

Walklate, S. 1995. Equal Opportunities and the Future of Policing. In *Core Issues in Policing*, F. Leishman, B. Loveday, S.P. Savage (eds), 191–204. London: Longman.

Wall, D.S. 1994a. The Ideology of Internal Recruitment: The Selection of Chief Constables and Changes Within the Tripartite Arrangement. *British Journal of Criminology* **34** (3), 322–38.

Wall, D. 1994b. Putting Freemasonry into Perspective: The Debate over Freemasonry and Policing. *Policing and Society* **3** (4), 257–68.

Wall, D. 1997. Policing the Virtual Community: The Internet, Cyberspace and Cyber-crime. In *Policing Futures: The Police, Law Enforcement and the Twenty-First Century*, P. Francis, P. Davies, V. Jupp (eds), 208–36. Houndmills, Basingstoke: Macmillan.

Wallington, P.T. (ed.) 1984. *Civil Liberties 1984.* Oxford: Martin Robertson/Cobden Trust.

Wambaugh, J. 1976. *The Choirboys.* London: Weidenfeld and Nicolson.

Wambaugh, J. 1981. *The Glitter Dome.* London: Futura.

Waters, I. 1995. Quality of Service: Politics or Paradigm Shift? In *Core Issues in Policing*, F. Leishman, B. Loveday, S.P. Savage (eds), 205–17. London: Longman.

Weatheritt, M. 1983. *Community Policing: Does It Work and How Do We Know? Cropwood Paper: 15.* Cambridge: Cambridge Institute of Criminology.

Weatheritt, M. 1985. Police Research. *Policing* **1** (2), 77–86.

Weatheritt, M. 1986. *Innovations in Policing.* London: Croom Helm/The Police Foundation.

Weatheritt, M. 1987. Community Policing Now. In *Policing and the Community*, P. Willmott (ed.), 7–20. London: Policy Studies Institute.

Weatheritt, M. 1989. Why Should the Police Use Police Research? In *Police Research: Some Future Prospects*, M. Weatheritt (ed.), 35–44. Aldershot: Avebury.

Websdale, N. 1991. Disciplining and Non-Disciplining Spaces: The Rise of Policing As an Aspect of Governmentality in 19th Century Eugene, Oregon. *Policing and Society* **2** (2), 89–116.

Websdale, N.S. 1994. Nonpolicing, Policing and Progressivism in Eugene, Oregon. *Policing and Society* **4** (2), 131–74.

Websdale, N.S. 1995. Police History and the Question of Gender: The Case of Eugene, Oregon in the Post-World War Two Era. *Policing and Society* **5** (4), 313–38.

Websdale, N. & B. Johnson 1997. The Policing of Domestic Violence in Rural and Urban Areas: The Voices of Battered Women in Kentucky. *Policing and Society* **6** (4), 297–317.

Webster, W.H. & H. Williams 1992. *The City in Crisis: A Report by the Special Advisor to the Board of Police Commissioners on the Civil Disorder in Los Angeles.* Los Angeles, Ca: Office of the Special Advisor to the Board of Police Commissioners City of Los Angeles.

Weeks, J. 1996. Forging New Links in the Justice Chain. *Police* (March), 17–18.

Weinberger, B. 1991. *Keeping the Peace? Policing Strikes in Britain, 1906–1926.* Oxford: Berg.

Weinberger, B. 1995. *The Best Police in the World: An Oral History of English Policing From the 1930s to the 1960s.* Aldershot: Scolar.

Weiner, N.L. & C.V. Willie 1971. Decisions By Juvenile Officers. *American Journal of Sociology* **77** (2), 199–210.

Weisel, D.L. & J.E. Eck 1994. Toward a Practical Approach to Organizational Change: Community Policing Initiatives in Six Cities. In *The Challenge of Community Policing: Testing the Promises*, D.P. Rosenbaum (ed.), 53–72. Thousand Oaks: Sage.

Weisheit, R.A., L.E. Wells, D.N. Falcone 1994. Community Policing in Small-Town and Rural America. *Crime and Delinquency* **40** (4, July), 549–67.

Weiss, R.P. 1987. From "Slugging Detective" to "Labor Relations": Policing Labour at Ford, 1930–1947. In *Private Policing. Sage Criminal Justice System Annuals.* Vol. 23, C.D. Shearing & P.C. Stenning (eds), 110–30. Newbury Park, California: Sage.

Weitzer, R. 1985. Policing a Divided Society: Obstacles to Normalization in Northern Ireland. *Social Problems* **33** (1, October), 41–55.

Weitzer, R. 1990. *Transforming Settler States: Communal Conflict and Internal Security in Northern Ireland and Zimbabwe.* Berkeley: University of California Press.

Weitzer, R. 1992. Northern Ireland's Police Liaison Committees. *Policing and Society* **2**, 233–43.

Weitzer, R. 1995. *Policing Under Fire: Ethnic Conflict and Police–Community Relations in Northern Ireland. New Directions in Crime and Justice Studies.* Albany: State University of New York.

Weitzer, R. & C. Beattie 1994. Police Killings in South Africa: Criminal Trials 1986–1992. *Policing and Society* **4** (2), 99–118.

Werthman, C. & I. Piliavin 1967. Gang Members and the Police. In *The Police: Six Sociological Essays*, D. Bordua (ed.). New York: Wiley.

Westley, W.A. 1953. Violence and the Police. *American Journal of Sociology* **59**, 34–41.

Westley, W.A. 1956. Secrecy and the Police. *Social Forces* **34** (3), 254–7.

Westley, W.A. 1970. *Violence and the Police.* Cambridge, Mass.: MIT Press.

Wheeler, S., E. Bonacich, M.R. Cramer, I.K. Zola 1968. Agents of Delinquency Control: A Comparative Analysis. In *Controlling Delinquents*, S. Wheeler (ed.), 31–60. New York: Wiley.

Which? 1990. The Police. (May):258–61.

White, R. 1994. Street Life: Police Practics and Youth Behaviour. In *The Police and Young People in Australia*, R. White & C. Alder (eds), 102–27. Cambridge: Cambridge University Press.

White, R. & C. Alder (eds) 1994. *The Police and Young People in Australia.* Cambridge: Cambridge University Press.

Whittaker, B. 1964. *The Police.* Harmondsworth, Middx.: Penguin.

Whittaker, B. 1979. *The Police in Society.* London: Eyre and Methuen.

Wilderman, J. 1991. When the State Fails: A Critical Assessment of Contract Policing in the United States. In *Crimes by the Capitalist State*, G. Barak (ed.), 219–32. Albany: State University of New York.

Wiles, P. 1971. Criminal Statistics and Sociological Explanations of Crime. In *The Sociology of Crime and Delinquency in Britain, vol. 1*, W.G. Carson & P. Wiles (eds). Oxford: Martin Robertson.

Wiles, P. 1993. Policing Structures, Organisational Change and Personnel Management. In *Reforming British Policing Missions and Structures*, R. Dingwall & J. Shapland (eds), 51–70. Sheffield: Faculty of Law, University of Sheffield.

Wilkins, L.T. 1964. *Social Deviance.* London: Tavistock.

Wilkinson, C. & R. Evans 1990. Police Cautioning of Juveniles: The Impact of Home Office Circular 14/85. *Criminal Law Review*, 165–76.

Wilkinson, D.L. & D.P. Rosenbaum 1994. The Effects of Organizational Structure on Community Policing: A Comparison of Two Cities. In *The Challenge of Community Policing: Testing the Promises*, D.P. Rosenbaum (ed.), 110–26. Thousand Oaks: Sage.

Williams, G. 1985. Letting Off the Guilty and Prosecuting the Innocent. *Criminal Law Review*, 115.

Willink, Sir Henry 1962. *Royal Commission on the Police, Final Report.* London: HMSO.

Willis, C. 1983. *The Use, Effectiveness and Impact of Police Stop and Search Powers. Research and Planning Unit Paper, No. 15.* London: Home Office.

Wilson, J.Q. 1968. Dilemmas in Police Administration. *Public Administration Review* **28** (September/October), 407–17.

Wilson, J.Q. 1969. *Varieties of Police Behaviour.* Cambridge, Mass.: Harvard University Press.

Wilson, J.Q. 1980. What Can the Police Do About Violence? *Annals of the American Academy of Political and Social Science* **452** (November), 13–21.

Wilson, J.Q. & B. Boland 1978a. The Effects of the Police on Crime. *Law and Society* **12** (3), 367–90.

Wilson, J.Q. & B. Boland 1978b. The Effects of the Police on Crime: A Response to Jacob and Rich. *Law and Society* **16** (1).

Wilson, J.Q. & G. Kelling 1982. Broken Windows. *The Atlantic Monthly* (March), 29–38.

Winter, M. 1998. *Police Philosophy and Protest Policing in the Federal Republic of Germany, 1960–1990.* See della Porta & Reiter (1998), 188–212.

Wintle, M. 1996. Policing the Liberal State in the Netherlands: The Historical Context of the Current Reorganization of the Dutch Police. *Policing and Society* **6** (3), 181–97.

Wisler, D. & H. Kriesi 1998. *Public Order, Protest Cycles and Political Process: Two Swiss Cities Compared.* See della Porta & Reiter (1998), 91–116.

Wolfe, N.T. 1992. *Policing a Socialist Society: The German Democratic Republic. Contributions in Criminology and Penology: Number 34.* New York: Greenwood Press.

Woodcock, J. 1991. Overturning Police Culture. *Policing* **7** (3), 172–83.

Worden, R.E. 1989. Situational and Attitudinal Explanations of Police Behaviour. A Theoretical Reappraisal and Empirical Reassessment. *Law and Society* **23** (4), 667–711.

Worden, R.E. 1996. The Causes of Police Brutality: Theory and Evidence on Police Use of Force. In *Police Violence: Understanding and Controlling Police Abuse of Force*, W.A. Geller & H. Toch (eds), 23–51. New Haven, Conn.: Yale University Press.

Worpole, K. 1979. Death in Southall. *New Society* (24, May), 458–59.

Wortley, R., R. Williams, M. Walker 1996. Perceptions of Policing by Australian Senior Secondary Students: Implications For Diversifying the Recruit Mix. *Policing and Society* **6** (2), 131–44.

Wright, A. & B. Irving 1996. Value Conflicts in Policing Crisis into Opportunity: Making Critical Use of Experience. *Policing and Society* **6** (3), 199–211.

Wright, S. 1978. New Police Technologies: An Exploration of the Social Implications and Unforseen Impacts of Some Recent Developments. *Journal of Peace Research* **XV** (4), 305–22.

Wycoff, M.A. 1982. Evaluating the Crime-Effectiveness of Municipal Police. In *Managing Police Work: Issues and Analysis. Perspectives in Criminal Justice*, No. 4, J.R. Greene (ed.), 15–36. Beverly Hills: Sage.

Wycoff, M.A. & W.G. Skogan 1994a. Community Policing in Madison: An Analysis of Implementation and Impact. In *The Challenge of Community Policing: Testing the Promises*, D.P. Rosenbaum (ed.), 75–91. Thousand Oaks: Sage.

Wycoff, M.A. & W.G. Skogan 1994b. The Effect of a Community Policing Management Style on Officers' Attitudes. *Crime and Delinquency* **40** (3, July), 371–83.

Yearnshire, S. 1996. Men of Violence. *Police Review* (30, August), 28–29.

Young, J. 1971. The Role of the Police As Amplifiers of Deviancy, Negotiators of Reality and Translators of Fantasy. In *Images of Deviance*, S. Cohen (ed.), 27–61. Harmondsworth, Middx.: Penguin.

Young, J. 1994. *Policing the Streets: Stops and Search in North London.* London: Centre for Criminology, Middlesex University.

Young, M. 1991. *An Inside Job.* Oxford: Clarendon.

Young, M. 1995. Black Humour – Making Light of Death. *Policing and Society* **5** (2), 151–68.

Index

Note: Most references are to the **police** and **Britain**, unless otherwise indicated.

abuse of authority 121–58, 189, 196–7
  see also bending *under* rules; excessive *under* force; invitational edges; regulating
accountability 192–3, 201–2, 222, 235, 236, 248
accreditation 182–3
action 99, 116
  attitudes, different 107–9
  defensive 130
  plans 235
  see also abuse of authority; regulating police wrongdoing
administration, time spent on 7–8
Africa 27, 65, 87
  see also South Africa
age *see* juveniles
Anglo-Saxon approach 24
  see also Britain; United States
anomie 112–13, 150
arrest 141–2
  concocted charge 135–7
  domestics 177–8, 237–8
  of good class villain 100–1
  instead of summons 142, 144
  not made *see* non-enforcement
  pressure to make and quotas 33, 132–3
  to prevent complaints 156, 170
  see also crime
Asia 65, 74, 89, 92, 219
  see also India; Japan
assassination 92, 157–8
assistance *see* care
attitudes, different 107–9
Australia 6, 37, 91, 110, 111
  organizations, police 193–4, 196, 200
  reform 206, 218
  regulating police wrongdoing 169–70, 171, 174–7 *passim*
authoritarianism 24, 27, 98, 101, 106, 116
authority 17, 19, 20, 63
  denied by suspect 153–5
  isolation 108, 109, 117
  not delegated 193
  psychology and subcultures 103, 112, 116
  see also abuse of authority
autonomy 186–8, 203

behaviour, police, explanation of 102–9
benefits in kind 122
Britain *see* London; Northern Ireland *and also* preliminary note to index
brutality *see* excessive *under* force
bureaucracy, punishment-centred 127–32, 134, 162
  see also managerialism; regulation; rules

Canada 3, 6, 55
  civil police 26
  discretion 32
  militarism 25
  organizations, police 188, 189–90, 196
  psychology and subcultures 111

reform 206, 210, 218–19, 245
regulating police wrongdoing 167–8, 177
care 14–15, 17, 208
case
building 135–7
against police 168–70
cautioning 37, 45–6
centre and periphery 27–8
charge
-bargaining *see* plea-bargaining
concocted 135–7
detention 142
children *see* juveniles
China 65, 89
citizenship 21–2, 26–7
of criminals 64–9, 138–9
dissent 73, 75–8, 79
exclusion 40–1
law 186
non-citizens *see* colonialism
of police 102–4
resistance 61–2
state 20–4, 64–9
see also civil rights
civil defence 82
civil rights 21, 224, 247
citizenship 29–30, 62
dissent 74, 75–8
silence 144–5
see also citizenship
civility 16–17, 43–4, 141
class 21–2, 210
abuse of authority 154
discretion 33, 35, 40, 54, 55, 56, 60–1
middle class resistance 154
regulating police wrongdoing 169, 178
subordination and exclusion 48–9
war, preparing for 79–80
see also working class
coercion *see* force/coercion
colonialism 23, 24–6, 27, 86, 189–90
see also Australia; Canada; India; Northern Ireland; South Africa
commonsense 45, 128, 133
Commonwealth *see* colonialism
communal values *see* values
community policing 92, 102, 206–26, 234–5, 250
dangers 220–5
failures 213–17
implementation and aims 208–13, 214
successes 217–20
theory 207–8
see also patrolling
complaints about police 119, 156
arresting to prevent 156, 170
conciliation 182
credibility 169–70
dissatisfaction with 163–4
informal resolution 165
numbers of 160–1, 162
unrecorded 164–5
see also substantiation
compliance strategies 10
conciliation 182
condemning police behaviour 106–7
confession 136–7
consent principle 125, 140–1, 143
conservatism 101, 116
conservative theory on riots 76
constitutional issues 185, 186–7, 195–6, 202, 203, 204–5
contempt for police 153–5
continuities in explanation of police behaviour 102–9
control 70–2
see also authority; dissent; force; keeping people in their place; militarism; order; regulating
control room operatives 32–3, 238, 240
corruption 121–5
see also abuse of authority; invitational edges
costs *see* expenditure
credibility of complaints 169–70
crime and criminals
citizenship 64–9, 138–9
criminal law *see* law
criminalization of exclusion 41–2
defining 33–5
fighting, delusion about 117–18
not arrested *see* non-enforcement
not reduced 9
prevention 4, 11, 23–4, 98, 208, 227
rate 11–12
state 64–9
unrecorded 33–4
waves and media 36, 37
see also arrest
crises 15, 218–19, 235
see also dissent
cynicism 97, 101–2, 114–15, 133, 134

danger and risk 112, 119, 131, 227
de-centralization 234–5
see also community policing

defensive action 130
deference, enforcing 154–5
democratic control *see* organizations
democratic solution to dissent 74–5
demonstrations *see* dissent
deprivation, poverty and marginalization 30, 37, 43, 57, 92, 117, 155
  organizations, police 192, 198–201, 204
  police wrongdoing 163, 168, 169–70
  reform and change 221, 224, 231, 244
  see also race; unemployment; working class
deviance concept and police wrongdoing 178–80, 181
dirty work concept 112–14, 117
discretion 31–45, 133
  law 191–5
  managerialism 229, 236–7, 238
  organizations, police 193–4
  policy-making 194–5
  source of 97
  see also non-enforcement
discrimination and prejudice 37, 38–9, 97
  see also class; juveniles; race; sexism
dissatisfaction with complaints 163–4
dissent (protests and riots), controlling 42, 62, 64–96, 175, 208, 222
  organizations, police 188, 197–9, 204
divided societies 84–6
  see also Northern Ireland
domestics 12, 15, 39, 57–62, 192, 194
  arrests 177–8, 237–8
domination 86
  see also colonialism; control; subordination

easing 130
efficiency and effectiveness of reform 216, 240–1, 243–5
emergencies *see* crises
enforcing *see* force
ethics *see* moral
ethnic minorities *see* race
Europe 4, 9, 21, 26, 111
  abuse of authority 124, 132, 150, 155
  dissent, control of 65, 69, 75, 79, 88, 91, 94
  organizations, police 190–1, 196, 200
  reform 206, 214, 218, 229, 237, 245
  regulating police wrongdoing 168, 175, 177
  see also France; Germany; Italy; Netherlands
evidence of police wrongdoing 160–1, 169–70, 174–5
excitement 99, 116
exclusion 56
  citizenship 40–1
  criminalizing 41–2
  of improper evidence 174–5
  rhetoric of 118–19
  subordination 45–61
expenditure/costs and resource allocation 9, 194–5
  reform 209, 227–8, 239–40, 244–5

fairness 138–9
feminists 41, 57, 59, 61–2, 178, 192, 237
  see also women
firearms *see* weapons
force/coercion 116
  abuse of authority 149–53
  duopoly of 69–70
  enforcing deference 154–5
  excessive 149–58, 168–9, 172–4, 177–9
    see also lethal force
  lack of 16–17
  monopoly of, custodians of state's 15–19, 20, 23, 26, 29, 116, 185
    see also dissent
  normal 149–50
  patrolling 18–19
  potential 16
  see also militarism; weapons
France 9, 175
  centre and periphery 27–8
  citizenship 21, 62
  militarism 26–7
  organizations, police 190–1, 196, 200
  reform 206, 218, 229, 245
  subordination and exclusion 55, 60

Germany 4, 26, 27, 55, 191
  dissent, control of 65, 75, 79
globalization 243
golden age of policing 218, 219, 222
good class villain 100–1
good stories 131–2

harassment 42, 43–4, 46–7, 140, 160
help *see* care
Hong Kong 88
humour 14, 102, 114–15
hypocrisy 128, 132

ideology and change *see* reform
illegality 16, 17, 19, 125–6
 see also abuse of authority; crime; law; non-enforcement
inaction *see* non-enforcement
inclusion 55–6
 control through 70–2
 reversing dissent 78–84
incorporation of working class 72, 80–1, 83, 95
independence and control 184–91, 202
 Britain 186–8
 Commonwealth 189–90
 Europe 190–1
 regulation of police wrongdoing 162, 167–8, 181
 United States 188–9
India 4, 15, 42, 111, 137, 196
 dissent, control of 65–6, 70, 95
ineffective crime-fighters 6–9
informants 124
information problems 238–9
international comparisons 3–4, 12, 37, 55
 see also Australia; Europe; India; Japan; South Africa; United States
interrogation 136–7, 145
intimidation 42
investigation 7–9
invitational edges of corruption 125–7, 134
 assassination 157–8
 bureaucratic 127–9
 force 149–53
 legal 133, 147–9
 performance 132–3
 rule-breaking 129–32
irony of militarization 92–4
isolation 97, 108, 109, 111, 117
Israel 65, 86–7, 177, 225
Italy 20, 26, 27, 75, 79, 91, 206

Japan 4, 26, 137, 175, 219
 force, monopoly of 18
 help and assistance 15
 patrolling 6, 18
 psychology and subcultures 111
 subordination and exclusion 55
justice *see* law
juveniles 134
 curfews 223, 225
 delinquent 8, 36, 37, 45–6
  parents of 146–7
 keeping in place 36, 37, 39, 45–8, 51–4

keeping dissent in its place *see* dissent
keeping people in their place 31–63
 subordination and exclusion 45–61
 see also discretion

labelling 35
labour movement *see* strikes; unions
Latin America 157, 204
law/legal system 4, 5, 247
 abuse of authority 133, 147–9
 fairness 138–9
 impartiality and discretion 191–5
 legal advice, right to 142–3, 145–6
 miscarriages 107, 137–8
 organizations, police 185–6, 191–5
 police wrongdoing 160, 163, 170–3
 procedural 115, 163
 as servant of order 39–40
 using and enforcing 133–8
 see also illegality; non-enforcement; rules
legitimacy
 crisis of 81, 92
 legitimation of reform 219–20
 of police wrongdoing 162–3
lethal force
 abuse of authority 131, 151–3, 156–8
 dissent 65, 66, 71, 87, 90–1, 92
 organizations, police 199–200
 police wrongdoing 164, 166–7, 174, 175, 179
 reform 229, 248
 subcultures 112–13
liberal-radical theory on riots 76–9
local policing *see* community policing
local values 44–5
London (and Metropolitan Police) 28
 abuse of authority 122, 124, 128, 155
 citizenship and state 21–2, 23, 24
 crime-fighting minimal 9
 discretion 35, 42
 dissent, control of 25, 71, 79, 84, 85, 91, 93–4
 force, monopoly of 18–19
 harassment 42
 organizations, police 186–7, 188, 192, 196–200 *passim*
 psychology and subcultures 100, 102, 103, 105, 107, 112
 reform 226, 248
  community policing 208, 209, 210, 211, 212, 213, 215, 219, 222–3
 regulating police wrongdoing 161, 175, 177

loyalty/solidarity 99–100, 119, 130–1, 164

malls 248–9
malpractice *see* abuse; regulating
managerialism 226–43
  bottom up 242
  conflict, internal 231–2
  devaluation by lower ranks 229–31
  discretion 229, 236–7, 238
  evaluation 240–1
  limits and constraints 236–40
  militarism 228–9, 238
  reform 234–6, 241–2
  specialists 232–3
marginalized people *see* deprivation
masculinity, cult of 99, 104, 114, 116, 117
media 5, 36, 37, 203
  see also moral panics
mentally ill 14, 17
Metropolitan Police *see* London
Middle East 65, 86–7, 177, 225
militarism/militarization 22–3, 25, 26–7
  as last resort 70
  managerialism 228–9, 238
  resurgence of 87–95
  see also weapons
mission 98–9
mobility 82–3, 84, 90–2, 95, 105
  of protesters 82, 83
  see also special squads
mobilization
  community 212–13
  political 176
monopoly of force *see under* force
mooching 122
moral order *see* values
moral panics 36, 46, 177, 199
mugging 36, 53, 54, 81, 202

negotiation 72, 74–5
neighbourhood watch 212–13
Netherlands 3, 55, 190
  abuse of authority 124, 132, 155, 177
  community values 44–5
  help and assistance 14
  psychology and subcultures 111
  reform 206, 214, 237, 245
neutrality 85, 163
neutralization 118
New Zealand 25, 26, 177, 190
noble cause corruption 148–9, 178
non-citizens *see* colonialism
non-enforcement 5–14, 31–2, 192
  see also discretion
non-police law enforcers 10–11, 211, 239–40, 243–9
norm, deviancy as 129–30
  see also abuse of authority
normal force 149–50
Northern Ireland 4, 18, 24–5, 196, 225
  abuse of authority 125, 157
  centre and periphery 27–8
  dissent, control of 67, 73, 84–92 *passim*
  psychology and subcultures 111, 114
  regulating police wrongdoing 161, 173, 174, 175
nostalgia 218, 219, 222

oral tradition of police 109–20
order and peacekeeping 12–14, 16, 56, 153, 207–8
  see also control; dissent; keeping people in their place
ordinary decent people *see* respectable
organizations, police, control of 180–1, 184–205
  law 185–6, 191–5
  restraint, mechanism for 197–201
  see also constitutional; independence and control; rules

para-military *see* militarism
parents of juveniles 146–7
patrolling 1–3, 10, 18–19, 99, 101–2, 245
  abuse of authority 131–7 *passim*
  foot 6–7
  managerialism 230, 231–2, 242
  see also community policing; stop and search
peacekeeping *see* control; order
peer evaluation 182–3
  see also loyalty
performance pressure 132–3, 137–8
personality, police 97–102, 103, 107
Peterloo 69–70
plea-bargaining 37, 135, 146
ploys 142–4, 165, 166
policing 1–30
  see also abuse of authority; authority; citizenship; crime; dissent; force; international comparisons; keeping people in their place; order; organizations; personality; reform; regulating; sub-culture; talking
policy, policing by 235–6, 237

see also bureaucracy
political
  control *see* organizations
  mobilization 176
  protests 73–4, 88
  rights 21
post-traumatic stress disorder 112–13
poverty *see* deprivation
prejudice *see* discrimination
presentational rules 128, 130–1
prevention *see under* crime
prisons 11–12
privacy 32, 61
  private and public blurred 248–9
privatization 243–9
professionalism and militarization 94–5
professionalization 234–5
proper police procedure 138–40
prostitution 44–5, 56, 123
protection 122
  see also care
protesters *see* dissent
psychological traits of police 97–102, 103, 107
public
  ignorant 117
  involvement *see* community policing
  as main informants/complainants 8, 56
  see also respectable people
punishment-centred bureaucracy 127–32, 134, 162

quality of life 43–4
quasi-judicial function 193–4
  see also discretion
quotas *see* pressure *under* arrest

race/racism (by police and community) 26, 29, 198
  abuse of authority 151–3, 156, 160
  discretion 35, 37, 49, 52, 57
  institutional 54
    see also South Africa
  keeping people in their place 51–5
  psychology and subcultures 98, 101, 102, 105, 108, 111, 118
  reform 210, 221, 225, 227
  regulating police wrongdoing 169, 175, 177
  riots and protests 75–6, 77, 78–9, 85
  subordination and exclusion 49–50
recording 33–4, 164–5
reform and change 206–50
  privatization 243–9
  see also community policing; managerialism
regulating police wrongdoing 159–83
  case making 168–70
  deviance concept 178–80, 181
  independent 162, 167–8, 181
  obstacles and barriers 164–7
  toleration 173–6
  see also abuse of authority; complaints; rules; substantiation
repeat offenders 7–8, 241
reported offences 8, 56
  lack of *see* non-enforcement
  and recorded, gap between 33–4
resistance 61–2, 210, 214–15
  see also dissent
resources *see* expenditure
respectable people 100, 117
  keeping people in their place 40–2, 43, 45, 49, 61, 62–3
  ordinary decent protesters 73–4, 83, 203
  organizations, police 194, 200, 203
restraint, mechanism for 197–201
rights *see* civil rights
riots 64–9 *passim*, 75–8, 87–9
  normative explanation 86–8
  see also dissent
risk *see* danger
rules 159–60, 163
  bending and breaking 127–49
    arrest, detention and charge 141–2
    obscure 147
    performance 132–3
    ploys 142–4
    proper procedure 138–40
    silence, right of 144–5
    street powers 140–1
    third party involvement 145–7
    using and enforcing law 133–8
    see also invitational edges
  see also law; regulating
Russia/Soviet Union 4, 26, 65

Scotland 155, 161, 166, 168, 174
  United States compared 4, 12, 37, 55
sexism (against women and men)
  discretion 33, 35, 39
  keeping people in their place 33, 35, 39, 57–60
  see also women
silence, right of 144–5
social rights *see* citizenship; civil rights

social values *see* values
social workers 149, 171, 181
South Africa 54, 157
  dissent, control of 65, 67, 86, 87, 93, 94–5
  force and militarism 18–19, 25, 87, 93, 94–5
  police wrongdoing 161, 175, 179
  reform 225, 247
Soviet Union/Russia 4, 26, 65
Spain 26, 27
special squads 82–3, 84, 90–2, 95, 105, 154–5, 157, 232
sport 72
squads *see* special squads
state 20–4, 27, 64–9
  control *see* force; law; organizations
stop and search 35, 42, 50–5, 127, 140–1, 143, 192
street powers *see* patrolling; stop and search
strikes and industrial disputes 12–13, 71–2, 74, 79–83, 188, 195, 230
sub-culture, police 98, 104–6, 108, 116
  talking and attitudes 107–20
  universality and tenacity of 111–12
subordination 40, 42, 86
  exclusion 45–61
  see also domination
substantiation of police wrongdoing 160–2, 165, 167, 168, 171
suppression *see* force
suspicion 101–2, 141
  see also cynicism
symbolism 237–8
  see also uniform

talking by police 109–20
team work 216
  see also community policing
technology 10, 88–9
tenacity of police sub-culture 111–12
termination of course of action 151–2
terrorism 4, 18, 89–92
third party involvement in rule bending 145–7
toleration of malpractice 173–6
traffic and traffic police 10, 16, 17, 33, 35, 73, 154, 195, 241
trouble, avoiding 130, 162

undercover work 122–3, 124
unemployment 54, 81, 244
uniform 9, 99, 102–4, 228
unions, police in 79–80
  see also strikes
United States 4, 5
  abuse of authority 124
    excessive force 151–3, 154, 156–7
    rule-breaking 127–8, 132, 133, 135, 138, 139, 146
  centre and periphery 28
  citizenship 23, 29–30, 62
  discretion 31–8 *passim*
  dissent, control of 64–78 *passim*, 85
    militarization 89, 91–2
  non-enforcement 6, 7, 8, 9
  organizations, police 185, 196, 198–204 *passim*
  patrolling 1–3, 6–7
  peacekeeping 12, 14
  psychology and subcultures 98, 101, 102–3, 109, 111, 112, 117, 119
  reform 245, 248
    community policing 206, 207, 209, 210, 212, 218, 219, 224, 225
    managerialism 227, 228, 229, 232, 234, 236–7, 238, 241
  regulating police wrongdoing 161, 167–9, 173–4, 176–7, 178–9, 181
  Scotland compared 4, 12, 37, 55
universality of police sub-culture 111–12
us and them 99–101

values and moral order 44–5, 194
  community/local 39–41, 44–5
  compromised *see* abuse of authority
  moral culpability 133–7
  moral status of protesters 66, 68
  virtuous policy, community policing as 217–18
  see also respectable
victimization 47–8, 60–1
victims of crime 5–6, 8, 16, 20, 53, 56–7
video surveillance 246–7
Vietnam War 65, 74, 92
vigilantism 225
violence *see* force/coercion; weapons

warnings (rights) to suspects 139, 141–2, 170
weapons 238
  non-lethal 66, 70, 88–9, 93
  see also lethal force; militarism
women
  keeping in place 51–5

in police and prejudice against 99, 103–4, 105, 111–12, 113, 116
vulnerable 43
see also feminists; sexism
working class, police as 97
see also class; deprivation; incorporation; strikes; unemployment
working rules 128–30
wrongdoing *see* abuse of authority; complaints; regulating police

young people *see* juveniles

zero tolerance 43–4, 92, 250
zero-sum game 84, 86

Printed in the United Kingdom
by Lightning Source UK Ltd.
123862UK00001B/23/A

9 781857 286939